of I

M000163791

GEORG TRAKL

THE

LAST GOLD

OF

EXPIRED STARS

Complete Poems 1908 – 1914

Translated by Jim Doss and Werner Schmitt

LOCH RAVEN PRESS   SYKESVILLE, MD   2023

Printed in the United States of America

Front Cover Art: Photo of Parco dei Mostri
 courtesy of http://philip.greenspun.com

Back Cover Art: Georg Trakl Self-Portait
 Created roughly November 30, 1913 in Innsbruck, Studio of Max von Esterle

Cover and book design: Jim Doss

Library of Congress Control Number: 2010922948
ISBN 978-0-9821854-5-2

Loch Raven Press
140 Milrey Drive, Suite L
Sykesville, MD 21784
www.lochravenpress.com

Table of Contents

Introduction
  Chronology   3
  Biographical Sketch   7
  Translator's Note   10

PART ONE: **Poems**   (1913)
  The Ravens   13
  The Young Maid   13
  Romance in the Night   19
  In Red Foliage Full of Guitars...   19
  Music in Mirabell *[version 3]*   21
  Melancholy of the Evening   21
  Winter Twilight   23
  Rondel   25
  Blessing of Women   25
  The Beautiful City   25
  In a Deserted Room   27
  To the Boy Elis   29
  The Thunderstorm Evening   31
  Evening Muse   31
  Dream of Evil *[version 1]*   33
  Spiritual Song   33
  In Autumn   35
  Toward Evening My Heart   37
  The Peasants   37
  All Souls' Day   39
  Melancholy *[version 3]*   39
  Soul of Life   41
  Transfigured Autumn   41
  Corner by the Forest   43
  In Winter   43
  In an Old Family Album   45
  Transformation *[version 2]*   45

Small Concert 47
Mankind 47
The Walk 49
De profundis 51
Trumpets 53
Dusk 53
Cheerful Spring *[version 2]* 55
Suburb in Foehn 57
The Rats 59
Doldrums *[version 1]* 59
Whispered in the Afternoon 61
Psalm *[version 2]* 61
Rosary Songs 65
    To the Sister 65
    Nearness of Death *[version 2]* 65
    Amen 65
Decay *[version 2]* 67
In the Homeland 67
An Autumn Evening 69
Human Misery *[version 2]* 69
In the Village 71
Evening Song 75
Three Gazes into an Opal 75
Night Song 79
Helian 79

PART TWO: Sebastian in Dream (1915)

Sebastian in Dream
Childhood 89
Hourly Song 89
On the Way 91
Landscape *[version 2]* 93
To the Boy Elis 93
Elis *[version 3]* 95
Hohenburg *[version 2]* 97
Sebastian in Dream 99
At the Moor *[version 3]* 101
In Spring 103
Evening in Lans *[version 2]* 103
At the Mönchsberg *[version 2]* 105
Kaspar Hauser Song 105
Nights 107

Metamorphosis of Evil *[version 2]*   107

Autumn of the Lonely

In the Park   111
A Winter Evening *[version 2]*   111
The Cursed   113
Sonja   115
Along   115
Autumn Soul *[version 2]*   117
Afra *[version 2]*   119
Autumn of the Lonely   119

Seven-song of Death

Rest and Silence   123
Anif   123
Birth   125
Decline *[version 5]*   127
To One Who Died Young   127
Spiritual Dusk *[version 2]*   129
Occidental Song   129
Transfiguration   131
Foehn   133
The Wanderer *[version 2]*   133
Karl Kraus   135
To the Muted   135
Passion *[version 3]*   137
Seven-song of Death   137
Winter Night   139

Song of the Departed

In Venice   143
Limbo *[verison 2]*   143
The Sun   145
Song of a Captive Blackbird   147
Summer   147
End of Summer   149
Year   149
Occident *[version 4]*   151
Springtime of the Soul   153
In Darkness *[version 2]*   155
Song of the Departed   157

Dream and Derangement

Dream and Derangement   159

PART THREE: **Der Brenner** (1914–1915)

In Hellbrunn 167
The Heart 167
Sleep *[version 2]* 169
The Thunderstorm 169
The Evening 171
The Night 173
The Gloom 175
The Homecoming *[version 2]* 175
Lament 177
Surrender at Night *[version 5]* 179
In the East 179
Lament 181
Grodek *[version 2]* 181
Revelation and Decline 183

PART FOUR: **Other Writings**

The Morning Song 189
Dream Wanderer 189
The Three Ponds of Hellbrunn *[version 2]* 191
The Three Ponds in Hellbrunn *[version 3]* 193
St. Peter's Cemetery 195
A Spring Evening 195
In an Old Garden 197
[Evening Round Dance] *[version 1]* 197
Evening Round Dance *[version 2]* 199
[Night Soul] *[version 1]* 199
Night Soul *[version 2]* 201
Night Soul *[version 3]* 203
Dream Country. An Episode. 203
From the Golden Chalice. Barrabas. A Fantasy. 209
From the Golden Chalice. Mary Magdalene. A Dialog. 213
Abandonment 217
Head Stage Director Friedheim 221
Gustav Streicher 225
Review of *Jakobus and the Women* 227

PART FIVE: *From* The Bequest

Collection 1909
Three Dreams 237

From the Still Days 239
Dusk 241
Autumn *[version 1]* 241
The Horror 243
Devotion 243
Sabbath 245
Song in the Night 247
The Deep Song 253
Ballad 255
Ballad 255
Ballad 257
Melusine 257
Decay 257
Poem 259
Night Song 259
By a Window 261
Colorful Autumn *[version 1]* 261
The Three Ponds in Hellbrunn *[version 1]* 263
On the Death of an Old Woman 265
Gypsy 265
Nature Theater 267
Exhausting 267
Closing Chord 269
Accord 269
Crucifixus 271
Confiteor 271
Silence 273
Before Sunrise 273
Blood Guilt 273
Encounter 275
Perfection 275
Metamorphosis 277
Evening Walk 277
The Saint 277
To a Woman Passer-by 279
The Dead Church 279

Poems 1909–1912

Melusine 283
The Night of the Poor 283
Night Song 285
De profundis 285
At the Cemetery 287
Sunny Afternoon 287
Age 289

The Shadow 289
Quaint Spring 289
The Dream of an Afternoon 291
Summer Sonata 291
Luminous Hour 293
Childhood Memory 295
An Evening 295
Season 297
In Wine Country 297
The Dark Valley 299
Summer Dawn 299
In the Moonlight 301
Fairy Tale 301
A Spring Evening 303
Elegy 305
Springtime of the Soul 305
Western Dusk 307
The Church 307
To Angela *[version 1]* 309
To Angela *[version 2]* 311
In milk and desolation... 315
Daydreaming in the Evening 317
Winter Walk in A-Minor 317
Always Darker 319
On the Way *[version 1]* 319
On the Way *[version 2]* 323
December *[version 1]* 325
December Sonnet *[version 2]* 325
Green-golden the day arises... 327
Hölderlin 327

Poems 1912–1914

A carpet, into which the suffering... 329
Rosy mirror: an ugly image... 329
The song of the spring rain... 331
Figure which has long dwelt... 331
[Deliriums] 333
Delirium 333
On the Edge of an Old Water *[version 1]* 333
On the Edge of an Old Well *[version 2]* 335
Along Walls 335
A paleness resting in the shadow... 335
The stillness of the deceased loves... 337
With rosy steps the stone sinks... 337
The blue night has gently risen... 339

O the dwelling in the stillness... 339
In the Evening 341
Justice 341
Sister's Garden *[version 1]* 343
Sister's Garden *[version 2]* 343
Wind, white voice... *[version 1]* 343
Wind, white voice... *[version 2]* 345
So softly in the evening... 345
The dew of spring... 347
O the beeches stripped of leaves... 347
To Novalis *[version 1]* 349
[To Novalis] *[version 2a]* 349
To Novalis *[version 2b]* 349
Hour of Grief 351
[Nocturnal Lament] *[version 1]* 351
[Nocturnal Lament] *[version 2]* 353
To Johanna 353
Melancholy 355
Please *[version 1]* 355
Please *[version 2]* 357
To Lucifer *[version 3]* 357
Blue evening take someone's temple... 357
[In the Evening] *[version 1]* 359
In the Evening *[version 2]* 359
With the Young Wine *[version 1]* 361
With the Young Wine *[version 2]* 361
The night devoured red faces... 363
Homecoming 363
Daydreaming *[version 1]* 365
Daydreaming *[version 2]* 365
Daydreaming *[version 3]* 367
Psalm 367
[Autumn Homecoming] *[version 1b]* 369
Autumn Homecoming *[version 2]* 369
Autumn Homecoming *[version 3]* 371
[Remnant] *[version 1]* 371
[Remnant] *[version 2]* 373
Age 373
The Sunflowers 373
So seriously o summer dusk... 375

Double Versions

Colorful Autumn *[version 2]* 377
Dream of Evil *[version 2]* 377
Dream of Evil *[version 3]* 379

Quietly *[version 1]*   379
Melancholia *[version 2]*   381
[Transformation] *[version 1]*   381
Cheerful Spring *[version 1]*   383
[Doldrums] *[version 2]*   385
Psalm *[version 1]*   387
[Nearness of Death] *[version 1]*   389
In the Hospital *[version 1]*   389
In the Hospital *[version 2]*   391
[Landscape] *[version 1]*   393
Elis *[version 1]*   393
Elis *[version 2]*   395
[Hohenburg] *[version 1]*   399
December *[version 1]*   399
[At the Moor] *[version 2]*   401
At the Moor *[version 4]*   401
Summer *[version 1]*   403
At the Mönchsberg *[version 1]*   403
Memory *[version 1]*   405
In Winter *[version 1]*   405
[Autumn Soul] *[version 1]*   407
Evening Mirror *[version 1]*   407
[Decline] *[version 1]*   409
[Decline] *[version 2]*   409
[Decline] *[version 3]*   411
Decline *[version 4]*   411
At the Hill *[version 1]*   413
Wanderer's Sleep *[version 1]*   413
Passion *[version 1]*   415
Passion *[version 2]*   419
[Limbo] *[version 1]*   423
Occident *[version 1a]*   423
Wanderings *[version 1b]*   425
Occident *[version 2]*   427
Occident *[version 3]*   435
Along Walls *[version 1]*   439
[Sleep] *[version 1]*   439
To *[version 1]*   441
In Snow *[version 1]*   441
Sight *[version 2]*   443
To the Night *[version 3]*   443
To the Night *[version 4]*   445

Complexes of Poems and Fragments
The monk listens long to the dying bird...   447

Where the possessed stand stand by black walls... 447
Through black forehead the dead city goes awry... 449
Those sing the decline of the sinister city... 449
Where by walls the shadows of the ancestors... 449
Sinisterly a brown deer bleeds in the bush... 451
Summer. In sunflowers yellow rotten bones... 451
Far away the mother sat in the shadow... 451
Or when he a gentle novice... 453
Childhood 453
A cross towers Elis... 455
Birth 455
In Spring 455
Night Transformation, Death and Soul 455
When the day sank K drove... 455
The homeless one turns... 455
At evening Münch awaked at the border... 455
In spring; a delicate corpse... 455
Nocturnal beeches; in the heart... 457
Snowy night! You dark sleepers... 457

Dramatic Fragments

Bluebeard 459
Don Juan's Death 475
Drama Fragment *[version 1]* 483
Drama Fragment *[version 2]* 487

Selected Letters

1. To Karl von Kalmár (in Vienna) 493
4. To Hermine Von Rauterberg 493
5. To Ludwig Von Ficker (In Innsbruck) 495
14. To Erhard Buschbeck (In Salzburg) 497
18. To Friedrich Trakl in Rovereto 499
29. To Erhard Buschbeck in Vienna 501
35. To Erhard Buschbeck in Vienna 501
50. To Erhard Buschbeck in Salzburg 501
53. To Erhard Buschbeck (in Vienna) 503
61. To Erhard Buschbeck (in Vienna) 503
66. To Erhard Buschbeck in Vienna (In Innsbruck) 505
77. To Kurt Wolff Publishing House (in Leipzig) 505
85. To Ludwig von Ficker (In Innsbruck) 507
100. To Ludwig von Ficker (In Innsbruck) 507
102a. To Rudolf von Ficker (In Innsbruck) 509
103. To Ludwig von Ficker in Innsbruck 509
104. To Ludwig von Ficker (In Innsbruck) 509
106. To Ludwig von Ficker (In Innsbruck) 511

110. To To Karl Borromaeus Heinrich (in Paris?)   511
112. To To Karl Borromaeus Heinrich (in Innsbruck)   513
113. To Ludwig von Ficker (In Innsbruck)   513
115. To the Kurt Wolff Publishing House (in Leipzig)   515
117. To the Kurt Wolff Publishing House (in Leipzig)   515
118. To Maria Geipel in Salzburg   517
122. To the Kurt Wolff Publishing House (in Leipzig)   517
127. To Ludwig von Ficker in Innsbruck   517
129. To Ludwig von Ficker (In Innsbruck)   519
129. To Karl Röck in Innsbruck   519
131. To Adolf Loos (In Vienna)   519
132. To Ludwig von Ficker in Innsbruck   521
133. To Ludwig von Ficker in Innsbruck   521
133a To Cäcile von Ficker in Innsbruck   521
133a To Cäcile von Ficker in Innsbruck   523
137. To Ludwig Von Ficker (In Innsbruck)   523
139. To Gustav Streicher in Vienna   523
144. To Irene Amtmann (in Vienna)   525

Suplemental Materials
    People Around Trakl   527
    Glossary   541

The Last Gold of Expired Stars

Chronology of Georg Trakl's Life

1887   2/3 – Georg Trakl is born at 14:30 in Salzburg, Waagplatz NR. 2 ("Schaffnerhouse," today NR, 1a). Father Tobias is a successful hardware goods dealer. Trakl is the fifth of seven children. Mother Maria, to a great extent, leaves the care of the children to the French Governess.
2/8 - Baptism in the Evangelical Christuskirche (Church of Christ), Salzburg.

1891   8/8 – Birth of sister Margarethe (Grete); she is often present in Trakl's writing, and is his only love.

1892   In autumn, begins attending an exercise school, which is affiliated with the catholic educational establishment. For religious education, he is enrolled in a Protestant school, where he becomes acquainted with his lifelong friend and promoter Erhard Buschbeck.

1893   Moves to the roomier dwelling, Waagplatz NR. 3. The living quarters are over the hardware store.

1897   Begins attending the Staatsgymnasium (Humanistic State Gymnasium) in autumn. Schoolmates: Buschbeck, Kalmár, Minnich among others.

1901   Trakl must repeat the fourth grade.

1904   First literary attempts, and membership in a poetry club ("Apollo," named later to "Minerva," until approximately 1906).

1905   Leaves High School after being forced to again repeat a grade. First drug experiences.
9/18 – Enrolled in the Practical Course in Pharmacy at dispensing pharmacy "The White Angel."

1906   3/31 – His one act play "Death Day" premieres at the City Theatre in Salzburg.
5/12 – His prose "Dream Country. An Episode" appears in the Salzburger People's Newspaper.
9/15 – His play "Fata Morgana" premiers at the City Theatre in Salzburg and is poorly received. Afterwards, Trakl destroys this text as well as "Death Day."

1907   Continual work crises; advancement to stronger drugs.

1908   2/26 – "The Morning Song," Georg's first published poem, appears in the Salzburger People's Newspaper.
9/20 – Conclusion of the Pharmacy Practical Course.
10/5 – Enrolls at the University of Vienna in pharmacy studies. Parallels Grete's study of piano at the Viennese music academy.

1909   Assembles his youthful poems in the "Collection 1909" and discovers new poetical stimulations in Baudelaire, Rimbaud and others.
7/17 – Georg receives a preliminary test certification ('sufficient') in his pharmaceutical studies.
10/17 – On Buschbeck's recommendation, the poems "Devotion," "Completion" and "A Passing" appear in the New Viennese Journal.

1910   Breakthrough to his mature lyric poetry.
6/18 – Death of the father Tobias; experiences financial problems from now on.
7/25 – Receives the degree Master of Pharmacy (cumulative rating of 'sufficient').
Late summer – Grete moves to Berlin to study piano.
10/1 – Begins active military service at the medical department in Vienna.

1911   Increasing depressions and drug excesses.
9/30 – End of military service.
10/15–12/20 – Employed in Salzburg as a pharmacist at "The White Angel."
12/1 – Appointment as a Military Medical Assistant (rank of second lieutenant).

1912   March – The poem "Cheerful Spring" appears in *Der Ruf*, Vienna.
4/1 – Start of semi-annual duties in the pharmacy of the Innsbruck Garrison Hospital.
5/1 – "Suburbs in Foehn" appears in the bi-monthly magazine *Der Brenner*, Innsbruck (on the recommendation of Buschbeck's friend Robert Müller). Its publisher, Ludwig von Ficker, begins publishing Trakl's newest works, rapidly becomes his mentor and friend, and often grants Trakl refuge at his house. In addition, Trakl develops acquaintances with *Der Brenner* coworkers (Karl Röck, Max von Esterle) as well as Karl Kraus, Adolf Loos, Oskar Kokoschka and Karl Borromaeus Heinrich.
7/17 – Grete marries bookseller Arthur Langen in Berlin.

10/1 – Based on positive appraisals of his duties in the Innsbruck Garrison Hospital, Trakl is transitioned into active duty as a Military Medical Civil Servant.

11/30 – Transitions into the reserves, in order to begin an Accounting Trainee position in the Viennese Ministry for Public Works.

12/31 – Start of the Accounting Trainee position in the Viennese Ministry for Public Works.

1913   1/1 – Requests dismissal from his Accounting Trainee position. Thereafter, unsteady efforts to obtain suitable employment have him oscillating between Salzburg, Vienna and Innsbruck.

2/1 – Dissolution of the paternal hardware store.

April – Georg receives an offer for the publication of his manuscript of "Poems" from the Kurt Wolff publishing house, Leipzig. The distribution takes place in July.

Second half of August – Journeys to Venice with Karl Kraus, Adolf Loos and wife Bessie, and Ficker.

12/10 – Only public reading given in Innsbruck, at an evening featuring *Der Brenner* writers.

1914   3/6 – The manuscript "Sebastian in Dream" is sent to the Kurt Wolff publishing house.

March – Journeys to Berlin to visit Grete, who has suffered after an abortion. Meets with Else Lasker-Schüler.

7/27 – At Ficker's suggestion, Ludwig Wittgenstein awards 20,000 crowns from his donation for needy artists to Trakl. Because of the outbreak of WWI, Trakl never receives the money.

8/24 – Begins his service as a medic in the Austrian army.

September – Attempts suicide with a pistol following the battle of Grodek after suffering a break-down while single-handed caring for close to one hundred seriously wounded soldiers, prevented from succeeding by comrades.

10/7 – Taken to a Krakow Military Garrison Hospital for observation of his mental condition.

10/25–26 – Ficker visits and is the last of his friends to see him alive.

11/3 – Death occurs at 21:00 from an overdose of cocaine (heart failure).

11/6 – Burial at the Rakoviczer cemetery in Krakow.

1915   His final poems are printed in *Der Brenner*. The book "Sebastian in Dream" appears from the Kurt Wolff publishing house.

1917   9/23 – Grete shoots herself after a party in Berlin.

1919 The initial publication of the complete poetical works from the Kurt Wolff publishing house, edited by Karl Röck.

1925 10/7 – Ludwig von Ficker arranges for the transfer of Trakl's remains from Krakow and organizes a funeral attended by friends and admirers in Mühlau, Innsbruck.

1939 Erhard Buschbeck publishes Trakl's youthful poems under the title "From the Golden Chalice" with the Otto Müller publishing house, Salzburg.

1950's The "re-discovery" of Trakl in German and American literary circles.

1969 The historical and critical edition of poems and letters appears (compiled by Walther Killy and Hans Szklenar) from the Otto Müller publishing house, Salzburg.

Biographical Sketch

Georg Trakl was born on February 3, 1887 in Salzburg, Austria, to Tobias Trakl and his second wife Maria. He was the fifth of seven children. His beloved sister, Margarette, usually called Gretl or Grete, was the youngest. Little is known of the family life, but it appears the father was detached and absorbed in his hardware business, while his mother was more of the neurotic artistic type who suffered from depression and would withdraw for days on end into her private rooms filled with antiques. Most of the children's upbringing was left to Maria Boring, their French governess, who taught them French and imposed a strict Catholic regime on the children. Although Trakl professed the Protestant beliefs of his father, his mother sent him to the Catholic Teacher Preparatory School from 1892 to 1897, and afterwards the Humanistic State Gymnasium of Salzburg from 1897 to 1905. Near the end of his school years, Trakl became moody and withdrawn, began to drink excessively, experiment with drugs, and occasionally spoke of suicide. Twice he failed to be promoted to the next grade, and following the second time refused to sit for his examinations. He left the Gymnasium after this, and was schooled at home for a time, where he discovered the poets Baudelaire and the French Symbolists Verlaine and Rimbaud, whose work and life deeply impressed him, and remained an influence throughout his writing career along with Nietzsche, Hölderlin, and Dostoevsky.

Trakl decided to train as a pharmacist, against his father's wishes, which gave him easy access to drugs his entire life. During his three year pharmaceutical apprenticeship, Trakl wrote several plays, inspired by the example of his friend Gustav Streicher. In 1906, the Salzburg City Theater staged his one act plays *Totentag* and *Fata Morgana* to poor reviews and later he destroyed all copies of the manuscripts. During this time, he published a few poems, prose sketches and critiques in local daily newspapers. He also assembled a collection of early poems that were published after his death together with the other juvenile pieces by childhood friend Erhard Buschbeck, and are contained in this volume as "Collection 1909."

From 1908 to 1911, Trakl lived in Vienna where he studied pharmacy, eventually graduating with a Master of Pharmacy degree before beginning a year's active military duty there. During this time he developed a hatred of cities, and the corrupting influence of refined civilization that is reflected in many of his poems. The death of his father in 1910 placed Trakl in a state of financial difficulty, when what seemed to be a prosperous hardware business ultimately proved to be insolvent. After this, his life grew more and more unstable; his depression, drinking and drug use escalated, yet amid this strife and misery he developed his mature poetic style. In October 1911, Trakl returned to Salzburg as a dispensing pharmacist at "The White Angel" apothecary. Before the end of the year, he received an appointment as a Military Medical Assistance with the rank of second lieutenant.

In November 1912, he switched to the reserves in order to accept an accounting position at the Ministry of Public works, a job he resigned after one day.

The year 1912 also saw Trakl's first publication in the monthly magazine, *Der Brenner*, published by Ludwig von Ficker, who rapidly became Trakl's friend and mentor. Trakl is often granted refuge from his worldly struggles by von Ficker at his Innsbruck house. A support group consisting of *Der Brenner* co-workers Karl Röck, and Max von Esterle, and the *Brenner* circle of friends including Karl Kraus, Adolf Loos, Oskar Kokoschka and Karl Borromaeus Heinrich formed around Trakl. 1913 found Trakl oscillating between employment opportunities in Salzburg, Vienna and Innsbruck as the paternal hardware store finally went out of business. In April, Trakl received an offer to publish his manuscript "Poems" from the Kurt Wolff Publishing House, and the distribution took place in July. In the later half of August, he journeyed to Venice with Karl Kraus, Adolf Loos and Ludwig von Ficker, his first trip outside of German speaking countries. In December, he gave his only public reading in Innsbruck at an evening featuring *Der Brenner* writers. Reviewers at the time described his poems as speaking "with the convincing strength of an odd spiritual personality," and "with him everything becomes image or parable, barters in his soul into other expressionistic possibilities, which are not appropriate for humans today, but nevertheless are delivered so convincingly that one believes their possibility." Yet he was "an outwardly strange person" whose "kind of reading is better suited for an intimate gathering than a large hall and occasionally he spoke so soft that his voice became barely audible."

In March 1914, his manuscript "Sebastian in Dream" was accepted by the Kurt Wolff Publishing House. He traveled to Berlin to attend to his sister Grete, who married a bookseller, and was seriously ill following an abortion. There he met the poetess Else Lasker Schüler, to whom he dedicates the poem "Occident," "with admiration." At the end of July, at von Ficker's suggestion, Ludwig Wittgenstein awarded Trakl 20,000 crowns from his donation to needy artists. Due to the outbreak of WWI, Trakl never received the money. He returned to his old rank of second lieutenant in the Austrian medical corp, and with an Innsbruck ambulance column journeyed to the eastern front in Galicia, now modern-day Poland. The army suffered terrible defeats at the hands of the Russians.

In September, following the battle of Grodek, Trakl was put in charge of caring for approximately 100 seriously wounded solders, to whom he could provide little help or comfort, since he was only a dispensing pharmacist. His already fragile mental state deteriorated further. This uninterrupted contact with mutilated soldiers and the morbidity of battle overwhelmed him. One evening, as he left the barn that served as an impromptu hospital, he was startled to see the bodies of disloyal townspeople hanged in a tree. He broke down and attempted to commit suicide with a pistol, only to be disarmed by his comrades. He calmed himself and performed his duties for several weeks without incident. A short time later, he received orders to report to the Krakow Military Garrison Hospital, where he thought he was to serve as a pharmacist, only to be placed in the psychiatric ward of the hospital for the observation of his mental condition. Suspected of being schizophrenic, Trakl was confined to a cell with another officer who suffered with

delirium tremors. Ludwig von Ficker visited Trakl there October 25th and 26th and was the last of his friends to see him alive. On November 3rd Trakl died from an overdose of cocaine, drugs that he had secretly concealed upon his detention. It will never be known if his death was a suicide due to depression or the fear of being court marshaled, or an accidental overdose. Wittgenstein arrived three days later to meet Trakl and inform him of the monetary award to relieve Trakl's financial hardships, only to be informed of his death. He said of Trakl's poetry: "I don't understand it; but its tone bewitched me. It is the tone of truly ingenious humans." Trakl was buried in the Rakoviczer cemetery in Krakow. In 1915, Trakl's final poems appeared in *Der Brenner*, and "Sebastian in Dream" was published. In the fall of 1925, Ludwig von Ficker moved Trakl's remains from Krakow to the Mühlau near Innsbruck.

Translator's Note

The material in this book represents all of Trakl's creative output during his short life. Included in the first half are the two books accepted for publication by the Kurt Wolff Publishing House while Trakl was still alive, as well as poems published in the magazine *Der Brenner* after his death, and some juvenile poems, prose, and articles. The second half, "The Bequest," is composed of the legacy of papers cataloged by Trakl scholars, including juvenile poems, mature work not contained in either of published books, multiple versions of published poems as he continued to refine his craft, a few surviving dramatic fragments, and a selection of letters.

In translating the German texts into English, we've attempted to preserve as much of the linguistic oddities of the original as possible, and tried to resisted the tendency of those who came before us to smooth over the peculiar phrase and bring Trakl's language into a format that may be more appealing to modern tastes. In addition, it should be noted we've coined a few new words in several of these poems trying to introduce the German concept of gendered nouns into largely gender-neutral English. Words like Jüngling-Jünglingin, Fremdling-Fremdlingin, Mönch-Mönchin, which Trakl used to describe the dual-natured relationship with his sister Grete, have become youth-youthtress, stranger-strangeress, monk-monkess. While these terms may seem a little odd to the English speaker, we think preserving this connection adds value to the overall understanding of Trakl's work.

Part One:

Poems

(Kurt Wolff Publishing House, Leipzig, 1913)

Die Raben

Über den schwarzen Winkel hasten
Am Mittag die Raben mit hartem Schrei.
Ihr Schatten streift an der Hirschkuh vorbei
Und manchmal sieht man sie mürrisch rasten.

O wie sie die braune Stille stören,
In der ein Acker sich verzückt,
Wie ein Weib, das schwere Ahnung berückt,
Und manchmal kann man sie keifen hören

Um ein Aas, das sie irgendwo wittern,
Und plötzlich richten nach Nord sie den Flug
Und schwinden wie ein Leichenzug
In Lüften, die von Wollust zittern.

Die junge Magd

Ludwig von Ficker zugeeignet

1

Oft am Brunnen, wenn es dämmert,
Sieht man sie verzaubert stehen
Wasser schöpfen, wenn es dämmert.
Eimer auf und nieder gehen.

In den Buchen Dohlen flattern
Und sie gleichet einem Schatten.
Ihre gelben Haare flattern
Und im Hofe schrein die Ratten.

Und umschmeichelt von Verfalle
Senkt sie die entzundenen Lider.
Dürres Gras neigt im Verfalle
Sich zu ihren Füßen nieder.

The Ravens

Over the black corner at midday
The ravens rush with hard cry.
Their shadow streaks past the doe
And sometimes they are seen in sullen rest.

O how they disturb the brown silence
Of a field lying ecstatic with itself,
Like a woman ensnared by heavy foreboding,
And sometimes one can hear their nagging

Around a carcass scented out somewhere,
And suddenly their flight bends northward
And disappears like a funeral procession
Into winds that tremble with lust.

The Young Maid

Dedicated to Ludwig von Ficker

1

Often at the well when it dawns
One sees her standing spellbound
Scooping water when it dawns.
Buckets go up and down.

In the beech trees jackdaws flutter
And she resembles a shadow.
Her golden hair flutters
And rats scream in the yard.

And enticed by decay
She lowers the inflamed eyelids.
Parched grass in decay
Bends down to her feet.

2

Stille schafft sie in der Kammer
Und der Hof liegt längst verödet.
Im Hollunder vor der Kammer
Kläglich eine Amsel flötet.

Silbern schaut ihr Bild im Spiegel
Fremd sie an im Zwielichtscheine
Und verdämmert fahl im Spiegel
Und ihr graut vor seiner Reine.

Traumhaft singt ein Knecht im Dunkel
Und sie starrt von Schmerz geschüttelt.
Röte träufelt durch das Dunkel.
Jäh am Tor der Südwind rüttelt.

3

Nächtens übern kahlen Anger
Gaukelt sie in Fieberträumen.
Mürrisch greint der Wind im Anger
Und der Mond lauscht aus den Bäumen.

Balde rings die Sterne bleichen
Und ermattet von Beschwerde
Wächsern ihre Wangen bleichen.
Fäulnis wittert aus der Erde.

Traurig rauscht das Rohr im Tümpel
Und sie friert in sich gekauert.
Fern ein Hahn kräht. Übern Tümpel
Hart und grau der Morgen schauert.

4

In der Schmiede dröhnt der Hammer
Und sie huscht am Tor vorüber.
Glührot schwingt der Knecht den Hammer
Und sie schaut wie tot hinüber.

Wie im Traum trifft sie ein Lachen;

2

Silently she works in the chamber
And the yard lies long desolate.
In the elder trees by the chamber
A blackbird flutes pitifully.

Silverly her image in the mirror
Gazes at her strangely in the twilight-glow
And dusks sickly in the mirror
And she shudders before its purity.

Dreamlike a farm boy sings in the darkness
And she stares shaken with pain.
Redness trickles through the darkness.
Suddenly at the gate the south wind rattles.

3

Nightly over the barren meadow
She totters in feverish dreams.
Morosely the wind whines in the meadow
And the moon listens from the trees.

Soon all around the stars pale
And exhausted from complaints
Her waxen cheeks become pale.
Putrefaction is scented from the earth.

Sadly the reeds rustle by the pond
And cowering she grows cold.
Far away a cock crows. Above the pond
Morning shivers hard and gray.

4

In the smithy the hammer
Clangs and she scurries past the gate.
In red glow the farm boy swings the hammer
And she looks over as if dead.

As in a dream she's struck by his laughter;

Und sie taumelt in die Schmiede,
Scheu geduckt vor seinem Lachen,
Wie der Hammer hart und rüde.

Hell versprühn im Raum die Funken
Und mit hilfloser Geberde
Hascht sie nach den wilden Funken
Und sie stürzt betäubt zur Erde.

5

Schmächtig hingestreckt im Bette
Wacht sie auf voll süßem Bangen
Und sie sieht ihr schmutzig Bette
Ganz von goldnem Licht verhangen,

Die Reseden dort am Fenster
Und den bläulich hellen Himmel.
Manchmal trägt der Wind ans Fenster
Einer Glocke zag Gebimmel.

Schatten gleiten übers Kissen,
Langsam schlagt die Mittagsstunde
Und sie atmet schwer im Kissen
Und ihr Mund gleicht einer Wunde.

6

Abends schweben blutige Linnen,
Wolken über stummen Wäldern,
Die gehüllt in schwarze Linnen.
Spatzen lärmen auf den Feldern.

Und sie liegt ganz weiß im Dunkel.
Unterm Dach verhaucht ein Girren.
Wie ein Aas in Busch und Dunkel
Fliegen ihren Mund umschwirren.

Traumhaft klingt im braunen Weiler
Nach ein Klang von Tanz und Geigen,
Schwebt ihr Antlitz durch den Weiler,
Weht ihr Haar in kahlen Zweigen.

And she reels into the smithy,
Shyly cowering before his laughter,
Like the hammer hard and coarse.

Brightly in the room sparks
Spray and with helpless gestures
She snatches after the wild sparks
And falls dazed to the earth.

5

Sprawled slenderly across the bed
She wakes filled with sweet tremblings
And she sees her soiled bed
Curtained by a golden light,

The mignonettes there at the window
And the bluish brightness of sky.
Sometimes the wind carries to the window
A bell's hesitant tinkling.

Shadows glide over the pillow,
The noon hour strikes slowly
And she breathes heavily on the pillow
And her mouth is like a wound.

6

In the evenings bloody linens float,
Clouds over silent forests,
That are wrapped in black linens.
Sparrows fuss in the fields.

And she lies completely white in darkness.
Under the roof a cooing wafts away.
Like carrion in bush and darkness
Flies swirl around her mouth.

Dreamlike in the brown hamlet
A sound of dance and fiddles echoes,
Floats her countenance through the hamlet,
Blows her hair in bare branches.

Romanze zur Nacht

Einsamer unterm Sternenzelt
Geht durch die stille Mitternacht.
Der Knab aus Träumen wirr erwacht,
Sein Antlitz grau im Mond verfällt.

Die Närrin weint mit offnem Haar
Am Fenster, das vergittert starrt.
Im Teich vorbei auf süßer Fahrt
Ziehn Liebende sehr wunderbar.

Der Mörder lächelt bleich im Wein,
Die Kranken Todesgrausen packt.
Die Nonne betet wund und nackt
Vor des Heilands Kreuzespein.

Die Mutter leis' im Schlafe singt.
Sehr friedlich schaut zur Nacht das Kind
Mit Augen, die ganz wahrhaft sind.
Im Hurenhaus Gelächter klingt.

Beim Talglicht drunt' im Kellerloch
Der Tote malt mit weißer Hand
Ein grinsend Schweigen an die Wand.
Der Schläfer flüstert immer noch.

Im roten Laubwerk voll Guitarren…

Im roten Laubwerk voll Guitarren
Der Mädchen gelbe Haare wehen
Am Zaun, wo Sonnenblumen stehen.
Durch Wolken fährt ein goldner Karren.

In brauner Schatten Ruh verstummen
Die Alten, die sich blöd umschlingen.
Die Waisen süß zur Vesper singen.
In gelben Dünsten Fliegen summen.

Romance in the Night

The lonely one under the tent of stars
Goes through the still midnight.
The boy woozily awakens out of dreams,
His countenance decays gray in moon.

The foolish woman with unbound hair weeps
By the window's gazing trellis.
On the pond passing by in sweet journey
Lovers drift most wonderfully.

The murderer smiles palely in wine,
Death's horror grips the sick.
The nun prays excoriated and naked
Before the Savior's agony on the cross.

The mother sings quietly in sleep.
Very peacefully the child gazes into the night
With eyes that are completely truthful.
Laughter rings out in the whorehouse.

By candlelight down in the cellar hole
The dead one paints with white hand
A grinning silence on the wall.
The sleeper whispers still.

In Red Foliage Full of Guitars...

In red foliage full of guitars
The girls' yellow hair blows
At the fence, where sunflowers stand.
A golden cart drives through the clouds.

In the repose of brown shadows
The old grow silent, embrace dim-wittedly.
Orphans sing sweetly for vespers.
Flies buzz in yellow streams.

Am Bache waschen noch die Frauen.
Die aufgehängten Linnen wallen.
Die Kleine, die mir lang gefallen,
Kommt wieder durch das Abendgrauen.

Vom lauen Himmel Spatzen stürzen
In grüne Löcher voll Verwesung.
Dem Hungrigen täuscht vor Genesung
Ein Duft von Brot und herben Würzen.

Musik im Mirabell

[3. Fassung]

Ein Brunnen singt. Die Wolken stehn
Im klaren Blau, die weißen, zarten.
Bedächtig stille Menschen gehn
Am Abend durch den alten Garten.

Der Ahnen Marmor ist ergraut.
Ein Vogelzug streift in die Weiten.
Ein Faun mit toten Augen schaut
Nach Schatten, die ins Dunkel gleiten.

Das Laub fällt rot vom alten Baum
Und kreist herein durchs offne Fenster.
Ein Feuerschein glüht auf im Raum
Und malet trübe Angstgespenster.

Ein weißer Fremdling tritt ins Haus.
Ein Hund stürzt durch verfallene Gänge.
Die Magd löscht eine Lampe aus,
Das Ohr hört nachts Sonatenklänge.

Melancholie des Abends

– Der Wald, der sich verstorben breitet –
Und Schatten sind um ihn, wie Hecken.
Das Wild kommt zitternd aus Verstecken,

By the brook women still wash.
The hung-up linens billow.
The small child, whom I have long liked,
Comes again through evening's grayness.

Sparrows fall from mild skies
Into green holes filled with rot.
An aroma of bread and harsh spices
Feigns recovery to the hungry one.

Music in Mirabell

[version 3]

A fountain sings. The clouds stand
In clear blueness, white, delicate.
Silent people wander thoughtfully
Through the old garden in the evening.

The ancestors' marble has turned gray.
A line of birds streaks into the distance.
A faun with dead eyes gazes
After shadows that glide into darkness.

The leaves fall red from the old tree
And whirl inside through an open window.
A firelight glows in the room
And paints dim specters of anxiety.

A white stranger enters the house.
A dog leaps through decayed lanes.
The maid extinguishes a lamp.
At night the ear hears the sounds of sonatas.

Melancholy of the Evening

—The forest which widens deceased—
And shadows are around it, like hedges.
The deer comes trembling out of hidden places

Indes ein Bach ganz leise gleitet

Und Farnen folgt und alten Steinen
Und silbern glänzt aus Laubgewinden.
Man hört ihn bald in schwarzen Schlünden –
Vielleicht, daß auch schon Sterne scheinen.

Der dunkle Plan scheint ohne Maßen,
Verstreute Dörfer, Sumpf und Weiher,
Und etwas täuscht dir vor ein Feuer.
Ein kalter Glanz huscht über Straßen.

Am Himmel ahnet man Bewegung,
Ein Heer von wilden Vögeln wandern
Nach jenen Ländern, schönen, andern.
Es steigt und sinkt des Rohres Regung.

Winterdämmerung

An Max von Esterle

Schwarze Himmel von Metall.
Kreuz in roten Stürmen wehen
Abends hungertolle Krähen
Über Parken gram und fahl.

Im Gewölk erfriert ein Strahl;
Und vor Satans Flüchen drehen
Jene sich im Kreis und gehen
Nieder siebenfach an Zahl.

In Verfaultem süß und schal
Lautlos ihre Schnäbel mähen.
Häuser dräu'n aus stummen Nähen;
Helle im Theatersaal.

Kirchen, Brücken und Spital
Grauenvoll im Zwielicht stehen.
Blutbefleckte Linnen blähen
Segel sich auf dem Kanal.

While a brook glides very quietly

And follows ferns and ancient stones
And gleams silverly from tangled foliage.
Soon one hears it in black gorges—
Perhaps, also that the stars already shine.

The dark plain seems endless,
Scattered villages, marsh and pond,
And something feigns a fire to you.
A cold gleam shoos over roads.

In the sky one anticipates movement,
A host of wild birds migrates
Towards those lands, beautiful, distant.
The stirring of reeds rises and sinks.

Winter Twilight

To Max von Esterle

Black skies of metal.
In the evening hunger-mad crows
Blow crosswise in red storms
Over parks sorrowful and sallow.

In the clouds a sunbeam freezes to death;
And before Satan's curses
Those turn within the circle and go
Down sevenfold in number.

In putrefaction sweet and stale
Their beaks mow noiselessly.
Houses threaten from mute proximities;
Brightness in the theater hall.

Churches, bridges, and hospitals
Stand gruesome in the twilight.
Blood-stained linens billow
Sails upon the canal.

Rondel

Verflossen ist das Gold der Tage,
Des Abends braun und blaue Farben:
Des Hirten sanfte Flöten starben
Des Abends blau und braune Farben
Verflossen ist das Gold der Tage.

Frauensegen

Schreitest unter deinen Frau'n
Und du lächelst oft beklommen:
Sind so bange Tage kommen.
Weiß verblüht der Mohn am Zaun.

Wie dein Leib so schön geschwellt
Golden reift der Wein am Hügel.
Ferne glänzt des Weihers Spiegel
Und die Sense klirrt im Feld.

In den Büschen rollt der Tau,
Rot die Blätter niederfließen.
Seine liebe Frau zu grüßen
Naht ein Mohr dir braun und rauh.

Die schöne Stadt

Alte Plätze sonnig schweigen.
Tief in Blau und Gold versponnen
Traumhaft hasten sanfte Nonnen
Unter schwüler Buchen Schweigen.

Aus den braun erhellten Kirchen
Schaun des Todes reine Bilder,
Großer Fürsten schöne Schilder.
Kronen schimmern in den Kirchen.

Rondel

Flown away is the gold of days,
The evening's brown and blue colors,
The shepherd's gentle flutes have died away,
The evening's blue and brown colors,
Flown away is the gold of days.

Blessing of Women

Walking among your women
And often you smile uneasily:
Anxious days have come.
The poppy withers white along the fence.

Like your belly so beautifully swollen
Wine ripens golden on the hill.
Far away the pond's mirror glimmers
And the scythe rattles in the field.

Dew rolls through the bushes,
The leaves flow down red.
To greet his beloved lady
A moor approaches you brown and rough.

The Beautiful City

Old plazas remain in sunny silence.
Deeply spun in blue and gold
Gentle nuns hasten dreamlike
Under the sultry beech trees' silence.

Out of brownly illuminated churches
Death's pure images gaze,
Mighty princes' beautiful emblems.
Crowns shimmer in the churches.

Rösser tauchen aus dem Brunnen.
Blütenkrallen drohn aus Bäumen.
Knaben spielen wirr von Träumen
Abends leise dort am Brunnen.

Mädchen stehen an den Toren,
Schauen scheu ins farbige Leben.
Ihre feuchten Lippen beben
Und sie warten an den Toren.

Zitternd flattern Glockenklänge,
Marschtakt hallt und Wacherufen.
Fremde lauschen auf den Stufen.
Hoch im Blau sind Orgelklänge.

Helle Instrumente singen.
Durch der Gärten Blätterrahmen
Schwirrt das Lachen schöner Damen.
Leise junge Mütter singen.

Heimlich haucht an blumigen Fenstern
Duft von Weihrauch, Teer und Flieder.
Silbern flimmern müde Lider
Durch die Blumen an den Fenstern.

In einem verlassenen Zimmer

Fenster, bunte Blumenbeeten,
Eine Orgel spielt herein.
Schatten tanzen an Tapeten,
Wunderlich ein toller Reihn.

Lichterloh die Büsche wehen
Und ein Schwarm von Mücken schwingt.
Fern im Acker Sensen mähen
Und ein altes Wasser singt.

Wessen Atem kommt mich kosen?
Schwalben irre Zeichen ziehn.
Leise fließt im Grenzenlosen

Steeds plunge out of the fountain.
Flower-claws threaten from trees.
Boys play woozy with dreams
Quietly in the evening there at the fountain.

Girls stand at the gates,
Peer timidly into the colorful life.
Their moist lips quiver
And they wait at the gates.

The trembling flutter of bell-sounds,
Rhythm of march and the guard's call resonate.
Strangers listen on the steps.
High in the blue are organ sounds.

Bright instruments sing.
Through the gardens' borders of foliage
The laughter of beautiful ladies whirs by.
Quietly young mothers sing.

Secretly at flowery windows
Scent of incense, tar and lilac wafts.
Tired eyelids flicker silverly
Through the flowers at the windows.

In a Deserted Room

Window, colorful flowerbeds,
An organ plays within.
Shadows dance on wallpapers,
Fantastically a mad succession.

Ablaze the bushes waver
And a swarm of gnats sways.
Far away scythes mow in the acre,
And an ancient water sings.

Whose breath comes to caress me?
Swallows draw insane signs.
Quietly there in the boundlessness

Dort das goldne Waldland hin.

Flammen flackern in den Beeten.
Wirr verzückt der tolle Reihn
An den gelblichen Tapeten.
Jemand schaut zur Tür herein.

Weihrauch duftet süß und Birne
Und es dämmern Glas und Truh.
Langsam beugt die heiße Stirne
Sich den weißen Sternen zu.

An den Knaben Elis

Elis, wenn die Amsel im schwarzen Wald ruft,
Dieses ist dein Untergang.
Deine Lippen trinken die Kühle des blauen Felsenquells.

Laß, wenn deine Stirne leise blutet
Uralte Legenden
Und dunkle Deutung des Vogelflugs.

Du aber gehst mit weichen Schritten in die Nacht,
Die voll purpurner Trauben hängt
Und du regst die Arme schöner im Blau.

Ein Dornenbusch tönt,
Wo deine mondenen Augen sind.
O, wie lange bist, Elis, du verstorben.

Dein Leib ist eine Hyazinthe,
In die ein Mönch die wächsernen Finger taucht.
Eine schwarze Höhle ist unser Schweigen,

Daraus bisweilen ein sanftes Tier tritt
Und langsam die schweren Lider senkt.
Auf deine Schläfen tropft schwarzer Tau,

Das letzte Gold verfallener Sterne.

The golden woodland flows out.

Flames flicker in the flowerbeds.
Woozily the mad succession enraptures
On the yellowish wallpapers.
Someone looks in through the door.

Incense smells sweet and pear-like,
And glass and chest darken with dusk.
Slowly the hot forehead
Bends toward white stars.

To the Boy Elis

Elis, when the blackbird calls in the black woods,
This is your decline.
Your lips drink the coolness of the blue rock-spring.

Cease, when your forehead bleeds quietly
Ancient legends
And dark interpretations of the flight of birds.

But with tender steps you walk into the night
That hangs full of purple grapes,
And you move the arms more beautifully in the blueness.

A thorn bush tinges
Where your moon-like eyes are.
O, how long, Elis, have you been dead.

Your body is a hyacinth
Into which a monk dips his waxy fingers.
Our silence is a black cavern

From which a gentle animal steps at times
And slowly lowers heavy eyelids.
On your temples black dew drips,

The last gold of expired stars.

Der Gewitterabend

O die roten Abendstunden!
Flimmernd schwankt am offenen Fenster
Weinlaub wirr ins Blau gewunden,
Drinnen nisten Angstgespenster.

Staub tanzt im Gestank der Gossen.
Klirrend stößt der Wind in Scheiben.
Einen Zug von wilden Rossen
Blitze grelle Wolken treiben.

Laut zerspringt der Weiherspiegel.
Möven schrein am Fensterrahmen.
Feuerreiter sprengt vom Hügel
Und zerschellt im Tann zu Flammen.

Kranke kreischen im Spitale.
Bläulich schwirrt der Nacht Gefieder.
Glitzernd braust mit einem Male
Regen auf die Dächer nieder.

Abendmuse

Ans Blumenfester wieder kehrt des Kirchturms Schatten
Und Goldnes. Die heiße Stirn verglüht in Ruh und Schweigen.
Ein Brunnen fällt im Dunkel von Kastanienzweigen;
Da fühlst du: es ist gut! in schmerzlichem Ermatten.

Der Markt ist leer von Sommerfrüchten und Gewinden.
Einträchtig stimmt der Tore schwärzliches Gepränge.
In einem Garten tönen sanften Spieles Klänge,
Wo Freunde nach dem Mahle sich zusammenfinden.

Des weißen Magiers Märchen lauscht die Seele gerne.
Rund saust das Korn, das Mäher nachmittags geschnitten.
Geduldig schweigt das harte Leben in den Hütten;
Der Kühle linden Schlaf bescheint die Stallaterne.

The Thunderstorm Evening

O the red evening hours!
Glimmering by the open window
Vine leaves sway woozily curled in the blue,
Within specters of fear nestle.

Dust dances in the stench of the gutters.
Rattling the wind knocks at the panes.
A herd of wild horses
Thunderbolts drive garish clouds.

Loudly the pond-mirror bursts.
Gulls cry near the window frames.
A fiery horseman gallops from the hill
And smashes to flames in the firs.

The sick shriek in the hospital.
Bluish the night's plumage whirs.
Glistening all at once
Rain roars down upon the roofs.

Evening Muse

Again at the flowering window the church tower's shadow
And golden shape return. The hot forehead burns down in rest and silence.
A fountain falls in the darkness of chestnut branches;
Here you feel: it is good! in painful exhaustion.

The market is empty of summer fruits and garlands.
Harmoniously the gates' blackish pageantry attunes.
In a garden the tones of gentle play sound,
Where friends find each other after the meal.

The soul likes to listen to the white magician's fairy tales.
Roundly the corn swishes cut by mowers in the afternoon.
The hard life grows patiently silent in the huts;
The stable lamp shines upon the dulcet slumber of cows.

Von Lüften trunken sinken balde ein die Lider
Und öffnen leise sich zu fremden Sternenzeichen.
Endymion taucht aus dem Dunkel alter Eichen
Und beugt sich über trauervolle Wasser nieder.

Traum des Bösen
[1. Fassung]

Verhallend eines Gongs braungoldne Klänge –
Ein Liebender erwacht in schwarzen Zimmern
Die Wang' an Flammen, die im Fenster flimmern.
Am Strome blitzen Segel, Masten, Stränge.

Ein Mönch, ein schwangres Weib dort im Gedränge.
Guitarren klimpern, rote Kittel schimmern.
Kastanien schwül in goldnem Glanz verkümmern;
Schwarz ragt der Kirchen trauriges Gepränge.

Aus bleichen Masken schaut der Geist des Bösen.
Ein Platz verdämmert grauenvoll und düster;
Am Abend regt auf Inseln sich Geflüster.

Des Vogelfluges wirre Zeichen lesen
Aussätzige, die zur Nacht vielleicht verwesen.
Im Park erblicken zitternd sich Geschwister.

Geistliches Lied

Zeichen, seltne Stickerein
Malt ein flatternd Blumenbeet.
Gottes blauer Odem weht
In den Gartensaal herein,
Heiter ein.
Ragt ein Kreuz im wilden Wein.

Hör' im Dorf sich viele freun,
Gärtner an der Mauer mäht,
Leise eine Orgel geht,

Drunk with air eyelids soon sink inward
And quietly open to foreign constellations.
Endymion rises from the darkness of ancient oaks
And bends down over mournful waters.

Dream of Evil
[version 1]

Fading away of a gong's brown-golden sounds—
A lover awakens in black rooms,
The cheek near flames that flicker in the window.
In the river sails, masts, and ropes flash.

A monk, a pregnant woman there in the crowd.
Guitars strum, red smocks gleam.
Chestnuts shrivel sultry in golden radiance;
The churches' sad pageantry towers black.

The spirit of evil watches from pale masks.
A square dusks gruesome and somber.
In the evening whispers stir on the islands.

Lepers, perhaps decaying during the night,
Read confused signs from the flight of birds.
In the park siblings behold each other trembling.

Spiritual Song

A fluttering flowerbed
Paints symbols, rare embroideries.
God's blue breath blows
Inside the garden hall,
Cheerfully inside.
A cross towers in wild vines.

Hear the villagers rejoicing,
The gardener mows by the wall,
Quietly an organ goes,

Mischet Klang und goldenen Schein,
Klang und Schein.
Liebe segnet Brot und Wein.

Mädchen kommen auch herein
Und der Hahn zum letzten kräht.
Sacht ein morsches Gitter geht
Und in Rosen Kranz und Reihn,
Rosenreihn
Ruht Maria weiß und fein.

Bettler dort am alten Stein
Scheint verstorben im Gebet,
Sanft ein Hirt vom Hügel geht
Und ein Engel singt im Hain,
Nah im Hain
Kinder in den Schlaf hinein.

Im Herbst

Die Sonnenblumen leuchten am Zaun,
Still sitzen Kranke im Sonnenschein.
Im Acker mühn sich singend die Frau'n,
Die Klosterglocken läuten darein.

Die Vögel sagen dir ferne Mär',
Die Klosterglocken läuten darein.
Vom Hof tönt sanft die Geige her.
Heut keltern sie den braunen Wein.

Da zeigt der Mensch sich froh und lind.
Heut keltern sie den braunen Wein.
Weit offen die Totenkammern sind
Und schön bemalt vom Sonnenschein.

Mixes sound and golden light,
Sound and light.
Love blesses bread and wine.

Girls also come in
And the cock crows to the last.
Gently a rotten trellis goes
And in rose wreath and rows,
Rose rows,
Mary rests white and fine.

The beggar there on the ancient stone
Seems to be deceased in prayer,
Quietly from the hill a shepherd goes
And an angel in the grove,
Nearby in the grove,
Sings the children to sleep.

In Autumn

The sunflowers shine near the fence,
Silently the sick sit in the sunshine.
Women toil singing in the acre
Into which monastery bells chime.

Birds tell you a far away tale
Into which monastery bells chime.
From the courtyard the violin sounds softly.
Today they press the brown wine.

Now man appears cheerful and dulcet.
Today they press the brown wine.
The chambers of the dead are open wide
And beautifully painted with sunshine.

Zu Abend mein Herz

Am Abend hört man den Schrei der Fledermäuse.
Zwei Rappen springen auf der Wiese.
Der rote Ahorn rauscht.
Dem Wanderer erscheint die kleine Schenke am Weg.
Herrlich schmecken junger Wein und Nüsse.
Herrlich: betrunken zu taumeln in dämmernden Wald.
Durch schwarzes Geäst tönen schmerzliche Glocken.
Auf das Gesicht tropft Tau.

Die Bauern

Vorm Fenster tönendes Grün und Rot.
Im schwarzverräucherten, niederen Saal
Sitzen die Knechte und Mägde beim Mahl;
Und sie schenken den Wein und sie brechen das Brot.

Im tiefen Schweigen der Mittagszeit
Fällt bisweilen ein karges Wort.
Die äcker flimmern in einem fort
Und der Himmel bleiern und weit.

Fratzenhaft flackert im Herd die Glut
Und ein Schwarm von Fliegen summt.
Die Mägde lauschen blöd und verstummt
Und ihre Schläfen hämmert das Blut.

Und manchmal treffen sich Blicke voll Gier,
Wenn tierischer Dunst die Stube durchweht.
Eintönig spricht ein Knecht das Gebet
Und ein Hahn kräht unter der Tür.

Und wieder ins Feld. Ein Grauen packt
Sie oft im tosenden ährengebraus
Und klirrend schwingen ein und aus
Die Sensen geisterhaft im Takt.

Toward Evening My Heart

At evening one hears the cry of bats.
Two black horses leap in the meadow.
The red maple rustles.
To the wanderer the small inn appears along the way.
Glorious taste the young wine and nuts.
Glorious: to stagger drunk in the dusking forest.
Through black branches grievous bells sound.
Dew drips on the face.

The Peasants

Resounding green and red before the window.
In the smoke-blackened, low hall
The farm boys and maids sit with the meal;
And they pour the wine and they break the bread.

In the deep silence of midday
Sometimes a meager word is spoken.
The fields glimmer on and on
And the sky leaden and wide.

Grotesquely the embers flicker in the hearth
And a swarm of flies buzzes.
The maids listen dim-witted and mute
And the blood pounds in their temples.

And sometimes looks meet filled with greed,
When animal vapors blow through the room.
Monotonously a farm boy says the prayer
And a cock crows under the door.

And again into the field. A horror seizes
Them often in the roaring bluster of corn
And the scythes swing back and forth
Clanking in a ghostly rhythm.

Allerseelen

Die Männlein, Weiblein, traurige Gesellen,
Sie streuen heute Blumen blau und rot
Auf ihre Grüfte, die sich zag erhellen.
Sie tun wie arme Puppen vor dem Tod.

O! wie sie hier voll Angst und Demut scheinen,
Wie Schatten hinter schwarzen Büschen stehn.
Im Herbstwind klagt der Ungebornen Weinen,
Auch sieht man Lichter in der Irre gehn.

Das Seufzen Liebender haucht in Gezweigen
Und dort verwest die Mutter mit dem Kind.
Unwirklich scheinet der Lebendigen Reigen
Und wunderlich zerstreut im Abendwind.

Ihr Leben ist so wirr, voll trüber Plagen.
Erbarm' dich Gott der Frauen Höll' und Qual,
Und dieser hoffnungslosen Todesklagen.
Einsame wandeln still im Sternensaal.

Melancholie
[3. Fassung]

Bläuliche Schatten. O ihr dunklen Augen,
Die lang mich anschaun im Vorübergleiten.
Guitarrenklänge sanft den Herbst begleiten
Im Garten, aufgelöst in braunen Laugen.
Des Todes ernste Düsternis bereiten
Nymphische Hände, an roten Brüsten saugen
Verfallne Lippen und in schwarzen Laugen
Des Sonnenjünglings feuchte Locken gleiten.

All Souls' Day

The little men, little women, sad companions,
Today they scatter flowers blue and red
On their crypts, which light up shyly.
They act like poor dolls before death.

O! how full of fear and humility they appear
Like shadows standing behind black bushes.
In the autumn wind the weeping of the unborn complains,
Also one sees lights lose their way.

The sighs of lovers breathe in the branches,
And there the mother with the child decays.
The dance of the living seems unreal
And strangely dispersed in the evening wind.

Their life is so confused, full of dim plagues.
God take pity on the women's hell and agony
And these hopeless lamentations of death.
The lonely ones walk silently in the hall of stars.

Melancholy
[version 3]

Bluish shadows. O you dark eyes
That gaze long at me gliding past.
Guitar chords softly accompany autumn
In the garden dissolved in brown lyes.
Nymph-like hands prepare
Death's earnest somberness, decayed lips
Suck at red breasts and in black lyes
The moist curls of the sun-youth glide.

Seele des Lebens

Verfall, der weich das Laub umdüstert,
Es wohnt im Wald sein weites Schweigen.
Bald scheint ein Dorf sich geisterhaft zu neigen.
Der Schwester Mund in schwarzen Zweigen flüstert.

Der Einsame wird bald entgleiten,
Vielleicht ein Hirt auf dunklen Pfaden.
Ein Tier tritt leise aus den Baumarkaden,
Indes die Lider sich vor Gottheit weiten.

Der blaue Fluß rinnt schön hinunter,
Gewölke sich am Abend zeigen;
Die Seele auch in engelhaftem Schweigen.
Vergängliche Gebilde gehen unter.

Verklärter Herbst

Gewaltig endet so das Jahr
Mit goldnem Wein und Frucht der Gärten.
Rund schweigen Wälder wunderbar
Und sind des Einsamen Gefährten.

Da sagt der Landmann: Es ist gut.
Ihr Abendglocken lang und leise
Gebt noch zum Ende frohen Mut.
Ein Vogelzug grüßt auf der Reise.

Es ist der Liebe milde Zeit.
Im Kahn den blauen Fluß hinunter
Wie schön sich Bild an Bildchen reiht –
Das geht in Ruh und Schweigen unter.

Soul of Life

Decay, which gently darkens the foliage,
Its vast silence dwells in the forest.
Soon a village seems to bend ghostly.
The sister's mouth whispers in black branches.

The lonely will soon slip away,
Perhaps a shepherd on dark paths.
An animal steps quietly from the arcade of trees
While the eyelids widen before divinity.

The blue river runs beautifully past.
Clouds appear in the evening;
The soul also in angelic silence.
Transient shapes go under.

Transfigured Autumn

So the year ends enormously
With golden wine and the fruit of the gardens.
All around forests grow wonderfully silent
And are the lonely one's companions.

Here the countryman says: it is good.
You evening bells long and quiet
Still give cheerful courage to the end.
A line of birds greets on the journey.

It is the tender time of love.
In the boat down the blue river
How beautifully image follows image—
That declines in rest and silence.

Winkel am Wald

An Karl Minnich

Braune Kastanien. Leise gleiten die alten Leute
In stilleren Abend; weich verwelken schöne Blätter.
Am Friedhof scherzt die Amsel mit dem toten Vetter,
Angelen gibt der blonde Lehrer das Geleite.

Des Todes reine Bilder schaun von Kirchenfenstern;
Doch wirkt ein blutiger Grund sehr trauervoll und düster.
Das Tor blieb heut verschlossen. Den Schlüssel hat der Küster.
Im Garten spricht die Schwester freundlich mit Gespenstern.

In alten Kellern reift der Wein ins Goldne, Klare.
Süß duften äpfel. Freude glänzt nicht allzu ferne.
Den langen Abend hören Kinder Märchen gerne;
Auch zeigt sich sanftem Wahnsinn oft das Goldne, Wahre.

Das Blau fließt voll Reseden; in Zimmern Kerzenhelle.
Bescheidenen ist ihre Stätte wohl bereitet.
Den Saum des Walds hinab ein einsam Schicksal gleitet;
Die Nacht erscheint, der Ruhe Engel, auf der Schwelle.

Im Winter

Der Acker leuchtet weiß und kalt.
Der Himmel ist einsam und ungeheuer.
Dohlen kreisen über dem Weiher
Und Jäger steigen nieder vom Wald.

Ein Schweigen in schwarzen Wipfeln wohnt.
Ein Feuerschein huscht aus den Hütten.
Bisweilen schellt sehr fern ein Schlitten
Und langsam steigt der graue Mond.

Ein Wild verblutet sanft am Rain
Und Raben plätschern in blutigen Gossen.
Das Rohr bebt gelb und aufgeschossen.
Frost, Rauch, ein Schritt im leeren Hain.

Corner by the Forest

To Karl Minnich

Brown chestnut trees. Quietly the old people glide
In more silent evening; tenderly beautiful leaves wither.
At the cemetery the blackbird jokes with the dead cousin,
The blond teacher escorts Angela.

Pure images of death gaze from church windows;
Yet a bloody cause seems very mournful and cheerless.
The gate remained locked today; the sexton has the key.
In the garden the sister speaks cordially with ghosts.

In old cellars the wine matures into gold, clarity.
Apples smell sweet. Joy shines not too far away.
Children gladly hear fairy tales through the long evening;
Also gold, truth often come out in gentle insanity.

The blue flows full of mignonettes; in rooms candlelight.
For the humble their place is well prepared.
Along the edge of the forest a lonely destiny glides;
Night appears, the angel of rest, on the threshold.

In Winter

The acre shines white and cold.
The sky is lonely and immense.
Jackdaws circle over the pond
And hunters climb down from the forest.

A silence dwells in black treetops.
A firelight flits from the huts.
Sometimes a sleigh rings far away
And slowly the gray moon rises.

Softly a deer bleeds to death at the field's edge
And ravens splash in bloody gutters.
The reeds tremble yellow and upraised.
Frost, smoke, a step in the empty grove.

In ein altes Stammbuch

Immer wieder kehrst du Melancholie,
O Sanftmut der einsamen Seele.
Zu Ende glüht ein goldener Tag.

Demutsvoll beugt sich dem Schmerz der Geduldige
Tönend von Wohllaut und weichem Wahnsinn.
Siehe! es dämmert schon.

Wieder kehrt die Nacht und klagt ein Sterbliches
Und es leidet ein anderes mit.

Schaudernd unter herbstlichen Sternen
Neigt sich jährlich tiefer das Haupt.

Verwandlung
[2. Fassung]

Entlang an Gärten, herbstlich, rotversengt:
Hier zeigt im Stillen sich ein tüchtig Leben.
Des Menschen Hände tragen braune Reben,
Indes der sanfte Schmerz im Blick sich senkt.

Am Abend: Schritte gehn durch schwarzes Land
Erscheinender in roter Buchen Schweigen.
Ein blaues Tier will sich vorm Tod verneigen
Und grauenvoll verfällt ein leer Gewand.

Geruhiges vor einer Schenke spielt,
Ein Antlitz ist berauscht ins Gras gesunken.
Hollunderfrüchte, Flöten weich und trunken,
Resedenduft, der Weibliches umspült.

In an Old Family Album

Always you return melancholy,
O the meekness of the lonely soul.
A golden day glows until the end.

Humbly the patient one yields to grief
Resounding with harmony and tender insanity.
See! It dusks already.

Again night descends and a mortal laments
And another commiserates.

Shuddering under autumn stars
The head bends deeper every year.

Transformation
[version 2]

Along gardens, autumnal, red-seared:
Here a strenuous life is revealed in stillness.
The hands of man carry brown vines
While the gentle pain subsides in the glance.

In the evening: steps go through black land,
Appearer in the silence of red beeches.
A blue animal wants to bow before death
And gruesomely an empty vestment decays.

Peacefulness plays before an inn,
A countenance has sunk intoxicated in the grass.
Fruits of the elder, flutes soft and drunk,
Mignonette-scent, which washes around females.

Kleines Konzert

Ein Rot, das traumhaft dich erschüttert –
Durch deine Hände scheint die Sonne.
Du fühlst dein Herz verrückt vor Wonne
Sich still zu einer Tat bereiten.

In Mittag strömen gelbe Felder.
Kaum hörst du noch der Grillen Singen,
Der Mäher hartes Sensenschwingen.
Einfältig schweigen goldene Wälder.

Im grünen Tümpel glüht Verwesung.
Die Fische stehen still. Gotts Odem
Weckt sacht ein Saitenspiel im Brodem.
Aussätzigen winkt die Flut Genesung.

Geist Dädals schwebt in blauen Schatten,
Ein Duft von Milch in Haselzweigen.
Man hört noch lang den Lehrer geigen,
Im leeren Hof den Schrei der Ratten.

Im Krug an scheußlichen Tapeten
Blühn kühlere Violenfarben.
Im Hader dunkle Stimmen starben,
Narziß im Endakkord von Flöten.

Menschheit

Menschheit vor Feuerschlünden aufgestellt,
Ein Trommelwirbel, dunkler Krieger Stirnen,
Schritte durch Blutnebel; schwarzes Eisen schellt,
Verzweiflung, Nacht in traurigen Gehirnen:
Hier Evas Schatten, Jagd und rotes Geld.
Gewölk, das Licht durchbricht, das Abendmahl.
Es wohnt in Brot und Wein ein sanftes Schweigen
Und jene sind versammelt zwölf an Zahl.
Nachts schrein im Schlaf sie unter Ölbaumzweigen;
Sankt Thomas taucht die Hand ins Wundenmal.

Small Concert

A red, which dreamily unsettles you—
Through your hands the sun shines.
You feel your heart crazy with bliss
Silently prepare itself for an act.

Yellow fields stream into noon.
You barely still hear the cricket's singing,
The mowers' hard scythe-swings.
Simple-mindedly golden forests fall silent.

Decay glows in the green pool.
The fish stand still. Softly God's breath
Awakens string music in the vapor.
The flood beckons recovery to lepers.

Daedalus' ghost floats in blue shadows,
A scent of milk in hazel branches.
One still hears the teacher's violin playing long,
The cry of the rats in the empty yard.

In the inn cooler violet colors
Bloom on hideous wallpapers.
Dark voices died in quarrel,
Narcissus in the final chord of flutes.

Mankind

Mankind placed before fiery gorges,
A drum roll, dark warriors' foreheads,
Steps through blood-fog; black iron resounds,
Despair, night in sad brains:
Here Eve's shadow, hunt and red money.
Clouds that light breaks through, the Last Supper.
A gentle silence dwells in bread and wine
And those are gathered twelve in number.
At night they scream in sleep under olive branches.
Saint Thomas dips the hand into the stigmata.

Der Spaziergang

1

Musik summt im Gehölz am Nachmittag.
Im Korn sich ernste Vogelscheuchen drehn.
Hollunderbüsche sacht am Weg verwehn;
Ein Haus zerflimmert wunderlich und vag.

In Goldnem schwebt ein Duft von Thymian,
Auf einem Stein steht eine heitere Zahl.
Auf einer Wiese spielen Kinder Ball,
Dann hebt ein Baum vor dir zu kreisen an.

Du träumst: die Schwester kämmt ihr blondes Haar,
Auch schreibt ein ferner Freund dir einen Brief.
Ein Schober flieht durchs Grau vergilbt und schief
Und manchmal schwebst du leicht und wunderbar.

2

Die Zeit verrinnt. O süßer Helios!
O Bild im Krötentümpel süß und klar;
Im Sand versinkt ein Eden wunderbar.
Goldammern wiegt ein Busch in seinem Schoß.

Ein Bruder stirbt dir in verwunschnem Land
Und stählern schaun dich deine Augen an.
In Goldnem dort ein Duft von Thymian.
Ein Knabe legt am Weiler einen Brand.

Die Liebenden in Faltern neu erglühn
Und schaukeln heiter hin um Stein und Zahl.
Aufflattern Krähen um ein ekles Mahl
Und deine Stirne tost durchs sanfte Grün.

Im Dornenstrauch verendet weich ein Wild.
Nachgleitet dir ein heller Kindertag,
Der graue Wind, der flatterhaft und vag
Verfallne Düfte durch die Dämmerung spült.

The Walk

1

In the afternoon music hums in the woods.
In the corn serious scarecrows revolve.
Along the way elder bushes are gently blown over;
A house glimmers strange and vague.

In gold a scent of thyme floats,
A humorous number stands on a stone.
In a meadow children play ball,
Then a tree begins to circle before you.

You dream: the sister combs her blond hair,
Also a far-away friend writes you a letter.
A haystack flees through grayness yellowed and askew
And sometimes you float light and miraculous.

2

Time trickles away. O sweet Helios!
O image sweet and clear in the toad pool;
Wonderfully an Eden sinks in sand.
A bush cradles yellowhammers in its lap.

A brother of yours dies in an execrated land
And steely your eyes behold yourself.
There in gold a scent of thyme.
A boy sets a fire in the hamlet.

The lovers glow anew among butterflies
And swing cheerfully around stone and number.
Crows flutter up around a nauseous meal
And your forehead roars through the soft green.

In the thorn bush a deer gently dies.
A happy day of childhood glides after you.
The gray wind, flighty and vague,
Swills decayed scents through the dusk.

3

Ein altes Wiegenlied macht dich sehr bang.
Am Wegrand fromm ein Weib ihr Kindlein stillt.
Traumwandelnd hörst du wie ihr Bronnen quillt.
Aus Apfelzweigen fällt ein Weiheklang.

Und Brot und Wein sind süß von harten Mühn.
Nach Früchten tastet silbern deine Hand.
Die tote Rahel geht durchs Ackerland.
Mit friedlicher Geberde winkt das Grün.

Gesegnet auch blüht armer Mägde Schoß,
Die träumend dort am alten Brunnen stehn.
Einsame froh auf stillen Pfaden gehn
Mit Gottes Kreaturen sündelos.

De profundis

Es ist ein Stoppelfeld, in das ein schwarzer Regen fällt.
Es ist ein brauner Baum, der einsam dasteht.
Es ist ein Zischelwind, der leere Hütten umkreist.
Wie traurig dieser Abend.

Am Weiler vorbei
Sammelt die sanfte Waise noch spärliche ähren ein.
Ihre Augen weiden rund und goldig in der Dämmerung
Und ihr Schoß harrt des himmlischen Bräutigams.

Bei der Heimkehr
Fanden die Hirten den süßen Leib
Verwest im Dornenbusch.

Ein Schatten bin ich ferne finsteren Dörfern.
Gottes Schweigen
Trank ich aus dem Brunnen des Hains.

Auf meine Stirne tritt kaltes Metall
Spinnen suchen mein Herz.
Es ist ein Licht, das in meinem Mund erlöscht.

3

An old lullaby makes you very anxious.
By the wayside a woman piously suckles her child.
Sleepwalking you hear her fountain well up.
A sound of consecration falls from the apple boughs.

And bread and wine are sweet from hard labor.
Silverly your hand fumbles for fruit.
The dead Rachel goes through farmland.
With peaceful gestures the green beckons.

Blessed also are the flowering wombs of poor maids,
Who stand dreaming there by the old fountain.
The lonely ones go gladly along silent paths
Among God's creatures without sin.

De profundis

It is a stubble field in which a black rain falls.
It is a brown tree that stands alone there.
It is a hissing wind that circles empty huts.
How sad is this evening.

Past the hamlet
The gentle orphan still gathers sparse ears of corn.
Her eyes graze round and golden in the dusk
And her womb awaits the heavenly bridegroom.

On the way home
Shepherds found the sweet body
Putrefied in the thorn bush.

I am a shadow far from sinister villages.
I drank God's silence
From the fountain in the grove.

Upon my forehead cold metal steps
Spiders seek my heart.
It is a light that extinguishes in my mouth.

Nachts fand ich mich auf einer Heide,
Starrend von Unrat und Staub der Sterne.
Im Haselgebüsch
Klangen wieder kristallne Engel.

Trompeten

Unter verschnittenen Weiden, wo braune Kinder spielen
Und Blätter treiben, tönen Trompeten. Ein Kirchhofsschauer.
Fahnen von Scharlach stürzen durch des Ahorns Trauer
Reiter entlang an Roggenfeldern, leeren Mühlen.

Oder Hirten singen nachts und Hirsche treten
In den Kreis ihrer Feuer, des Hains uralte Trauer,
Tanzende heben sich von einer schwarzen Mauer;
Fahnen von Scharlach, Lachen, Wahnsinn, Trompeten.

Dämmerung

Im Hof, verhext von milchigem Dämmerschein,
Durch Herbstgebräuntes weiche Kranke gleiten.
Ihr wächsern-runder Blick sinnt goldner Zeiten,
Erfüllt von Träumerei und Ruh und Wein.

Ihr Siechentum schließt geisterhaft sich ein.
Die Sterne weiße Traurigkeit verbreiten.
Im Grau, erfüllt von Täuschung und Geläuten,
Sieh, wie die Schrecklichen sich wirr zerstreun.

Formlose Spottgestalten huschen, kauern
Und flattern sie auf schwarz-gekreuzten Pfaden.
O! trauervolle Schatten an den Mauern.

Die andern fliehn durch dunkelnde Arkaden;
Und nächtens stürzen sie aus roten Schauern
Des Sternenwinds, gleich rasenden Mänaden.

At night I found myself on a heath
Covered with rubbish and the dust of stars.
In the hazel bush
Crystal angels sounded once more.

Trumpets

Under pruned willows, where brown children play
And leaves drift, trumpets resound. A churchyard's shudder.
Flags of scarlet fall through the maple's sadness,
Horsemen along rye fields, empty mills.

Or shepherds sing at night and stags step
Into the circle of their fire, the grove's ancient sorrow,
Dancers rise from a black wall;
Flags of scarlet, laughter, insanity, trumpets.

Dusk

In the courtyard, bewitched by milky twilight,
Gentle sick people glide through autumn-bronze.
Their waxy-round gaze ponders golden times
Fulfilled with daydream and rest and wine.

Ghostly their wasting illness entraps them.
The stars spread white sadness.
In grayness, fulfilled with delusion and pealing of bells,
See how the frightful scatter in confusion.

Formless figures of ridicule, they shoo, crouch down
And flutter on black-crossed paths.
O! mournful shadows on the walls.

The others escape through darkening arcades
And at night they fall from red shudders
Of the starry wind like raging Maenads.

Heiterer Frühling
[2. Fassung]

1

Am Bach, der durch das gelbe Brachfeld fließt,
Zieht noch das dürre Rohr vom vorigen Jahr.
Durchs Graue gleiten Klänge wunderbar,
Vorüberweht ein Hauch von warmem Mist.

An Weiden baumeln Kätzchen sacht im Wind,
Sein traurig Lied singt träumend ein Soldat.
Ein Wiesenstreifen saust verweht und matt,
Ein Kind steht in Konturen weich und lind.

Die Birken dort, der schwarze Dornenstrauch,
Auch fliehn im Rauch Gestalten aufgelöst.
Hell Grünes blüht und anderes verwest
Und Kröten schliefen durch den jungen Lauch.

2

Dich lieb ich treu du derbe Wäscherin,
Noch trägt die Flut des Himmels goldene Last.
Ein Fischlein blitzt vorüber und verblaßt;
Ein wächsern Antlitz fließt durch Erlen hin.

In Gärten sinken Glocken lang und leis
Ein kleiner Vogel trällert wie verrückt.
Das sanfte Korn schwillt leise und verzückt
Und Bienen sammeln noch mit ernstem Fleiß.

Komm Liebe nun zum müden Arbeitsmann!
In seine Hütte fällt ein lauer Strahl.
Der Wald strömt durch den Abend herb und fahl
Und Knospen knistern heiter dann und wann.

3

Wie scheint doch alles Werdende so krank!

Cheerful Spring

[version 2]

1

Beside the brook, which flows through the yellow fallow field,
The dry reed from last year still moves.
Sounds glide wonderfully through grayness,
A whiff of warm muck blows by.

From willows catkins dangle placidly in the wind.
Dreamily a soldier sings his sad song.
A strip of meadow swishes blown and dull,
A child stands in silhouette gentle and dulcet.

The birches there, the black thorn bush,
Also shapes flee dissolved in smoke.
Brightly green blooms and another rots
And toads slept among the young leeks.

2

I love you truly, sturdy laundress,
Still the flood bears the sky's golden burden.
A small fish flashes past and fades;
A waxy countenance flows along through the alders.

In gardens bells sink long and quiet
A small bird warbles like crazy.
The gentle corn swells quiet and ecstatic
And bees still gather with earnest diligence.

Love, come now to the weary laborer!
Into his hut a mild beam falls.
The forest streams through the evening harsh and sallow
And now and then buds crackle cheerfully.

3

Yet how all that is being born seems so ill!

Ein Fieberhauch um einen Weiler kreist;
Doch aus Gezweigen winkt ein sanfter Geist
Und öffnet das Gemüte weit und bang.

Ein blühender Erguß verrinnt sehr sacht
Und Ungebornes pflegt der eignen Ruh.
Die Liebenden blühn ihren Sternen zu
Und süßer fließt ihr Odem durch die Nacht.

So schmerzlich gut und wahrhaft ist, was lebt;
Und leise rührt dich an ein alter Stein:
Wahrlich! Ich werde immer bei euch sein.
O Mund! der durch die Silberweide bebt.

Vorstadt im Föhn

Am Abend liegt die Stätte öd und braun,
Die Luft von gräulichem Gestank durchzogen.
Das Donnern eines Zugs vom Brückenbogen –
Und Spatzen flattern über Busch und Zaun.

Geduckte Hütten, Pfade wirr verstreut,
In Gärten Durcheinander und Bewegung,
Bisweilen schwillt Geheul aus dumpfer Regung,
In einer Kinderschar fliegt rot ein Kleid.

Am Kehricht pfeift verliebt ein Rattenchor.
In Körben tragen Frauen Eingeweide,
Ein ekelhafter Zug voll Schmutz und Räude,
Kommen sie aus der Dämmerung hervor.

Und ein Kanal speit plötzlich feistes Blut
Vom Schlachthaus in den stillen Fluß hinunter.
Die Föhne färben karge Stauden bunter
Und langsam kriecht die Röte durch die Flut.

Ein Flüstern, das in trübem Schlaf ertrinkt.
Gebilde gaukeln auf aus Wassergräben,
Vielleicht Erinnerung an ein früheres Leben,
Die mit den warmen Winden steigt und sinkt.

A whiff of fever encircles a hamlet.
Yet from the branches a gentle spirit beckons
And opens the mind wide and frightened.

A blooming outpour trickles away very gradually
And the unborn tends to its own repose.
The lovers bloom toward their stars
And sweeter their breath flows through the night.

So painfully good and true is, what lives;
And quietly an old stone touches you:
Truly! I will always be with you.
O mouth! that trembles through the white willow.

Suburb in Foehn

In the evening the site lies deserted and brown,
The air pervaded with a horrid stench.
The thunder of a train from the bridge arch—
And sparrows flutter about bush and fence.

Cowering huts, paths scattered chaotically,
In the gardens confusion and movement,
Sometimes howls swell out of muffled stirring,
In a group of children a red dress flies.

By the rubbish a rat's choir whistles amorously.
In baskets women carry entrails,
A vile procession full of filth and mange,
They emerge from the twilight.

And a sewer suddenly vomits fatty blood
From the slaughterhouse down into the still river.
The foehn tinges meager shrubs more colorfully
And the redness slowly creeps through the flood.

A whispering that drowns in bleary sleep.
Shapes juggle up on the drains,
Perhaps the memory of an earlier life,
Which rises and sinks with the warm winds.

Aus Wolken tauchen schimmernde Alleen,
Erfüllt von schönen Wägen, kühnen Reitern.
Dann sieht man auch ein Schiff auf Klippen scheitern
Und manchmal rosenfarbene Moscheen.

Die Ratten

In Hof scheint weiß der herbstliche Mond.
Vom Dachrand fallen phantastische Schatten.
Ein Schweigen in leeren Fenstern wohnt;
Da tauchen leise herauf die Ratten

Und huschen pfeifend hier und dort
Und ein gräulicher Dunsthauch wittert
Ihnen nach aus dem Abort,
Den geisterhaft der Mondschein durchzittert

Und sie keifen vor Gier wie toll
Und erfüllen Haus und Scheunen,
Die von Korn und Früchten voll.
Eisige Winde im Dunkel greinen.

Trübsinn
[1. Fassung]

Weltunglück geistert durch den Nachmittag.
Baraken fliehn durch Gärtchen braun und wüst.
Lichtschnuppen gaukeln um verbrannten Mist,
Zwei Schläfer schwanken heimwärts, grau und vag.

Auf der verdorrten Wiese läuft ein Kind
Und spielt mit seinen Augen schwarz und glatt.
Das Gold tropft von den Büschen trüb und matt.
Ein alter Mann dreht traurig sich im Wind.

Am Abend wieder über meinem Haupt
Saturn lenkt stumm ein elendes Geschick.
Ein Baum, ein Hund tritt hinter sich zurück

From clouds gleaming avenues surface
Fulfilled with beautiful chariots, daring riders.
Then one also sees a boat foundering on rocks
And sometimes rose-colored mosques.

The Rats

In the courtyard the autumn moon shines white.
From the eaves phantom-like shadows drop.
A silence dwells in empty windows;
Then the rats dip quietly upstairs

And scurry whistling here and there
And a grayish whiff of vapor drifts
After them from the outhouse
Through which the moonlight trembles ghostly

And they nag as if mad from greed
And crowd house and barns
Filled with corn and fruits.
Icy winds whine in the darkness.

Doldrums
[version 1]

World misfortune wanders ghostly through the afternoon.
Shanties flee through small gardens brown and deserted.
Sparks flitter around burnt muck.
Two sleepers stagger homeward, gray and vague.

On the withered meadow a child runs
And plays with his eyes black and smooth.
Gold drips from the bushes murky and dull.
An old man turns sadly in the wind.

In the evening above my head
Saturn again mutely guides a wretched fate.
A tree, a dog scratches behind itself

Und schwarz schwankt Gottes Himmel und entlaubt.

Ein Fischlein gleitet schnell hinab den Bach;
Und leise rührt des toten Freundes Hand
Und glättet liebend Stirne und Gewand.
Ein Licht ruft Schatten in den Zimmern wach.

In den Nachmittag geflüstert

Sonne, herbstlich dünn und zag,
Und das Obst fällt von den Bäumen.
Stille wohnt in blauen Räumen
Einen langen Nachmittag.

Sterbeklänge von Metall;
Und ein weißes Tier bricht nieder.
Brauner Mädchen rauhe Lieder
Sind verweht im Blätterfall.

Stirne Gottes Farben träumt,
Spürt des Wahnsinns sanfte Flügel.
Schatten drehen sich am Hügel
Von Verwesung schwarz umsäumt.

Dämmerung voll Ruh und Wein;
Traurige Guitarren rinnen.
Und zur milden Lampe drinnen
Kehrst du wie im Traume ein.

Psalm
[2. Fassung]

Karl Kraus zugeeignet

Es ist ein Licht, das der Wind ausgelöscht hat.
Es ist ein Heidekrug, den am Nachmittag ein Betrunkener verläßt.
Es ist ein Weinberg, verbrannt und schwarz mit Löchern voll Spinnen.
Es ist ein Raum, den sie mit Milch getüncht haben.

And God's sky sways black and defoliated.

Swiftly a small fish glides down the brook;
And quietly the dead friend's hand stirs
And lovingly smooths forehead and robe.
A light rouses shadows in the rooms.

Whispered in the Afternoon

Sun, autumn thin and apprehensive,
And the fruit falls from the trees.
Stillness dwells in blue rooms
A long afternoon.

Dying-sounds of metal;
And a white animal breaks down.
The coarse songs of brown girls
Have blown away in the falling leaves.

The forehead dreams God's colors,
Feels the gentle wings of insanity.
Shadows revolve on the hill
Fringed blackly by rot.

Dusk full of rest and wine;
Sad guitars flow.
And as if in a dream
You turn to the calm lamp within.

Psalm
[version 2]

Dedicated to Karl Kraus

It is a light, which the wind has extinguished.
It is a village inn, which a drunkard abandons in the afternoon.
It is a vineyard, burned and black with holes full of spiders.
It is a room, which they have whitewashed with milk.

Der Wahnsinnige ist gestorben. Es ist eine Insel der Südsee,
Den Sonnengott zu empfangen. Man rührt die Trommeln.
Die Männer führen kriegerische Tänze auf.
Die Frauen wiegen die Hüften in Schlinggewächsen und Feuerblumen,
Wenn das Meer singt. O unser verlorenes Paradies.

Die Nymphen haben die goldenen Wälder verlassen.
Man begräbt den Fremden. Dann hebt ein Flimmerregen an.
Der Sohn des Pan erscheint in Gestalt eines Erdarbeiters,
Der den Mittag am glühenden Asphalt verschläft.
Es sind kleine Mädchen in einem Hof in Kleidchen voll herzzerreißender
    Armut.
Es sind Zimmer, erfüllt von Akkorden und Sonaten.
Es sind Schatten, die sich vor einem erblindeten Spiegel umarmen.
An den Fenstern des Spitals wärmen sich Genesende.
Ein weißer Dampfer am Kanal trägt blutige Seuchen herauf.

Die fremde Schwester erscheint wieder in jemands bösen Träumen.
Ruhend im Haselgebüsch spielt sie mit seinen Schatten.
Der Student, vielleicht ein Doppelgänger, schaut ihr lange vom Fenster
    nach.
Hinter ihm steht sein toter Bruder, oder er geht die alte Wendeltreppe
    herab.
Im Dunkel brauner Kastanien verblaßt die Gestalt des jungen Novizen.
Der Garten ist im Abend. Im Kreuzgang flattern die Fledermäuse umher.
Die Kinder des Hausmeisters hören zu spielen auf und suchen das Gold des
    Himmels.
Endakkorde eines Quartetts. Die kleine Blinde läuft zitternd durch die
    Allee,
Und später tastet ihr Schatten an kalten Mauern hin, umgeben vom Märchen
    und heiligen Legenden.

Es ist ein leeres Boot, das am Abend den schwarzen Kanal heruntertreibt.
In der Düsternis des alten Asyls verfallen menschliche Ruinen.
Die toten Waisen liegen an der Gartenmauer.
Aus grauen Zimmern treten Engel mit kotgefleckten Flügeln.
Würmer tropfen von ihren vergilbten Lidern.
Der Platz vor der Kirche ist finster und schweigsam, wie in den Tagen der
    Kindheit.
Auf silbernen Sohlen gleiten frühere Leben vorbei
Und die Schatten der Verdammten steigen zu den seufzenden Wassern nieder.
In seinem Grab spielt der weiße Magier mit seinen Schlangen.

Schweigsam über der Schädelstätte öffnen sich Gottes goldene Augen.

The lunatic is dead. It is an island in the South Pacific
To receive the sun god. One beats the drums.
The men perform warlike dances.
When the sea sings, women sway the hips
Between climbing plants and fire flowers. O our lost paradise.

The nymphs have left the golden forests.
One buries the stranger. Then a shimmering rain begins.
The son of Pan appears in the guise of an excavator
Who sleeps away the midday near the glowing asphalt.
There are small girls in a courtyard in little dresses full of heartbreaking
    poverty!
There are rooms fulfilled with chords and sonatas.
There are shadows that embrace before a blind mirror.
By the windows of the hospital convalescents warm themselves.
A white steamboat in the canal bears bloody epidemics along.

The strange sister appears again in someone's evil dreams.
Resting in the hazel bush she plays with his stars.
The student, possibly a double, looks after her from the window for a long
    time.
His dead brother stands behind him, or he descends the old spiral staircase.
In the darkness of brown chestnuts the figure of the young novice grows
    pale.
The garden is in evening. In the cloister the bats flutter about.
The caretaker's children stop to play and search the gold of heaven.
Closing chords of a quartet. The small blind girl runs trembling through
    the avenue,
And later her shadow gropes along cold walls surrounded by fairy tales
    and holy legends.

It is an empty boat, which drifts down the black canal in the evening.
In the somberness of the old asylum human ruins decay.
The dead orphans lie by the garden wall.
From gray rooms angels step with excrement-splattered wings.
Worms drip from their yellowed eyelids.
The plaza before the church is sinister and taciturn, like in the days of
    childhood.
On silver soles former lives glide past
And the shadows of the damned descend to the sighing waters.
In his grave the white magician plays with his snakes.

Taciturnly over the place of skulls God's golden eyes open.

Rosenkranzlieder

An die Schwester

Wo du gehst wird Herbst und Abend,
Blaues Wild, das unter Bäumen tönt,
Einsamer Weiher am Abend.

Leise der Flug der Vögel tönt,
Die Schwermut über deinen Augenbogen.
Dein schmales Lächeln tönt.

Gott hat deine Lider verbogen.
Sterne suchen nachts, Karfreitagskind,
Deinen Stirnenbogen.

Nähe des Todes
  [2. Fassung]

O der Abend, der in die finsteren Dörfer der Kindheit geht.
Der Weiher unter den Weiden
Füllt sich mit den verpesteten Seufzern der Schwermut.

O der Wald, der leise die braunen Augen senkt,
Da aus des Einsamen knöchernen Händen
Der Purpur seiner verzückten Tage hinsinkt.

O die Nähe des Todes. Laß uns beten.
In dieser Nacht lösen auf lauen Kissen
Vergilbt von Weihrauch sich der Liebenden schmächtige Glieder.

Amen

Verwestes gleitend durch die morsche Stube;
Schatten an gelben Tapeten; in dunklen Spiegeln wölbt
Sich unserer Hände elfenbeinerne Traurigkeit.

Braune Perlen rinnen durch die erstorbenen Finger.
In der Stille
Tun sich eines Engels blaue Mohnaugen auf.

Rosary Songs

To the Sister

Wherever you go becomes autumn and evening,
Blue deer, which sounds under trees,
Lonely pond in the evening.

Quietly the flight of birds sounds,
The gloom above the arches of your eyes.
Your narrow smile sounds.

God has twisted your eyelids.
At night, Good Friday's child, stars seek
The arch of your brow.

Nearness of Death
[version 2]

O the evening, which goes into the sinister villages of childhood.
The pond under the willows
Fills with the contaminated sighs of gloom.

O the forest, which quietly lowers brown eyes,
When from the lonely one's bony hands
The purple of his ecstatic days sinks down.

O the nearness of death. Let us pray.
During this night on warm pillows yellowed by incense
The slender limbs of lovers release.

Amen

Putrid shape gliding through the moldered room;
Shadows on yellow wallpapers; in dark mirrors
The ivory sadness of our hands arches.

Brown beads run through dead fingers.
In the stillness
The blue poppy-eyes of an angel open.

Blau ist auch der Abend;
Die Stunde unseres Absterbens, Azraels Schatten,
Der ein braunes Gärtchen verdunkelt.

Verfall

[2. Fassung]

Am Abend, wenn die Glocken Frieden läuten,
Folg ich der Vögel wundervollen Flügen,
Die lang geschart, gleich frommen Pilgerzügen,
Entschwinden in den herbstlich klaren Weiten.

Hinwandelnd durch den dämmervollen Garten
Träum ich nach ihren helleren Geschicken
Und fühl der Stunden Weiser kaum mehr rücken.
So folg ich über Wolken ihren Fahrten.

Da macht ein Hauch mich von Verfall erzittern.
Die Amsel klagt in den entlaubten Zweigen.
Es schwankt der rote Wein an rostigen Gittern,

Indes wie blasser Kinder Todesreigen
Um dunkle Brunnenränder, die verwittern,
Im Wind sich fröstelnd blaue Astern neigen.

In der Heimat

Resedenduft durchs kranke Fenster irrt;
Ein alter Platz, Kastanien schwarz und wüst.
Das Dach durchbricht ein goldener Strahl und fließt
Auf die Geschwister traumhaft und verwirrt.

Im Spülicht treibt Verfallnes, leise girrt
Der Föhn im braunen Gärtchen; sehr still genießt
Ihr Gold die Sonnenblume und zerfließt.
Durch blaue Luft der Ruf der Wache klirrt.

Resedenduft. Die Mauern dämmern kahl.

The evening is also blue;
The hour of our dying, Azreal's shadow,
Which darkens a brown garden.

Decay

[version 2]

In the evening, when the bells ring peace,
I follow the wonderful flights of birds
That in long rows, like devout processions of pilgrims,
Disappear into the clear autumn vastness.

Wandering through the dusk-filled garden
I dream after their brighter destinies
And barely feel the motion of the hour hands.
Thus I follow their journeys over the clouds.

Then a whiff of decay makes me tremble.
The blackbird complains in defoliated branches.
The red wine sways on rusty trellises.

While like the death-dances of pale children
Around dark fountain edges that weather,
Shivering blue asters bend in the wind.

In the Homeland

Mignonette-scent strays through the sick window;
An old plaza, chestnut trees black and wasted.
A golden ray breaks through the roof and flows
Over the siblings dreamlike and confused.

Decay drifts in the dishwater, the foehn
Quietly coos through the small brown garden; very still
The sunflower savors its gold and melts away.
Through blue air the call of the guard rattles.

Mignonette-scent. The walls dusk bleakly.

Der Schwester Schlaf ist schwer. Der Nachtwind wühlt
In ihrem Haar, das mondner Glanz umspült.

Der Katze Schatten gleitet blau und schmal
Vom morschen Dach, das nahes Unheil säumt,
Die Kerzenflamme, die sich purpurn bäumt.

Ein Herbstabend

An Karl Röck

Das braune Dorf. Ein Dunkles zeigt im Schreiten
Sich oft an Mauern, die im Herbste stehn,
Gestalten: Mann wie Weib, Verstorbene gehn
In kühlen Stuben jener Bett bereiten.

Hier spielen Knaben. Schwere Schatten breiten
Sich über braune Jauche. Mägde gehn
Durch feuchte Bläue und bisweilen sehn
Aus Augen sie, erfüllt von Nachtgeläuten.

Für Einsames ist eine Schenke da;
Das säumt geduldig unter dunklen Bogen,
Von goldenem Tabaksgewölk umzogen.

Doch immer ist das Eigne schwarz und nah.
Der Trunkne sinnt im Schatten alter Bogen
Den wilden Vögeln nach, die ferngezogen.

Menschliches Elend
[2. Fassung]

Die Uhr, die vor der Sonne fünfe schlägt –
Einsame Menschen packt ein dunkles Grausen,
Im Abendgarten kahle Bäume sausen.
Des Toten Antlitz sich am Fenster regt.

Vielleicht, daß diese Stunde stille steht.

The sister's sleep is heavy. The night wind rummages
Through her hair, bathed in lunar brilliance.

The cat's shadow glides blue and slender
From the moldered roof which borders near mischief,
The candle flame that rears up purple.

An Autumn Evening

To Karl Röck

The brown village. A darkness is often reflected
By striding along walls that stand in autumn,
Figures: both man and woman, deceased walk
In cool rooms to prepare their bed.

Here boys play. Heavy shadows broaden
Over brown manure. Maids walk
Through moist blueness and sometimes they look
Out of eyes filled with night-chimes.

For the lonely one there is an inn;
It waits patiently under dark arches
Where golden clouds of tobacco move around.

Yet always the self is black and near.
The drunk ponders in the shadow of ancient arches
After wild birds that are drawn far away.

Human Misery
[version 2]

The clock that strikes five before the sun—
A dark horror grips lonely people,
In the evening garden bleak trees swish,
The dead one's countenance stirs at the window.

Perhaps this hour stands still.

Vor trüben Augen blaue Bilder gaukeln
Im Takt der Schiffe, die am Flusse schaukeln.
Am Kai ein Schwesternzug vorüberweht.

Im Hasel spielen Mädchen blaß und blind,
Wie Liebende, die sich im Schlaf umschlingen.
Vielleicht, daß um ein Aas dort Fliegen singen,
Vielleicht auch weint im Mutterschoß ein Kind.

Aus Händen sinken Astern blau und rot,
Des Jünglings Mund entgleitet fremd und weise;
Und Lider flattern angstverwirrt und leise;
Durch Fieberschwärze weht ein Duft von Brot.

Es scheint, man hört auch gräßliches Geschrei;
Gebeine durch verfallne Mauern schimmern.
Ein böses Herz lacht laut in schönen Zimmern;
An einem Träumer lauft ein Hund vorbei.

Ein leerer Sarg im Dunkel sich verliert.
Dem Mörder will ein Raum sich bleich erhellen,
Indes Laternen nachts im Sturm zerschellen.
Des Edlen weiße Schläfe Lorbeer ziert.

Im Dorf

1

Aus braunen Mauern tritt ein Dorf, ein Feld.
Ein Hirt verwest auf einem alten Stein.
Der Saum des Walds schließt blaue Tiere ein,
Das sanfte Laub, das in die Stille fällt.

Der Bauern braune Stirnen. Lange tönt
Die Abendglocke; schön ist frommer Brauch,
Des Heilands schwarzes Haupt im Dornenstrauch,
Die kühle Stube, die der Tod versöhnt.

Wie bleich die Mütter sind. Die Bläue sinkt
Auf Glas und Truh, die stolz ihr Sinn bewahrt;
Auch neigt ein weißes Haupt sich hochbejahrt

Before dull eyes blue images flutter
To the rhythm of ships which rock in the river.
At the wharf a row of nuns blows by.

In the hazel bush girls play pale and blind
Like lovers who embrace in sleep.
Perhaps flies linger around a carcass there,
Perhaps also a child weeps in the mother's lap.

From hands asters sink blue and red,
The youth's mouth slips away strange and wise;
And eyelids flutter confused with fear and quiet;
Through fevered blackness an aroma of bread blows.

It seems one also hears horrible screaming;
Bones shimmer through decayed walls.
An evil heart laughs loudly in beautiful rooms;
A dog runs past a dreamer.

An empty coffin gets lost in the darkness.
A room wants to light up palely for the murderer,
While lanterns are smashed in the night's storm.
Laurel adorns the noble one's white temple.

In the Village

1

A village, a field step from brown walls.
A shepherd molders on an old stone.
The edge of the forest includes blue animals,
The soft leaves that fall in the stillness.

The peasants' brown foreheads. The evening bell
Sounds long; beautiful are pious customs,
The Savior's black head in the thorn bush,
The cool room that death reconciles.

How pale the mothers are. The blueness sinks
On glass and chest, which their mind proudly preserves;
Also a white head bends highly aged

Aufs Enkelkind, das Milch und Sterne trinkt.

2

Der Arme, der im Geiste einsam starb,
Steigt wächsern über einen alten Pfad.
Die Apfelbäume sinken kahl und stad
Ins Farbige ihrer Frucht, die schwarz verdarb.

Noch immer wölbt das Dach aus dürrem Stroh
Sich übern Schlaf der Kühe. Die blinde Magd
Erscheint im Hof; ein blaues Wasser klagt;
Ein Pferdeschädel starrt vom morschen Tor.

Der Idiot spricht dunklen Sinns ein Wort
Der Liebe, das im schwarzen Busch verhallt,
Wo jene steht in schmaler Traumgestalt.
Der Abend tönt in feuchter Bläue fort.

3

Ans Fenster schlagen äste föhnentlaubt.
Im Schoß der Bäurin wächst ein wildes Weh.
Durch ihre Arme rieselt schwarzer Schnee;
Goldäugige Eulen flattern um ihr Haupt.

Die Mauern starren kahl und grauverdreckt
Ins kühle Dunkel. Im Fieberbette friert
Der schwangere Leib, den frech der Mond bestiert.
Vor ihrer Kammer ist ein Hund verreckt.

Drei Männer treten finster durch das Tor
Mit Sensen, die im Feld zerbrochen sind.
Durchs Fenster klirrt der rote Abendwind;
Ein schwarzer Engel tritt daraus hervor.

Over the grandchild who drinks milk and stars.

2

The poor one, who died lonely in spirit,
Rises waxen over an old path.
The apple trees sink bleak and calm
Into the colors of their fruit which spoiled blackly.

Still the roof of dried straw arches
Over the sleep of cows. The blind maid
Appears in the yard; a blue water laments;
A horse's skull stares from the rotten gate.

With dark mind the idiot speaks a word
Of love, which fades away in the black bush
Where the other stands as a slender dream-figure.
The evening sounds forth in moister blue.

3

At the window branches knock stripped bare by the foehn.
In the womb of the peasant woman a wild pain grows.
Black snow trickles through her arms;
Golden-eyed owls flutter around her head.

The walls stare bleak and gray-soiled
In the cool darkness. In the fever-bed
The pregnant belly freezes, insolently ogled by the moon.
In front of her chamber a dog has died.

Sinisterly three men step through the gate
With scythes broken in the field.
Through the window the red evening wind rattles;
From it a black angel steps out.

Abendlied

Am Abend, wenn wir auf dunklen Pfaden gehn,
Erscheinen unsere bleichen Gestalten vor uns.

Wenn uns dürstet,
Trinken wir die weißen Wasser des Teichs,
Die Süße unserer traurigen Kindheit.

Erstorbene ruhen wir unterm Hollundergebüsch,
Schaun den grauen Möven zu.

Frühlingsgewölke steigen über die finstere Stadt,
Die der Mönche edlere Zeiten schweigt.

Da ich deine schmalen Hände nahm
Schlugst du leise die runden Augen auf,
Dieses ist lange her.

Doch wenn dunkler Wohllaut die Seele heimsucht,
Erscheinst du Weiße in des Freundes herbstlicher Landschaft.

Drei Blicke in einen Opal

An Erhard Buschbeck

1

Blick in Opal: ein Dorf umkränzt von dürrem Wein,
Der Stille grauer Wolken, gelber Felsenhügel
Und abendlicher Quellen Kühle: Zwillingsspiegel
Umrahmt von Schatten und von schleimigem Gestein.

Des Herbstes Weg und Kreuze gehn in Abend ein,
Singende Pilger und die blutbefleckten Linnen.
Des Einsamen Gestalt kehrt also sich nach innen
Und geht, ein bleicher Engel, durch den leeren Hain.

Aus Schwarzem bläst der Föhn. Mit Satyrn im Verein
Sind schlanke Weiblein; Mönche der Wollust bleiche Priester,

Evening Song

In the evening, when we go on dark paths,
Our pale figures appear before us.

If we thirst,
We drink the white water of the pond,
The sweetness of our sad childhood.

Deceased we rest under the elder bushes,
Watch the gray gulls.

Spring clouds rise over the sinister city
That silences the nobler times of monks.

When I took your slender hands
You quietly opened round eyes,
This is long ago.

Yet when the dark harmony visits my soul,
You appear white in the friend's autumn landscape.

Three Gazes into an Opal

To Erhard Buschbeck

1

Gaze into an opal: a village wreathed in dry vines,
The stillness of gray clouds, yellow cliff,
And the coolness of evening springs: twin mirrors
Framed by shadows and by slimy stone.

The way and crosses of autumn are received into evening,
Singing pilgrims and the bloodstained linens.
The lonely one's figure turns inward,
A pale angel, and goes through the empty grove.

Out of blackness the foehn blows. Slender women
Are together with satyrs; monks, pale priests of lust,

Ihr Wahnsinn schmückt mit Lilien sich schön und düster
Und hebt die Hände auf zu Gottes goldenem Schrein.

2

Der ihn befeuchtet, rosig hängt ein Tropfen Tau
Im Rosmarin: hinfließt ein Hauch von Grabgerüchen,
Spitälern, wirr erfüllt von Fieberschrein und Flüchen.
Gebein steigt aus dem Erbbegräbnis morsch und grau.

In blauem Schleim und Schleiern tanzt des Greisen Frau,
Das schmutzstarrende Haar erfüllt von schwarzen Tränen,
Die Knaben träumen wirr in dürren Weidensträhnen
Und ihre Stirnen sind von Aussatz kahl und rauh.

Durchs Bogenfenster sinkt ein Abend lind und lau.
Ein Heiliger tritt aus seinen schwarzen Wundenmalen.
Die Purpurschnecken kriechen aus zerbrochenen Schalen
Und speien Blut in Dorngewinde starr und grau.

3

Die Blinden streuen in eiternde Wunden Weiherauch.
Rotgoldene Gewänder; Fackeln; Psalmensingen;
Und Mädchen, die wie Gift den Leib des Herrn umschlingen.
Gestalten schreiten wächsernstarr durch Glut und Rauch.

Aussätziger mitternächtigen Tanz führt an ein Gauch
Dürrknöchern. Garten wunderlicher Abenteuer;
Verzerrtes; Blumenfratzen, Lachen; Ungeheuer
Und rollendes Gestirn im schwarzen Dornenstrauch.

O Armut, Bettelsuppe, Brot und süßer Lauch;
Des Lebens Träumerei in Hütten vor den Wäldern.
Grau härtet sich der Himmel über gelben Feldern
Und eine Abendglocke singt nach altem Brauch.

Their insanity adorns itself beautifully and somberly with lilies
And lifts the hands to God's golden shrine.

2

Rosily a drop of dew hangs in the rosemary
Which it moistens: a whiff of grave-smells flows away,
Of hospitals, woozily fulfilled by fever-screams and curses.
Skeletons rise from the family vault moldered and gray.

In blue slime and veils the old man's wife dances,
Her dirt-stiffen hair fulfilled with black tears,
The boys dream woozily in dry strands of willows
And their foreheads are bald and rough with leprosy.

Through the arched window an evening sinks dulcet and lukewarm.
A saint steps out of his black wound stigmata.
Purple snails creep from broken shells
And spew blood in thorn-threads stiff and gray.

3

The blind sprinkle incense into ulcerating wounds.
Red-golden robes; torches; singing of psalms;
And girls who embrace the Lord's body like poison.
Figures walk rigid as wax through embers and smoke.

A fool leads the midnight dance of lepers
With dry bones. Garden of fantastical adventures;
Distorted; flower-grimaces, laughter; monsters
And rolling stars in a black thorn bush.

O poverty, beggar's soup, bread and sweet leek;
Daydreaming of life in huts before the forests.
The sky above yellow fields hardens into gray
And an evening bell sings according to old custom.

Nachtlied

Des Unbewegten Odem. Ein Tiergesicht
Erstarrt vor Bläue, ihrer Heiligkeit.
Gewaltig ist das Schweigen im Stein;

Die Maske eines nächtlichen Vogels. Sanfter Dreiklang
Verklingt in einem. Elai! dein Antlitz
Beugt sich sprachlos über bläuliche Wasser.

O! ihr stillen Spiegel der Wahrheit.
An des Einsamen elfenbeinerner Schläfe
Erscheint der Abglanz gefallener Engel.

Helian

In den einsamen Stunden des Geistes
Ist es schön, in der Sonne zu gehn
An den gelben Mauern des Sommers hin.
Leise klingen die Schritte im Gras; doch immer schläft
Der Sohn des Pan im grauen Marmor.

Abends auf der Terrasse betranken wir uns mit braunem Wein.
Rötlich glüht der Pfirsich im Laub;
Sanfte Sonate, frohes Lachen.

Schön ist die Stille der Nacht.
Auf dunklem Plan
Begegnen wir uns mit Hirten und weißen Sternen.

Wenn es Herbst geworden ist
Zeigt sich nüchterne Klarheit im Hain.
Besänftigte wandeln wir an roten Mauern hin
Und die runden Augen folgen dem Flug der Vögel.
Am Abend sinkt das weiße Wasser in Graburnen.

In kahlen Gezweigen feiert der Himmel.
In reinen Händen trägt der Landmann Brot und Wein
Und friedlich reifen die Früchte in sonniger Kammer.

Night Song

The breath of the unmoved. An animal face
Stiffens in blueness, its holiness.
Enormous is the silence in stone;

The mask of a nocturnal bird. Soft triad
Fades into one sound. Elai! your countenance
Bends speechless over bluish waters.

O! you still mirrors of truth.
On the ivory temple of the lonely one
The reflection of fallen angels appears.

Helian

In the lonely hours of the spirit
It is beautiful to walk in the sun
Along the yellow walls of summer.
Quietly the steps sound in the grass; but always
The son of Pan sleeps in the gray marble.

Evenings on the terrace we got drunk with brown wine.
The peach glows reddish in the foliage;
Soft sonata, glad laughter.

Beautiful is the stillness of night.
On a dark plain
We meet ourselves with shepherds and white stars.

When autumn has come
A sober clarity appears in the grove.
Calmed we stroll along red walls
And the round eyes follow the flight of birds.
In the evening the white water sinks into funeral urns.

The sky celebrates in bare branches.
In pure hands the countryman carries bread and wine
And the fruits ripen peacefully in a sunny chamber.

O wie ernst ist das Antlitz der teueren Toten.
Doch die Seele erfreut gerechtes Anschaun.

Gewaltig ist das Schweigen des verwüsteten Gartens,
Da der junge Novize die Stirne mit braunem Laub bekränzt,
Sein Odem eisiges Gold trinkt.

Die Hände rühren das Alter bläulicher Wasser
Oder in kalter Nacht die weißen Wangen der Schwestern.

Leise und harmonisch ist ein Gang an freundlichen Zimmern hin,
Wo Einsamkeit ist und das Rauschen des Ahorns,
Wo vielleicht noch die Drossel singt.

Schön ist der Mensch und erscheinend im Dunkel,
Wenn er staunend Arme und Beine bewegt,
Und in purpurnen Höhlen stille die Augen rollen.

Zur Vesper verliert sich der Fremdling in schwarzer Novemberzerstörung,
Unter morschem Geäst, an Mauern voll Aussatz hin,
Wo vordem der heilige Bruder gegangen,
Versunken in das sanfte Saitenspiel seines Wahnsinns,

O wie einsam endet der Abendwind.
Ersterbend neigt sich das Haupt im Dunkel des Ölbaums.

Erschütternd ist der Untergang des Geschlechts.
In dieser Stunde füllen sich die Augen des Schauenden
Mit dem Gold seiner Sterne.

Am Abend versinkt ein Glockenspiel, das nicht mehr tönt,
Verfallen die schwarzen Mauern am Platz,
Ruft der tote Soldat zum Gebet.

Ein bleicher Engel
Tritt der Sohn ins leere Haus seiner Väter.

Die Schwestern sind ferne zu weißen Greisen gegangen.
Nachts fand sie der Schläfer unter den Säulen im Hausflur,
Zurückgekehrt von traurigen Pilgerschaften.

O how earnest is the countenance of the beloved dead.
But righteous viewing delights the soul.

The silence of the ravaged garden is immense,
When the young novice wreaths his forehead with brown leaves,
His breath drinks icy gold.

The hands touch the age of bluish waters
Or in cold night the white cheeks of the sisters.

Quiet and harmonious is a walk along friendly rooms
Where solitude is and the maple's rustling,
Where perhaps the thrush still sings.

Beautiful is man and appearing in darkness,
When marveling he moves arms and legs,
And the eyes roll silently in purple sockets.

At vespers the stranger loses himself in November's black destruction,
Under rotten branches, along walls full of leprosy,
Where the holy brother had walked before
Rapt in the gentle string music of his insanity,

O how lonely the evening wind ends.
Dying away the head bends down in the darkness of the olive tree.

Devastating is the decline of the race.
In this hour the eyes of the beholder fill
With the gold of his stars.

In the evening a glockenspiel that no longer rings sinks down,
The black walls decay by the square,
The dead soldier calls for prayer.

A pale angel
The son steps into the empty house of his fathers.

The sisters have gone far away to white old men.
At night the sleeper found them under columns in the hallway
Returned from sad pilgrimages.

O wie starrt von Kot und Würmern ihr Haar,
Da er darein mit silbernen Füßen steht,
Und jene verstorben aus kahlen Zimmern treten.

O ihr Psalmen in feurigen Mitternachtsregen,
Da die Knechte mit Nesseln die sanften Augen schlugen,
Die kindlichen Früchte des Hollunders
Sich staunend neigen über ein leeres Grab.

Leise rollen vergilbte Monde
über die Fieberlinnen des Jünglings,
Eh dem Schweigen des Winters folgt.

Ein erhabenes Schicksal sinnt den Kidron hinab,
Wo die Zeder, ein weiches Geschöpf,
Sich unter den blauen Brauen des Vaters entfaltet,
über die Weide nachts ein Schäfer seine Herde führt.
Oder es sind Schreie im Schlaf,
Wenn ein eherner Engel im Hain den Menschen antritt,
Das Fleisch des Heiligen auf glühendem Rost hinschmilzt.

Um die Lehmhütte rankt purpurner Wein,
Tönende Bündel vergilbten Korns,
Das Summen der Bienen, der Flug des Kranichs.
Am Abend begegnen sich Auferstandene auf Felsenpfaden.

In schwarzen Wassern spiegeln sich Aussätzige;
Oder sie öffnen die kotbefleckten Gewänder
Weinend dem balsamischen Wind, der vom rosigen Hügel weht.

Schlanke Mägde tasten durch die Gassen der Nacht,
Ob sie den liebenden Hirten fänden.
Sonnabends tönt in den Hütten sanfter Gesang.

Lasset das Lied auch des Knaben gedenken,
Seines Wahnsinns, und weißer Brauen und seines Hingangs,
Des Verwesten, der bläulich die Augen aufschlägt.
O wie traurig ist dieses Wiedersehn.

O how their hair stiffens with excrement and worms
When he stands in it with silver feet,
And they step deceased from bleak rooms.

O you psalms in fiery midnight rains
When servants smite the mild eyes with nettles,
The childlike fruits of the elderberry
Bend astonished over an empty grave.

Quietly yellowed moons roll
Over the youth's feverish linen
Before the silence of winter follows.

An exalted destiny ponders down the Kidron,
Where the cedar, a gentle creature,
Unfolds under the blue brows of the father,
Over the meadow at night a shepherd leads his flock.
Or there are screams in sleep,
When a brazen angel approaches man in the grove,
The saint's flesh melts on the glowing grate.

Around the clay huts purple vines climb,
Resounding sheaves of yellowed corn,
The humming of bees, the flight of the crane.
In the evening the resurrected meet on rocky paths.

In black waters lepers are reflected;
Or they open their excrement-tainted robes
Weeping to the balmy wind that blows from the rosy hill.

Slender maids grope through the alleys of the night
So they might find the loving shepherd.
Saturdays a soft singing sounds in the huts.

Let the song also commemorate the boy,
His insanity, and white brows and his passing away,
The decayed one, who bluishly opens the eyes.
O how sad is this reunion.

Die Stufen des Wahnsinns in schwarzen Zimmern,
Die Schatten der Alten unter der offenen Tür,
Da Helians Seele sich im rosigen Spiegel beschaut
Und Schnee und Aussatz von seiner Stirne sinken.

An den Wänden sind die Sterne erloschen
Und die weißen Gestalten des Lichts.

Dem Teppich entsteigt Gebein der Gräber,
Das Schweigen verfallener Kreuze am Hügel,
Des Weihrauchs Süße im purpurnen Nachtwind.

O ihr zerbrochenen Augen in schwarzen Mündern,
Da der Enkel in sanfter Umnachtung
Einsam dem dunkleren Ende nachsinnt,
Der stille Gott die blauen Lider über ihn senkt.

The stages of insanity in black rooms,
The shadows of the aged under the open door,
When Helian's soul looks at itself in the rosy mirror
And snow and leprosy sink from his forehead.

On the walls the stars have expired
And the white figures of the light.

Skeletons from the graves rise out of the carpet,
The silence of decayed crosses on the hill,
The sweetness of incense in the purple night wind.

O you shattered eyes in black mouths,
When the grandson in gentle derangement
Ponders the darker ending alone,
The silent God lowers blue eyelids over him.

Part Two:

Sebastian in Dream

(Kurt Wolff Publishing House, Leipzig, 1915)

Sebastian im Traum

Kindheit

Voll Früchten der Hollunder; ruhig wohnte die Kindheit
In blauer Höhle. Über vergangenen Pfad,
Wo nun bräunlich das wilde Gras saust,
Sinnt das stille Geäst; das Rauschen des Laubs

Ein gleiches, wenn das blaue Wasser im Felsen tönt.
Sanft ist der Amsel Klage. Ein Hirt
Folgt sprachlos der Sonne, die vom herbstlichen Hügel rollt.

Ein blauer Augenblick ist nur mehr Seele.
Am Waldsaum zeigt sich ein scheues Wild und friedlich
Ruhn im Grund die alten Glocken und finsteren Weiler.

Frömmer kennst du den Sinn der dunklen Jahre,
Kühle und Herbst in einsamen Zimmern;
Und in heiliger Bläue läuten leuchtende Schritte fort.

Leise klirrt ein offenes Fenster; zu Tränen
Rührt der Anblick des verfallenen Friedhofs am Hügel,
Erinnerung an erzählte Legenden; doch manchmal erhellt sich die Seele,
Wenn sie frohe Menschen denkt, dunkelgoldene Frühlingstage.

Stundenlied

Mit dunklen Blicken sehen sich die Liebenden an,
Die Blonden, Strahlenden. In starrender Finsternis
Umschlingen schmächtig sich die sehnenden Arme.

Purpurn zerbrach der Gesegneten Mund. Die runden Augen
Spiegeln das dunkle Gold des Frühlingsnachmittags,
Saum und Schwärze des Walds, Abendängste im Grün;
Vielleicht unsäglichen Vogelflug, des Ungeborenen
Pfad an finsteren Dörfern, einsamen Sommern hin
Und aus verfallener Bläue tritt bisweilen ein Abgelebtes.

Sebastian in Dream

Childhood

The elder bush full of fruit; calmly childhood dwelled
In a blue cave. Over the bygone path,
Where brownly the wild grass now swishes,
Silent branches ponder; the rustle of leaves

The same as when blue water resounds in stone.
Gentle is the blackbirds' lament. Speechlessly
A shepherd follows the sun that rolls down the autumn hill.

A blue moment is only more soul.
A shy deer appears along the forest edge and peacefully
The old bells and sinister hamlets rest in the valley.

More devoutly you know the meaning of the dark years,
Coolness and autumn in lonely rooms;
And shining footsteps ring forth in holy blueness.

Quietly an open window rattles; tears flow
At the sight of the decayed cemetery by the hill,
Memories of retold legends; but the soul sometimes brightens
When it thinks glad people, dark-gold spring days.

Hourly Song

With dark gazes the lovers look upon each other,
The blonde, radiant ones. In stiffening gloom
Their yearning arms delicately entwine.

Purple the blessed one's mouth broke. The round eyes
Mirror the dark gold of the spring afternoon,
Edge and blackness of the forest, evening fears in the green;
Perhaps the unspeakable flight of birds, the unborn's
Path past sinister villages, lonely summers
And sometimes a deceased shape steps out of decayed blueness.

Leise rauscht im Acker das gelbe Korn.
Hart ist das Leben und stählern schwingt die Sense der Landmann,
Fügt gewaltige Balken der Zimmermann.

Purpurn färbt sich das Laub im Herbst; der mönchische Geist
Durchwandelt heitere Tage; reif ist die Traube
Und festlich die Luft in geräumigen Höfen.
Süßer duften vergilbte Früchte; leise ist das Lachen
Des Frohen, Musik und Tanz in schattigen Kellern;
Im dämmernden Garten Schritt und Stille des verstorbenen Knaben.

Unterwegs

Am Abend trugen sie den Fremden in die Totenkammer;
Ein Duft von Teer; das leise Rauschen roter Platanen;
Der dunkle Flug der Dohlen; am Platz zog eine Wache auf.
Die Sonne ist in schwarze Linnen gesunken; immer wieder kehrt dieser
    vergangene Abend.
Im Nebenzimmer spielt die Schwester eine Sonate von Schubert.
Sehr leise sinkt ihr Lächeln in den verfallenen Brunnen,
Der bläulich in der Dämmerung rauscht. O, wie alt ist unser Geschlecht.
Jemand flüstert drunten im Garten; jemand hat diesen schwarzen Himmel
    verlassen.
Auf der Kommode duften Äpfel. Großmutter zündet goldene Kerzen an.

O, wie mild ist der Herbst. Leise klingen unsere Schritte im alten Park
Unter hohen Bäumen. O, wie ernst ist das hyazinthene Antlitz der Dämmerung.
Der blaue Quell zu deinen Füßen, geheimnisvoll die rote Stille deines Munds,
Umdüstert vom Schlummer des Laubs, dem dunklen Gold verfallener
    Sonnenblumen.
Deine Lider sind schwer von Mohn und träumen leise auf meiner Stirne.
Sanfte Glocken durchzittern die Brust. Eine blaue Wolke
Ist dein Antlitz auf mich gesunken in der Dämmerung.

Ein Lied zur Guitarre, das in einer fremden Schenke erklingt,
Die wilden Hollunderbüsche dort, ein lang vergangener Novembertag,
Vertraute Schritte auf der dämmernden Stiege, der Anblick gebräunter
    Balken,
Ein offenes Fenster, an dem ein süßes Hoffen zurückblieb –
Unsäglich ist das alles, o Gott, daß man erschüttert ins Knie bricht.

Quietly the yellow corn rustles in the acre.
Life is hard and steely the countryman swings the scythe,
The carpenter joins enormous rafters.

The leaves in autumn tinge purple; the monastic spirit
Wanders through cheerful days; the grape is ripe
And the air festive in spacious courtyards.
Yellowed fruits smell sweeter; quiet is the laughter
Of the joyful, music and dance in shady cellars;
In the dusking garden step and silence of the dead boy.

On the Way

In the evening they carried the stranger into the chamber of the dead;
A smell of tar; the quiet rustling of red sycamores;
The dark flight of jackdaws; a guard entered the square.
The sun has sunk into black linens; always this bygone evening returns.
From an adjoining room the sister plays a sonata from Schubert.
Very quietly her smile sinks into the decayed fountain
Which murmurs bluish in the dusk. O how old is our race.
Someone whispers down there in the garden; someone has left this black
      sky.
On the cabinet apples smell sweet. Grandmother lights golden candles.

O, how mild is the autumn. Quietly our steps sound in the old park
Under tall trees. O, how earnest is the hyacinthine countenance of the
      dusk.
The blue spring by your feet, mysteriously the red silence of your mouth,
Overshadowed by the slumber of foliage, the dark gold of decayed sunflowers.
Your eyelids are heavy from poppy and dream quietly on my forehead.
Gentle bells tremble through the breast. A blue cloud
Your countenance has sunk over me in the dusk.

A song with guitar that sounds out in a strange tavern,
The wild elder bushes there, a bygone November day,
Familiar steps on the dusking staircase, the sight of brown rafters,
An open window in which a sweet hope stayed behind—
All this is so unspeakable, o God, that one breaks down on the knees
      shaken.

O, wie dunkel ist diese Nacht. Eine purpurne Flamme
Erlosch an meinem Mund. In der Stille
Erstirbt der bangen Seele einsames Saitenspiel.
Laß, wenn trunken von Wein das Haupt in die Gosse sinkt.

Landschaft
[2. Fassung]

Septemberabend; traurig tönen die dunklen Rufe der Hirten
Durch das dämmernde Dorf; Feuer sprüht in der Schmiede.
Gewaltig bäumt sich ein schwarzes Pferd; die hyazinthenen Locken
    der Magd
Haschen nach der Inbrunst seiner purpurnen Nüstern.
Leise erstarrt am Saum des Waldes der Schrei der Hirschkuh
Und die gelben Blumen des Herbstes
Neigen sich sprachlos über das blaue Antlitz des Teichs.
In roter Flamme verbrannte ein Baum; aufflattern mit dunklen Gesichtern
    die Fledermäuse.

An den Knaben Elis

Elis, wenn die Amsel im schwarzen Wald ruft,
Dieses ist dein Untergang.
Deine Lippen trinken die Kühle des blauen Felsenquells.

Laß, wenn deine Stirne leise blutet
Uralte Legenden
Und dunkle Deutung des Vogelflugs.

Du aber gehst mit weichen Schritten in die Nacht,
Die voll purpurner Trauben hängt
Und du regst die Arme schöner im Blau.

Ein Dornenbusch tönt,
Wo deine mondenen Augen sind.
O, wie lange bist, Elis, du verstorben.

O, how dark is this night. A purple flame
Expired at my mouth. In the stillness
The anxious soul's lonely string music dies down.
Cease, when drunk with wine the head sinks into the gutter.

Landscape
[version 2]

September evening; sadly the shepherds' dark calls sound
Through the dusking village; fire sprays in the smithy.
Enormously a black horse rears up; the hyacinthine locks of the maid
Snatch after the fervor of its crimson nostrils.
Quietly the cry of the doe stiffens at the edge of the forest
And the yellow flowers of autumn
Bend speechless over the blue countenance of the pond.
In red flame a tree burned; with dark faces the bats flutter up.

To the Boy Elis

Elis, when the blackbird calls in the black woods,
This is your decline.
Your lips drink the coolness of the blue rock-spring.

Cease, when your forehead bleeds quietly
Ancient legends
And dark interpretations of the flight of birds.

But with tender steps you walk into the night
That hangs full of purple grapes,
And you move the arms more beautifully in the blueness.

A thorn bush tinges
Where your moon-like eyes are.
O, how long, Elis, have you been dead.

Dein Leib ist eine Hyazinthe,
In die ein Mönch die wächsernen Finger taucht.
Eine schwarze Höhle ist unser Schweigen,

Daraus bisweilen ein sanftes Tier tritt
Und langsam die schweren Lider senkt.
Auf deine Schläfen tropft schwarzer Tau,

Das letzte Gold verfallener Sterne.

Elis

[3. Fassung]

1

Vollkommen ist die Stille dieses goldenen Tags.
Unter alten Eichen
Erscheinst du, Elis, ein Ruhender mit runden Augen.

Ihre Bläue spiegelt den Schlummer der Liebenden.
An deinem Mund
Verstummten ihre rosigen Seufzer.

Am Abend zog der Fischer die schweren Netze ein.
Ein guter Hirt
Führt seine Herde am Waldsaum hin.
O! wie gerecht sind, Elis, alle deine Tage.

Leise sinkt
An kahlen Mauern des Ölbaums blaue Stille,
Erstirbt eines Greisen dunkler Gesang.

Ein goldener Kahn
Schaukelt, Elis, dein Herz am einsamen Himmel.

2

Ein sanftes Glockenspiel tönt in Elis' Brust
Am Abend,
Da sein Haupt ins schwarze Kissen sinkt.

Your body is a hyacinth
Into which a monk dips his waxy fingers.
Our silence is a black cavern

From which a gentle animal steps at times
And slowly lowers heavy eyelids.
On your temples black dew drips,

The last gold of expired stars.

Elis

[version 3]

1

Perfect is the stillness of this golden day.
Under ancient oaks
You appear, Elis, as one at rest with round eyes.

Their blue mirrors the slumber of lovers.
By your mouth
Their rosy sighs fell silent.

In the evening the fisherman hauled in the heavy nets.
A good shepherd
Leads his flock along the forest's edge.
O! how righteous, Elis, are all your days.

Quietly
Along bleak walls the olive tree's blue stillness sinks,
Causing the dark song of an old man to fade away.

A golden boat
Rocks your heart, Elis, in the lonely sky.

2

A gentle glockenspiel sounds in Elis' breast
In the evening,
When his head sinks into the black pillow.

Ein blaues Wild
Blutet leise im Dornengestrüpp.

Ein brauner Baum steht abgeschieden da;
Seine blauen Früchte fielen von ihm.

Zeichen und Sterne
Versinken leise im Abendweiher.

Hinter dem Hügel ist es Winter geworden.

Blaue Tauben
Trinken nachts den eisigen Schweiß,
Der von Elis' kristallener Stirne rinnt.

Immer tönt
An schwarzen Mauern Gottes einsamer Wind.

Hohenburg
[2. Fassung]

Es ist niemand im Haus. Herbst in Zimmern;
Mondeshelle Sonate
Und das Erwachen am Saum des dämmernden Walds.

Immer denkst du das weiße Antlitz des Menschen
Ferne dem Getümmel der Zeit;
Über ein Träumendes neigt sich gerne grünes Gezweig,

Kreuz und Abend;
Umfängt den Tönenden mit purpurnen Armen sein Stern,
Der zu unbewohnten Fenstern hinaufsteigt.

Also zittert im Dunkel der Fremdling,
Da er leise die Lider über ein Menschliches aufhebt,
Das ferne ist; die Silberstimme des Windes im Hausflur.

A blue deer
Quietly bleeds in the thorn brush.

A brown tree stands isolated there;
Its blue fruits have fallen from it.

Signs and stars
Sink quietly in the evening pond.

Behind the hill it has become winter.

Blue doves
Drink at night the icy sweat
Which runs from Elis' crystal forehead.

Always
God's lonely wind sounds along black walls.

Hohenburg

[version 2]

There is no one in the house. Autumn in rooms;
Moon-bright sonata
And the awakening at the edge of the dusking forest.

Always you imagine the white countenance of man
Far from the turmoil of time;
Over a dreaming shape green branches bend with pleasure,

Cross and evening;
With purple arms the resounding one is embraced by his star
Which climbs up to uninhabited windows.

Thus the stranger trembles in darkness
As he quietly lifts the eyelids over a human shape
Far away; the silver voice of the wind in the hallway.

Sebastian im Traum

Für Adolf Loos

Mutter trug das Kindlein im weißen Mond,
Im Schatten des Nußbaums, uralten Hollunders,
Trunken vom Safte des Mohns, der Klage der Drossel;
Und stille
Neigte in Mitleid sich über jene ein bärtiges Antlitz

Leise im Dunkel des Fensters; und altes Hausgerät
Der Väter
Lag im Verfall; Liebe und herbstliche Träumerei.

Also dunkel der Tag des Jahrs, traurige Kindheit,
Da der Knabe leise zu kühlen Wassern, silbernen Fischen hinabstieg,
Ruh und Antlitz;
Da er steinern sich vor rasende Rappen warf,
In grauer Nacht sein Stern über ihn kam;

Oder wenn er an der frierenden Hand der Mutter
Abends über Sankt Peters herbstlichen Friedhof ging,
Ein zarter Leichnam stille im Dunkel der Kammer lag
Und jener die kalten Lider über ihn aufhob.

Er aber war ein kleiner Vogel im kahlen Geist,
Die Glocke lang im Abendnovember,
Des Vaters Stille, da er im Schlaf die dämmernde Wendeltreppe hinabstieg.

2

Frieden der Seele. Einsamer Winterabend,
Die dunklen Gestalten der Hirten am alten Weiher;
Kindlein in der Hütte von Stroh; o wie leise
Sank in schwarzem Fieber das Antlitz hin.
Heilige Nacht.

Oder wenn er an der harten Hand des Vaters
Stille den finstern Kalvarienberg hinanstieg
Und in dämmernden Felsennischen
Die blaue Gestalt des Menschen durch seine Legende ging,
Aus der Wunde unter dem Herzen purpurn das Blut rann.

Sebastian in Dream

For Adolf Loos

Mother bore the infant in the white moon,
In the shadow of the walnut tree, the ancient elder,
Drunk with the juice of the poppy, the lament of the thrush;
And silently
A bearded face bent over her in compassion

Quietly in the darkness of the window; and the old household goods
Of the fathers
Lay in decay; love and autumn reverie.

So dark the day of the year, sad childhood,
When quietly the boy climbed down to cool waters, silvery fishes,
Rest and countenance;
When stony he cast himself before raving black horses,
In gray night his star came over him;

Or when he walked at the freezing hand of the mother
In the evening over Saint Peter's autumn cemetery,
A delicate corpse lay still in the darkness of the chamber
And the other one raised the cold eyelids over him.

But he was a small bird in bleak branches,
The bell long into the November evening,
The father's stillness as in sleep he descended the dusking spiral stair.

2

Peace of the soul. Lonesome winter evening,
The dark figures of the shepherds by the old pond;
Infant in the hut of straw; o how quietly
The countenance sank into black fever.
Holy night.

Or when he at the hard hand of the father
Silently climbed sinister Mount Calvary
And in dusking rock-niches
The blue figure of man passed through His legend,
Blood ran purple from the wound under the heart.

O wie leise stand in dunkler Seele das Kreuz auf.

Liebe; da in schwarzen Winkeln der Schnee schmolz,
Ein blaues Lüftchen sich heiter im alten Hollunder fing,
In dem Schattengewölbe des Nußbaums;
Und dem Knaben leise sein rosiger Engel erschien.

Freude; da in kühlen Zimmern eine Abendsonate erklang,
Im braunen Holzgebälk
Ein blauer Falter aus der silbernen Puppe kroch.

O die Nähe des Todes. In steinerner Mauer
Neigte sich ein gelbes Haupt, schweigend das Kind,
Da in jenem März der Mond verfiel.

3

Rosige Osterglocke im Grabgewölbe der Nacht
Und die Silberstimmen der Sterne,
Daß in Schauern ein dunkler Wahnsinn von der Stirne des Schläfers sank.

O wie stille ein Gang den blauen Floß hinab
Vergessenes sinnend, da im grünen Geäst
Die Drossel ein Fremdes in den Untergang rief.

Oder wenn er an der knöchernen Hand des Greisen
Abends vor die verfallene Mauer der Stadt ging
Und jener in schwarzem Mantel ein rosiges Kindlein trug,
Im Schatten des Nußbaums der Geist des Bösen erschien.

Tasten über die grünen Stufen des Sommers. O wie leise
Verfiel der Garten in der braunen Stille des Herbstes,
Duft und Schwermut des alten Hollunders,
Da in Sebastians Schatten die Silberstimme des Engels erstarb.

Am Moor
[3. Fassung]

Wanderer im schwarzen Wind; leise flüstert das dürre Rohr
In der Stille des Moors. Am grauen Himmel

O how quietly the cross rose up in the dark soul.

Love; when in black corners the snow melted,
A blue breeze was cheerfully snared in the old elder,
In the shadowy arch of the walnut tree;
And quietly a rosy angel appeared to the boy.

Joy; when in cool rooms an evening sonata sounded,
In the brown rafters
A blue moth crept from its silver chrysalis.

O the nearness of death. In stony wall
A yellow head bowed, silencing the child,
When in that March the moon decayed.

3

Rosy Easter Bell in the burial vault of night
And the silver voices of the stars,
So that in showers a dark insanity sank from the forehead of the sleeper.

O how silent a walk down the blue river,
Pondering on things forgotten, when in green branches
The thrush calls a stranger into decline.

Or when he walked at the bony hand of the old man
Evenings before the decayed wall of the city,
And the other one bore a rosy infant in a black coat,
The spirit of evil appeared in the shadow of the walnut tree.

Groping over the green steps of summer. O how quietly
The garden decayed in autumn's brown stillness,
Scent and gloom of the old elder tree,
When in Sebastian's shadow the silver voice of the angel died.

At the Moor
[version 3]

Wanderer in the black wind; quietly the dry reeds whisper
In the stillness of the moor. In the gray sky

Ein Zug von wilden Vögeln folgt;
Quere über finsteren Wassern.

Aufruhr. In verfallener Hütte
Aufflattert mit schwarzen Flügeln die Fäulnis;
Verkrüppelte Birken seufzen im Wind.

Abend in verlassener Schenke. Den Heimweg umwittert
Die sanfte Schwermut grasender Herden,
Erscheinung der Nacht: Kröten tauchen aus silbernen Wassern.

Im Frühling

Leise sank von dunklen Schritten der Schnee,
Im Schatten des Baums
Heben die rosigen Lider Liebende.

Immer folgt den dunklen Rufen der Schiffer
Stern und Nacht;
Und die Ruder schlagen leise im Takt.

Balde an verfallener Mauer blühen
Die Veilchen,
Ergrünt so stille die Schläfe des Einsamen.

Abend in Lans
[2. Fassung]

Wanderschaft durch dämmernden Sommer
An Bündeln vergilbten Korns vorbei. Unter getünchten Bogen,
Wo die Schwalbe aus und ein flog, tranken wir feurigen Wein.

Schön: o Schwermut und purpurnes Lachen.
Abend und die dunklen Düfte des Grüns
Kühlen mit Schauern die glühende Stirne uns.

Silberne Wasser rinnen über die Stufen des Walds,
Die Nacht und sprachlos ein vergessenes Leben.

A flock of wild birds follows;
Slanting over sinister waters.

Turmoil. In decayed hut
Putrefaction flutters up with black wings.
Crippled birches sigh in the wind.

Evening in deserted tavern. The way home is scented all around
By the gentle gloom of grazing herds,
Apparition of the night: toads plunge out of silver waters.

In Spring

Quietly snow sank from dark steps,
In the shadow of the trees
Lovers raise the rosy eyelids.

Always star and night
Follow the mariner's dark calls;
And the oars beat quietly in time.

Soon by the decayed wall
Violets bloom,
So silently the temple of the lonely one turns green.

Evening in Lans
[version 2]

Wanderings through the dusking summer
Past bundles of yellowed corn. Beneath whitewashed arches,
Where the swallow flew out and in, we drank fiery wine.

Beautiful: o gloom and purple laughter.
Evening and the dark scents of green
Cool our glowing foreheads with showers.

Silver waters trickle over the steps of the forest,
The night and a forgotten life speechless.

Freund; die belaubten Stege ins Dorf.

Am Mönchsberg
[2. Fassung]

Wo im Schatten herbstlicher Ulmen der verfallene Pfad hinabsinkt,
Ferne den Hütten von Laub, schlafenden Hirten,
Immer folgt dem Wandrer die dunkle Gestalt der Kühle

Über knöchernen Steg, die hyazinthene Stimme des Knaben,
Leise sagend die vergessene Legende des Walds,
Sanfter ein Krankes nun die wilde Klage des Bruders.

Also rührt ein spärliches Grün das Knie des Fremdlings,
Das versteinerte Haupt;
Näher rauscht der blaue Quell die Klage der Frauen.

Kaspar Hauser Lied

Für Bessie Loos

Er wahrlich liebte die Sonne, die purpurn den Hügel hinabstieg,
Die Wege des Walds, den singenden Schwarzvogel
Und die Freude des Grüns.

Ernsthaft war seinen Wohnen im Schatten des Baums
Und rein sein Antlitz.
Gott sprach eine sanfte Flamme zu seinem Herzen:
O Mensch!

Stille fand sein Schritt die Stadt am Abend;
Die dunkle Klage seines Munds:
Ich will ein Reiter werden.

Ihm aber folgte Busch und Tier,
Haus und Dämmergarten weißer Menschen
Und sein Mörder suchte nach ihm.

Friend; the leafy footbridges into the village.

At the Mönchsberg
[version 2]

Where in the shadow of autumn elms the decayed path sinks downward,
Far from the huts of foliage, sleeping shepherds,
Always the dark figure of coolness follows the wanderer

Over the bony footbridge, the hyacinthine voice of the boy
Quietly telling the forgotten legend of the forest,
Gentler a sick shape now the wild lament of the brother.

Thus a scanty green touches the knee of the stranger,
The petrified head;
Nearer the blue spring murmurs the lament of women.

Kaspar Hauser Song

To Bessie Loos

Truly he loved the sun which descended crimson behind the hill,
The paths of the forest, the singing blackbird,
And the joy of green.

Earnest was his dwelling in the shadow of the tree
And his countenance pure.
God spoke a soft flame into his heart:
O man!

Silently his footstep found the city in the evening;
The dark lament of his mouth:
I want to be a horseman.

But bush and animal followed him,
House and the dusking garden of white humans
And his murderer searched for him.

Frühling und Sommer und schön der Herbst
Des Gerechten, sein leiser Schritt
An den dunklen Zimmern Träumender hin.
Nachts blieb er mit seinem Stern allein;

Sah, daß Schnee fiel in kahles Gezweig
Und im dämmernden Hausflur den Schatten des Mörders.

Silbern sank des Ungeborenen Haupt hin.

Nachts

Die Bläue meiner Augen ist erloschen in dieser Nacht,
Das rote Gold meines Herzens. O! wie stille brannte das Licht.
Dein blauer Mantel umfing den Sinkenden;
Dein roter Mund besiegelte des Freundes Umnachtung.

Verwandlung des Bösen
[2. Fassung]

Herbst: schwarzes Schreiten am Waldsaum; Minute stummer Zerstörung; auf-
lauscht die Stirne des Aussätzigen unter dem kahlen Baum. Langvergangener
Abend, der nun über die Stufen von Moos sinkt; November. Eine Glocke läutet
und der Hirt führt eine Herde von schwarzen und roten Pferden ins Dorf. Unter
dem Haselgebüsch weidet der grüne Jäger ein Wild aus. Seine Hände rauchen
von Blut und der Schatten des Tiers seufzt im Laub über den Augen des Mannes,
braun und schweigsam; der Wald. Krähen, die sich zerstreuen; drei. Ihr Flug gle-
icht einer Sonate, voll verblichener Akkorde und männlicher Schwermut; leise löst
sich eine goldene Wolke auf. Bei der Mühle zünden Knaben ein Feuer an. Flamme
ist des Bleichsten Bruder und jener lacht vergraben in sein purpurnes Haar; oder
es ist ein Ort des Mordes, an dem ein steiniger Weg vorbeiführt. Die Berberitzen
sind verschwunden, jahrlang träumt es in bleierner Luft unter den Föhren; Angst,
grünes Dunkel, das Gurgeln eines Ertrinkenden: aus dem Sternenweiher zieht der
Fischer einen großen, schwarzen Fisch, Antlitz voll Grausamkeit und Irrsinn. Die
Stimmen des Rohrs, hadernder Männer im Rücken schaukelt jener auf rotem Kahn
über frierende Herbstwasser, lebend in dunklen Sagen seines Geschlechts und die
Augen steinern über Nächte und jungfräuliche Schrecken aufgetan. Böse.

Was zwingt dich still zu stehen auf der verfallenen Stiege, im Haus deiner Väter?

Spring and summer and beautiful the autumn
Of the righteous one, his quiet step
Past the dark rooms of dreamers.
At night he remained alone with his star;

Saw snow falling into bleak branches
And in the dusking hallway the shadow of the murderer.

Silverly the head of the unborn sank.

Nights

The blueness of my eyes is extinguished in this night,
The red gold of my heart. O! how still the light burned.
Your blue coat surrounded the sinking one;
Your red mouth sealed the friend's derangement.

Metamorphosis of Evil
[version 2]

Autumn: black striding along the forest edge; moment of mute destruction; the
forehead of the leper eavesdrops under the bleak tree. Bygone evening that now
sinks over steps of moss; November. A bell rings and the shepherd leads a herd
of black and red horses into the village. Under the hazel bush, the green hunter
disembowels a deer. His hands smoke with blood and the shadow of the deer sighs
in leaves over the eyes of the man, brown and taciturn; the forest. Crows that scat-
ter; three. Their flight resembles a sonata full of faded chords and manly gloom;
quietly a golden cloud dissolves. By the mill boys light a fire. Flame is the brother
of the palest one, and the other one laughs buried in his purple hair; or it is a place
of murder passed by a stony path. The barberries are gone, year-long it dreams in
leaden air under the pines; fear, green darkness, the gurgling of a drowning man;
from the starry pond the fisherman pulls a large black fish, countenance filled with
cruelty and madness. The voices of reeds, of quarreling men in the back, the other
one sways in a red boat across the freezing waters of autumn, living in dark legends
of his race and stony the eyes opened over nights and virgin terrors. Evil.

What forces you to stand silently on the decayed stair in the house of your fa-
thers? Leaden blackness. What do you lift with silver hand to the eyes; and the
eyelids sink as if drunk from poppy? But through the wall of stone you see the

Bleierne Schwärze. Was hebst du mit silberner Hand an die Augen; und die Lider sinken wie trunken von Mohn? Aber durch die Mauer von Stein siehst du den Sternenhimmel, die Milchstraße, den Saturn; rot. Rasend an die Mauer von Stein klopft der kahle Baum. Du auf verfallenen Stufen: Baum, Stern, Stein! Du, ein blaues Tier, das leise zittert; du, der bleiche Priester, der es hinschlachtet am schwarzen Altar. O dein Lächeln im Dunkel, traurig und böse, daß ein Kind im Schlaf erbleicht. Eine rote Flamme sprang aus deiner Hand und ein Nachtfalter verbrannte daran. O die Flöte des Lichts; o die Flöte des Tods. Was zwang dich still zu stehen auf verfallener Stiege, im Haus deiner Väter? Drunten ans Tor klopft ein Engel mit kristallnem Finger.

O die Hölle des Schlafs; dunkle Gasse, braunes Gärtchen. Leise läutet im blauen Abend der Toten Gestalt. Grüne Blümchen umgaukeln sie und ihr Antlitz hat sie verlassen. Oder es neigt sich verblichen über die kalte Stirne des Mörders im Dunkel des Hausflurs; Anbetung, purpurne Flamme der Wollust; hinsterbend stürzte über schwarze Stufen der Schläfer ins Dunkel.

Jemand verließ dich am Kreuzweg und du schaust lange zurück. Silberner Schritt im Schatten verkrüppelter Apfelbäumchen. Purpurn leuchtet die Frucht im schwarzen Geist und im Gras häutet sich die Schlange. O! das Dunkel; der Schweiß, der auf die eisige Stirne tritt und die traurigen Träume im Wein, in der Dorfschenke unter schwarzverrauchtem Gebälk. Du, noch Wildnis, die rosige Inseln zaubert aus dem braunen Tabaksgewölk und aus dem Innern den wilden Schrei eines Greifen holt, wenn er um schwarze Klippen jagt in Meer, Sturm und Eis. Du, ein grünes Metall und innen ein feuriges Gesicht, das hingehen will und singen vom Beinerhügel finstere Zeiten und den flammenden Sturz des Engels. O! Verzweiflung, die mit stummem Schrei ins Knie bricht.

Ein Toter besucht dich. Aus dem Herzen rinnt das selbstvergossene Blut und in schwarzer Braue nistet unsäglicher Augenblick; dunkle Begegnung. Du – ein purpurner Mond, da jener im grünen Schatten des Ölbaums erscheint. Dem folgt unvergängliche Nacht.

starry sky, the Milky Way, Saturn; red. Raging a bleak tree knocks against the wall of stone. You on decayed stairs: tree, star, stone! You, a blue animal that quietly trembles; you, the pale priest who slaughters it on the black altar. O your smile in the darkness, sad and evil, so that a child turns pale in sleep. A red flame jumped out of your hand and a moth burned up in it. O the flute of light; o the flute of death. What forced you to stand silently on the decayed stair in the house of your fathers? Below at the gate an angel knocks with crystalline finger.

O the hell of sleep; dark alley, small brown garden. Quietly in the blue evening the figures of the dead ring. Little green flowers surround them and their countenance has left them. Or it bends faded over the cold forehead of the murderer in the darkness of the hallway; adoration, purple flame of lust; dying, the sleeper fell over black steps into the darkness.

Somebody left you at the crossroads and you gaze back for a long time. Silver step in the shadow of small crippled apple trees. The fruit shines purple in black branches and in the grass the snake molts. O! the darkness; the sweat that appears on the icy forehead, and the sad dreams in the wine, in the village tavern under the smoke-blackened rafters. You, still the wilderness that conjures rosy islands from the brown tobacco clouds, and draws from its core the wild cry of a rapter that hunts around black cliffs in sea, storm and ice. You, a green metal and within a fiery face that wants to go there and sing away gloomy times and the flaming fall of the angel from the hill of skeletons. O! desperation, which with mute cry breaks to the knee.

A dead person visits you. From the heart self-spilt blood runs and in the black eyebrow an unspeakable moment nests; dark encounter. You—a purple moon, as the other one appears in the green shadow of the olive tree. After this everlasting night follows.

Der Herbst des Einsamen

Im Park

Wieder wandelnd im alten Park,
O! Stille gelb und roter Blumen.
Ihr auch trauert, ihr sanften Götter,
Und das herbstliche Gold der Ulme.
Reglos ragt am bläulichen Weiher
Das Rohr, verstummt am Abend die Drossel.
O! dann neige auch du die Stirne
Vor der Ahnen verfallenem Marmor.

Ein Winterabend
[2. Fassung]

Wenn der Schnee ans Fenster fällt,
Lang die Abendglocke läutet,
Vielen ist der Tisch bereitet
Und das Haus ist wohlbestellt.

Mancher auf der Wanderschaftv
Kommt ans Tor auf dunklen Pfaden.
Golden blüht der Baum der Gnaden
Aus der Erde kühlem Saft.

Wanderer tritt still herein;
Schmerz versteinerte die Schwelle.
Da erglänzt in reiner Helle
Auf dem Tische Brot und Wein.

Autumn of the Lonely

In the Park

Again wandering in the old park,
O! stillness of yellow and red flowers.
You mourn also, you gentle gods,
And the autumn gold of the elm.
Motionless in the bluish pond the reeds
Rise, the thrush falls silent in the evening.
O! then you too should bow the forehead
Before the ancestor's decayed marble.

A Winter Evening
[version 2]

When the snow falls against the window,
The evening bell rings long,
The table is prepared for many,
And the house is well appointed.

Some in their wanderings
Come to the gate on dark paths.
The tree of grace blooms golden
From the earth's cool sap.

Wanderer step silently inside;
Pain has petrified the threshold.
There in pure radiance
Bread and wine glow upon the table.

Die Verfluchten

1

Es dämmert. Zum Brunnen gehn die alten Fraun.
Im Dunkel der Kastanien lacht ein Rot.
Aus einem Laden rinnt ein Duft von Brot
Und Sonnenblumen sinken übern Zaun.

Am Fluß die Schenke tönt noch lau und leis.
Guitarre summt; ein Klimperklang von Geld.
Ein Heiligenschein auf jene Kleine fallt,
Die vor der Glastür wartet sanft und weiß.

O! blauer Glanz, den sie in Scheiben weckt,
Umrahmt von Dornen, schwarz und starrverzückt.
Ein krummer Schreiber lächelt wie verrückt
Ins Wasser, das ein wilder Aufruhr schreckt.

2

Am Abend säumt die Pest ihr blau Gewand
Und leise schließt die Tür ein finstrer Gast.
Durchs Fenster sinkt des Ahorns schwarze Last;
Ein Knabe legt die Stirn in ihre Hand.

Oft sinken ihre Lider bös und schwer.
Des Kindes Hände rinnen durch ihr Haar
Und seine Tränen stürzen heiß und klar
In ihre Augenhöhlen schwarz und leer.

Ein Nest von scharlachfarbnen Schlangen bäumt
Sich träg in ihrem aufgewühlten Schoß.
Die Arme lassen ein Erstorbenes los,
Das eines Teppichs Traurigkeit umsäumt.

3

Ins braune Gärtchen tönt ein Glockenspiel.
Im Dunkel der Kastanien schwebt ein Blau,
Der süße Mantel einer fremden Frau.

The Cursed

Dusk falls. The old women go to the well.
In the darkness of the chestnuts a red laughs.
From a shop the aroma of bread trickles
And sunflowers sink over the fence.

By the river the tavern still sounds mild and quiet.
A guitar hums; a jingling of money.
A halo falls upon that small child
Who waits before the glass door gentle and white.

O! blue radiance which she awakens in the panes
Framed by thorns, black and rigidly enraptured.
A crooked writer smiles as if crazy
Into water which a wild uproar startles.

2

In the evening the plague borders her blue garment
And quietly a sinister guest closes the door.
The black burden of the maple sinks through the window;
A boy lays the forehead in her hand.

Often her eyelids sink evil and heavy.
The child's hands run through her hair
And his tears fall hot and clear
Into her eye sockets black and empty.

A nest of scarlet colored snakes rears up
Lethargically in her troubled womb.
The arms release a dead shape
That is surrounded by a carpet's sadness.

Into the brown garden a glockenspiel sounds.
In the darkness of the chestnuts a blueness floats,
The sweet coat of a strange woman.

Resedenduft; und glühendes Gefühl

Des Bösen. Die feuchte Stirn beugt kalt und bleich
Sich über Unrat, drin die Ratte wühlt,
Vom Scharlachglanz der Sterne lau umspült;
Im Garten fallen Äpfel dumpf und weich.

Die Nacht ist schwarz. Gespenstisch bläht der Föhn
Des wandelnden Knaben weißes Schlafgewand
Und leise greift in seinen Mund die Hand
Der Toten. Sonja lächelt sanft und schön.

Sonja

Abend kehrt in alten Garten;
Sonjas Leben, blaue Stille.
Wilder Vögel Wanderfahrten;
Kahler Baum in Herbst und Stille.

Sonnenblume, sanftgeneigte
Über Sonjas weißes Leben.
Wunde, rote, niegezeigte
Läßt in dunklen Zimmern leben,

Wo die blauen Glocken läuten;
Sonjas Schritt und sanfte Stille.
Sterbend Tier grüßt im Entgleiten,
Kahler Baum in Herbst und Stille.

Sonne alter Tage leuchtet
Über Sonjas weiße Brauen,
Schnee, der ihre Wangen feuchtet,
Und die Wildnis ihrer Brauen.

Entlang

Geschnitten sind Korn und Traube,
Der Weiler in Herbst und Ruh.

Fragrance of mignonettes; and a glowing sense

Of evil. The damp forehead bends cold and pale
Over muck where the rat digs
Bathed by the mild scarlet glow of stars;
In the garden apples fall dull and soft.

The night is black. Ghostly the foehn billows
Through the sleepwalking boy's white nightgown
And quietly the hand of the dead reaches
In his mouth. Sonja smiles soft and beautiful.

Sonja

Evening returns to the old garden.
Sonja's life, blue stillness.
Wild birds' migrations;
Bare tree in autumn and stillness.

Sunflower, gently bowed
Over Sonja's white life.
Wound, red, never shown,
Requires dark rooms to live

Where the blue bells ring;
Sonja's step and gentle stillness.
A dying animal salutes in parting,
Bare tree in autumn and stillness.

The sun of ancient days shines
Over Sonja's white brow,
Snow moistens her cheeks
And the wilderness of her brow.

Along

Corn and grape are cut,
The hamlet in autumn and rest.

Hammer und Amboß klingt immerzu,
Lachen in purpurner Laube.

Astern von dunklen Zäunen
Bring dem weißen Kind.
Sag wie lang wir gestorben sind;
Sonne will schwarz erscheinen.

Rotes Fischlein im Weiher;
Stirn, die sich fürchtig belauscht;
Abendwind leise ans Fenster rauscht,
Blaues Orgelgeleier.

Stern und heimlich Gefunkel
Läßt noch einmal aufschaun.
Erscheinung der Mutter in Schmerz und Graun;
Schwarze Reseden im Dunkel.

Herbstseele
[2. Fassung]

Jägerruf und Blutgebell;
Hinter Kreuz und braunem Hügel
Blindet sacht der Weiherspiegel,
Schreit der Habicht hart und hell.

Über Stoppelfeld und Pfad
Banget schon ein schwarzes Schweigen;
Reiner Himmel in den Zweigen;
Nur der Bach rinnt still und stad.

Bald entgleitet Fisch und Wild.
Blaue Seele, dunkles Wandern
Schied uns bald von Lieben, Andern.
Abend wechselt Sinn und Bild.

Rechten Lebens Brot und Wein,
Gott in deine milden Hände
Legt der Mensch das dunkle Ende,
Alle Schuld und rote Pein.

Hammer and anvil clang incessantly,
Laughter in purple bower.

Bring asters from dark fences
To the white child.
Say how long we've been dead;
Sun wants to appear black.

Small red fish in the pond;
Forehead that listens fearfully to itself;
Evening wind quietly rustles at the window,
Blue singsong of an organ.

Star and secret glittering
Allow still one more glance up.
Phantom of the mother in pain and dread;
Black mignonettes in the dark.

Autumn Soul
[version 2]

Hunter's call and bloody baying;
Behind cross and brown hill
The pond-mirror gently blinds,
The hawk cries harsh and clear.

Over stubble field and path
A black silence already trembles;
Pure sky in the branches;
Only the brook trickles still and calm.

Soon fish and deer slip away.
Blue soul, dark wandering
Separated us soon from loves, others.
Evening changes sense and image.

Bread and wine of the righteous life,
God in your mild hands
Man lays the dark end,
All guilt and red anguish.

Afra

[2. Fassung]

Ein Kind mit braunem Haar. Gebet und Amen
Verdunkeln still die abendliche Kühle
Und Afras Lächeln rot in gelbem Rahmen
Von Sonnenblumen, Angst und grauer Schwüle.

Gehüllt in blauen Mantel sah vor Zeiten
Der Mönch sie fromm gemalt an Kirchenfenstern;
Das will in Schmerzen freundlich noch geleiten,
Wenn ihre Sterne durch sein Blut gespenstern.

Herbstuntergang; und des Hollunders Schweigen.
Die Stirne rührt des Wassers blaue Regung,
Ein härnes Tuch gelegt auf eine Bahre.

Verfaulte Früchte fallen von den Zweigen;
Unsäglich ist der Vögel Flug, Begegnung
Mit Sterbenden; dem folgen dunkle Jahre.

Der Herbst des Einsamen

Der dunkle Herbst kehrt ein voll Frucht und Fülle,
Vergilbter Glanz von schönen Sommertagen.
Ein reines Blau tritt aus verfallener Hülle;
Der Flug der Vögel tönt von alten Sagen.
Gekeltert ist der Wein, die milde Stille
Erfüllt von leiser Antwort dunkler Fragen.

Und hier und dort ein Kreuz auf ödem Hügel;
Im roten Wald verliert sich eine Herde.
Die Wolke wandert übern Weiherspiegel;
Es ruht des Landmanns ruhige Geberde.
Sehr leise rührt des Abends blauer Flügel
Ein Dach von dürrem Stroh, die schwarze Erde.

Afra

[version 2]

A child with brown hair. Prayer and amen
Darken silently the coolness of evening
And Afra's smile red in yellow frame
Of sunflowers, fear and gray sultriness.

Wrapped in blue coat the monk saw her
In former times devoutly painted in church windows;
This should still be friendly escort through pain
When her stars haunt his blood.

Autumn decline; and the elder-trees' silence.
The water's blue moving stirs the forehead,
A hairy cloth is laid upon a bier.

Rotten fruits fall from the branches;
Unspeakable is the flight of birds, encounter
With the dying; after this dark years follow.

Autumn of the Lonely

The dark autumn returns filled with fruit and abundance,
Yellow brilliance of beautiful summer days.
A pure blueness steps from a decayed sheath;
The flight of birds sounds with ancient legends.
The wine is pressed, the mild stillness
Fulfilled with the quiet answer of dark questions.

And here and there a cross on barren hill;
In the red forest a herd trails away.
The cloud roams over the pond-mirror;
The countryman's calm gesture rests.
Very quietly the blue wing of the evening stirs
A roof of dried straw, the black earth.

Bald nisten Sterne in des Müden Brauen;
In kühle Stuben kehrt ein still Bescheiden
Und Engel treten leise aus den blauen
Augen der Liebenden, die sanfter leiden.
Es rauscht das Rohr; anfällt ein knöchern Grauen,
Wenn schwarz der Tau tropft von den kahlen Weiden.

Soon stars nest in the brows of the weary one;
In cool rooms a silent modesty enters
And angels step quietly from the blue
Eyes of lovers, who suffer more gently.
The reed murmurs; a bony horror attacks
When dew drips blackly from bare willows.

Siebengesang des Todes

Ruh und Schweigen

Hirten begruben die Sonne im kahlen Wald.
Ein Fischer zog
In härenem Netz den Mond aus frierendem Weiher.

In blauem Kristall
Wohnt der bleiche Mensch, die Wang' an seine Sterne gelehnt;
Oder er neigt das Haupt in purpurnem Schlaf.

Doch immer rührt der schwarze Flug der Vögel
Den Schauenden, das Heilige blauer Blumen,
Denkt die nahe Stille Vergessenes, erloschene Engel.

Wieder nachtet die Stirne in mondenem Gestein;
Ein strahlender Jüngling
Erscheint die Schwester in Herbst und schwarzer Verwesung.

Anif

Erinnerung: Möven, gleitend über den dunklen Himmel
Männlicher Schwermut.
Stille wohnst du im Schatten der herbstlichen Esche,
Versunken in des Hügels gerechtes Maß;

Immer gehst du den grünen Fluß hinab,
Wenn es Abend geworden,
Tönende Liebe; friedlich begegnet das dunkle Wild,

Ein rosiger Mensch. Trunken von bläulicher Witterung
Rührt die Stirne das sterbende Laub
Und denkt das ernste Antlitz der Mutter;
O, wie alles ins Dunkel hinsinkt;

Die gestrengen Zimmer und das alte Gerät

Seven-song of Death

Rest and Silence

Shepherds buried the sun in the bare forest.
A fisherman drew
The moon from the freezing pond in a hairy net.

In blue crystal
The pale man dwells, the cheek leaned on his stars;
Or he bends the head in purple sleep.

But always the black flight of birds moves
The beholder, the sanctity of blue flowers,
The nearby stillness ponders forgotten things, extinct angels.

Again the forehead nightfalls into lunar stone.
A radiant youth
The sister appears in autumn and black decay.

Anif

Memory: gulls, gliding over the dark sky
Of manly gloom.
Silently you dwell in the shadow of the autumn ash tree,
Sunken into the hill's righteous dimension;

Always you walk down the green river
When evening has come
Sounding love; peacefully the dark deer encounters,

A rosy man; drunk with bluish weather
The forehead stirs the dying leaves
And thinks the earnest countenance of the mother;
O, how everything sinks into darkness;

The austere rooms and the old utensils

Der Väter.
Dieses erschüttert die Brust des Fremdlings.
O, ihr Zeichen und Sterne.

Groß ist die Schuld des Geborenen. Weh, ihr goldenen Schauer
Des Todes,
Da die Seele kühlere Blüten träumt.

Immer schreit im kahlen Gezweig der nächtliche Vogel
Über des Mondenen Schritt,
Tönt ein eisiger Wind an den Mauern des Dorfs.

Geburt

Gebirge: Schwärze, Schweigen und Schnee.
Rot vom Wald niedersteigt die Jagd;
O, die moosigen Blicke des Wilds.

Stille der Mutter; unter schwarzen Tannen
Öffnen sich die schlafenden Hände,
Wenn verfallen der kalte Mond erscheint.

O, die Geburt des Menschen. Nächtlich rauscht
Blaues Wasser im Felsengrund;
Seufzend erblickt sein Bild der gefallene Engel,

Erwacht ein Bleiches in dumpfer Stube.
Zwei Monde
Erglänzen die Augen der steinernen Greisin.

Weh, der Gebärenden Schrei. Mit schwarzem Flügel
Rührt die Knabenschläfe die Nacht,
Schnee, der leise aus purpurner Wolke sinkt.

Of the ancestors.
This shakes the breast of the stranger.
O, you signs and stars.

Great is the guilt of the born. Woe, you golden shudders
Of death
When the soul dreams cooler blooms.

Always the nocturnal bird cries in bare branches
Over the lunar one's steps,
An icy wind sounds by the walls of the village.

Birth

Mountains: blackness, silence and snow.
The hunt descends red from the forest.
O, the mossy gazes of the deer.

The mother's stillness; under black firs
Sleeping hands open
When the cold moon appears decayed.

O, the birth of man. Nocturnally blue water
Murmers in the rocky ground;
Sighing the fallen angel beholds his image,

A pale shape awakens in stuffy room.
Two moons
The ancient eyes of the stony old lady gleam.

Woe, the birthing woman's scream. With black wings
The night touches the boy's temple,
Snow that falls quietly from a purple cloud.

Untergang
[5. Fassung]

An Karl Borromaeus Heinrich

Über den weißen Weiher
Sind die wilden Vögel fortgezogen.
Am Abend weht von unseren Sternen ein eisiger Wind.

Über unsere Gräber
Beugt sich die zerbrochene Stirne der Nacht.
Unter Eichen schaukeln wir auf einem silbernen Kahn.

Immer klingen die weißen Mauern der Stadt.
Unter Dornenbogen
O mein Bruder klimmen wir blinde Zeiger gen Mitternacht.

An einen Frühverstorbenen

O, der schwarze Engel, der leise aus dem Innern des Baums trat,
Da wir sanfte Gespielen am Abend waren,
Am Rand des bläulichen Brunnens.
Ruhig war unser Schritt, die runden Augen in der braunen Kühle des
    Herbstes,
O, die purpurne Süße der Sterne.

Jener aber ging die steinernen Stufen des Mönchsbergs hinab,
Ein blaues Lächeln im Antlitz und seltsam verpuppt
In seine stillere Kindheit und starb;
Und im Garten blieb das silberne Antlitz des Freundes zurück,
Lauschend im Laub oder im alten Gestein.

Seele sang den Tod, die grüne Verwesung des Fleisches
Und es war das Rauschen des Walds,
Die inbrünstige Klage des Wildes.
Immer klangen von dämmernden Türmen die blauen Glocken des Abends.

Stunde kam, da jener die Schatten in purpurner Sonne sah,
Die Schatten der Fäulnis in kahlem Geäst;
Abend, da an dämmernder Mauer die Amsel sang,
Der Geist des Frühverstorbenen stille im Zimmer erschien.

Decline

[version 5]

To Karl Borromaeus Heinrich

Over the white pond
The wild birds have migrated.
In the evening an icy wind blows from our stars.

Over our graves
The broken forehead of night bends.
Under oaks we sway in a silver boat.

Always the white walls of the city resound.
Under arches of thorns
O my brother we climb blind clock-hands toward midnight.

To One Who Died Young

O, the black angel who stepped quietly from inside the tree
When we were gentle playmates in the evening
At the edge of the bluish fountain.
Calm was our step, the round eyes in the brown coolness of autumn,
O, the purple sweetness of the stars.

But the other one descended the stony steps of the Mönchsberg,
A blue smile on the countenance and strangely pupated
Into his silenter childhood and died;
And in the garden the silver countenance of the friend remained
Listening in leaf or in ancient stones.

Soul sang death, the green decay of the flesh
And it was the murmur of the forest,
The fervent lament of the deer.
Always the blue evening bells rang from the dusky towers.

Hour came when the other one saw the shadows in the purple sun,
The shadows of putrescence in bleak branches;
Evening when the blackbird sang by the dusking wall,
The ghost of the one who died young silently appeared in the room.

O, das Blut, das aus der Kehle des Tönenden rinnt,
Blaue Blume; o die feurige Träne
Geweint in die Nacht.

Goldene Wolke und Zeit. In einsamer Kammer
Lädst du öfter den Toten zu Gast,
Wandelst in trautem Gespräch unter Ulmen den grünen Fluß hinab.

Geistliche Dämmerung
[2. Fassung]

Stille begegnet am Saum des Waldes
Ein dunkles Wild;
Am Hügel endet leise der Abendwind,

Verstummt die Klage der Amsel,
Und die sanften Flöten des Herbstes
Schweigen im Rohr.

Auf schwarzer Wolke
Befährst du trunken von Mohn
Den nächtigen Weiher,

Den Sternenhimmel.
Immer tönt der Schwester mondene Stimme
Durch die geistliche Nacht.

Abendländisches Lied

O der Seele nächtlicher Flügelschlag:
Hirten gingen wir einst an dämmernden Wäldern hin
Und es folgte das rote Wild, die grüne Blume und der lallende Quell
Demutsvoll. O, der uralte Ton des Heimchens,
Blut blühend am Opferstein
Und der Schrei des einsamen Vogels über der grünen Stille des Teichs.

O, ihr Kreuzzüge und glühenden Martern

O, the blood that runs from the throat of the resounding one,
Blue flower; o the fiery tear
Wept in the night.

Golden cloud and time. In a lonely chamber
You invite the dead person to be a guest more often,
Wander in intimate conversation under elms along the green river.

Spiritual Dusk
[version 2]

Silently a dark deer encounters at the edge
Of the forest;
The evening wind ends quietly on the hill,

The blackbird's lament grows mute
And the gentle flutes of autumn
Silence in the reeds.

On a black cloud
Drunk with poppy you travel
The nocturnal pond,

The starry sky.
Always the lunar voice of the sister sounds
Through the spiritual night.

Occidental Song

O the soul's nocturnal wing beat:
Shepherds we once moved along dusking forests
And the red deer, the green flower and the babbling spring followed
Full of humbleness. O, the ancient tone of the cricket,
Blood blooming on the sacrificial stone,
And the cry of a lonely bird over the pond's green stillness.

O, you crusades and glowing tortures

Des Fleisches, Fallen purpurner Früchte
Im Abendgarten, wo vor Zeiten die frommen Jünger gegangen,
Kriegsleute nun, erwachend aus Wunden und Sternenträumen.
O, das sanfte Zyanenbündel der Nacht.

O, ihr Zeiten der Stille und goldener Herbste,
Da wir friedliche Mönche die purpurne Traube gekeltert;
Und rings erglänzten Hügel und Wald.
O, ihr Jagden und Schlösser; Ruh des Abends,
Da in seiner Kammer der Mensch Gerechtes sann,
In stummem Gebet um Gottes lebendiges Haupt rang.

O, die bittere Stunde des Untergangs,
Da wir ein steinernes Antlitz in schwarzen Wassern beschaun.
Aber strahlend heben die silbernen Lider die Liebenden:
E i n Geschlecht. Weihrauch strömt von rosigen Kissen
Und der süße Gesang der Auferstandenen.

Verklärung

Wenn es Abend wird,
Verläßt dich leise ein blaues Antlitz.
Ein kleiner Vogel singt im Tamarindenbaum.

Ein sanfter Mönch
Faltet die erstorbenen Hände.
Ein weißer Engel sucht Marien heim.

Ein nächtiger Kranz
Von Veilchen, Korn und purpurnen Trauben
Ist das Jahr des Schauenden.

Zu deinen Füßen
Öffnen sich die Gräber der Toten,
Wenn du die Stirne in die silbernen Hände legst.

Stille wohnt
An deinem Mund der herbstliche Mond,
Trunken von Mohnsaft dunkler Gesang;

Blaue Blume,

Of the flesh, the fall of purple fruit
In the evening garden where in bygone times the pious disciples walked,
Warriors now, awakened out of wounds and starry dreams.
O, the soft cyan-bundle of night.

O, you times of stillness and golden autumns
When we peaceful monks pressed the purple grape;
And hill and forest shone all around.
O, you hunts and castles, repose of evening,
When in his chamber man pondered over the righteous,
Struggled in silent prayer for the living head of God.

O, the bitter hour of decline,
When we behold a stony countenance in black waters.
But in radiance the lovers lift the silver eyelids:
O n e gender. Incense flows from rosy pillows
And the sweet song of the resurrected.

Transfiguration

When evening appears
A blue countenance quietly leaves you.
A small bird sings in the tamarind tree.

A gentle monk
Folds the deceased hands.
A white angel haunts Mary.

A nocturnal wreath
Of violets, corn and purple grapes
Is the year of the beholder.

By your feet
The graves of the dead open
When you lay the forehead in silver hands.

Silently the autumn moon
Dwells upon your mouth,
Dark song drunk with poppy juice;

Blue flower

Die leise tönt in vergilbtem Gestein.

Föhn

Blinde Klage im Wind, mondene Wintertage,
Kindheit, leise verhallen die Schritte an schwarzer Hecke,
Langes Abendgeläut.
Leise kommt die weiße Nacht gezogen,

Verwandelt in purpurne Träume Schmerz und Plage
Des steinigen Lebens,
Daß nimmer der dornige Stachel ablasse vom verwesenden Leib.

Tief im Schlummer aufseufzt die bange Seele,

Tief der Wind in zerbrochenen Bäumen,
Und es schwankt die Klagegestalt
Der Mutter durch den einsamen Wald

Dieser schweigenden Trauer; Nächte,
Erfüllt von Tränen, feurigen Engeln.
Silbern zerschellt an kahler Mauer ein kindlich Gerippe

Der Wanderer
[2. Fassung]

Immer lehnt am Hügel die weiße Nacht,
Wo in Silbertönen die Pappel ragt,
Stern' und Steine sind.

Schlafend wölbt sich über den Gießbach der Steg,
Folgt dem Knaben ein erstorbenes Antlitz,
Sichelmond in rosiger Schlucht

Ferne preisenden Hirten. In altem Gestein
Schaut aus kristallenen Augen die Kröte,
Erwacht der blühende Wind, die Vogelstimme des Totengleichen
Und die Schritte ergrünen leise im Wald.

That quietly sounds in yellowed stones.

Foehn

Blind lament in the wind, lunar winter days,
Childhood, quietly the steps fade near black hedge,
Long evening bells.
Quietly the white night approaches,

Transforms pain and worriment into purple dreams
Of stony living
So the thorny sting will never leave the rotting body.

Deep in slumber the anxious soul heaves a sigh,

The wind deep in broken trees,
And the lamenting figure
Of the mother staggers through the lonely forest

Of this speechless grief; nights,
Fulfilled with tears, fiery angels.
Silverly a childlike skeleton smashes against a bleak wall.

The Wanderer
[version 2]

Always the white night leans upon the hill,
Where the poplar towers in silver tones
Are stars and stones.

Asleep the footbridge arches over the flooding brook,
A deceased countenance follows the boy,
Sickle moon in rosy ravine

Far from eulogizing shepherds. In old rocks
The toad gazes out of crystalline eyes,
Awakens the flowering wind, the birdcall of the deathlike man
And the footsteps quietly turn green in the forest.

Dieses erinnert an Baum und Tier. Langsame Stufen von Moos;
Und der Mond,
Der glänzend in traurigen Wassern versinkt.

Jener kehrt wieder und wandelt an grünem Gestade,
Schaukelt auf schwarzem Gondelschiffchen durch die verfallene Stadt.

Karl Kraus

Weißer Hohepriester der Wahrheit,
Kristallne Stimme, in der Gottes eisiger Odem wohnt,
Zürnender Magier,
Dem unter flammendem Mantel der blaue Panzer des Kriegers klirrt.

An die Verstummten

O, der Wahnsinn der großen Stadt, da am Abend
An schwarzer Mauer verkrüppelte Bäume starren,
Aus silberner Maske der Geist des Bösen schaut;
Licht mit magnetischer Geißel die steinerne Nacht verdrängt.
O, das versunkene Läuten der Abendglocken.

Hure, die in eisigen Schauern ein totes Kindlein gebärt.
Rasend peitscht Gottes Zorn die Stirne des Besessenen,
Purpurne Seuche, Hunger, der grüne Augen zerbricht.
O, das gräßliche Lachen des Golds.

Aber stille blutet in dunkler Höhle stummere Menschheit,
Fügt aus harten Metallen das erlösende Haupt.

This reminds of tree and animal. Slow steps of moss;
And the moon
That sinks glowing in sad waters.

The other one returns again and walks on the green shore,
Sways in a black gondola through the decayed city.

Karl Kraus

White pontiff of truth,
Crystalline voice in which God's icy breath dwells,
Angry magician
Under whose flaming coat the armor of the warrior rattles.

To the Muted

O, the insanity of the great city, when in the evening
At the black wall the stunted trees stare,
The spirit of evil gazes from a silver mask;
Light dislodges the stony night with a magnetic scourge.
O, the rapt sound of evening bells.

Whore, who in icy shudders bears a dead babe.
Raging God's wrath lashes the forehead of the possessed,
Purple pestilence, hunger that breaks green eyes.
O, the horrible laughter of gold.

But muter humanity calmly bleeds in a dark cave,
Assembles the redeeming head out of hard metals.

Passion

[3. Fassung]

Wenn Orpheus silbern die Laute rührt,
Beklagend ein Totes im Abendgarten,
Wer bist du Ruhendes unter hohen Bäumen?
Es rauscht die Klage das herbstliche Rohr,
Der blaue Teich,
Hinsterbend unter grünenden Bäumen
Und folgend dem Schatten der Schwester;
Dunkle Liebe
Eines wilden Geschlechts,
Dem auf goldenen Rädern der Tag davonrauscht.
Stille Nacht.

Unter finsteren Tannen
Mischten zwei Wölfe ihr Blut
In steinerner Umarmung; ein Goldnes
Verlor sich die Wolke über dem Steg,
Geduld und Schweigen der Kindheit.
Wieder begegnet der zarte Leichnam
Am Tritonsteich
Schlummernd in seinem hyazinthenen Haar.
Daß endlich zerbräche das kühle Haupt!

Denn immer folgt, ein blaues Wild,
Ein Äugendes unter dämmernden Bäumen,
Dieser dunkleren Pfaden
Wachend und bewegt von nächtigem Wohllaut,
Sanftem Wahnsinn;
Oder es tönte dunkler Verzückung
Voll das Saitenspiel
Zu den kühlen Füßen der Büßerin
In der steinernen Stadt.

Siebengesang des Todes

Bläulich dämmert der Frühling; unter saugenden Bäumen
Wandert ein Dunkles in Abend und Untergang,
Lauschend der sanften Klage der Amsel.

Passion
[version 3]

When Orpheus silverly stirs the lyre,
Lamenting the dead in the evening garden,
Who are you resting under tall trees?
The lament rustles the autumn reeds,
The blue pond,
Dying away under greening trees
And following the shadow of the sister;
Dark love
Of a wild race
From which the day rushes away on golden wheels.
Silent night.

Under sinister firs
Two wolves mixed their blood
In stony embrace; a golden shape
The cloud disappeared over the footbridge,
Patience and silence of childhood.
Again encounter the delicate corpse
By the Triton pond
Slumbering in his hyacinthine hair.
That the cool head would finally burst!

Because always a blue deer follows,
An eyeing shape under dusking trees,
The gentle insanity
Of these darker paths
Waking and moved by nocturnal harmonies;
Or the string music sounded
Full of dark ecstasy
At the cool feet of the penitent woman
In the stony city.

Seven-song of Death

Bluish spring dusks: under sucking trees
A dark shape wanders into evening and decline
Listening to the blackbird's gentle lament.

Schweigend erscheint die Nacht, ein blutendes Wild,
Das langsam hinsinkt am Hügel.

In feuchter Luft schwankt blühendes Apfelgezweig,
Löst silbern sich Verschlungenes,
Hinsterbend aus nächtigen Augen; fallende Sterne;
Sanfter Gesang der Kindheit.

Erscheinender stieg der Schläfer den schwarzen Wald hinab,
Und es rauschte ein blauer Quell im Grund,
Daß jener leise die bleichen Lider aufhob
Über sein schneeiges Antlitz;

Und es jagte der Mond ein rotes Tier
Aus seiner Höhle;
Und es starb in Seufzern die dunkle Klage der Frauen.

Strahlender hob die Hände zu seinem Stern
Der weiße Fremdling;
Schweigend verläßt ein Totes das verfallene Haus.

O des Menschen verweste Gestalt: gefügt aus kalten Metallen,
Nacht und Schrecken versunkener Wälder
Und der sengenden Wildnis des Tiers;
Windesstille der Seele.

Auf schwärzlichem Kahn fuhr jener schimmernde Ströme hinab,
Purpurner Sterne voll, und es sank
Friedlich das ergrünte Gezweig auf ihn,
Mohn aus silberner Wolke.

Winternacht

Es ist Schnee gefallen. Nach Mitternacht verläßt du betrunken von purpurnem Wein den dunklen Bezirk der Menschen, die rote Flamme ihres Herdes. O die Finsternis!

Schwarzer Frost. Die Erde ist hart, nach Bitterem schmeckt die Luft. Deine Sterne schließen sich zu bösen Zeichen.

Mit versteinerten Schritten stampfst du am Bahndamm hin, mit runden Augen, wie ein Soldat, der eine schwarze Schanze stürmt. Avanti!

Bitterer Schnee und Mond!

Silently the night appears, a bleeding deer
That slowly sinks down at the hill.

In damp air blossoming apple branches sway,
Labyrinthine shapes that release silverly,
Dying away from nocturnal eyes; falling stars;
Gentle song of childhood.

Appearing more the sleeper descended the black forest
And a blue spring murmured from the ground
So that the other one quietly lifted pale eyelids
Over his snowy countenance;

And the moon chased a red animal
From its cave;
And in sighs the dark lament of women died.

More radiant the white stranger lifted the hands
Toward his star;
Silently a dead shape leaves the decayed house.

O the putrefied figure of man: formed from cold metals,
Night and terror of sunken forests
And the singeing wilderness of the animal;
Wind lull of the soul.

In a blackish boat the other one rode down shimmering rivers
Filled with purple stars, and the greening branches
Sank peacefully over him,
Poppy from silver clouds.

Winter Night

Snow has fallen. After midnight drunk with purple wine you leave the dark domain of men, the red flame of their hearth. O the sinisterness!

Black frost. The earth is hard, the air tastes of bitterness. Your stars close into evil signs.

With petrified steps you tramp along the railroad embankment, with round eyes, like a soldier who storms a black entrenchment. Avanti!

Bitter snow and moon!

A red wolf which an angel chokes. Your legs rattle in stride like blue ice and a

Ein roter Wolf, den ein Engel würgt. Deine Beine klirren schreitend wie blaues Eis und ein Lächeln voll Trauer und Hochmut hat dein Antlitz versteinert und die Stirne erbleicht vor der Wollust des Frostes;

oder sie neigt sich schweigend über den Schlaf eines Wächters, der in seiner hölzernen Hütte hinsank.

Frost und Rauch. Ein weißes Sternenhemd verbrennt die tragenden Schultern und Gottes Geier zerfleischen dein metallenes Herz.

O der steinerne Hügel. Stille schmilzt und vergessen der kühle Leib im silbernen Schnee hin.

Schwarz ist der Schlaf. Das Ohr folgt lange den Pfaden der Sterne im Eis.

Beim Erwachen klangen die Glocken im Dorf. Aus dem östlichen Tor trat silbern der rosige Tag.

smile full of sadness and pride has petrified your face and the forehead pales before the lust of frost;

or it bends silently over the sleep of a watchman, who sank down in his wooden hut.

Frost and smoke. A white star-shirt burns the bearing shoulders and God's vultures mangle your metallic heart.

O the stony hill. Still and forgotten the cool body melts in silver snow.

Black is the sleep. Long the ear follows the paths of the stars in the ice.

At the awakening the church bells rang in the village. Silverly the rosy day stepped from the eastern gate.

Gesang des Abgeschiedenen

In Venedig

Stille in nächtigem Zimmer
Silbern flackert der Leuchter
Vor dem singenden Odem
Des Einsamen;
Zaubrisches Rosengewölk.

Schwärzlicher Fliegenschwarm
Verdunkelt den steinernen Raum
Und es starrt von der Qual
Des goldenen Tags das Haupt
Des Heimatlosen.

Reglos nachtet das Meer.
Stern und schwärzliche Fahrt
Entschwand am Kanal.
Kind, dein kränkliches Lächeln
Folgte mir leise im Schlaf.

Vorhölle
[2. Fassung]

An herbstlichen Mauern, es suchen Schatten dort
Am Hügel das tönende Gold
Weidende Abendwolken
In der Ruh verdorrter Platanen.
Dunklere Tränen odmet diese Zeit,
Verdammnis, da des Träumers Herz
Überfließt von purpurner Abendröte,
Der Schwermut der rauchenden Stadt;
Dem Schreitenden nachweht goldene Kühle
Dem Fremdling, vom Friedhof,
Als folgte im Schatten ein zarter Leichnam.

Song of the Departed

In Venice

Stillness in nocturnal room.
Silverly the candlestick flickers
Before the singing breath
Of the lonely one;
Enchanting rose-clouds.

Blackish swarm of flies
Darkens the stony room
And the head of the homeless one
Stares from the agony
Of the golden day.

Motionless the sea falls into night.
Star and blackish travel
Vanished by the canal.
Child, your sickly smile
Followed me quietly during sleep.

Limbo
[verison 2]

By autumn walls, there shadows seek
On the hill the singing gold
Grazing evening clouds
In the repose of withered sycamores.
This time breathes darker tears,
Damnation, since the dreamer's heart
Overflows with purple glow of sunset,
The gloom of the smoking city;
From the cemetery a golden coolness drifts after
The walker, the stranger,
As if a tender corpse followed in the shadow.

Leise läutet der steinerne Bau;
Der Garten der Waisen, das dunkle Spital,
Ein rotes Schiff am Kanal.
Träumend steigen und sinken im Dunkel
Verwesende Menschen
Und aus schwärzlichen Toren
Treten Engel mit kalten Stirnen hervor;
Bläue, die Todesklagen der Mütter.
Es rollt durch ihr langes Haar,
Ein feuriges Rad, der runde Tag
Der Erde Qual ohne Ende.

In kühlen Zimmern ohne Sinn
Modert Gerät, mit knöchernen Händen
Tastet im Blau nach Märchen
Unheilige Kindheit,
Benagt die fette Ratte Tür und Truh,
Ein Herz
Erstarrt in schneeiger Stille.
Nachhallen die purpurnen Flüche
Des Hungers in faulendem Dunkel,
Die schwarzen Schwerter der Lüge,
Als schlüge zusammen ein ehernes Tor.

Die Sonne

Täglich kommt die gelbe Sonne über den Hügel.
Schön ist der Wald, das dunkle Tier,
Der Mensch; Jäger oder Hirt.

Rötlich steigt im grünen Weiher der Fisch.
Unter dem runden Himmel
Fährt der Fischer leise im blauen Kahn.

Langsam reift die Traube, das Korn.
Wenn sich stille der Tag neigt,
Ist ein Gutes und Böses bereitet.

Wenn es Nacht wird,
Hebt der Wanderer leise die schweren Lider;
Sonne aus finsterer Schlucht bricht.

Quietly the stone building rings;
The garden of the orphans, the dark hospital,
A red ship in the canal.
Dreaming in the darkness
Rotting people rise and sink
And from black gates
Angels with cold foreheads emerge;
Blueness, the death-laments of the mothers.
Through their long hair
A fiery wheel rolls, the round day
Of earth's agony without end.

Utensils molder in cool rooms
Without meaning, with bony hands
Unholy childhood
Gropes in the blueness after fairy tales,
The plump rat gnaws door and chest,
A heart
Stiffens in snowy stillness.
Purple curses of hunger reverberate
In putrefying darkness,
The black swords of the lie,
As if a brazen gate slammed shut.

The Sun

Daily the yellow sun comes over the hill.
Beautiful is the forest, the dark animal,
Man; hunter or shepherd.

Reddish the fish rises in the green pond.
Under the round sky
The fisherman quietly sails in the blue boat.

Slowly the grape ripens, the corn.
When the day ends silently
A good and evil is prepared.

When night comes
The wanderer quietly lifts the heavy eyelids;
Sun breaks out of a sinister ravine.

Gesang einer gefangenen Amsel

Für Ludwig von Ficker

Dunkler Odem im grünen Gezweig.
Blaue Blümchen umschweben das Antlitz
Des Einsamen, den goldnen Schritt
Ersterbend unter dem Ölbaum.
Aufflattert mit trunkenem Flügel die Nacht.
So leise blutet Demut,
Tau, der langsam tropft vom blühenden Dorn.
Strahlender Arme Erbarmen
Umfängt ein brechendes Herz.

Sommer

Am Abend schweigt die Klage
Des Kuckucks im Wald.
Tiefer neigt sich das Korn,
Der rote Mohn.

Schwarzes Gewitter droht
Über dem Hügel.
Das alte Lied der Grille
Erstirbt im Feld.

Nimmer regt sich das Laub
Der Kastanie.
Auf der Wendeltreppe
Rauscht dein Kleid.

Stille leuchtet die Kerze
Im dunklen Zimmer;
Eine silberne Hand
Löschte sie aus;

Windstille, sternlose Nacht.

Song of a Captive Blackbird

For Ludwig von Ficker

Dark breath in the green branches.
Small blue flowers hover around the countenance
Of the lonely one, the golden step
Dying under the olive tree.
Night flutters up with drunken wing.
So quietly humility bleeds,
Dew that slowly drips from blossoming thorn.
The compassion of radiant arms
Embraces a breaking heart.

Summer

In the evening the cuckoo's lament
Grows silent in the forest.
The corn bends deeper,
The red poppy.

Black thunderstorm threatens
Over the hill.
The old song of the cricket
Dies off in the field.

The leaves of the chestnut
Never stir.
Your gown rustles
On the spiral stair.

Silently the candle glows
In the dark room;
A silver hand
Extinguished it;

Wind lull, starless night.

Sommersneige

Der grüne Sommer ist so leise
Geworden, dein kristallenes Antlitz.
Am Abendweiher starben die Blumen,
Ein erschrockener Amselruf.

Vergebliche Hoffnung des Lebens. Schon rüstet
Zur Reise sich die Schwalbe im Haus
Und die Sonne versinkt am Hügel;
Schon winkt zur Sternenreise die Nacht.

Stille der Dörfer; es tönen rings
Die verlassenen Wälder. Herz,
Neige dich nun liebender
Über die ruhige Schläferin.

Der grüne Sommer ist so leise
Geworden und es läutet der Schritt
Des Fremdlings durch die silberne Nacht.
Gedächte ein blaues Wild seines Pfads,

Des Wohllauts seiner geistlichen Jahre!

Jahr

Dunkle Stille der Kindheit. Unter grünenden Eschen
Weidet die Sanftmut bläulichen Blickes; goldene Ruh.
Ein Dunkles entzückt der Duft der Veilchen; schwankende Ähren
Im Abend, Samen und die goldenen Schatten der Schwermut.
Balken behaut der Zimmermann; im dämmernden Grund
Mahlt die Mühle; im Hasellaub wölbt sich ein purpurner Mund,
Männliches rot über schweigende Wasser geneigt.
Leise ist der Herbst, der Geist des Waldes; goldene Wolke
Folgt dem Einsamen, der schwarze Schatten des Enkels.
Neige in steinernem Zimmer; unter alten Zypressen
Sind der Tränen nächtige Bilder zum Quell versammelt;
Goldenes Auge des Anbeginns, dunkle Geduld des Endes.

End of Summer

The green summer has grown
So quiet, your crystalline countenance.
By the evening pond the flowers died,
A frightened call of a blackbird.

Futile hope of life. Already the swallow
In the house prepares for the journey
And the sun sinks at the hill;
Already the night beckons to the starry journey.

Silence of villages; the abandoned forests
Resound all around. Heart,
Now bend more lovingly
Over the woman peacefully sleeping.

The green summer has grown
So quiet; and the stranger's footstep
Rings through the silver night.
May a blue deer remember his path,

The harmony of his spiritual years!

Year

Dark stillness of childhood. Under greening ash trees
The meekness of the bluish gaze feasts; golden repose.
A dark shape is charmed by the fragrance of violets; swaying ears of corn
In the evening, seed and the golden shadows of gloom.
The carpenter trims the beams; in the dusking valley
The mill grinds; a purple mouth swells in hazel leaves,
Masculine bent red over silent waters.
Autumn is quiet, the spirit of the forest; a golden cloud
Follows the lonely one, the black shadow of the grandson.
Ending in a stony room; under old cypress trees
The nightly images of tears are gathered in a well;
Golden eye of the beginning, dark patience of the end.

Abendland

[4. Fassung]

Else Lasker-Schüler in Verehrung

1

Mond, als träte ein Totes
Aus blauer Höhle,
Und es fallen der Blüten
Viele über den Felsenpfad.
Silbern weint ein Krankes
Am Abendweiher,
Auf schwarzem Kahn
Hinüberstarben Liebende.

Oder es läuten die Schritte
Elis' durch den Hain
Den hyazinthenen
Wieder verhallend unter Eichen.
O des Knaben Gestalt
Geformt aus kristallenen Tränen,
Nächtigen Schatten.
Zackige Blitze erhellen die Schläfe
Die immerkühle,
Wenn am grünenden Hügel
Frühlingsgewitter ertönt.

2

So leise sind die grünen Wälder
Unsrer Heimat,
Die kristallne Woge
Hinsterbend an verfallner Mauer
Und wir haben im Schlaf geweint;
Wandern mit zögernden Schritten
An der dornigen Hecke hin
Singende im Abendsommer,
In heiliger Ruh
Des fern verstrahlenden Weinbergs;
Schatten nun im kühlen Schoß

Occident

[version 4]

To Else Lasker-Schüler, with admiration

1

Moon, as if a dead thing would step
From a blue cave,
And many blossoms fall
Across the rock path.
Silverly a sickly shape weeps
By the evening pond,
In a black boat
Lovers have died crossing over.

Or Elis' footsteps
Ring through the grove,
The hyacinthine
Again fading under oaks.
O the boy's figure
Formed from crystalline tears,
Nocturnal shadows.
Jagged lightning illuminates the temple
That is always cool,
When by the greening hill
Spring thunderstorm resounds.

2

So quiet are the green forests
Of our homeland,
The crystalline wave
Dying on a decayed wall
And we have wept in sleep;
Singers wandering with hesitant steps
Along the thorny hedge
In the summer evening,
In holy peace
Of the distant radiant vineyard;
Shadows now in the cool lap

Der Nacht, trauernde Adler.
So leise schließt ein mondener Strahl
Die purpurnen Male der Schwermut.

3

Ihr großen Städte
Steinern aufgebaut
In der Ebene!
So sprachlos folgt
Der Heimatlose
Mit dunkler Stirne dem Wind,
Kahlen Bäumen am Hügel.
Ihr weithin dämmernden Ströme!
Gewaltig ängstet
Schaurige Abendröte
Im Sturmgewölk.
Ihr sterbenden Völker!
Bleiche Woge
Zerschellend am Strande der Nacht,
Fallende Sterne.

Frühling der Seele

Aufschrei im Schlaf; durch schwarze Gassen stürzt der Wind,
Das Blau des Frühlings winkt durch brechendes Geäst,
Purpurner Nachttau und es erlöschen rings die Sterne.
Grünlich dämmert der Fluß, silbern die alten Alleen
Und die Türme der Stadt. O sanfte Trunkenheit
Im gleitenden Kahn und die dunklen Rufe der Amsel
In kindlichen Gärten. Schon lichtet sich der rosige Flor.

Feierlich rauschen die Wasser. O die feuchten Schatten der Au,
Das schreitende Tier; Grünendes, Blütengezweig
Rührt die kristallene Stirne; schimmernder Schaukelkahn.
Leise tönt die Sonne im Rosengewölk am Hügel.
Groß ist die Stille des Tannenwalds, die ernsten Schatten am Fluß.

Reinheit! Reinheit! Wo sind die furchtbaren Pfade des Todes,
Des grauen steinernen Schweigens, die Felsen der Nacht

Of night, mourning eagles.
So quietly a moonbeam closes
The purple stigmata of gloom.

3

You mighty cities
Built from stone
On the plain!
So speechless
The homeless one follows
The wind with dark forehead,
Bare trees by the hill.
You widely dusking rivers!
In storm clouds
The scary glow of sunset
Frightens enormously.
You dying people!
Pale wave
Breaking on the beach of night,
Falling stars.

Springtime of the Soul

Outcry in sleep; through black alleys the wind rushes,
The blue of spring beckons through breaking branches,
Purple night dew and stars extinguish all around.
Greenish the river dawns, silverly the old avenues
And the towers of the city. O gentle drunkenness
In the gliding boat and the dark calls of the blackbird
In childlike gardens. Already the rosy veil thins.

Solemnly the waters murmur. O the moist shadows of the floodplain,
The striding animal; greening shapes, flowering branches
Touch the crystal forehead; shimmering boat-sway.
Quietly the sun sounds in the rose-colored clouds by the hill.
Great is the stillness of the fir forest, the serious shadows at the river.

Purity! Purity! Where are the terrible paths of death,
Of gray stony silence, the rocks of the night

Und die friedlosen Schatten? Strahlender Sonnenabgrund.

Schwester, da ich dich fand an einsamer Lichtung
Des Waldes und Mittag war und groß das Schweigen des Tiers;
Weiße unter wilder Eiche, und es blühte silbern der Dorn.
Gewaltiges Sterben und die singende Flamme im Herzen.

Dunkler umfließen die Wasser die schönen Spiele der Fische.
Stunde der Trauer, Schweigender Anblick der Sonne;
Es ist die Seele ein Fremdes auf Erden. Geistlich dämmert
Bläue über dem verhauenen Wald und es läutet
Lange eine dunkle Glocke im Dorf; friedlich Geleit.
Stille blüht die Myrthe über den weißen Lidern des Toten.

Leise tönen die Wasser im sinkenden Nachmittag
Und es grünet dunkler die Wildnis am Ufer, Freude im rosigen Wind;

Der sanfte Gesang des Bruders am Abendhügel.

Im Dunkel
[2. Fassung]

Es schweigt die Seele den blauen Frühling.
Unter feuchtem Abendgezweig
Sank in Schauern die Stirne den Liebenden.

O das grünende Kreuz. In dunklem Gespräch
Erkannten sich Mann und Weib.
An kahler Mauer
Wandelt in seinen Gestirnen der Einsame.

Über die mondbeglänzten Wege des Walds
Sank die Wildnis
Vergessener Jagden; Blick der Bläue
Aus verfallenen Felsen bricht.

And the peaceless shadows? Radiant abyss of sun.

Sister, when I found you at the lonely clearing
In the forest, it was midday and the silence of the animal great;
Whiteness under wild oak, and the thorn bloomed silver.
Enormous dying and the singing flame in the heart.

Darker the waters flow around the beautiful play of fishes.
Hour of mourning, silent vision of the sun;
The soul is a strange shape on earth. Spiritually blueness
Dusks over the pruned forest; and a dark bell rings
Long in the village; peaceful escort.
Silently the myrtle blooms over the white eyelids of the dead.

Quietly the waters resound in the sinking afternoon
And the wilderness on the bank greens more darkly; joy in the rosy wind;

The brother's gentle song by the evening hill.

In Darkness
[version 2]

The soul silences the blue springtime.
Under damp evening branches
The forehead of lovers sank in shudders.

O the greening cross. In dark conversation
Man and woman knew each other.
Along the bare wall
The lonely one wanders with his stars.

Over the moon-brightened forest paths
The wilderness
Of forgotten hunts sank; glimpse of blue
Breaks from moldered rocks.

Gesang des Abgeschiedenen

An Karl Borromaeus Heinrich

Voll Harmonien ist der Flug der Vögel. Es haben die grünen Wälder
Am Abend sich zu stilleren Hütten versammelt;
Die kristallenen Weiden des Rehs.
Dunkles besänftigt das Plätschern des Bachs, die feuchten Schatten

Und die Blumen des Sommers, die schön im Winde läuten.
Schon dämmert die Stirne dem sinnenden Menschen.

Und es leuchtet ein Lämpchen, das Gute, in seinem Herzen
Und der Frieden des Mahls; denn geheiligt ist Brot und Wein
Von Gottes Händen, und es schaut aus nächtigen Augen
Stille dich der Bruder an, daß er ruhe von dorniger Wanderschaft.
O das Wohnen in der beseelten Bläue der Nacht.

Liebend auch umfängt das Schweigen im Zimmer die Schatten der Alten,
Die purpurnen Martern, Klage eines großen Geschlechts,
Das fromm nun hingeht im einsamen Enkel.

Denn strahlender immer erwacht aus schwarzen Minuten des Wahnsinns
Der Duldende an versteinerter Schwelle
Und es umfangt ihn gewaltig die kühle Bläue und die leuchtende Neige des
    Herbstes,

Das stille Haus und die Sagen des Waldes,
Maß und Gesetz und die mondenen Pfade der Abgeschiedenen.

Song of the Departed

To Karl Borromaeus Heinrich

The flight of birds is full of harmonies. The green forests
In the evening have gathered to quieter huts;
The crystal meadows of the doe.
A dark shape calms the ripple of the brook, the damp shadows,

And the flowers of summer which ring beautifully in the wind.
Already the forehead of the pondering man darkens with dusk.

And a small lamp shines, the goodness in his heart
And the peace of the meal; because bread and wine are sanctified
By God's hands, and out of nocturnal eyes
The brother silently gazes at you so that he rests from thorny wanderings.
O the dwelling in the soulful blueness of night.

Lovingly the silence in the room also embraces the shadows of the ancestors,
The purple martyrs, lament of a mighty race
That now dies piously in the lonely grandchild.

Because from black minutes of insanity the sufferer
Always awakens more radiant at the petrified threshold
And the cool blueness embraces him enormously and the bright end of
    autumn,

The still house and the telling of the forest,
Measure and law and the lunar paths of the departed.

Traum und Umnachtung

Traum und Umnachtung

Am Abend ward zum Greis der Vater; in dunklen Zimmern versteinerte das Antlitz der Mutter und auf dem Knaben lastete der Fluch des entarteten Geschlechts. Manchmal erinnerte er sich seiner Kindheit, erfüllt von Krankheit, Schrecken und Finsternis, verschwiegener Spiele im Sternengarten, oder daß er die Ratten fütterte im dämmernden Hof. Aus blauem Spiegel trat die schmale Gestalt der Schwester und er stürzte wie tot ins Dunkel. Nachts brach sein Mund gleich einer roten Frucht auf und die Sterne erglänzten über seiner sprachlosen Trauer. Seine Träume erfüllten das alte Haus der Väter. Am Abend ging er gerne über den verfallenen Friedhof, oder er besah in dämmernder Totenkammer die Leichen, die grünen Flecken der Verwesung auf ihren schönen Händen. An der Pforte des Klosters bat er um ein Stück Brot; der Schatten eines Rappen sprang aus dem Dunkel und erschreckte ihn. Wenn er in seinem kühlen Bette lag, überkamen ihn unsägliche Tränen. Aber es war niemand, der die Hand auf seine Stirne gelegt hätte. Wenn der Herbst kam, ging er, ein Hellseher, in brauner Au. O, die Stunden wilder Verzückung, die Abende am grünen Fluß, die Jagden. O, die Seele, die leise das Lied des vergilbten Rohrs sang; feurige Frömmigkeit. Stille sah er und lang in die Sternenaugen der Kröte, befühlte mit erschauernden Händen die Kühle des alten Steins und besprach die ehrwürdige Sage des blauen Quells. O, die silbernen Fische und die Früchte, die von verkrüppelten Bäumen fielen. Die Akkorde seiner Schritte erfüllten ihn mit Stolz und Menschenverachtung. Am Heimweg traf er ein unbewohntes Schloß. Verfallene Götter standen im Garten, hintrauernd am Abend. Ihm aber schien: hier lebte ich vergessene Jahre. Ein Orgelchoral erfüllte ihn mit Gottes Schauern. Aber in dunkler Höhle verbrachte er seine Tage, log und stahl und verbarg sich, ein flammender Wolf, vor dem weißen Antlitz der Mutter. O, die Stunde, da er mit steinernem Munde im Sternengarten hinsank, der Schatten des Mörders über ihn kam. Mit purpurner Stirne ging er ins Moor und Gottes Zorn züchtigte seine metallenen Schultern; o, die Birken im Sturm, das dunkle Getier, das seine umnachteten Pfade mied. Haß verbrannte sein Herz, Wollust, da er im grünen den Sommergarten dem schweigenden Kind Gewalt tat, in dem strahlenden sein umnachtetes Antlitz erkannte. Weh, des Abends am Fenster, da aus purpurnen Blumen, ein gräulich Gerippe, der Tod trat. O, ihr Türme und Glocken; und die Schatten der Nacht fielen steinern auf ihn.

Niemand liebte ihn. Sein Haupt verbrannte Lüge und Unzucht in dämmern-den Zimmern. Das blaue Rauschen eines Frauengewandes ließ ihn zur Säule erstarren und in der Tür stand die nächtige Gestalt seiner Mutter. Zu seinen Häupten

Dream and Derangement

Dream and Derangement

In the evening the father became an old man; in dark rooms the countenance of the mother turned to stone and the curse of the degenerated race weighed on the boy. Sometimes he remembered his childhood, fulfilled with sickness, terror and sinisterness, secret games in the star-garden, or feeding rats in the dusking courtyard. From the blue mirror the slender figure of the sister stepped and he fell into darkness as if dead. At night his mouth burst open like a red fruit and stars gleamed over his speechless grief. His dreams fulfilled the ancient house of the fathers. In the evening he liked to walk over the decayed cemetery, or he watched the corpses in the dusking crypts, the green stains of rot on their beautiful hands. At the gate of the monastery he asked for a piece of bread; the shadow of a black horse jumped out of darkness and frightened him. When he lay in his cool bed, unspeakable tears overcame him. But there was no one who might have put a hand on his forehead. When autumn came, he walked, a clairvoyant, in brown floodplain. O, the hours of wild ecstasy, the evenings by the green river, the hunting. O, the soul which quietly sang the song of the yellowed reed; fiery piety. Silent and long he looked into the starry eyes of the toad, felt with trembling hands the coolness of the old stone and consulted with the revered legend of the blue well. O, the silver fish and fruits which fell from crippled trees. The chords of his steps fulfilled him with pride and contempt of men. On the way home he encountered an uninhabited palace. Decayed gods stood in the garden mourning in the evening. But it seemed to him: here I lived forgotten years. An organ choral fulfilled him with God's trembling. But in a dark cave he spent his days, lied and stole and hid, a flaming wolf before the white countenance of the mother. O, the hour when with stony mouth he sank down in the star-garden, the shadow of the murderer came over him. With purple forehead he walked into the moor and God's wrath castigated his metal shoulders; o, the birches in the storm; the dark animals which avoided his deranged paths. Hate burned his heart, lust, when in the green summer garden he violated the silent child and recognized in the radiance his own deranged countenance. Woe, in the evening at the window, when out of purple flowers a grayish skeleton, death stepped. O, you towers and bells; and the shadows of night fell stony upon him.

No one loved him. Lie and lechery burned his head in dusking rooms. The blue rustle of a woman's dress made him stiffen into a column and the nocturnal figure of his mother stood in the doorway. Above his head the shadow of evil rose up. O, you nights and stars. In the evening he walked past the mountain with the cripple;

erhob sich der Schatten des Bösen. O, ihr Nächte und Sterne. Am Abend ging er mit dem Krüppel am Berge hin; auf eisigem Gipfel lag der rosige Glanz der Abendröte und sein Herz läutete leise in der Dämmerung. Schwer sanken die stürmischen Tannen über sie und der rote Jäger trat aus dem Wald. Da es Nacht ward, zerbrach kristallen sein Herz und die Finsternis schlug seine Stirne. Unter kahlen Eichbäumen erwürgte er mit eisigen Händen eine wilde Katze. Klagend zur Rechten erschien die weiße Gestalt eines Engels, und es wuchs im Dunkel der Schatten des Krüppels. Er aber hob einen Stein und warf ihn nach jenem, daß er heulend floh, und seufzend verging im Schatten des Baums das sanfte Antlitz des Engels. Lange lag er auf steinigem Acker und sah staunend das goldene Zelt der Sterne. Von Fledermäusen gejagt, stürzte er fort ins Dunkel. Atemlos trat er ins verfallene Haus. Im Hof trank er, ein wildes Tier, von den blauen Wassern des Brunnens, bis ihn fror. Fiebernd saß er auf der eisigen Stiege, rasend gen Gott, daß er stürbe. O, das graue Antlitz des Schreckens, da er die runden Augen über einer Taube zerschnittener Kehle aufhob. Huschend über fremde Stiegen begegnete er einem Judenmädchen und er griff nach ihrem schwarzen Haar und er nahm ihren Mund. Feindliches folgte ihm durch finstere Gassen und sein Ohr zerriß ein eisernes Klirren. An herbstlichen Mauern folgte er, ein Mesnerknabe, stille dem schweigenden Priester; unter verdorrten Bäumen atmete er trunken den Scharlach jenes ehrwürdigen Gewands. O, die verfallene Scheibe der Sonne. Süße Martern verzehrten sein Fleisch. In einem verödeten Durchhaus erschien ihm starrend von Unrat seine blutende Gestalt. Tiefer liebte er die erhabenen Werke des Steins; den Turm, der mit höllischen Fratzen nächtlich den blauen Sternenhimmel stürmt; das kühle Grab, darin des Menschen feuriges Herz bewahrt ist. Weh, der unsäglichen Schuld, die jenes kundtut. Aber da er Glühendes sinnend den herbstlichen Fluß hinabging unter kahlen Bäumen hin, erschien in härenem Mantel ihm, ein flammender Dämon, die Schwester. Beim Erwachen erloschen zu ihren Häuptern die Sterne.

O des verfluchten Geschlechts. Wenn in befleckten Zimmern jegliches Schicksal vollendet ist, tritt mit modernden Schritten der Tod in das Haus. O, daß draußen Frühling wäre und im blühenden Baum ein lieblicher Vogel singe. Aber gräulich verdorrt das spärliche Grün an den Fenstern der Nächtlichen und es sinnen die blutenden Herzen noch Böses. O, die dämmernden Früh-lingswege des Sinnenden. Gerechter erfreut ihn die blühende Hecke, die junge Saat des Landmanns und der singende Vogel, Gottes sanftes Geschöpf; die Abendglocke und die schöne Gemeine der Menschen. Daß er seines Schicksals vergäße und des dornigen Stachels. Frei ergrünt der Bach, wo silbern wandelt sein Fuß, und ein sagender Baum rauscht über dem umnachteten Haupt ihm. Also hebt er mit schmächtiger Hand die Schlange, und in feurigen Tränen schmolz ihm das Herz hin. Erhaben ist das Schweigen des Walds, ergrüntes Dunkel und das moosige Getier, aufflatternd, wenn es Nacht wird. O der Schauer, da jegliches seine Schuld weiß, dornige Pfade geht. Also fand er im Dornenbusch die weiße Gestalt des Kindes, blutend nach dem Mantel seines Bräutigams. Er aber stand vergraben in sein stählernes Haar stumm und leidend vor ihr. O die strahlenden Engel, die der purpurne Nacht-

the rosy splendor of the glow of sunset lay on the icy peak and his heart quietly rang in the dusk. The stormy firs sank heavily upon them and the red hunter stepped out of the forest. When night came his heart broke crystal-like and sinisterness beat his forehead. Under bleak oak trees he strangled a wild cat with icy hands. Lamenting to his right, the white figure of an angel appeared, and in the darkness the shadow of the cripple grew. But he lifted a rock and threw it at the other so that he fled howling and in the shadow of the tree the soft countenance of the angel faded away sighing. Long he lay on a stony acre and gazed with astonishment at the golden tent of the stars. Chased by bats, he fell away into darkness. Breathless he entered the decayed house. In the courtyard he, a wild animal, drank the well's blue water until he became cold. Feverish he sat upon the icy stairs, raging against God that he might die. O, the gray countenance of terror when he raised the round eyes over a dove's slit throat. Shooing over strange stairs he met a Jewish girl and he grabbed at her black hair and he seized her mouth. Hostile shapes followed him through sinister streets and an iron clinking tore his ear. Along autumn walls he, an acolyte, quietly followed the silent priest; drunkenly he breathed in the scarlet of his reverend vestment under withered trees. O, the decayed disk of the sun. Sweet torments consumed his flesh. In a deserted passageway his own bleeding figure covered with refuse appeared to him. He loved the noble works of stone more deeply; the tower that nightly storms the blue starry sky with hellish grimaces; the cool grave in which man's fiery heart is preserved. Woe, to the unspeakable guilt signified by it. But when he walked along the autumn river under bleak trees pondering something blazing, a flaming daemon appeared to him in hairy coat, the sister. Awaking the stars expired above their heads.

O of the cursed race. When in defiled rooms every destiny has been fulfilled, death enters the house in moldering steps. O, that it were spring outdoors and a lovely bird was singing in the blossoming tree. But grayish the scanty green withers around the windows of the nocturnal ones and bleeding hearts still think evil. O, the dusking spring paths of the pondering. More righteously he rejoices in the blossoming hedge, the countryman's young seed, and the singing bird, God's gentle creature; the evening bell and the beautiful community of men. So that he might forget his fate and the thorny sting. Freely the brook turns green, where silverly his foot wanders, and a telling tree rustles above his deranged head. Thus he lifts the serpent with slender hand and in fiery tears his heart melted away. The silence of the forest is sublime, greening darkness, and the mossy animals fluttering up when night comes. O the shiver when every being knows its guilt, walks thorny paths. Thus he found the white figure of the child in the thorn bush bleeding for the coat of its bridegroom. But he stood buried in his steely hair mute and suffering before her. O the radiant angels whom the purple night wind dispersed. Nightlong he dwelled in a crystalline cave and silverly leprosy grew on his forehead. A shadow he walked down the mule track under autumn stars. Snow fell, and blue sinisterness filled the house. The harsh voice of the father called out like a blind man and evoked dread. Woe of the bowed appearance of women. Under rigid hands

wind zerstreute. Nachtlang wohnte er in kristallener Höhle und der Aussatz wuchs silbern auf seiner Stirne. Ein Schatten ging er den Saumpfad hinab unter herbstlichen Sternen. Schnee fiel, und blaue Finsternis erfüllte das Haus. Eines Blinden klang die harte Stimme des Vaters und beschwor das Grauen. Weh der gebeugten Erscheinung der Frauen. Unter erstarrten Händen verfielen Frucht und Gerät dem entsetzten Geschlecht. Ein Wolf zerriß das Erstgeborene und die Schwestern flohen in dunkle Gärten zu knöchernen Greisen. Ein umnachteter Seher sang jener an verfallenen Mauern und seine Stimme verschlang Gottes Wind. O die Wollust des Todes. O ihr Kinder eines dunklen Geschlechts. Silbern schimmern die bösen Blumen des Bluts an jenes Schläfe, der kalte Mond in seinen zerbrochenen Augen. O, der Nächtlichen; o, der Verfluchten.

Tief ist der Schlummer in dunklen Giften, erfüllt von Sternen und dem weißen Antlitz der Mutter, dem steinernen. Bitter ist der Tod, die Kost der Schuldbeladenen; in dem braunen Geäst des Stamms zerfielen grinsend die irdenen Gesichter. Aber leise sang jener im grünen Schatten des Hollunders, da er aus bösen Träumen erwachte; süßer Gespiele nahte ihm ein rosiger Engel, daß er, ein sanftes Wild, zur Nacht hinschlummerte; und er sah das Sternenantlitz der Reinheit. Golden sanken die Sonnenblumen über den Zaun des Gartens, da es Sommer ward. O, der Fleiß der Bienen und das grüne Laub des Nußbaums; die vorüberziehenden Gewitter. Silbern blühte der Mohn auch, trug in grüner Kapsel unsere nächtigen Sternenträume. O, wie stille war das Haus, als der Vater ins Dunkel hinging. Purpurn reifte die Frucht am Baum und der Gärtner rührte die harten Hände; o die härenen Zeichen in strahlender Sonne. Aber stille trat am Abend der Schatten des Toten in den trauernden Kreis der Seinen und es klang kristallen sein Schritt über die grünende Wiese vorm Wald. Schweigende versammelten sich jene am Tisch; Sterbende brachen sie mit wächsernen Händen das Brot, das blutende. Weh der steinernen Augen der Schwester, da beim Mahle ihr Wahnsinn auf die nächtige Stirne des Bruders trat, der Mutter unter leidenden Händen das Brot zu Stein ward. O der Verwesten, da sie mit silbernen Zungen die Hölle schwiegen. Also erloschen die Lampen im kühlen Gemach und aus purpurnen Masken sahen schweigend sich die leidenden Menschen an. Die Nacht lang rauschte ein Regen und erquickte die Flur. In dorniger Wildnis folgte der Dunkle den vergilbten Pfaden im Korn, dem Lied der Lerche und der sanften Stille des grünen Gezweigs, daß er Frieden fände. O, ihr Dörfer und moosigen Stufen, glühender Anblick. Aber beinern schwanken die Schritte über schlafende Schlangen am Waldsaum und das Ohr folgt immer dem rasenden Schrei des Geiers. Steinige Öde fand er am Abend, Geleite eines Toten in das dunkle Haus des Vaters. Purpurne Wolke umwölkte sein Haupt, daß er schweigend über sein eigenes Blut und Bildnis herfiel, ein mondenes Antlitz; steinern ins Leere hinsank, da in zerbrochenem Spiegel, ein sterbender Jüngling, die Schwester erschien, die Nacht das verfluchte Geschlecht verschlang.

the terrified race's progeny and utensils decayed. A wolf tore the firstborn and the sisters fled into dark gardens to bony old men. A deranged seer the other one sang along the decayed walls and God's wind engulfed his voice. O, the lust of death. O you children of a dark race. Silverly the evil flowers of the blood glimmer on the other one's temple, the cold moon in his broken eyes. O, of the nocturnal ones; o, of the cursed.

Deep is the slumber in dark poisons, fulfilled with stars and the white countenance of the mother, the stony one. Bitter is death, the fare of the guilt-laden; in the brown branches of the family tree the earthen faces decayed grinning. But quietly the other one sang in the green shadow of the elderberry, when he woke from evil dreams; sweet playmate, a rosy angel, approached him, so that he, a gentle deer, slumbered into the night; and he saw the starry countenance of purity. The sunflowers sank golden over the garden fence when the summer came. O, the diligence of bees and the green leaves of the walnut tree; the thunderstorms passing by. Silverly the poppy bloomed also, bore in green bud our nocturnal star-dreams. O, how silent the house was when the father passed away into darkness. The fruit ripened purple on the tree and the gardener moved his hard hands; o the hairy signs in the radiant sun. But silently in the evening the shadow of the dead man entered the grieving family circle and his step sounded crystalline over the green meadow before the forest. Muted ones those gathered around the table; dying ones with waxen hands they broke the bread, the bleeding. Woe of the sister's stony eyes, when at the meal her insanity appeared on the brother's forehead, when under the mother's suffering hands the bread turned to stone. O, of the putrefied ones, when with silver tongues they silenced hell. Thus the lamps in the cool room died out and through purple masks the suffering humans looked at each other silently. Nightlong the rain poured down, and refeshed the meadow. In thorny wilderness the dark one followed the yellowed paths in the corn, the song of the lark and the gentle stillness of green branches so that he might find peace. O, you villages and mossy steps, radiant view. But bonily the footsteps stagger over sleeping serpents at the forest edge and the ear always follows the raving scream of the vulture. In the evening he found a stony solitude, a dead man's escort into the dark house of the father. Purple cloud covered his head so that he silently attacked his own blood and likeness, a lunar countenance; stonily sank away into emptiness, when in a broken mirror a dying youth, the sister, appeared; the night engulfed the cursed race.

Part Three:

Der Brenner

(Published by Ludwig von Ficker, 1914-1915)

In Hellbrunn

Wieder folgend der blauen Klage des Abends
Am Hügel hin, am Frühlingsweiher –
Als schwebten darüber die Schatten lange Verstorbener,
Die Schatten der Kirchenfürsten, edler Frauen –
Schon blühen ihre Blumen, die ernsten Veilchen
Im Abendgrund, rauscht des blauen Quells
Kristallne Woge. So geistlich ergrünen
Die Eichen über den vergessenen Pfaden der Toten,
Die goldene Wolke über dem Weiher.

Das Herz

Das wilde Herz ward weiß am Wald;
O dunkle Angst
Des Todes, so das Gold
In grauer Wolke starb.
Novemberabend.
Am kahlen Tor am Schlachthaus stand
Der armen Frauen Schar;
In jeden Korb
Fiel faules Fleisch und Eingeweid;
Verfluchte Kost!

Des Abends blaue Taube
Brachte nicht Versöhnung.
Dunkler Trompetenruf
Durchfuhr der Ulmen
Nasses Goldlaub,
Eine zerfetzte Fahne
Vom Blute rauchend,
Daß in wilder Schwermut
Hinlauscht ein Mann.
O! ihr ehernen Zeiten
Begraben dort im Abendrot.

Aus dunklem Hausflur trat
Die goldne Gestalt
Der Jünglingin

In Hellbrunn

Again following the blue lament of the evening
Along the hill, by the spring pond—
As if the shadows of those long dead float above,
Shadows of church princes, noble women—
Already their flowers bloom, the earnest violets
In evening ground, murmur of the blue spring's
Crystal wave. So spiritually the oaks turn green
Over the forgotten paths of the dead,
The golden cloud over the pond.

The Heart

The wild heart turned white by the forest;
O dark fear
Of death as the gold
Died in a gray cloud.
November evening.
The crowd of poor women stood
At the bare gate by the slaughterhouse;
Into every basket
Rotten flesh and entrails fall;
Cursed food!

The evening's blue dove
Brought no reconciliation.
Dark trumpeting
Passes through the elm's
Wet golden foliage,
A tattered flag
Smoking with blood
So that in wild gloom
A man listens.
O! you brazen ages
Buried there in the glow of sunset.

From the dark hallway
The golden figure
Of the youthtress

Umgeben von bleichen Monden,
Herbstlicher Hofstaat,
Zerknickten schwarze Tannen
Im Nachtsturm,
Die steile Festung.
O Herz
Hinüberschimmernd in schneeige Kühle.

Der Schlaf
[2. Fassung]

Verflucht ihr dunklen Gifte,
Weißer Schlaf!
Dieser höchst seltsame Garten
Dämmernder Bäume
Erfüllt von Schlangen, Nachtfaltern,
Spinnen, Fledermäusen.
Fremdling! Dein verlorner Schatten
Im Abendrot,
Ein finsterer Korsar
Im salzigen Meer der Trübsal.
Aufflattern weiße Vögel am Nachtsaum
Über stürzenden Städten
Von Stahl.

Das Gewitter

Ihr wilden Gebirge, der Adler
Erhabene Trauer.
Goldnes Gewölk
Raucht über steinerner öde.
Geduldige Stille odmen die Föhren,
Die schwarzen Lämmer am Abgrund,
Wo plötzlich die Bläue
Seltsam verstummt,
Das sanfte Summen der Hummeln.
O grüne Blume –
O Schweigen.

Stepped surrounded by pale moons,
Autumn court,
Black firs buckled
In the night storm,
The steep fortress.
O heart
Shimmering across in snowy coolness.

Sleep
[version 2]

Cursed you dark poisons,
White sleep!
This most strange garden
Of dusking trees
Fulfilled with snakes, moths,
Spiders, bats.
Stranger! Your doomed shadow
In the glow of sunset,
A sinister corsair
In the salty sea of misery.
White birds flutter up on the edge of night
Over toppling cities
Of steel.

The Thunderstorm

You wild mountains, the eagles'
Lofty mourning.
Golden clouds
Smoke over stony wasteland.
The pines breathe patient stillness,
The black lambs at the abyss
Where suddenly the blueness
Falls strangely mute,
The soft hum of the bumblebees.
O green flower—
O silence.

Traumhaft erschüttern des Wildbachs
Dunkle Geister das Herz,
Finsternis,
Die über die Schluchten hereinbricht!
Weiße Stimmen
Irrend durch schaurige Vorhöfe,
Zerrißne Terrassen,
Der Väter gewaltiger Groll, die Klage
Der Mütter,
Des Knaben goldener Kriegsschrei
Und Ungebornes
Seufzend aus blinden Augen.

O Schmerz, du flammendes Anschaun
Der großen Seele!
Schon zuckt im schwarzen Gewühl
Der Rosse und Wagen
Ein rosenschauriger Blitz
In die tönende Fichte.
Magnetische Kühle
Umschwebt dies stolze Haupt,
Glühende Schwermut
Eines zürnenden Gottes.

Angst, du giftige Schlange,
Schwarze, stirb im Gestein!
Da stürzen der Tränen
Wilde Ströme herab,
Sturm-Erbarmen,
Hallen in drohenden Donnern
Die schneeigen Gipfel rings.
Feuer
Läutert zerrissene Nacht.

Der Abend

Mit toten Heldengestalten
Erfüllst du Mond
Die schweigenden Wälder,
Sichelmond –

Dreamlike the dark spirits
Of the wild brook shake the heart,
Sinisterness
That descends upon the ravines!
White voices
Straying through dreadful courtyards,
Torn terraces,
The fathers' immense resentment, the lament
Of the mothers,
The boy's golden battle cry
And the unborn
Sighing from blind eyes.

O pain, you flaming contemplation
Of the great soul!
Already in the black melee
Of horses and wagons
An eerie rose-colored lightning
Flashes in the sounding spruce.
Magnetic coolness
Floats around this proud head,
Glowing gloom
Of an angering God.

Fear, you venomous snake,
Black, die in stone!
There the tears' wild streams
Fall down,
Storm-mercy,
The snowy peaks all around
Resound in menacing thunders.
Fire
Purifies torn night.

The Evening

Moon, with dead heroic figures
You fulfill
The silent forests,
Sickle moon—

Mit der sanften Umarmung
Der Liebenden,
Den Schatten berühmter Zeiten
Die modernden Felsen rings;
So bläulich erstrahlt es
Gegen die Stadt hin,
Wo kalt und böse
Ein verwesend Geschlecht wohnt,
Der weißen Enkel
Dunkle Zukunft bereitet.
Ihr mondverschlungnen Schatten
Aufseufzend im leeren Kristall
Des Bergsees.

Die Nacht

Dich sing ich wilde Zerklüftung,
Im Nachtsturm
Aufgetürmtes Gebirge;
Ihr grauen Türme
Überfließend von höllischen Fratzen,
Feurigem Getier,
Rauhen Farnen, Fichten,
Kristallnen Blumen.
Unendliche Qual,
Daß du Gott erjagtest
Sanfter Geist,
Aufseufzend im Wassersturz,
In wogenden Föhren.

Golden lodern die Feuer
Der Völker rings.
Über schwärzliche Klippen
Stürzt todestrunken
Die erglühende Windsbraut,
Die blaue Woge
Des Gletschers
Und es dröhnt
Gewaltig die Glocke im Tal:
Flammen, Flüche
Und die dunklen

With the gentle embrace
Of lovers,
The shadows of famous ages
All around the moldering rocks;
So bluish it shines
Against the city
Where cold and evil
A decaying race dwells
Preparing the dark future
Of white grandchildren.
You moon-engulfed shadows
Sighing in the empty crystal
Of the mountain lake.

The Night

I sing you wild fissure,
In the night storm
Looming mountains;
You gray towers
Overflowing with hellish grimaces,
Fiery beasts,
Rough ferns, spruces,
Crystal flowers.
Unending agony,
Which makes you hunt down God
Gentle spirit,
Sighing in the waterfall,
In billowing pines.

The fires of the people
Blaze golden all around.
Over blackish cliffs
Drunk with death
The glowing wind-bride plummets,
The blue wave
Of the glacier,
And the bell in the valley
Peals mightily:
Flames, curses
And the dark

Spiele der Wollust,
Stürmt den Himmel
Ein versteinertes Haupt.

Die Schwermut

Gewaltig bist du dunkler Mund
Im Innern, aus Herbstgewölk
Geformte Gestalt,
Goldner Abendstille;
Ein grünlich dämmernder Bergstrom
In zerbrochner Föhren
Schattenbezirk;
Ein Dorf,
Das fromm in braunen Bildern abstirbt.

Da springen die schwarzen Pferde
Auf nebliger Weide.
Ihr Soldaten!
Vom Hügel, wo sterbend die Sonne rollt
Stürzt das lachende Blut –
Unter Eichen
Sprachlos! O grollende Schwermut
Des Heers; ein strahlender Helm
Sank klirrend von purpurner Stirne.

Herbstesnacht so kühle kommt,
Erglänzt mit Sternen
Über zerbrochenem Männergebein
Die stille Mönchin.

Die Heimkehr
[2. Fassung]

Die Kühle dunkler Jahre,
Schmerz und Hoffnung
Bewahrt zyklopisch Gestein,
Menschenleeres Gebirge,

Games of lust,
A petrified head
Storms heaven.

The Gloom

You are enormous dark mouth
Within, figure formed
From autumn clouds,
Golden evening stillness;
A greenish dusking mountain stream
In the shadowy area
Of broken pines;
A village
That dies off devoutly in brown images.

There the black horses leap
On misty meadow.
You soldiers!
From the hill where the sun rolls dying
The laughing blood falls—
Speechless
Under oaks! O resentful gloom
Of the army; a radiant helmet
Sank rattling from a purple forehead.

Autumn night comes so cool,
Over broken bones of men
The silent monkess
Gleams with stars.

The Homecoming
[version 2]

The coolness of dark years,
Cyclopean stone preserves
Pain and hope,
Mountains without people,

Des Herbstes goldner Odem,
Abendwolke –
Reinheit!

Anschaut aus blauen Augen
Kristallne Kindheit;
Unter dunklen Fichten
Liebe, Hoffnung,
Daß von feurigen Lidern
Tau ins starre Gras tropft –
Unaufhaltsam!

O! dort der goldene Steg
Zerbrechend im Schnee
Des Abgrunds!
Blaue Kühle
Odmet das nächtige Tal,
Glaube, Hoffnung!
Gegrüßt du einsamer Friedhof!

Klage

Jüngling aus kristallnem Munde
Sank dein goldner Blick ins Tal;
Waldes Woge rot und fahl
In der schwarzen Abendstunde.
Abend schlägt so tiefe Wunde!

Angst! des Todes Traumbeschwerde,
Abgestorben Grab und gar
Schaut aus Baum und Wild das Jahr;
Kahles Feld und Ackererde.
Ruft der Hirt die bange Herde.

Schwester, deine blauen Brauen
Winken leise in der Nacht.
Orgel seufzt und Hölle lacht
Und es faßt das Herz ein Grauen;
Möchte Stern und Engel schauen.

Mutter muß ums Kindlein zagen;

The autumn's golden breath,
Evening cloud—
Purity!

Crystal childhood
Gazes from blue eyes;
Under dark spruces
Love, hope,
So that from fiery eyelids
Dew drips into stiff grass—
Irresistibly!

O! there the golden footbridge
Breaking up in the snow
Of the abyss!
The nocturnal valley
Breathes blue coolness,
Belief, hope!
Hail you lonely graveyard!

Lament

Youth out of crystal mouth
Your golden gaze sank into the valley;
Forest's wave red and pale
In the black evening hour.
Evening strikes such deep wound!

Fear! death's dream-grievance,
Defunct grave and yet
The year looks from trees and deer;
Barren field and soil.
The shepherd calls the frightened flock.

Sister, your blue brows
Beckon quietly in the night.
Organ sighs and hell laughs;
And a dread seizes the heart;
Would like to see star and angel.

Mother must fear for her babe;

Rot ertönt im Schacht das Erz,
Wollust, Tränen, steinern Schmerz,
Der Titanen dunkle Sagen.
Schwermut! einsam Adler klagen.

Nachtergebung

[5. Fassung]

Mönchin! schließ mich in dein Dunkel,
Ihr Gebirge kühl und blau!
Niederblutet dunkler Tau;
Kreuz ragt steil im Sterngefunkel.

Purpurn brachen Mund und Lüge
In verfallner Kammer kühl;
Scheint noch Lachen, golden Spiel,
Einer Glocke letzte Züge.

Mondeswolke! Schwärzlich fallen
Wilde Früchte nachts vom Baum
Und zum Grabe wird der Raum
Und zum Traum dies Erdenwallen.

Im Osten

Den wilden Orgeln des Wintersturms
Gleicht des Volkes finstrer Zorn,
Die purpurne Woge der Schlacht,
Entlaubter Sterne.

Mit zerbrochnen Brauen, silbernen Armen
Winkt sterbenden Soldaten die Nacht.
Im Schatten der herbstlichen Esche
Seufzen die Geister der Erschlagenen.

Dornige Wildnis umgürtet die Stadt.
Von blutenden Stufen jagt der Mond
Die erschrockenen Frauen.

The ore resounds red in the shaft.
Lust, tears, stony anguish,
Dark legends of the Titans.
Gloom! lonely eagles lament.

Surrender at Night
[version 5]

Monkess! enclose me in your darkness,
You mountains cool and blue!
Dark dew bleeds down;
Cross towers steeply in the star-glitter.

Purply mouth and lies broke
Cool in the decayed chamber;
Laughter still shines, golden play,
A bell's final knells.

Moon-cloud! Blackish
Wild fruits fall at night from the tree
And the room becomes the grave
And this earthly wandering the dream.

In the East

The people's dark rage resembles
The wild organs of the winter storm,
The purple wave of battle,
Stars stripped of leaves.

With broken brows, silver arms
The night beckons dying soldiers.
In the shadows of the autumn ash tree
The ghosts of the slain sigh.

Thorny wilderness girds the city.
The moon chases the terrified women
Away from bleeding stairs.

Wilde Wölfe brachen durchs Tor.

Klage

Schlaf und Tod, die düstern Adler
Umrauschen nachtlang dieses Haupt:
Des Menschen goldnes Bildnis
Verschlänge die eisige Woge
Der Ewigkeit. An schaurigen Riffen
Zerschellt der purpurne Leib
Und es klagt die dunkle Stimme
Über dem Meer.
Schwester stürmischer Schwermut
Sieh ein ängstlicher Kahn versinkt
Unter Sternen,
Dem schweigenden Antlitz der Nacht.

Grodek
[2. Fassung]

Am Abend tönen die herbstlichen Wälder
Von tödlichen Waffen, die goldnen Ebenen
Und blauen Seen, darüber die Sonne
Düstrer hinrollt; umfängt die Nacht
Sterbende Krieger, die wilde Klage
Ihrer zerbrochenen Münder.
Doch stille sammelt im Weidengrund
Rotes Gewölk, darin ein zürnender Gott wohnt
Das vergoßne Blut sich, mondne Kühle;
Alle Straßen münden in schwarze Verwesung.
Unter goldnem Gezweig der Nacht und Sternen
Es schwankt der Schwester Schatten durch den schweigenden Hain,
Zu grüßen die Geister der Helden, die blutenden Häupter;
Und leise tönen im Rohr die dunkeln Flöten des Herbstes.
O stolzere Trauer! ihr ehernen Altäre
Die heiße Flamme des Geistes nährt heute ein gewaltiger Schmerz,
Die ungebornen Enkel.

Wild wolves broke through the gate.

Lament

Sleep and death, the somber eagles,
Swoop around this head all night long:
The icy wave of eternity
Would engulf the golden image
Of man. On horrible reefs
The purple body is shattered
And the dark voice laments
Over the sea.
Sister of stormy gloom,
Look a frightened boat sinks
Under stars,
The silent countenance of night.

Grodek
[version 2]

In the evening the autumn forests resound
With deadly weapons, the golden plains
And blue lakes above which the sun
Rolls more somberly; night embraces
Dying warriors, the wild lament
Of their broken mouths.
Yet silently in the meadow
A red cloud, in which an angry god dwells,
Gathers spilled blood, lunar coolness;
All roads end in black decay.
Under golden branches of night and stars
The sister's shadow staggers through the silent grove
To greet the ghosts of heroes, the bleeding heads;
And quietly the dark autumn flutes resound in the reeds.
O prouder grief! you brazen altars
Today an enormous pain nourishes the hot flame of the spirit,
The unborn grandchildren.

Offenbarung und Untergang

Seltsam sind die nächtigen Pfade des Menschen. Da ich nachtwandelnd an steinernen Zimmern hinging und es brannte in jedem ein stilles Lämpchen, ein kupferner Leuchter, und da ich frierend aufs Lager hinsank, stand zu Häupten wieder der schwarze Schatten der Fremdlingin und schweigend verbarg ich das Antlitz in den langsamen Händen. Auch war am Fenster blau die Hyazinthe aufgeblüht und es trat auf die purpurne Lippe des Odmenden das alte Gebet, sanken von den Lidern kristallne Tränen geweint um die bittere Welt. In dieser Stunde war ich im Tod meines Vaters der weiße Sohn. In blauen Schauern kam vom Hügel der Nachtwind, die dunkle Klage der Mutter, hinsterbend wieder und ich sah die schwarze Hölle in meinem Herzen; Minute schimmernder Stille. Leise trat aus kalkiger Mauer ein unsägliches Antlitz – ein sterbender Jüngling – die Schönheit eines heimkehrenden Geschlechts. Mondesweiß umfing die Kühle des Steins die wachende Schläfe, verklangen die Schritte der Schatten auf verfallenen Stufen, ein rosiger Reigen im Gärtchen.

Schweigend saß ich in verlassener Schenke unter verrauchtem Holzgebälk und einsam beim Wein; ein strahlender Leichnam über ein Dunkles geneigt und es lag ein totes Lamm zu meinen Füßen. Aus verwesender Bläue trat die bleiche Gestalt der Schwester und also sprach ihr blutender Mund: Stich schwarzer Dorn. Ach noch tönen von wilden Gewittern die silbernen Arme mir. Fließe Blut von den mondenen Füßen, blühend auf nächtigen Pfaden, darüber schreiend die Ratte huscht. Aufflackert ihr Sterne in meinengewölbten Brauen; und es läutet leise das Herz in der Nacht. Einbrach ein roter Schatten mit flammendem Schwert in das Haus, floh mit schneeiger Stirne. O bitterer Tod.

Und es sprach eine dunkle Stimme aus mir: Meinem Rappen brach ich im nächtigen Wald das Genick, da aus seinen purpurnen Augen der Wahnsinn sprang; die Schatten der Ulmen fielen auf mich, das blaue Lachen des Quells und die schwarze Kühle der Nacht, da ich ein wilder Jäger aufjagte ein schneeiges Wild; in steinerner Hölle mein Antlitz erstarb.

Und schimmernd fiel ein Tropfen Blutes in des Einsamen Wein; und da ich davon trank, schmeckte er bitterer als Mohn; und eine schwärzliche Wolke umhüllte mein Haupt, die kristallenen Tränen verdammter Engel; und leise rann aus silberner Wunde der Schwester das Blut und fiel ein feuriger Regen auf mich.

Am Saum des Waldes will ich ein Schweigendes gehn, dem aus sprachlosen Händen die härene Sonne sank; ein Fremdling am Abendhügel, der weinend aufhebt die Lider über die steinerne Stadt; ein Wild, das stille steht im Frieden des alten Hollunders; o ruhlos lauscht das dämmernde Haupt, oder es folgen die zögernden Schritte der blauen Wolke am Hügel, ernsten Gestirnen auch. Zur Seite geleitet stille die grüne Saat, begleitet auf moosigen Waldespfaden scheu das Reh. Es haben die Hütten der Dörfler sich stumm verschlossen und es ängstigt in schwarzer

Revelation and Decline

Strange are the nightly paths of men. As I moved sleepwalking past rooms of stone, and in each a still lamp burned, a copper candlestick, and as I sank freezing onto the bed, the black shadow of strangeress stood overhead, and silently I hid my countenance in the slow moving hands. Also the hyacinth had blossomed blue at the window and the old prayer rose on the purple lips of the breathing, crystalline tears sank from the eyelids wept over the bitter world. In this hour I was the white son in my father's death. In blue showers the night wind came from the hill, the dark lament of the mother dying away again and I saw the black hell in my heart; minute of shimmering stillness. Quietly an unspeakable countenance stepped from the chalky wall—a dying youth—the beauty of a race returning home. Lunar-white the coolness of stone embraced the waking temple, the steps of the shadows faded on decayed stairs, a rosy round dance in the small garden.

Silently I sat in a deserted inn under smoky rafters and lonely with wine; a radiant corpse bent over a dark shape and a dead lamb lay at my feet. Out of rotting blueness the pale figure of the sister stepped and her bleeding mouth spoke thus: stab black thorn. O my silver arms still resound from wild thunderstorms. Flow blood from the lunar feet blossoming on nightly paths over which the rat shoos screaming. You stars flicker in my arched brows; and the heart rings quietly in the night. A red shadow with a flaming sword broke into the house, fled with snowy forehead. O bitter death.

And a dark voice spoke out of me: I broke my black horse's neck in the nocturnal forest because insanity leaped from his purple eyes; the shadows of elms fell on me, the blue laughter of the well, and the black coolness of the night, as I a wild hunter roused a snowy deer; my countenance died off in stony hell.

And shimmering a drop of blood fell into the wine of the lonely one; and when I drank, it tasted more bitter than poppy; and a blackish cloud encircled my head, the crystal tears of damned angels; and quietly blood ran from the silver wound of the sister and a fiery rain fell over me.

At the edge of the forest, I will walk, a silent shape, from whose speechless hands the hairy sun sank; a stranger at the evening hill, who weeping lifts eyelids over the stony city; a deer that stands silently in the peace of the old elder tree; o restlessly the dusking head listens, or the hesitating steps follow the blue cloud at the hill, also earnest stars. To the side the green seed guides silently, shyly accompanies the doe on mossy forest paths. The huts of the villagers are mutely closed in silence, and the blue lament of the wild brook is frightening in the black wind-lull.

But as I climbed down the rocky path, insanity seized me and I screamed loudly in the night; and as I bent with silver fingers over the silent waters, I saw that my countenance had left me. And the white voice spoke to me: kill yourself! Sighing the shadow of a young boy arose in me and gazed at me radiantly out of crystal

Windesstille die blaue Klage des Wildbachs.

Aber da ich den Felsenpfad hinabstieg, ergriff mich der Wahnsinn und ich schrie laut in der Nacht; und da ich mit silbernen Fingern mich über die schweigenden Wasser bog, sah ich daß mich mein Antlitz verlassen. Und die weiße Stimme sprach zu mir: Töte dich! Seufzend erhob sich eines Knaben Schatten in mir und sah mich strahlend aus kristallnen Augen an, daß ich weinend unter den Bäumen hinsank, dem gewaltigen Sternengewölbe.

Friedlose Wanderschaft durch wildes Gestein ferne den Abendweilern, heim-kehrenden Herden; ferne weidet die sinkende Sonne auf kristallner Wiese und es erschüttert ihr wilder Gesang, der einsame Schrei des Vogels, ersterbend in blauer Ruh. Aber leise kommst du in der Nacht, da ich wachend am Hügel lag, oder rasend im Frühlingsgewitter; und schwärzer immer umwölkt die Schwermut das abgeschiedene Haupt, erschrecken schaurige Blitze die nächtige Seele, zerreißen deine Hände die atemlose Brust mir.

Da ich in den dämmernden Garten ging, und es war die schwarze Gestalt des Bösen von mir gewichen, umfing mich die hyazinthene Stille der Nacht; und ich fuhr auf gebogenem Kahn über den ruhenden Weiher und süßer Frieden rührte die versteinerte Stirne mir. Sprachlos lag ich unter den alten Weiden und es war der blaue Himmel hoch über mir und voll von Sternen; und da ich anschauend hinstarb, starben Angst und der Schmerzen tiefster in mir; und es hob sich der blaue Schatten des Knaben strahlend im Dunkel, sanfter Gesang; hob sich auf mondenen Flügeln über die grünenden Wipfel, kristallene Klippen das weiße Antlitz der Schwester.

Mit silbernen Sohlen stieg ich die dornigen Stufen hinab und ich trat ins kalkgetünchte Gemach. Stille brannte ein Leuchter darin und ich verbarg in purpurnen Linnen schweigend das Haupt; und es warf die Erde einen kindlichen Leichnam aus, ein mondenes Gebilde, das langsam aus meinem Schatten trat, mit zerbrochenen Armen steinerne Stürze hinabsank, flockiger Schnee.

eyes, so that I sank down weeping beneath the trees, the mighty star-firmament.

Peaceless wanderings through wild stone far away from evening hamlets, flocks returning home; far away the sinking sun grazes on a crystal meadow and its wild song convulses, the lonely cry of the bird fading away in blue rest. But quietly you come in the night as I lay waking on a hill, or raging in a spring thunderstorm; and always blacker gloom clouds the abandoned head, horrible lightning bolts terrify the nocturnal soul, your hands tear my breathless breast.

As I walked in the dusking garden, and the black figure of evil left me, the hyacinthine stillness of the night embraced me; and I rode in a curved boat over the resting pond and a sweet peace touched my petrified forehead. Speechless I lay under the old willows and the blue sky was high above me and filled with stars; and as I died off beholding, fear and the deepest pain died inside me; and the blue shadow of the boy rose, radiant in darkness, a gentle song; over greening treetops, crystal cliffs, the white countenance of the sister rose on lunar wings.

With silver soles I descended thorny stairs and I stepped into the whitewashed chamber. Calmly a candlestick burned inside and I buried my head silently in purple linen; and the earth ejected a childish corpse, a lunar shape, which slowly stepped out of my shadow, plunged with broken arms down stony abysses, flaky snow.

Part Four:

Other Writings Published During Lifetime

Das Morgenlied

Nun schreite herab, titanischer Bursche,
Und wecke die vielgeliebte Schlummernde dir!
Schreite herab, und umgürte
Mit zartlichten Blüten das träumende Haupt.
Entzünde den bangenden Himmel mit lodernder Fackel,
Daß die erblassenden Sterne tanzend ertönen
Und die fliegenden Schleier der Nacht
Aufflammend vergehen,
Daß die zyklopischen Wolken zerstieben,
In denen der Winter, der Erde entfliehend,
Noch heulend droht mit eisigen Schauern,
Und die himmlischen Fernen sich auftun in leuchtender Reinheit.
Und steigst dann, Herrlicher du, mit fliegenden Locken
Zur Erde herab, empfängt sie mit seligem Schweigen
Den brünstigen Freier, und in tiefen Schauern erbebend
Von deiner so wilden, sturmrasenden Umarmung,
Öffnet sie dir ihren heiligen Schoß.
Und es erfaßt die Trunkene süßeste Ahnung,
Wenn Blütenglühender du das keimende Leben
Ihr weckest, des hohe Vergangenheit
Höherer Zukunft sich zudrängt,
Das dir gleich ist, wie du dir selber gleichst,
Und deinem Willen ergeben, stets Bewegter,
Daß an ihr ein ewig Rätselvolles
In hoher Schönheit sich wieder künftig erneuert.

Traumwandler

Wo bist du, die mir zur Seite ging,
Wo bist du, Himmelsangesicht?
Ein rauher Wind höhnt mir ins Ohr: du Narr!
Ein Traum! Ein Traum! Du Tor!
Und doch, und doch! Wie war es einst,
Bevor ich in Nacht und Verlassenheit schritt?
Weißt du es noch, du Narr, du Tor!
Meiner Seele Echo, der rauhe Wind:
O Narr! O Tor!
Stand sie mit bittenden Händen nicht,

The Morning Song

Now stride down, titanic fellow,
And awaken the much loved slumbering woman!
Stride down, and gird
The dreaming head with tender blossoms.
Ignite the fearing sky with blazing torch,
So that the paling stars ring out dancing
And the flying veils of the night
Vanish flaming up,
So that the cyclopean clouds scatter,
In which the winter, escaping from the earth,
Still howling threats with icy showers,
And the celestial distances open in bright purity.
And then gloriously with flying tresses you climb
Down to earth, she receives the rutting suitor
With blessed silence, and trembling in deep shudders
From your wild, storm-racing embrace,
She opens her holy womb to you.
And the drunkard is seized by sweetest intuition,
When glowing with blooms you awaken
The germinating life for her, its exulted past presses
To a higher future,
That resembles you, as you resemble yourself,
Loyal to your will, ever moved,
So that in her an eternal mystery
Renews itself in exulted beauty again in the future.

Dream Wanderer

Where are you, who walked by my side,
Where are you, countenance of heaven?
A rough wind jeers in my ear: you fool!
A dream! A dream! You jester!
And yet, and yet! How was it once,
Before I walked into night and loneliness?
Do you know it still, you fool, you jester!
My soul's echo, the raw wind:
O fool! O jester!
Didn't she stand with pleading hands,

Ein trauriges Lächeln um den Mund,
Und rief in Nacht und Verlassenheit!
Was rief sie nur! Weißt du es nicht?
Wie Liebe klang's. Kein Echo trug
Zu ihr zurück, zu ihr dies Wort.
War's Liebe? Weh, daß ich's vergaß!
Nur Nacht um mich und Verlassenheit,
Und meiner Seele Echo – der Wind!
Der höhnt und höhnt: O Narr! O Tor!

Die drei Teiche von Hellbrunn
[2. Fassung]

Der erste

Um die Blumen taumelt das Fliegengeschmeiß
Um die bleichen Blumen auf dumpfer Flut,
Geh fort! Geh fort! Es brennt die Luft!
In der Tiefe glüht der Verwesung Glut!
Die Weide weint, das Schweigen starrt,
Auf den Wassern braut ein schwüler Dunst.
Geh fort! Geh fort! Dies ist der Ort
Für schwarzer Kröten ekle Brunst.

Der zweite

Bilder von Wolken, Blumen und Menschen –
Singe, singe, freudige Welt!
Lächelnde Unschuld spiegelt dich wider –
Himmlisch wird alles, was ihr gefällt:
Dunkles wandelt sie freundlich in Helle,
Fernes wird nah. O Freudiger du!
Sonne, Wolken, Blumen und Menschen
Atmen selige Gottesruh.

Der dritte

Die Wasser schimmern grünlich-blau
Und ruhig atmen die Zypressen,
Es tönt der Abend glockentief –
Da wächst die Tiefe unermessen.

A sad smile around the mouth,
And called in night and loneliness!
What did she call! Don't you know?
It sounded like love. No echo bore
This word back to her, to her.
Was it love? Woe, that I have forgotten!
Only night around me and loneliness,
And my soul's echo—the wind!
That jeers and jeers: O fool! O jester!

The Three Ponds of Hellbrunn
[version 2]

The First

Around the flowers the blowflies reel
Around the pale flowers on murky waters,
Go away! Go away! The air burns!
In the depths the smolder of putrefaction glows!
The willow weeps, the silence stares,
A sultry vapor brews on the waters.
Go away! Go away! This is the place
For black toads' disgusting rut.

The Second

Images of clouds, flowers, and people—
Sing, sing, joyful world!
Smiling innocence reflects you—
Everything it likes becomes heavenly:
It amicably transforms darkness into light,
Distant things become near. O joyful you!
Sun, clouds, flowers and people
Blessedly breathe the peace of God.

The Third

The waters shimmer greenish blue
And calmly the cypresses breathe,
The evening sounds bell-deep—
Then the depth grows immeasurably.

Der Mond steigt auf, es blaut die Nacht,
Erblüht im Widerschein der Fluten –
Ein rätselvolles Sphinxgesicht,
Daran mein Herz sich will verbluten.

Die drei Teiche von Hellbrunn
[3. Fassung]

Hinwandelnd an den schwarzen Mauern
Des Abends, silbern tönt die Leier
Des Orpheus fort im dunklen Weiher
Der Frühling aber tropft in Schauern
Aus dem Gezweig in wilden Schauern
Des Nachtwinds silbern tönt die Leier
Des Orpheus fort im dunklen Weiher
Hinsterbend an ergrünten Mauern.

Ferne leuchten Schloß und Hügel.
Stimmen von Frauen, die längst verstarben
Weben zärtlich und dunkelfarben
Über den weißen nymphischen Spiegel.
Klagen ihr vergänglich Geschicke
Und der Tag zerfließt im Grünen
Flüstern im Rohr und schweben zurücke –
Eine Drossel scherzt mit ihnen.

Die Wasser schimmern grünlichblau
Und ruhig atmen die Zypressen
Und ihre Schwermut unermessen
Fließt über in das Abendblau.
Tritonen tauchen aus der Flut,
Verfall durchrieselt das Gemäuer
Der Mond hüllt sich in grüne Schleier
Und wandelt langsam auf der Flut.

The moon rises, the night turns blue,
Blossoms in the reflection of the waters—
An enigmatic Sphinx face
On which my heart wants to bleed to death.

The Three Ponds in Hellbrunn
[version 3]

Wandering along the black walls
Of evening, silverly the lyre
Of Orpheus sounds forth in the dark pond
But spring drips in showers
From the branches in wild showers
Of the night wind silverly the lyre
Of Orpheus sounds forth in the dark pond
Dying away at greening walls.

Far away palace and hill shine.
Voices of women, who died long ago,
Weave delicately and dark-colored
Over the white nymphlike mirror.
Lament their fleeting fate
And the day dissolves in the green
Whispers in the reeds and floats back—
A thrush frolics with them.

The waters shimmer greenish-blue
And calmly the cypresses breathe
And their gloom immeasurable
Flows over into the evening-blue.
Tritons emerge from the waters,
Decay trickles through the walls
The moon wraps itself in green veils
And wanders slowly on the waters.

St.-Peters-Friedhof

Ringsum ist Felseneinsamkeit.
Des Todes bleiche Blumen schauern
Auf Gräbern, die im Dunkel trauern –
Doch diese Trauer hat kein Leid.

Der Himmel lächelt still herab
In diesen traumverschlossenen Garten,
Wo stille Pilger seiner warten.
Es wacht das Kreuz auf jedem Grab.

Die Kirche ragt wie ein Gebet
Vor einem Bilde ewiger Gnaden,
Manch Licht brennt unter den Arkaden,
Das stumm für arme Seelen fleht –

Indes die Bäume blüh'n zur Nacht,
Daß sich des Todes Antlitz hülle
In ihrer Schönheit schimmernde Fülle,
Die Tote tiefer träumen macht.

Ein Frühlingsabend

Ein Strauch voll Larven; Abendföhn im März;
Ein toller Hund läuft durch ein ödes Feld
Durchs braune Dorf des Priesters Glocke schellt;
Ein kahler Baum krümmt sich in schwarzem Schmerz.

Im Schatten alter Dächer blutet Mais;
O Süße, die der Spatzen Hunger stillt.
Durch das vergilbte Rohr bricht scheu ein Wild.
O Einsamstehn vor Wassern still und weiß.

Unsäglich ragt des Nußbaums Traumgestalt.
Den Freund erfreut der Knaben bäurisch Spiel.
Verfallene Hütten, abgelebt' Gefühl;
Die Wolken wandern tief und schwarz geballt.

St. Peter's Cemetery

Rocky isolation is all around.
Death's pale flowers shudder
On graves which mourn in darkness—
But this mourning has no agony.

Silently heaven smiles down
In this dream-locked garden
Where silent pilgrims wait.
On each grave the cross wakes.

The church rises up like a prayer
Before a picture of eternal grace,
A few lights burn under the arcades
Mutely pleading for poor souls—

While the trees bloom in the night
To wrap the countenance of death
In their beauty's glimmering abundance,
Making the dead dream deeper.

A Spring Evening

A shrub filled with larvae; evening foehn in March;
A mad dog runs through a desolate field
The priest's bell is ringing through the brown village;
A bare tree writhes in black pain.

In the shadow of old roofs maize bleeds;
O sweetness which satisfies the hunger of the sparrows.
Through the yellowed reed a deer breaks shyly.
O lonely-standing before waters silent and white.

Unspeakably the walnut tree's dream shape rises.
The friend is pleased by the countrified play of the boys.
Decayed huts, decrepit feelings;
The clouds wander deeply and blackly massed.

In einem alten Garten

Resedaduft entschwebt im braunen Grün,
Geflimmer schauert auf den schönen Weiher,
Die Weiden stehn gehüllt in weiße Schleier
Darinnen Falter irre Kreise ziehn.

Verlassen sonnt sich die Terrasse dort,
Goldfische glitzern tief im Wasserspiegel,
Bisweilen schwimmen Wolken übern Hügel,
Und langsam gehn die Fremden wieder fort.

Die Lauben scheinen hell, da junge Frau'n
Am frühen Morgen hier vorbeigegangen,
Ihr Lachen blieb an kleinen Blättern hangen,
In goldenen Dünsten tanzt ein trunkener Faun.

[Abendlicher Reigen]
[1. Fassung]

Asternfelder, braun und blau
Kinder spielen dort an Grüften
In den hell beschwingten Lüften
Hángen Möven silbergrau.

Seltsam Leben lebt im Wein.
Lauter spielet auf ihr Geigen
Welche Wollust! Rasend Reigen
Fröstelnd kommt die Nacht herein.

Lachst so laut du braune Gret
Wirr das Meer tráumt im Gemüte
Während eine just verblühte
Rose vor mir niederweht.

In an Old Garden

Mignonette fragrance drifts away in the brown greenness,
Glimmering shivers on the beautiful pond,
The willows stand wrapped in white veils
Therein moths draw errant circles.

Deserted the terrace suns itself there,
Goldfish glisten deeply in the water-mirror,
Sometimes clouds swim over the hill,
And slowly the strangers go forth again.

The bowers shine bright, since young women
Passed here in the early morning,
Their laughter remained hanging on small leaves,
In golden hazes a drunken Faun dances.

[Evening Round Dance]
[version 1]

Aster fields, brown and blue
Children play there by crypts
In the bright lilting air
Gulls hover silver-gray.

Strange life lives in the vine.
Play louder you violins
Which lust! Racing round dance
Shivering the night comes in.

You laugh so loud brown Gret
The sea dreams woozy in the mind
While a just withered rose
Blows down before me.

Abendlicher Reigen

[2. Fassung]

Asternfelder braun und blau,
Kinder spielen dort an Grüften,
In den abendlichen Lüften,
Hingehaucht in klaren Lüften
Hängen Möven silbergrau.
Hörnerschall hallt in der Au.

In der alten Schenke schrein
Toller auf verstimmte Geigen,
An den Fenstern rauscht ein Reigen,
Rauscht ein bunter Ringelreigen,
Rasend und berauscht von Wein.
Fröstelnd kommt die Nacht herein.

Lachen flattert auf, verweht,
Spöttisch klimpert eine Laute,
Leise eine stille Raute,
Eine schwermutvolle Raute
An der Schwelle niedergeht.
Klingklang! Eine Sichel mäht.

Traumhaft webt der Kerzen Schein,
Malt dies junge Fleisch verfallen,
Klingklang! Hörs im Nebel hallen,
Nach dem Takt der Geigen hallen,
Und vorbei tanzt nackt Gebein.
Lange schaut der Mond herein.

[Nachtseele]

[1. Fassung]

Stille wieder empfängt der modernde Wald
Den lallenden Quell,
Klage, die kristallen im Dunkel forttönt.

Schweigsam stieg von schwarzen Wäldern ein blaues Wild
Die Seele nieder,

Evening Round Dance
[version 2]

Aster fields brown and blue,
Children play there by crypts,
In the evening winds,
Wafted past in clear winds
Gulls hover silver-gray.
Horn sounds echo in the floodplain.

At the old inn out-of-tune fiddles
Scream more insanely,
By the windows a round dance sweeps,
A multi-colored ringlet round dance sweeps,
Raging and drunk from wine.
Shivering the night comes in.

Laughter flutters up, drifts away,
Mockingly a lute strums,
Quietly a still rhombus,
Full of gloom a rhombus
Descends at the threshold.
Clingclang! A sickle mows.

Dreamlike the candle's light weaves,
Paints this young flesh decayed,
Clingclang! In the fog hear it echo,
After the rhythm of the fiddles echo,
And beyond a naked skeleton dances.
For a long time the moon looks inside.

[Night Soul]
[version 1]

Silently the moldering forest again receives
The babbling spring,
Lament that sounds forth crystalline in the darkness.

Taciturnly a blue deer descended from black forests,
The soul

Da es Nacht war; über moosige Stufen ein schneeiger Quell.

Blut und Waffengetümmel vergessener Zeiten
Rauscht das Wasser im Föhrengrund.
Der Mond scheint immer in verfallene Zimmer,

Trunken von Frösten silberne Larve
Über den Schlaf des Jägers geneigt,
Haupt, das seine Sagen verlasse

O dann öffnet jener die langsamen Hände,
Daß er das Licht empfange,
Seufzend in gewaltiger Finsternis.

Nachtseele
[2. Fassung]

Schweigsam stieg von schwarzen Wäldern ein blaues Wild
Die Seele nieder,
Da es Nacht war, über moosige Stufen ein schneeiger Quell.

Blut und Waffengetümmel vergangener Zeiten
Rauscht im Föhrengrund,
Der Mond scheint immer in verfallene Zimmer;

Trunken von dunklen Giften, silberne Larve
Über den schlummernde Hirten geneigt,
Haupt, das schweigend seine Sagen verlassen.

O, dann öffnet jenes langsam die kalten Hände
Unter steinernen Bogen
Leise steigt ein goldener Sommer ans erblindete Fenster

Und es läuten im Grün die Schritte der Tänzerin
Die Nacht lang,
Öfter ruft in purpurner Schwermut das Käuzchen den Trunkenen.

When it was night; a snowy wellspring over mossy steps.

The water murmurs blood and weapon-turmoil
From forgotten times in the pine ground.
The moon shines always in decayed rooms,

Drunk with dark frosts silver larva
Bent over the sleep of the hunter,
Head that abandons its legends.

O then the other opens the slow hands,
So that he receives the light,
Sighing in enormous sinisterness.

Night Soul
[version 2]

Taciturnly a blue deer descended from black forests,
The soul
When it was night, a snowy wellspring over mossy steps.

Blood and weapon-turmoil from bygone times
Murmur in the pine ground,
The moon shines always in decayed rooms;

Drunk with dark poisons, silver larva
Bent over slumbering shepherds,
Head that silently abandons its legends.

O, then the other slowly opens the cold hands
Under stony arches
Quietly a golden summer rises in the blinded window

And the steps of the dancing woman ring in the green
The night long,
More often in purple gloom the screech owl calls the drunkard.

Nachtseele
[3. Fassung]

Schweigsam stieg vom schwarzen Wald ein blaues Wild
Die Seele nieder,
Da es Nacht war, über moosige Stufen ein schneeiger Quell.

Blut und Waffengetümmel vergangner Zeiten
Rauscht im Föhrengrund.
Der Mond scheint leise in verfallene Zimmer,

Trunken von dunklen Giften, silberne Larve
Über den Schlummer der Hirten geneigt;
Haupt, das schweigend seine Sagen verlassen.

O, dann öffnet jener die langsamen Hände
Verwesend in purpurnem Schlaf
Und silbern erblühen die Blumen des Winters

Am Waldsaum, erstrahlen die finstern Wege
In die steinerne Stadt;
Öfter ruft aus schwarzer Schwermut das Käuzchen den Trunkenen.

Traumland
Eine Episode

Manchmal muß ich wieder jener stillen Tage gedenken, die mir sind wie ein wundersames, glücklich verbrachtes Leben, das ich fraglos genießen konnte, gleich einem Geschenk aus gütigen, unbekannten Händen. Und jene kleine Stadt im Talesgrund ersteht da wieder in meiner Erinnerung mit ihrer breiten Hauptstraße, durch die sich eine lange Allee prachtvoller Lindenbäume hinzieht, mit ihren winkeligen Seitengassen, die erfüllt sind von heimlich schaffendem Leben kleiner Kaufleute und Handwerker – und mit dem alten Stadtbrunnen mitten auf dem Platze, der im Sonnenschein so verträumt plätschert, und wo am Abend zum Rauschen des Wassers Liebesgeflüster klingt. Die Stadt aber scheint von vergangenem Leben zu träumen.

Und sanft geschwungene Hügel, über die sich feierliche, schweigsame Tannenwälder ausdehnen, schließen das Tal von der Außenwelt ab. Die Kuppen schmiegen sich weich an den fernen, lichten Himmel, und in dieser Berührung von Himmel und Erde scheint einem der Weltraum ein Teil der Heimat zu sein. Menschenge-

Night Soul
[version 3]

Taciturnly a blue deer descended from the black forest,
The soul
When it was night, a snowy wellspring over mossy steps.

Blood and weapon-turmoil from bygone times
Murmur in the pine ground.
The moon shines quietly in decayed rooms;

Drunk with dark poisons, silver larva
Bent over the slumber of the shepherds;
Head that silently abandons its legends.

O, then the other one rotting in purple sleep
Opens slow hands
And silverly the flowers of winter bloom

At the forest's edge, the sinister ways
Into the stony city glisten;
More often out of black sorrow the screech owl calls the drunkard.

Dream Country
An Episode

Sometimes I must think back to those silent days, which are like a wondrous, fortunately spent life to me, which I could unquestionably enjoy like a gift from kindly, unknown hands. And that small city in the valley rises again in my memory with its broad main street, through which a long avenue of gorgeous linden trees stretches, with its angular alleyways filled by the secret working lives of small buyers and craftsmen—and with the old town fountain in the middle of the plaza, that so dreamily splashes in the sunshine, and where in the evening love-whispers sound in the murmur of water. But the city seems to dream of a past life.

And softly curved hills, over which solemn, taciturn fir forests stretch, lock the valley away from the external world. The summits nestle gently against the far, light-filled sky, and in this contact of sky and earth it seems to one that space is part of the homeland. All at once the figures of people come to my senses, and before me again the life of their past renews, with all its small sufferings and joys, which these people dare to confide to one another without shyness.

stalten kommen mir auf einmal in den Sinn, und vor mir lebt wieder das Leben ihrer Vergangenheit auf, mit all' seinen kleinen Leiden und Freuden, die diese Menschen ohne Scheu einander anvertrauen durften.

Acht Wochen habe ich in dieser Entlegenheit verlebt; diese acht Wochen sind mir wie ein losgelöster, eigener Teil meines Lebens – ein Leben für sich – voll eines unsäglichen, jungen Glückes, voll einer starken Sehnsucht nach fernen, schönen Dingen. Hier empfing meine Knabenseele zum erstenmale den Eindruck eines großen Erlebens.

Ich sehe mich wieder als Schulbube in dem kleinen Haus mit einem kleinen Garten davor, das, etwas abgelegen von der Stadt, von Bäumen und Gesträuch beinahe ganz versteckt liegt. Dort bewohnte ich eine kleine Dachstube, die mit wunderlichen alten, verblaßten Bildern ausgeschmückt war, und manchen Abend habe ich hier verträumt in der Stille, und die Stille hat meine himmelhohen, närrisch-glücklichen Knabenträume liebevoll in sich aufgenommen und bewahrt und hat sie mir später noch oft genug wiedergebracht – in einsamen Dämmerstunden. Oft auch ging ich am Abend zu meinem alten Onkel hinunter, der beinahe den ganzen Tag bei seiner kranken Tochter Maria verbrachte. Dann saßen wir drei stundenlang schweigend beisammen. Der laue Abendwind wehte zum Fenster herein und trug allerlei verworrenes Geräusch an unser Ohr, das einem unbestimmte Traumbilder vorgaukelte. Und die Luft war voll von dem starken, berauschenden Duft der Rosen, die am Gartenzaune blühten. Langsam schlich die Nacht ins Zimmer und dann stand ich auf, sagte »Gute Nacht« und begab mich in meine Stube hinauf, um dort noch eine Stunde am Fenster in die Nacht hinaus zu träumen.

Anfangs fühlte ich in der Nähe der kleinen Kranken etwas wie eine angstvolle Beklemmung, die sich später in eine heilige, ehrfurchtsvolle Scheu vor diesem stummen, seltsam ergreifenden Leiden wandelte. Wenn ich sie sah, stieg in mir ein dunkles Gefühl auf, daß sie sterben werde müssen. Und dann fürchtete ich sie anzusehen.

Wenn ich tagsüber in den Wäldern herumstreifte, mich in der Einsamkeit und Stille so froh fühlte, wenn ich mich müde dann ins Moos streckte, und stundenlang in den lichten, flimmernden Himmel blickte, in den man so weit hineinsehen konnte, wenn ein seltsam tiefes Glücksgefühl mich dann berauschte, da kam mir plötzlich der Gedanke an die kranke Maria – und ich stand auf und irrte, von unerklärlichen Gedanken überwältigt, ziellos umher und fühlte in Kopf und Herz einen dumpfen Druck, daß ich weinen hätte mögen.

Und wenn ich am Abend manchmal durch die staubige Hauptstraße ging, die erfüllt war vom Dufte der blühenden Linden, und im Schatten der Bäume flüsternde Paare stehen sah; wenn ich sah, wie beim leise plätschern-den Brunnen im Mondenschein zwei Menschen enge aneinander geschmiegt langsam dahinwandelten, als wären sie ein Wesen, und mich da ein ahnungsvoller heißer Schauer überlief, da kam die kranke Maria mir in den Sinn; dann überfiel mich eine leise Sehnsucht nach irgend etwas Unerklärlichem, und plötzlich sah ich mich mit ihr Arm in Arm die Straße hinab im Schatten der duftenden Linden lustwandeln. Und in Marias großen, dunklen Augen leuchtete ein seltsamer Schimmer, und der Mond

I spent eight weeks in this remoteness; these eight weeks are to me like a detached, separate part of my life—a life unto itself—full of an inexpressible, youthful happiness, full of a strong longing after far away, beautiful things. Here my boyish soul received for the first time the impact of an important experience.

I see myself again as a schoolboy living in a small house with a small garden in front of it, somewhat remote from the city, hidden almost completely by trees and bushes. There I inhabited a small garret, which was decorated with wonderfully old, faded pictures and I dreamed some evenings away here in the stillness, and the stillness took into itself and lovingly preserved my sky-high, foolishly-fortunate boyish dreams and later brought them back to me often enough—in the lonely dusk hours. Often in the evening I also went down to my old uncle who spent nearly the entire day by his ill daughter Maria. Then we three sat for hours in silence together. The tepid evening wind blew in through the window and bore all sorts of confused noise to our ear, simulating vague dream images. And the air was filled with the strong, intoxicating perfume of roses flowering by the garden fence. Slowly the night crept into the room and then I stood up, said "good night," and went back to my room to dream for yet another hour into the night outside.

At first I felt something like a fearful anxiety in the presence of the small invalid, which later changed into a holy, reverent shyness at this silent, strangely poignant suffering. When I saw her, a dark feeling arose in me that she will have to die. And then I was afraid to look at her.

When I roamed the forests during the day, I felt glad in the isolation and stillness when I stretched myself out tiredly then in the moss, and for hours glanced into the light, flickering sky that one could see so far into, when a strange, deep feeling of happiness befuddled me there, then suddenly I thought of the ill Maria—and I stood up and meandered around aimlessly overpowered by unexplainable thoughts and felt a dull pressure in head and heart that made me want to weep.

And when sometimes in the evening I went through the dusty main street which was filled with the perfume of flowering linden trees, and saw whispering couples standing around in the shadow of the trees; when I saw how two people slowly strolled near the quietly splashing well in the moonlit, nestled close together as if they were one, and there an ominous hot shiver flowed over me, at which the ill Maria came into my senses; then a quiet yearning to something unexplainable overtook me, and suddenly I saw myself with her, strolling arm in arm down the street in the shadow of the fragrant linden trees. And in Maria's large, dark eyes a strange glimmer shone, and the moon let her narrow face appear still more pale and transparent. Then I fled back to my garret, leaned at the window, saw in the dark sky where the stars seemed to expire, and for hours I was gripped by confusing daydreams until sleep overtook me.

And still—and still I had not exchanged ten words with Maria. She never spoke. I sat by her side for hours and looked into her sick, suffering face and felt again and again that she had to die.

In the garden, I lay in the grass and inhaled the perfume of a thousand flowers; my eye got drunk on the bright colors of the blooms over which sunlight flooded

ließ ihr schmales Gesichtchen noch blasser und durchsichtiger erscheinen. Dann flüchtete ich mich in meine Dachstube hinauf, lehnte mich ans Fenster, sah in den tiefdunklen Himmel hinauf, in dem die Sterne zu erlöschen schienen und hing stundenlang wirren, sinnverwirrenden Träumen nach, bis der Schlaf mich übermannte.

Und doch – und doch habe ich mit der kranken Maria keine zehn Worte gewechselt. Sie sprach nie. Nur stundenlang an ihrer Seite bin ich gesessen und habe in ihr krankes, leidendes Gesicht geblickt und immer wieder gefühlt, daß sie sterben müsse.

Im Garten habe ich im Gras gelegen und habe den Duft von tausend Blumen eingeatmet; mein Auge berauschte sich an den leuchtenden Farben der Blüten, über die das Sonnenlicht hinflutete, und auf die Stille in den Lüften habe ich gehorcht, die nur bisweilen unterbrochen wurde durch den Lockruf eines Vogels. Ich vernahm das Gären der fruchtbaren, schwülen Erde, dieses geheimnisvolle Geräusch des ewig schaffenden Lebens. Damals fühlte ich dunkel die Größe und Schönheit des Lebens. Damals auch war mir, als gehörte das Leben mir. Da aber fiel mein Blick auf das Erkerfenster des Hauses. Dort sah ich die kranke Maria sitzen – still und unbeweglich, mit geschlossenen Augen. Und all' mein Sinnen wurde wieder angezogen von dem Leiden dieses einen Wesens, verblieb dort – ward zu einer schmerzlichen, nur scheu eingestandenen Sehnsucht, die mich rätselhaft und verwirrend dünkte. Und scheu, still verließ ich den Garten, als hätte ich kein Recht, in diesem Tempel zu verweilen.

Sooft ich da am Zaun vorüberkam, brach ich wie in Gedanken eine von den großen, leuchtendroten, duftschweren Rosen. Leise wollte ich dann am Fenster vorüberhuschen, als ich den zitternden, zarten Schatten von Marias Gestalt sich vom Kiesweg abheben sah. Und mein Schatten berührte den ihrigen wie in einer Umarmung. Da nun trat ich, wie von einem flüchtigen Gedanken erfaßt, zum Fenster und legte die Rose, die ich eben erst gebrochen, in Marias Schoß. Dann schlich ich lautlos davon, als fürchtete ich, ertappt zu werden.

Wie oft hat dieser kleine, mich so bedeutsam dünkende Vorgang sich wiederholt! Ich weiß es nicht. Mir ist es, als hätte ich der kranken Maria tausend Rosen in den Schoß gelegt, als hätten unsere Schatten sich unzählige Male umarmt. Nie hat Maria dieser Episode Erwähnung getan; aber gefühlt habe ich aus dem Schimmer ihrer großen leuchtenden Augen, daß sie darüber glücklich war.

Vielleicht waren diese Stunden, da wir zwei beisammen saßen und schweigend ein großes, ruhiges, tiefes Glück genossen, so schön, daß ich mir keine schöneren zu wünschen brauchte. Mein alter Onkel ließ uns still gewähren. Eines Tages aber, da ich mit ihm im Garten saß, inmitten all' der leuchtenden Blumen, über die verträumt große gelbe Schmetterlinge schwebten, sagte er zu mir mit einer leisen, gedankenvollen Stimme: »Deine Seele geht nach dem Leiden, mein Junge.« Und dabei legte er seine Hand auf mein Haupt und schien noch etwas sagen zu wollen. Aber er schwieg. Vielleicht wußte er auch nicht, was er dadurch in mir geweckt hatte und was seither mächtig in mir auflebte.

Eines Tages, da ich wiederum zum Fenster trat, an dem Maria wie gewöhnlich saß, sah ich, daß ihr Gesicht im Tode erbleicht und erstarrt war. Sonnenstrah-

and I listened to the stillness in the air, only occasionally interrupted by the call of a bird. I heard the fermenting of the fruitful, sultry earth, the mysterious noise of the eternally creating life. At the time I darkly felt the greatness and beauty of life. At that time it also seemed that life belonged to me. But then my gaze fell on the bay window of the house. There I saw the sick Maria sitting—silent and immobile, with closed eyes. And all my pondering was again drawn in by the suffering of that one being, and remained there—became a grievous, only shyly admitted yearning, which I found puzzling and confusing. And shyly, silently, I left the garden, as I had no right to remain in this temple.

Whenever I came by the fence there, I broke off one of the large, shiny red, heavily perfumed roses like in my thoughts. Quietly I wanted to scurry past the window, as I saw the trembling, delicate shadow of Maria's figure defined against the gravel path. And my own shadow touched hers as if in an embrace. Yet I now came to the window, as if kept by a fleeting thought, and placed the rose I just broke off in Maria's lap. Then I slipped away noiselessly, as if I was afraid of being caught.

How often has this little process that seemed so significant for me been repeated! I don't know. For me, it was as if I put one thousand roses into the ill Maria's lap, as if our shadows embraced innumerable times. Maria has never mentioned this episode; but I have felt from the gleam of her large shinning eyes that she was happy about it.

Perhaps these hours, when we two sat together and silently enjoyed a large, calm, deep happiness were so beautiful that I did not need to wish any more beautiful. My old uncle silently approved of us. But one day, when I sat with him in the garden amid all the bright flowers, over which dreamily large yellow butterflies hovered, he said to me with a quiet, thoughtful voice: "Your soul goes out to the suffering, my boy." And in doing so he lay his hand on my head and appeared to want to say something more. But he was silent. Perhaps he also did not know what he had thereby awaken in me and what has revived powerfully in me since that time.

One day, when I again came to the window where Maria usually sat, I saw that her face was paled and had paralyzed in death. Sunbeams flitted over her light, delicate figure; her free-flowing golden hair fluttered in the wind, it seemed to me as if she had not been carried off by an illness, as if she would be dead without visible cause—a mystery. I put the last rose into her hand, she took it to the grave.

Soon after Maria's death I traveled off to a large city. But the memory of those still days filled with sunshine stayed alive in me, perhaps more alive than the noisy present. I will never see that small city in the valley again—yes, I avoid visiting it once more. I believe I could not do it, even if sometimes a strong longing overcomes me after those eternally young things of the past. Because I know I would only look in vain for what went by without a trace; I wouldn't find there what is only still alive in my memory—like the present—and that would probably be a useless agony for me.

len huschten über ihre lichte, zarte Gestalt hin; ihr gelöstes Goldhaar flatterte im Wind, mir war, als hätte sie keine Krankheit dahingerafft, als wäre sie gestorben ohne sichtbare Ursache – ein Rätsel. Die letzte Rose habe ich ihr in die Hand gelegt, sie hat sie ins Grab genommen.

Bald nach dem Tode Marias reiste ich ab in die Großstadt. Aber die Erinnerung an jene stillen Tage voll Sonnenschein sind in mir lebendig geblieben, lebendiger vielleicht als die geräuschvolle Gegenwart. Die kleine Stadt im Talesgrund werde ich nie mehr wiedersehen – ja, ich trage Scheu, sie wieder aufzusuchen. Ich glaube, ich könnte es nicht, wenn mich auch manchmal eine starke Sehnsucht nach jenen ewig jungen Dingen der Vergangenheit überfällt. Denn ich weiß, ich würde nur vergeblich nach dem suchen, was spurlos dahingegangen ist; ich würde dort das nicht mehr finden, was nur in meiner Erinnerung noch lebendig ist – wie das Heute – und das wäre mir wohl nur eine unnütze Qual.

Aus goldenem Kelch
Barrabas
Eine Phantasie

Es geschah aber zur selbigen Stunde, da sie des Menschen Sohn hinausführ-ten gen Golgatha, das da ist die Stätte, wo sie Räuber und Mörder hinrichten.   Es geschah zur selbigen hohen und glühenden Stunde, da er sein Werk vollendete.

Es geschah, daß zur selbigen Stunde eine große Menge Volks lärmend Jerusalems Straßen durchzog – und inmitten des Volkes schritt Barrabas, der Mörder, und trug sein Haupt trotzig hoch.

Und um ihn waren aufgeputzte Dirnen mit rotgemalten Lippen und geschminkten Gesichtern und haschten nach ihm. Und um ihn waren Männer, deren Augen trunken blickten von Wein und Lastern. In aller Reden aber lauerte die Sünde ihres Fleisches, und die Unzucht ihrer Geberden war der Ausdruck ihrer Gedanken.

Viele, die dem trunkenen Zuge begegneten, schlossen sich ihm an und riefen: »Es lebe Barrabas!« Und alle schrieen: »Barrabas lebe!« Jemand hatte auch »Hosiannah!« gerufen. Den aber schlugen sie – denn erst vor wenigen Tagen hatten sie Einem »Hosiannah!« zugerufen, der da in die Stadt gezogen kam als ein König, und hatten frische Palmenzweige auf seinen Weg gestreut. Heute aber streuten sie rote Rosen und jauchzten: »Barrabas!«

Und da sie an einem Palaste vorbeikamen, hörten sie drinnen Saitenspiel und Gelächter und den Lärm eines großen Gelages. Und aus dem Haus trat ein junger Mensch in reichem Festgewand. Und sein Haar glänzte von wohlriechenden Ölen und sein Körper duftete von den kostbarsten Essenzen Arabiens. Sein Auge leuchtete von den Freuden des Gelages und das Lächeln seines Mundes war geil von den Küssen seiner Geliebten.

Als der Jüngling Barrabam erkannte, trat er vor und sprach also:

From the Golden Chalice
Barrabas
A Fantasy

But it happened at the same hour when the Son of Man was lead out to Golgotha, which is the place where they execute thieves and murders.

It happened at the same exulted and glowing hour when He completed his work.

It happened that at the same hour a large number of people drew noisily along Jerusalem's streets—and in the midst of these people Barabbas, the murderer, walked and carried his head defiantly high.

And decorated strumpets with red-painted lips and made up faces were all around him and grabbed at him. And men were around him, whose eyes gazed drunk with wine and vice. But the sin of the flesh lurked in their talking, and the fornication of their gestures was the expression of their thoughts.

Many who met this drunken procession, joined it and cried: "Long live Barrabas!" And all screamed: "Live Barrabas!" Someone also cried: "Hosiannah." But they hit this one—because only a few days ago they had shouted "Hosiannah" to One who came drawn into town as a king, and they had scattered fresh palm branches before Him. But today they spread red roses and cheered: "Barrabas!"

And as they passed by a palace, they heard string-play and laughter and the noise of a great revelry. And from the house a young person stepped in a solemn vestment. And his hair shone from perfumed oils and his body smelled of the most precious Arabian essences. His eye shone from the joys of the revelry and the smile of his mouth was lustful from the kisses of his lover.

When the young man recognized Barrabas, he came forward to him and spoke:

"Step into my house, o Barrabas, and you shall rest on my softest pillows; step inside, o Barrabas, and my maids will anoint your body with the most precious

»Tritt ein in mein Haus, o Barrabas, und auf meinen weichsten Kissen sollst du ruhen; tritt ein, o Barrabas, und meine Dienerinnen sollen deinen Leib mit den kostbarsten Narden salben. Dir zu Füßen soll ein Mädchen auf der Laute seine süßesten Weisen spielen und aus meinem kostbarsten Becher will ich dir meinen glühendsten Wein darreichen. Und in den Wein will ich die herrlichste meiner Perlen werfen. O Barrabas, sei mein Gast für heute – und meinem Gast gehört für diesen Tag meine Geliebte, die schöner ist als die Morgenröte im Frühling. Tritt ein, Barrabas, und kränze dein Haupt mit Rosen, freu' dich dieses Tages, da jener stirbt, dem sie Dornen aufs Haupt gesetzt.«

Und da der Jüngling so gesprochen, jauchzte ihm das Volk zu und Barrabas stieg die Marmorstufen empor, gleich einem Sieger. Und der Jüngling nahm die Rosen, die sein Haupt bekränzten, und legte sie um die Schlafen des Mörders Barrabas.

Dann trat er mit ihm in das Haus, derweil das Volk auf den Straßen jauchzte.

Auf weichen Kissen ruhte Barrabas; Dienerinnen salbten seinen Leib mit den köstlichsten Narden und zu seinen Füßen tönte das liebliche Saitenspiel eines Mädchens und auf seinem Schoß saß des Jünglings Geliebte, die schöner war denn die Morgenröte im Frühling. Und Lachen tönte – und an unerhörten Freuden berauschten sich die Gäste, die sie alle waren des Einzigen Feinde und Verächter – Pharisäer und Knechte der Priester.

Zu Einer Stunde gebot der Jüngling Schweigen, und aller Lärm verstummte.

Da nun füllte der Jüngling seinen goldenen Becher mit dem köstlichsten Wein, und in dem Gefäß ward der Wein wie glühendes Blut. Eine Perle warf er hinein und reichte den Becher Barrabas dar. Der Jüngling aber griff nach einem Becher von Kristall und trank Barrabas zu:

»Der Nazarener ist tot! Es lebe Barrabas!«

Und alle im Saale jauchzten:

»Der Nazarener ist tot! Es lebe Barrabas!«

Und das Volk in den Straßen schrie:

»Der Nazarener ist tot! Es lebe Barrabas!«

Plötzlich aber erlosch die Sonne, die Erde erbebte in ihren Grundfesten und ein ungeheures Grauen ging durch die Welt. Und die Kreatur erzitterte.

Zur selbigen Stunde ward das Werk der Erlösung vollbracht!

balms. By your feet a girl will play on the lute its sweetest tunes and from my most precious chalice I will offer you my fieriest wine. And into the wine I want to throw the most glorious of my pearls. O Barabbas, be my guest for today—and for this day my love, who is more beautiful than the red of a morning in spring, belongs to my guest. Step inside, Barabbas, and wreath your head with roses, enjoy this day, since the One whom they set thorns on the head dies."

And as the youth spoke thus, the people cheered him and Barabbas climbed onto the marble stage like a victor. And the youth took the roses that wreathed his head and put them around the temples of the murderer Barabbas.

Then he stepped with him into the house, meanwhile the people on the streets were cheering.

On soft pillows, Barabbas rested; maids anointed his body with the most delicious balms and by his feet the lovely string play of a girl sounded and on his lap the lover of the youth sat, more beautiful than the red of a morning in spring. And laughter resounded—and the guests intoxicated themselves with egregious joys, because they all were enemies and despisers of the only One—Pharisees and subjugates of the priests.

At the appointed hour, the youth ordered silence, and all noise muted.

Then the youth filled his golden chalice with the most delicious wine, and in the vessel the wine became like glowing blood. He threw a pearl in and handed the chalice to Barabbas. The youth, however, reached for a chalice of crystal and drank to Barabbas:

"The Nazarene is dead! Long live Barabbas!"

And everyone in the hall cheered:

"The Nazarene is dead! Long live Barabbas!"

And the people in the roads cheered:

"The Nazarene is dead! Long live Barabbas!"

But suddenly the sun expired, the earth shook in its bedrock and a monstrous horror came over the world. And the creatures trembled.

In this same hour the work of redemption was accomplished!

Aus goldenem Kelch
Maria Magdalena
Ein Dialog

Vor den Toren der Stadt Jerusalem. Es wird Abend.

AGATHON: Es ist Zeit, in die Stadt zurückzukehren. Die Sonne ist untergegangen und über der Stadt dämmert es schon. Es ist sehr still geworden. – Doch was antwortest du nicht, Marcellus; was blickst du so abwesend in die Ferne?

MARCELLUS: Ich habe daran gedacht, daß dort in der Ferne das Meer die Ufer dieses Landes bespült; daran habe ich gedacht, daß jenseits des Meeres das ewige, göttergleiche Rom sich zu den Gestirnen erhebt, wo kein Tag eines Festes entbehrt. Und ich bin hier in fremder Erde. An alles das habe ich gedacht. Doch ich vergaß. Es ist wohl Zeit, daß du in die Stadt zurückkehrst. Es dämmert. Und zur Zeit der Dämmerung harrt ein Mädchen vor den Toren der Stadt Agathons. Laß sie nicht warten, Agathon, laß sie nicht warten, deine Geliebte. Ich sage dir, die Frauen dieses Landes sind sehr sonderbar; ich weiß, sie sind voller Rätsel. Laß sie nicht warten, deine Geliebte; denn man weiß nie, was geschehen kann. In einem Augenblick kann Furchtbares geschehen. Man sollte den Augenblick nie versäumen.

AGATHON: Warum sprichst du so zu mir?

MARCELLUS: Ich meine, wenn sie schön ist, deine Geliebte, sollst du sie nicht warten lassen. Ich sage dir, ein schönes Weib ist etwas ewig Unerklärliches. Die Schönheit des Weibes ist ein Rätsel. Man durchschaut sie nicht. Man weiß nie, was ein schönes Weib sein kann, was sie zu tun gezwungen ist. Das ist es, Agathon! Ach du – ich kannte eine. Ich kannte eine, ich sah Dinge geschehen, die ich nie ergründen werde. Kein Mensch würde sie ergründen können. Wir schauen nie den Grund der Geschehnisse.

AGATHON: Was sahst du geschehen? Ich bitte dich, erzähle mir mehr davon!

MARCELLUS: So gehen wir. Vielleicht ist eine Stunde gekommen, da ich es sagen werde können, ohne vor meinen eigenen Worten und Gedanken erschaudern zu müssen. *(Sie gehen langsam den Weg nach Jerusalem zurück. Es ist Stille um sie.)*

MARCELLUS: Es ging vor sich in einer glühenden Sommernacht, da in der Luft das Fieber lauert und Mond die Sinne verwirrt. Da sah ich sie. Es war in einer kleinen Schenke. Sie tanzte dort, tanzte mit nackten Füßen auf einem kostbaren Teppich. Niemals sah ich ein Weib schöner tanzen, nie berauschter; der Rhythmus ihres Körpers ließ mich seltsam dunkle Traumbilder schauen, daß heiße Fieberschauer meinen Körper durchbebten. Mir war, als spiele dieses Weib im Tanz mit unsichtbaren, köstlichen, heimlichen Dingen, als umarmte sie göttergleiche Wesen, die niemand sah, als küßte sie rote Lippen, die sich verlangend den ihren neigten; ihre Bewegungen waren die höchster Lust; es schien, als würde sie von Liebkosungen überschüttet. Sie schien Dinge zu sehen, die wir nicht sahen und

212

From the Golden Chalice
Mary Magdalene
A Dialog

Before the gates of the city Jerusalem. Evening appears.

AGATHON: It is time to return to the city. The sun has set and it is dusking over the city already. It has become very silent.—But why don't you answer, Marcellus, why do you look so absent-mindedly into the distance?

MARCELLUS: I remembered that there in the distance the sea washes the shores of this country; I remembered that beyond the sea, the eternal, god-like Rome rises to the stars, where no day lacks a celebration. And I am here on this strange earth. All this I remembered. But I forgot. It is probably time that you return to the city. Dusk falls. And at the time of twilight a girl is waiting before the gates of the city for Agathon. Don't let her wait, Agathon, don't let her wait, your beloved. I say to you the women of this country are very peculiar; I know they are full of mysteries. Do not let your beloved wait; because one never knows what can happen. In a moment dreadfulness can occur. One should never miss the moment.

AGATHON: Why do you speak like this to me?

MARCELLUS: I mean if she is beautiful, your beloved, you should not let her wait. I say to you a beautiful woman is something eternally unexplainable. The beauty of woman is a mystery. One does not see through her. One never knows what a beautiful woman can be, what she is forced to do. That is it, Agathon! Alas you—I knew one. I knew one, I saw things happen which I shall never fathom. No person could ever fathom them. We never see the reason for the events.

AGATHON: What did you see happening? I beg you, tell me more about this!

MARCELLUS: Let us go. Perhaps an hour has come when I am able to say it without trembling before my own words and thoughts. *(They slowly walk the road back to Jerusalem. Stillness is around them.)*

MARCELLUS: It took place on a glowing summer night, when fever lurks in the air and moon confuses the senses. There I saw her. It was in a small tavern. She danced there, danced with naked feet on an expensive carpet. I never saw a woman dancing more beautifully, more intoxicated; the rhythm of her body showed me strange dark dream images, so that hot feverish shudders shook through my body. It looked to me as if this woman played in dance with invisible, delicious, hidden things, as if she embraced god-like beings that no one saw, as if she kissed red lips bending to her demandingly; her movements were those of the highest lust; it seemed as if she was overwhelmed with caresses. She seemed to see things which we could not see, and played with them in dance, relished them in the egregious ecstasies of her body. Perhaps she lifted her mouth to delicious, sweet fruits and sipped fiery wine when she threw back her head and demandingly her look was directed upward. No! I did not understand this, nevertheless everything was strangely alive—it was there. And then sank cloakless, only her hair overflowing

spielte mit ihnen im Tanze, genoß sie in unerhörten Verzückungen ihres Körpers. Vielleicht hob sie ihren Mund zu köstlichen, süßen Früchten und schlürfte feurigen Wein, wenn sie ihren Kopf zurückwarf und ihr Blick verlangend nach oben gerichtet war. Nein! Ich habe das nicht begriffen, und doch war alles seltsam lebendig – es war da. Und sank dann hüllenlos, nur von ihren Haaren überflutet, zu unseren Füßen nieder. Es war, als hätte sich die Nacht in ihrem Haar zu einem schwarzen Knäuel zusammengeballt und entrückte sie uns. Sie aber gab sich hin, gab ihren herrlichen Leib hin, gab ihn einem jeden, der ihn haben wollte, hin. Ich sah sie Bettler und Gemeine, sah sie Fürsten und Könige lieben. Sie war die herrlichste Hetäre. Ihr Leib war ein köstliches Gefäß der Freude, wie es die Welt nicht schöner sah. Ihr Leben gehörte der Freude allein. Ich sah sie bei Gelagen tanzen und ihr Leib wurde von Rosen überschüttet. Sie aber stand inmitten leuchtender Rosen wie eine eben aufgeblühte, einzig schöne Blume. Und ich sah sie die Statue des Dionysos mit Blumen kränzen, sah sie den kalten Marmor umarmen, wie sie ihre Geliebten umarmte, sie erstickte mit ihren brennenden, fiebernden Küssen. – Und da kam einer, der ging vorbei, wortlos, ohne Geberde, und war gekleidet in ein härenes Gewand, und Staub war auf seinen Füßen. Der ging vorbei und sah sie an – und war vorüber. Sie aber blickte nach Ihm, erstarrte in ihrer Bewegung – und ging, ging, und folgte jenem seltsamen Propheten, der sie vielleicht mit den Augen gerufen hatte, folgte Seinem Ruf und sank zu Seinen Füßen nieder. Erniedrigte sich vor Ihm – und sah zu Ihm auf wie zu einem Gott; diente Ihm, wie Ihm die Männer dienten, die um Ihn waren.

AGATHON: Du bist noch nicht zu Ende. Ich fühle, du willst noch etwas sagen.

MARCELLUS: Mehr weiß ich nicht. Nein! Aber eines Tages erfuhr ich, daß sie jenen sonderlichen Propheten ans Kreuz schlagen wollten. Ich erfuhr es von unserem Statthalter Pilatus. Und da wollte ich hinausgehen nach Golgatha, wollte Jenen sehen, wollte Ihn sterben sehen. Vielleicht wäre mir ein rätselhaftes Geschehnis offenbar geworden. In Seine Augen wollte ich blicken; Seine Augen würden vielleicht zu mir gesprochen haben. Ich glaube, sie hätten gesprochen.

AGATHON: Und du gingst nicht!

MARCELLUS: Ich war auf dem Wege dahin. Aber ich kehrte um. Denn ich fühlte, ich würde jene draußen treffen, auf den Knien vor dem Kreuz, zu Ihm beten, auf das Fliehen Seines Lebens lauschend. In Verzückung. Und da kehrte ich wieder um. Und in mir ist es dunkel geblieben.

AGATHON: Doch jener Seltsame? – Nein, wir wollen nicht davon sprechen!

MARCELLUS: Laß uns darüber schweigen, Agathon! Wir können nichts anderes tun. – Sieh nur, Agathon, wie es in den Wolken seltsam dunkel glüht. Man könnte meinen, daß hinter den Wolken ein Ozean von Flammen loderte. Ein göttliches Feuer! Und der Himmel ist wie eine blaue Glocke. Es ist, als ob man sie tönen hörte, in tiefen, feierlichen Tönen. Man könnte sogar vermuten, daß dort oben in den unerreichbaren Höhen etwas vorgeht, wovon man nie etwas wissen wird. Aber ahnen kann man es manchmal, wenn auf die Erde die große Stille herabgestiegen ist. Und doch! Alles das ist sehr verwirrend. Die Götter lieben es, uns Menschen unlösbare Rätsel aufzugeben. Die Erde aber rettet uns nicht vor der Arglist der

down to our feet. It was as if the night had gathered into a black ball in her hair and removed her from us. But she gave herself, gave her wonderful body, gave to everyone who wanted to have it. I saw her love beggars and commoners, princes and kings. She was the most lovely hetaera. Her body was a delicious vessel of joy, the world has not seen more beautiful. Her life belonged to joy alone. I saw her dancing during binges and her body was showered with roses. But she stood in the midst of bright roses like a just opened, single beautiful flower. And I saw her crowning the statue of Dionysus with flowers, saw her embrace the cold marble like she embraced her lovers that she smothered with her burning, feverish kisses.—And then One came, who walked by, wordless, without gesture, and was clothed in a hairy garment, and dust was on his feet. He walked by and looked on her—and went past. But she gazed after Him, paralyzed in her movement—and walked, walked, and followed that strange prophet, who had perhaps called her with the eyes, followed His call and sank down at His feet. Humbled herself before Him—and looked up to Him as if to a god; served Him, like the men served Him who were around Him.

AGATHON: You are not yet at the end. I feel you want to say more.

MARCELLUS: I do not know more. No! But one day I found out they would nail that eccentric prophet to the cross. I found it out from our governor Pilate. And then I wanted to go out to Golgotha, wanted to see that One, wanted to see Him die. Perhaps a mysterious event would become obvious to me. I wanted to gaze into His eyes; perhaps His eyes would have spoken to me. I believe they would have spoken.

AGATHON: And you did not go!

MARCELLUS: I was on the way there. But I turned back. Because I felt I would meet her outside, on the knees before the cross to pray to Him, listening to the fleeing of His life. In rapture. And then I turned back again. And in me it remained dark.

AGATHON: But that strange one?—No, we will not speak of that.

MARCELLUS: Let us be silent about it, Agathon! We can do nothing else.—But look, Agathon, how it glows strangely dark in the clouds. One could guess that behind the clouds an ocean of flames blazes. A godly fire! And the sky is like a blue bell. It is as if one heard it ring in deep, solemn tones. One could even suspect that there above in the unreachable heights something happens which one will never know anything about. But one can sense it sometimes when the large silence has descended over the earth. And still! All this is very confusing. The gods love to give us humans unsolvable mysteries. But the earth does not save us from the guile of the gods; because it is also full of bewitching. Things and people confuse me. Certainly! Things are very tight-lipped! And the human soul does not give away its mysteries. When one asks, it is silent.

AGATHON: We want to live and not question. Life is full of beauty.

MARCELLUS: We will never know much. Yes! And hence it would be desirable to forget what we know. Enough of that! We are soon at the goal. But look how abandoned the roads are. One sees no more people. *(A wind rises up.)* This is a

Götter; denn auch sie ist voll des Sinnbetörenden. Mich verwirren die Dinge und die Menschen. Gewiß! Die Dinge sind sehr schweigsam! Und die Menschenseele gibt ihre Rätsel nicht preis. Wenn man fragt, so schweigt sie.

AGATHON: Wir wollen leben und nicht fragen. Das Leben ist voll des Schönen.

MARCELLUS: Wir werden vieles nie wissen. Ja! Und deshalb wäre es wünschenswert, das zu vergessen, was wir wissen. Genug davon! Wir sind bald am Ziel. Sieh nur, wie verlassen die Straßen sind. Man sieht keinen Menschen mehr. *(Ein Wind erhebt sich.)* Es ist dies eine Stimme, die uns sagt, daß wir zu den Gestirnen aufblicken sollen. Und schweigen.

AGATHON: Marcellus, sieh, wie hoch das Getreide auf den Äckern steht. Jeder Halm beugt sich zur Erde – früchteschwer. Es werden herrliche Erntetage sein.

MARCELLUS: Ja! Festtage! Festtage, mein Agathon!

AGATHON: Ich gehe mit Rahel durch die Felder, durch die früchteschweren, gesegneten Äcker! O du herrliches Leben!

MARCELLUS: Du hast recht! Freue dich deiner Jugend. Jugend allein ist Schönheit! Mir geziemt es, im Dunkel zu wandern. Doch hier trennen sich unsere Wege. Deiner harrt die Geliebte, meiner – das Schweigen der Nacht! Leb' wohl, Agathon! Es wird eine herrlich schöne Nacht sein. Man kann lange im Freien bleiben.

AGATHON: Und kann zu den Gestirnen emporblicken – zur großen Gelassenheit. Ich will fröhlich meiner Wege gehen und die Schönheit preisen. So ehrt man sich und die Götter.

MARCELLUS: Tu, wie du sagst, und du tust recht! Leb' wohl, Agathon!

AGATHON *(nachdenklich)*: Nur eines will ich dich noch fragen. Du sollst nichts dabei denken, daß ich dich darnach frage. Wie hieß doch jener seltsame Prophet? Sag'!

MARCELLUS: Was nützt es dir, das zu wissen! Ich vergaß seinen Namen. Doch nein! Ich erinnere mich. Ich erinnere mich. Er hieß Jesus und war aus Nazareth!

AGATHON: Ich danke dir! Leb' wohl! Die Götter mögen dir wohlgesinnt sein, Marcellus! *(Er geht.)*

MARCELLUS *(in Gedanken verloren)*: Jesus! – Jesus! Und war aus Nazareth! *(Er geht langsam und gedankenvoll seiner Wege. Es ist Nacht geworden und am Himmel leuchten unzählige Sterne.)*

Verlassenheit

Nichts unterbricht mehr das Schweigen der Verlassenheit. Über den dunklen, uralten Gipfeln der Bäume ziehn die Wolken hin und spiegeln sich in den grünlichblauen Wassern des Teiches, der abgründlich scheint. Und unbeweglich, wie in trauervolle Ergebenheit versunken, ruht die Oberfläche – tagein, tagaus.

Inmitten des schweigsamen Teiches ragt das Schloß zu den Wolken empor mit spitzen, zerschlissenen Türmen und Dächern. Unkraut wuchert über die schwar-

voice that says to us we are to look to the stars. And silence.

AGATHON: Marcellus, see how high the grain stands in the acres. Each blade bends earthward—heavy with fruit. The harvest days will be wonderful.

MARCELLUS: Yes! Festive days! Festive days, my Agathon!

AGATHON: I will go with Rachel through the fields, through the fruit-heavy, blessed acres! O you wonderful life!

MARCELLUS: You are right! Be happy with your youth. Youth alone is beauty! It suits me to wander in the darkness. But here our ways separate. Your beloved waits for you, for me—the silence of the night! Farewell, Agathon! It will be a wonderfully beautiful night. One can remain outdoors a long time.

AGATHON: And can look up to the stars—to the mighty tranquility. I will go merrily on my way and praise the beauty. Thus one honors oneself and the gods.

MARCELLUS: Do as you say, and you'll do well! Farewell, Agathon!

AGATHON *(contemplative)*: Only one thing I still want to ask you. You shouldn't think anything by it that I ask this. What was the name of that strange prophet? Tell me!

MARCELLUS: What use is it to you to know! I forgot his name. But no! I remember! I remember! He was called Jesus and was from Nazareth! **AGATHON**: I thank you! Farwell! May the gods be kind to you, Marcellus! *(He goes.)*

MARCELLUS: *(lost in thought)* Jesus!—Jesus! And was from Nazareth. *(He goes slowly and pensively on his way. Night has appeared and in the sky innumerable stars shine.)*

Abandonment

Nothing interrupts the silence of abandonment anymore. Over the dark, aged tree-tops the clouds expand and are reflected in the greenish-blue waters of the pond that shines like an abyss. And unmoving, as if sunken in mournful surrender, the surface rests—day-in, day-out.

In the middle of the taciturn pond the palace rises up to the clouds with pointed, ramshackled towers and roofs. Weeds grow rampantly over the black, worn out

zen, geborstenen Mauern, und an den runden, blinden Fenstern prallt das Sonnenlicht ab. In den düsteren, dunklen Höfen fliegen Tauben umher und suchen sich in den Ritzen des Gemäuers ein Versteck.

Sie scheinen immer etwas zu befürchten, denn sie fliegen scheu und hastend an den Fenstern hin. Drunten im Hof plätschert die Fontäne leise und fein. Aus bronzener Brunnenschale trinken dann und wann die dürstenden Tauben.

Durch die schmalen, verstaubten Gänge des Schlosses streift manchmal ein dumpfer Fieberhauch, daß die Fledermäuse erschreckt aufflattern. Sonst stört nichts die tiefe Ruhe.

Die Gemächer aber sind schwarz verstaubt! Hoch und kahl und frostig und voll erstorbener Gegenstände. Durch die blinden Fenster kommt bisweilen ein winziger Schein, den das Dunkel wieder aufsaugt. Hier ist die Vergangenheit gestorben.

Hier ist sie eines Tages erstarrt in einer einzigen, verzerrten Rose. An ihrer Wesenlosigkeit geht die Zeit achtlos vorüber.

Und alles durchdringt das Schweigen der Verlassenheit.

2

Niemand vermag mehr in den Park einzudringen. Die Äste der Bäume halten sich tausendfach umschlungen, der ganze Park ist nur mehr ein einziges, gigantisches Lebewesen.

Und ewige Nacht lastet unter dem riesigen Blätterdach. Und tiefes Schweigen! Und die Luft ist durchtränkt von Vermoderungsdünsten!

Manchmal aber erwacht der Park aus schweren Träumen. Dann strömt er ein Erinnern aus an kühle Sternennächte, an tief verborgene heimliche Stellen, da er fiebernde Küsse und Umarmungen belauschte, an Sommernächte, voll glühender Pracht und Herrlichkeit, da der Mond wirre Bilder auf den schwarzen Grund zauberte, an Menschen, die zierlich galant, voll rhythmischer Bewegungen unter seinem Blätterdache dahinwandelten, die sich süße, verrückte Worte zuraunten, mit feinem verheißenden Lächeln.

Und dann versinkt der Park wieder in seinen Todesschlaf.

Auf den Wassern wiegen sich die Schatten von Blutbuchen und Tannen und aus der Tiefe des Teiches kommt ein dumpfes, trauriges Murmeln.

Schwäne ziehen durch die glänzenden Fluten, langsam, unbeweglich, starr ihre schlanken Hälse emporrichtend. Sie ziehen dahin! Rund um das erstorbene Schloß! Tagein! tagaus!

Bleiche Lilien stehn am Rande des Teiches mitten unter grellfarbigen Gräsern. Und ihre Schatten im Wasser sind bleicher als sie selbst.

Und wenn die einen dahinsterben, kommen andere aus der Tiefe. Und sie sind wie kleine, tote Frauenhände.

Große Fische umschwimmen neugierig, mit starren, glasigen Augen die bleichen Blumen, und tauchen dann wieder in die Tiefe – lautlos!

Und alles durchdringt das Schweigen der Verlassenheit.

walls, and at the round, blind windows the sunlight recoils. In the gloomy, dark yards pigeons fly around and seek a hiding place in the chinks of the walls.

They always seem to fear something, because they fly timidly and scurry past the windows. Down there in the yard the fountain splashes quiet and dignified. From the fountain basin the thirsty pigeons drink now and then.

Through the narrow, dusty hallways of the palace sometimes a musty whiff of fever streaks, so that the bats flutter up terrified. Otherwise nothing disturbs the deep rest.

But the bedrooms are dusty black. High and bleak and frosty and full of deceased objects. Through the blind windows sometimes a tiny light comes that is absorbed by the dark again. Here the past has died.

Here one day it stiffened into a single, distorted rose. In its unsubstantialness time passes carelessly.

And the silence of abandonment permeates everything.

2

No one is able to enter the park anymore. The branches of the trees are entangled a thousandfold, the whole park is nothing more than one gigantic organism.

And eternal night weighs under the vast roof of leaves. And deep silence! And the air is soaked with mists of decay.

But sometimes the park awakens from heavy dreams. Then it floats out a remembrance to cool, starry nights, to deeply hidden, clandestine places, when it eavesdropped on feverish kisses and embraces, to summer nights full of glowing splendor and glory when the moon conjured up woozy images on the black ground, to people who strolled with a graceful gallantry full of rhythmic movements under its roof of leaves, who murmured sweet, kind words to each other with delicate, promising smiles.

And then the park sinks again into its death-sleep.

The shadows of blood-beeches and firs sway on the waters and from the pond's depth a dull, sad mumbling comes.

Swans move through the shining floods, slowly, motionless, their slender necks stiffy upright. They move along! Around the deceased palace! Day-in, day-out!

Pale lilies stand at the edge of the pond among sharply colored grasses. And their shadows in the water are paler than they are.

And when they die away others come from the depths. And they are like small, dead woman-hands.

Large fish swim curiously around the pale flowers with rigid, glassy eyes, and then dive into the depth again—soundlessly!

And the silence of abandonment permeates everything.

3

Und droben in einem rissigen Turmgemach sitzt der Graf. Tagein, tagaus.

Er sieht den Wolken nach, die über den Gipfeln der Bäume hinziehen, leuchtend und rein. Er sieht es gern, wenn die Sonne in den Wolken glüht, am Abend, da sie untersinkt. Er horcht auf die Geräusche in den Höhen: auf den Schrei eines Vogels, der am Turm vorbeifliegt oder auf das tönende Brausen des Windes, wenn er das Schloß umfegt.

Er sieht wie der Park schläft, dumpf und schwer, und sieht die Schwäne durch die glitzernden Fluten ziehn – die das Schloß umschwimmen. Tagein! Tagaus!

Und die Wasser schimmern grünlich-blau. In den Wassern aber spiegeln sich die Wolken, die über das Schloß hinziehen; und ihre Schatten in den Fluten leuchten strahlend und rein, wie sie selbst. Die Wasserlilien winken ihm zu, wie kleine, tote Frauenhände, und wiegen sich nach den leisen Tönen des Windes, traurig träumerisch.

Auf alles, was ihn da sterbend umgibt, blickt der arme Graf, wie ein kleines, irres Kind, über dem ein Verhängnis steht, und das nicht mehr Kraft hat, zu leben, das dahinschwindet, gleich einem Vormittagsschatten.

Er horcht nur mehr auf die kleine, traurige Melodie seiner Seele: Vergangenheit!

Wenn es Abend wird, zündet er seine alte, verrußte Lampe an und liest in mächtigen, vergilbten Büchern von der Vergangenheit Größe und Herrlichkeit.

Er liest mit fieberndem, tönendem Herzen, bis die Gegenwart, der er nicht angehört, versinkt. Und die Schatten der Vergangenheit steigen herauf – riesengroß. Und er lebt das Leben, das herrlich schöne Leben seiner Väter.

In Nächten, da der Sturm um den Turm jagt, daß die Mauern in ihren Grundfesten dröhnen und die Vögel angstvoll vor seinem Fenster kreischen, überkommt den Grafen eine namenlose Traurigkeit.

Auf seiner jahrhundertalten, müden Seele lastet das Verhängnis.

Und er drückt das Gesicht an das Fenster und sieht in die Nacht hinaus. Und da erscheint ihm alles riesengroß traumhaft, gespensterlich! Und schrecklich. Durch das Schloß hört er den Sturm rasen, als wollte er alles Tote hinausfegen und in Lüfte zerstreuen.

Doch wenn das verworrene Trugbild der Nacht dahinsinkt wie ein heraufbeschworener Schatten – durchdringt alles wieder das Schweigen der Verlassenheit.

Oberregisseur Friedheim

Es ist ein schwieriges Unternehmen, die fruchtbare, reiche Tätigkeit eines Mannes zu überblicken, der jahrelang in der Öffentlichkeit gewirkt und deshalb auch von der Allgemeinheit seine Beurteilung erfahren hat; es ist schwer, aus solche einem Wirken das Wesentlichste hervorzuheben, es dadurch zu charakterisieren,

3

And up there in a cracked tower the count sits. Day-in, day-out.

He looks after the clouds which move over the treetops brightly and purely. He likes to view the sun glowing in the clouds in the evening when it sets. He listens to the noises in the heights: to the cry of a bird that flies past the tower or to the sounding roar of the wind when it sweeps around the palace.

He sees how the park sleeps, dull and heavy, and sees the swans gliding through the glittering floods—which swim around the palace. Day-in! Day-out!

And the waters shimmer greenish-blue. But the clouds that move over the palace reflect in the waters; and their shadows shine in the floods, radiant and pure, like themselves. The water lilies wave to him, like small, dead woman-hands, and rock in the quiet sounds of the wind, sadly dreamy.

On everything that surrounds him here dying, the poor count glances like a small, crazy child over whom a doom stands, and no longer has the strength to live, who dwindles like a morning shadow.

He listens to only the small, sad melody of his soul: the past!

When evening comes, he lights his old, sooted lamp and reads in huge, yellowed books about the past's greatness and glory.

He reads with a fevered, resounding heart until the present, where he does not belong, sinks away. And the shadows of the past rise up—gigantic. And he lives the life, the superb, beautiful life of his fathers.

At nights, when the storm hunts around the tower so that the walls creak in their bedrocks and birds shriek fearfully before his windows, the count is overcome with a nameless sadness.

Doom weighs on his centuries-old, exhausted soul.

And he presses his face to the window and looks into the night outside. And there everything appears to him vastly dreamlike, ghostly! And frightful. Through the palace he hears the storm race as if it wanted to sweep all the dead things out and scatter them into the air.

But if the confused phantom of the night sinks away like a conjured shadow—again the silence of abandonment permeates everything.

Head Stage Director Friedheim

It is a difficult undertaking to survey the fruitful, rich activity of a man who worked in public for many years and therefore received his assessment from the world at large; it is difficult to emphasize out of such work what is most essential, to thereby characterize it, and to bring all the intentions, that must remain undone

und all' das Gewollte, das nur durch die Ungunst der Verhältnisse ungetan bleiben mußte, in Einklang mit dem Geschehenen zu bringen – wie Saat und Ernte.

Drei Jahre steht Herr Friedheim als künstlerischer Leider dem Stadttheater vor – drei Jahre rastloser, ernster Arbeit kann er überblicken und sich sagen: Ich habe mein Bestes gegeben, ich habe nach bestem künstlerischen Wissen und Gewissen getan. Und so ist es nur billig, daß die Öffentlichkeit der Tätigkeit dieses Mannes jederzeit die Anerkennung zuteil werden ließ, die er ganz verdiente, deshalb auch will ich mich mit der Vorführung des Wesentlichsten genügen.

Die Saison 1903, die besonders reich an Novitäten war, brachte uns die mustergiltigen Inszenierungen von Halbes "Strom", Werkmanns "Kreuzwegstürmer", Gustav Streichers "Stephan Fadinger", Schönherrs "Sonnwendtag", Beyerleins "Zapfenstreich." Diese Inszenierungen, die zum Teile ungeheure Anforderungen stellten, ließen Herrn Friedhelm als tüchtigen, unermüdlichen Regisseur erkennen. Daß Herr Friedheim als Schauspieler dem Regisseur in keiner Weise nachsteht, davon legten Zeugnis ab Leistungen, die er z.B. im Pfarrer v. Kirchfeld als Wurzelsepp, als Wachtmeister im Zapfenstreich, als Striese, als Stauffacher, als Pater in Renaissance bot. Von den Neuerscheinungen der nächsten Jahre sind besonders zu nennen "Traumulus," der zum Benefize Friedheims in Szene gesetzt wurde, ferner der "Schleier der Maya" und Seebachs "Die Unsichtbaren." In jedem dieser Werke hatte Herr Friedheim die Hauptgestalt zu verkörpern, seine glänzenden Leistungen als Direktor Niemeyer, als Sokrates und Baumeister werden noch in aller Erinnerung sein. Sein Spiel als Franz Moor trug ihm ein Anerkennungsschreiben von Herrn Bürgermeister Berger ein. Nicht unerwähnt seien die Verdienste gelassen, die Friedheim sich um die Aufführung von Wallensteins Lager und des Demetriusfragmentes erwarb. Eine reiche Auslese von Gutem und Bestem gab das heurige Spieljahr. Salzburg war die erste Provinzbühne, die nach Wien Schönherrs "Familie" brachte. Für seine glänzende Regieführung wurde Herrn Friedheim der persönliche Dank des Dichters zuteil. Ferner ist die Aufführung der "Brüder von St. Bernhard" zu nennen, des "Privatdozenten" (Prutz), "Klein Dorrits," und des Tendenzstückes "Stein unter Steinen." Eine Tat, auf die Herr Friedheim mit berechtigtem Stolz zurückblicken kann, war die wunderbare Inszenierung der "Salome."

Ununterbrochen, tatenfreudig hat Herr Friedheim bis an das Ende sein verantwortungsvolles Amt ausgefüllt, trotz der sich besonders in letzter Zeit häufenden Schwierigkeiten, die ihm von gewisser Seite in den Weg gelegt wurden. Am Samstag nimmt Herr Friedheim in "Narziß" von Salzburg Abschied. An das Publikum zu appellieren, ist wohl in diesem Falle nicht nötig, denn es wird Herrn Oberregisseur Friedheim in Erinnerung an das, was er unserem Theater gewesen, einen Ehrenabend veranstalten – ein kleiner Dank für große Mühe! In der Geschichte unseres Theater aber wird Herr Friedheim einen Ehrenplatz einnehmen, wie wenige – in der Geschichte, wie in der Erinnerung derer, die ihn in diesen Jahren seiner Tätigkeit hochschätzen lernten.

only through the disfavor of circumstances, in harmony with the events—like seed and harvest.

For three years Mr. Friedheim presided over the city theater as artistic leader—three years of restless, serious work he can look over and say to himself: I gave it my best, I applied my best artistic knowledge and conscience. And so it is only fair, that the public bestow their approval at all times on the activities of this man, which he completely earned, that is why I also want to satisfy myself with a presentation of the essentials.

The season of 1903, which was particularly rich with novelties, brought us the exemplary productions of Halbe's "River," Werkmann's "Crossroads' Attacker," Gustav Streicher's "Stephan Fadinger," Schönherr's "Solstice Day," Beyerlein's "Taps." These productions, which placed tremendous demands on details, showed Mr. Friedheim as an efficient, untiring stage director. That Mr. Friedheim is in no way inferior as actor than director is proven by his achievements, e.g. in "The Vicar from Kirchfeld" as Wurzelsepp, as the police constable in "Taps," as Striese, as Stauffacher, as Padre in "Renaissance." From the new productions of the next year, I want to single out "Traumulus," which was staged for Friedheim's benefit, and furthermore the "Veil of the Maya," and Seebach's "The Invisible Ones." In each of these works, Mr. Friedheim had to embody the major figure, his shining achievements as Headmaster Niemeyer, as Socrates and Master Builder should be still in the memories of everyone. His acting as Franz Moor resulted in a letter of commendation from Mayor Berger. Not to be omitted are the merits Friedheim earned with the performance of "Wallenstein's Encampment" and the fragment "Demetrius." A rich selection of the good and the best was presented during this year's play season. Salzburg was the first stage in the province that featured Schönherr's "Family" after Vienna. For his shining direction Mr. Friedheim received the personal thanks of the poet. Furthermore the performance of the "Brothers of St. Bernard" is to be mentioned, of the "Private Lecturer" (Prutz), "Small Dorrits," and the tendentious play "Stone between Stones." An act, which Mr. Friedheim can look back on with justifiable pride, is the wonderful production of "Salome."

Uninterrupted, joyful in deeds, Mr. Friedheim has fulfilled his responsible office until the end, despite several lately accumulating difficulties, which particular groups placed in his way. On Saturday, Mr. Friedheim takes his leave from Salzburg in "Narcissus." To appeal to the audience now is probably not necessary, because an evening of honor is prepared for Mr. Friedheim in memory of what he has been to our theater—a small thanks for great effort. However, in the history of our theater, Mr. Friedheim will have an esteemed place—in history, like in the memory of those who have learned to prize him in these years of his activity.

Gustav Streicher

Dieser Schriftsteller ist aus der österreichischen Provinzliteraturbewegung, einer Folge- und Begleiterscheinung des Naturalismus, hervorgegangen, die ihr Programm mit dem Schlagwort "Heimatkunst" formulierte und die, obwohl über sie genug geschrieben wurde, doch nicht jene Würdigung erfuhr, die ihr wohl hätte zukommen sollen. Mit dem plötzlichen Verebben des Naturalismus, der wie ein Sturm kam und ging, verlor selbstverständlich die Heimatkunst den Boden, in dem sie so tief Wurzel geschlagen hatte, und die ganze Bewegung, die, getragen von der jugendlich überquellenden Kraft eines guten und tapferen Willens, daran war, sich ihre eigensten Bahnen zu brechen, sah sich nun der nährenden und treibenden Kräfte beraubt. Und heute, da ungeahnte Möglichkeiten zu einer zukunftsträchtigen Kunst und dornicht- gefahrvolle Wege sich dem suchenden Blick offenbaren, ist der Sturm und Drang letzter Jahrzehnte eine Erinnerung, die eine erste Blässe deckt.

Unter den Vertretern ehemaliger Heimatkunst ist Gustav Streicher eine der markantesten Persönlichkeiten, und sein künstlerischer Werdegang ist ebenso interessant als lehrreich. Er fing mit dem Naturalismus an – sein Erstlingswerk "Am Nikolotag" ist von jener schweren, düsteren, heldenmütig-fanatischen Bodenständigkeit, die den konsequentesten Naturalisten eigen ist –, suchte in seinem folgenden Werk "Stephan Fadinger" den Weg zur historischen Tragödie großen Stils, immer noch auf Grund und mit den dichterischen Mitteln des Naturalismus, und fand sich endlich bei Ibsen, in seinem bisher nur wenig bekannten Drama "Liebesopfer", das ein psychologisches Problem subtilster Art mit den Mitteln der modernen Seelenanalyse zu lösen versucht; nach etlichen Jahren scheinbarer Untätigkeit (eine Komödie, die das Problem der modernen Frau umfassend gestalten will, blieb Fragment) zeigt Gustav Streicher sich in einer neuen Phase seiner Entwicklung, als Neuromantiker.

Die Entwicklung dieses Schriftstellers könnte verwunderlich und seltsam erscheinen, wenn sie nicht aus den zu Anfang geschilderten Verhältnissen ihre natürliche Erklärung fände. Und erklärlich ist es, wenn ein Dichter, dessen Eigenart eine so ausgesprochen dramatische ist, dessen Talent für eine geradlinige Entwicklung vorgeschaffen erscheinen mußte, solch tiefe Krisen durchzumachen hatte. Sein Drama "Mona Violanta", das Streicher Freitag abends im Mirabellsaale las, ist von der Art jener Seelentragödien, wie die Neuromantiker sie lieben. Die einen in kühle Ekstase versetzen, die einen träumen machen, deren Handlung man nicht erzählen sollte, weil soviel dabei verloren geht. Man denkt und träumt dieser seltsamen Violanta nach, die wie ein kühler Schatten durch einen Traum schreitet, fühlt den Ekel, der ihren Leib schüttelt, gedenkt sie des toten Gatten, der mit senilen Perversionen ihren blütenjungen Leib begeifert hat; man glaubt das Gespenst des Toten zu sehen, wenn Violanta ihn an ihrer Seite schreiten sieht, mit scheußlichen, lasterhaften Geberden widerliche Berührung mit seinem Weibe suchend, hört das Weib aufschreien und zusammenbrechen unter der Gewalt der toten Macht, und

Gustav Streicher

This writer has arisen out of the Austrian provincial literary movement, a follower and by-product of naturalism, which formulated its program with the catchword "homeland-art" and which, although enough was written over it, still did not experience the appreciation that should have come. With the sudden ebbing away of naturalism, which came and went like a storm, naturally homeland-art lost its ground, in which it had become deeply rooted, and the whole movement, based on the juvenile overflowing strength of a good and valiant will, was to break its most innate course, and saw itself now robbed of its nourishing and impelling forces. And today, when the unforeseen possibilities of a promising art and thorny, dangerous ways reveal themselves to the searching view, the storm and stress of the last decades become just a memory that covers a first pallor.

Among the representatives of this former homeland-art movement, Gustav Streicher is one of the most distinctive personalities, and his artistic development is just as interesting as instructive. He began with naturalism—his first work "On Nikolo Day" is from that heavy, dark, heroic-fanatical grassrootedness which is peculiar to the most consistent naturalists—, sought in his next work, "Stephan Fadinger," the way to a historical tragedy in an ample style, still based on and within the poetic methods of naturalism, and found himself finally beside Ibsen, with a little known drama called "Love's Sacrifice" that tries to solve a psychological problem of the subtlest kind through the methods of modern soul-analysis; after some years of apparent inactivity (a comedy, which would extensively shape the problem of the modern woman, remained a fragment) Gustav Streicher shows up in a new phase of his development as a new-romantic.

The development of this writer could appear astonishing and strange, if it did not find its natural explanation from the conditions described at the beginning. And it is explainable, if a poet, whose essence is so pronounced dramatically, whose talent for a linear development had to appear before, had gone through such deep crises. His drama "Mona Violanta" that Streicher read Friday evening in Mirabell Hall is from the tradition of soulful tragedies the new-romantics love. They move one into cool ecstasies, which make one dream, whose plot one should not tell because in doing so much gets lost. One ponders and dreams about this strange Violanta, who walks like a cool shadow through a dream, feels the disgust that shakes her body when she remembers her dead husband, who with senile perversion drools over her body blossoming with youth; one believes to see the ghost of the dead when Violanta sees him walking at her side, with abhorrent, vicious gestures seeking sickening contact with his wife, hears the woman scream out and break down under the terrible force of the dead power, and knows: she must summon the rawest forces of life to get rid of the dead, must become a strumpet in order not to die away in hysterical convulsions. It is strange how these verses penetrate the problem, how often the sound of the word expresses an unspeakable thought and sets the volatile mood. In these verses is something of the sweet, woman-like

weiß: die muß des Lebens roheste Gewalten herbeirufen, um den Toten loszuwerden, muß Dirne werden, um nicht in hysterischen Krämpfen zu vergehen. Es ist seltsam, wie diese Verse das Problem durchdringen, wie oft der Klang des Wortes einen unaussprechlichen Gedanken ausdrückt und die flüchtige Stimmung festhält. In diesen Versen ist etwas von der süßen, frauenhaften Überredungskunst, die uns verführt, dem Melos des Wortes zu lauschen und nicht zu achten des Wortes Inhalt und Gewicht; der Mollklang dieser Sprache stimmt die Sinne nachdenklich und erfüllt das Blut mit träumerischer Müdigkeit. Erst in der letzten Szene, da der Kondottiere auftritt, schmettert ein voller, eherner Ton in Dur über die Szene, und in fliegender Steigerung löst sich das Drama in einem dionysischen Gesang der Lebensfreudigkeit.

Daß der vortragende Dichter nicht völlig vermochte, die ganze Stimmungsgewalt seines Werkes zur Geltung zu bringen, daß manches von den glitzernden Schönheiten seines Dialogs verloren ging, das soll liebenswürdig entschuldigt werden. Das Publikum ist ihm gerne in seine Welt gefolgt und hat's ihm mit Dankbarkeit gelohnt, daß er für eine Stunde sie in die Tiefe eines seltsamen Daseins schauen ließ.

[Jakobus und die Frauen. Roman von Franz Karl Ginskey; L. Staackmanns Verlag, Leipzig.]

In diesem Buch ist Stimmung, leider nur Stimmung. In Stimmung ertrinkt die an und für sich schwächliche Handlung, die Psychologie ist unklar und plätschert auf lieblicher Oberfläche, die Charakteristik der Personen ist dürftig, schemenhaft, verworren. Und für all diese kapitalen Mängel sollen einige hübsche Stimmungsbilder und Lyrismen entschädigen. Nein! Diesem Buch fehlt alles zum Roman, darüber täuscht einen nicht die gesuchte Feierlichkeit eines Stils, der seit Jakob Wassermanns "Renate Fuchs" so fleißig gehandhabt wird, und mit dem die verschrobensten, langweiligsten, seichtesten Dinge pomphaft aufgebauscht werden. Mauvaise music! Und wenn ich überdenke, daß der gallische Roman den Gipfelpunkt eines beispiellosen Formenkults darstellt, und die russischen Epopöen der Urquell der gewaltigsten Geistesrevolution geworden sind, so gilt mir der Großteil unserer mitteleuropäischen Romanproduktion nicht mehr, als – bedrucktes Papier.

art of persuasion which seduces us to listen to the melody of the word, and not to notice the word's substance and weight; the minor-sound of this language tunes the senses thoughtfully and fulfills the blood with dreamy tiredness. Foremost in the last scene, when the condottiere rises, a full, brazen tone blares in major key over the scene and the drama loosens up with a flying culmination into a Dionysian song of life's joyfulness.

That the lecturing poet was not completely able to emphasize the entire force of mood of his work, that much of the glittering beauty of the dialogues was lost, should be kindly excused. The public followed him gladly into his world and rewarded with gratitude for an hour of having a look into the depths of a strange existence.

[Jakobus and the Women. A novel by Franz Karl Ginskey; L. Staackmann's Publishing House, Leipzig.]

In this book mood is, unfortunately, just mood. The already weak action drowns in mood, the psychology is unclear and splashes on a lovely surface, the characterizations of the people are meager, unrealistic, confusing. And for all these principal defects there should be some pretty affected sceneries or lyricisms to compensate. No! This book is missing everything to make it a novel, about which nobody is mislead by the sought-after solemnity of style that is handled so industriously since Jakob Wassermann's "Renate Fuchs," and with which the most eccentric, boring, and shallow things become exaggerated. *Mauvaise music!* And if I consider that the Gallic novel represents the zenith of an unparalleled cult of form, and that the Russian epic became the fountainhead of the most enormous spiritual revolution, then the majority of our novels produced in Central Europe strike me as nothing more than—printed paper.

The poet's circle Minerva (Georg sitting left), Salzburg about 1906

1908

1909

Military Medical Assistance, 1912

Military Service, 1910–1911

1911

Venice, 1913

Trakl with Paula Kopie, 1913

May, 1914

May, 1914

May, 1914

Silhouettes of Georg and Grete, made
1910 in the Prater, Vienna

Grete, 1912

Grete, after 1912

Grete, passport photo 1912 or later

Georg's parents in the garden

Ludwig von Ficker, mentor, and
publisher of *Der Brenner*

Karl Röck, editor of Trakl's Complete
Poetical Works

Karl Kraus, publisher of *Die Frackle*

Erhard Buschbeck, 1913

Karl Borromäus Heinrich

Adolf Loos

Oskar Kokoschka, 1914

Program of Trakl's only public reading in Innsbruck

Program sheet with the premiere of "Totentag" in 1906

Trakl's Grave Site in Mühlau near Innsbruck. He is buried beside Ludwig von Ficker.

Trakl's Grave Site Plaque

Part Five:

The Bequest

Sammlung 1909

Von Trakl selbst als Sichtung seiner Lyrik
bis zu diesem Jahr zusammengestellt. Später hat er
diese Texte nicht mehr gelten lassen.

Drei Träume

I

Mich däucht, ich träumte von Blätterfall,
Von weiten Wäldern und dunklen Seen,
Von trauriger Worte Widerhall –
Doch konnt' ich ihren Sinn nicht verstehn.

Mich däucht, ich träumte von Sternenfall,
Von blasser Augen weinendem Flehn,
Von eines Lächelns Widerhall –
Doch konnt' ich seinen Sinn nicht verstehn.

Wie Blätterfall, wie Sternenfall,
So sah ich mich ewig kommen und gehn,
Eines Traumes unsterblicher Widerhall –
Doch konnt' ich seinen Sinn nicht verstehn.

II

In meiner Seele dunklem Spiegel
Sind Bilder niegeseh'ner Meere,
Verlass'ner, tragisch phantastischer Länder,
Zerfließend ins Blaue, Ungefähre.

Meine Seele gebar blut-purpurne Himmel
Durchglüht von gigantischen, prasselnden Sonnen,
Und seltsam belebte, schimmernde Gärten,
Die dampften von schwülen, tödlichen Wonnen.

Und meiner Seele dunkler Bronnen

Collection 1909

Arranged by Trakl as a survey of his poems
written up to 1909. Later he did not consider
these texts to be of any importance.

Three Dreams

I

I think I dreamed of falling leaves,
Of wide forests and dark lakes,
Of sad words' echo—
Yet I could not understand their meaning.

I think I dreamed of falling stars,
Of the weeping entreaty of pale eyes,
Of a smile's echo—
Yet I could not understand its meaning.

Like falling leaves, like falling stars,
So I saw myself eternally coming and going,
An immortal dream's echo—
Yet I could not understand its meaning.

II

In my soul's dark mirror
Are pictures of never-seen seas,
Of abandoned, tragic imaginary lands,
Dissolving into blue, vagueness.

My soul bore blood-purple skies
Aglow with gigantic, crackling suns,
And strangely animated, shimmering gardens
That steamed with muggy, deadly delights.

And my soul's dark fountain

Schuf Bilder ungeheurer Nächte,
Bewegt von namenlosen Gesängen
Und Atemwehen ewiger Mächte.

Meine Seele schauert erinnerungsdunkel,
Als ob sie in allem sich wiederfände –
In unergründlichen Meeren und Nächten,
Und tiefen Gesängen, ohn' Anfang und Ende.

III

Ich sah viel Städte als Flammenraub
Und Greuel auf Greuel häuften die Zeiten,
Und sah viel Völker verwesen zu Staub,
Und alles in Vergessenheit gleiten.

Ich sah die Götter stürzen zur Nacht,
Die heiligsten Harfen ohnmächtig zerschellen,
Und aus Verwesung neu entfacht,
Ein neues Leben zum Tage schwellen.

Zum Tage schwellen und wieder vergehn,
Die ewig gleiche Tragödia,
Die also wir spielen sonder Verstehn,

Und deren wahnsinnsnächtige Qual
Der Schönheit sanfte Gloria
Umkränzt als lächelndes Dornenall.

Von den stillen Tagen

So geisterhaft sind diese späten Tage
Gleichwie der Blick von Kranken, hergesendet
Ins Licht. Doch ihrer Augen stumme Klage
Beschattet Nacht, der sie schon zugewendet.

Sie lächeln wohl und denken ihrer Feste,
Wie man nach Liedern bebt, die halb vergessen,
Und Worte sucht für eine traurige Geste,
Die schon verblaßt in Schweigen ungemessen.

Created pictures of immense nights,
Moved by nameless cantos
And the breaths of eternal powers.

My soul shudders dark with memory,
As if it found itself in everything—
In unfathomable seas and nights,
And deep cantos without beginning and end.

III

I saw many towns as if robbed by flame
And the times accumulated atrocity after atrocity,
And saw a lot of people putrefy to dust,
And everything float into oblivion.

I saw the gods fall to the night,
The holiest harps powerlessly smashed,
And kindled anew from putrefaction,
A new life swelling to the day.

Swelling to the day and again passing,
The eternally identical tragedy,
That thus we play without understanding,

And its insanity's nightly torture
Wreathes the gently glory of beauty
Like a smiling universe of thorns.

From the Still Days

So ghostly are these late days
Just like the look of sick people sent here
In the light. Yet the night, toward which they already turn,
Shades the muted lament of their eyes.

They probably smile and recall their celebrations,
How one is moved after songs, half forgotten,
And searches words for a sad gesture,
Already grown pale in silence unmeasured.

So spielt um kranke Blumen noch die Sonne
Und läßt von einer todeskühlen Wonne
Sie schauern in den dünnen, klaren Lüften.

Die roten Wälder flüstern und verdämmern,
Und todesnächtiger hallt der Spechte Hämmern
Gleichwie ein Widerhall aus dumpfen Grüften.

Dämmerung

Zerwühlt, verzerrt bist du von jedem Schmerz
Und bebst vom Mißton aller Melodien,
Zersprungne Harfe du – ein armes Herz,
Aus dem der Schwermut kranke Blumen blühn.

Wer hat den Feind, den Mörder dir bestellt,
Der deiner Seele letzten Funken stahl,
Wie er entgöttert diese karge Welt
Zur Hure, häßlich, krank, verwesungsfahl!

Von Schatten schwingt sich noch ein wilder Tanz,
Zu kraus zerrißnem, seelenlosem Klang,
Ein Reigen um der Schönheit Dornenkranz,

Der welk den Sieger, den verlornen, krönt
– Ein schlechter Preis, um den Verzweiflung rang,
Und der die lichte Gottheit nicht versöhnt.

Herbst
[1. Fassung]

Am Abend, wenn die Glocken Frieden läuten,
Folg' ich der Vögel wundervollen Flügen,
Die lang geschart, gleich frommen Pilgerzügen,
Entschwinden in den herbstlich klaren Weiten.

Hinwandelnd durch den nachtverschloßnen Garten,

So the sun still plays around ill flowers
And lets them shiver in the thin, clear airs
With a death-cool delight.

The red forests whisper and darken,
And with more nightly-death the woodpeckers' hammering resounds
Just like an echo from airless crypts.

Dusk

You are rumpled, distorted by every pain
And shake with the discord of all melodies,
You broken harp—a poor heart,
From which gloom's sick flowers bloom.

Who has ordered the enemy, the murderer for you,
Who stole the last spark of your soul,
How he makes this scanty world godless
To a whore, ugly, ill, pale with putrefaction!

From shadows a wild dance still swings
To fuzzily ruptured, soulless sound,
A round dance around beauty's thorn wreath,

Which witheringly crowns the lost winner,
—A wretched prize, wrung from despair,
And that fails to reconcile the bright divinity.

Autumn
[version 1 of 'Decay']

In the evening, when the bells ring peace,
I follow the wonderful flights of birds
That in long rows, like devout processions of pilgrims,
Disappear into the clear autumn vastness.

Wandering through the garden closed for the night

Träum' ich nach ihren helleren Geschicken,
Und fühl' der Stunden Weiser kaum mehr rücken –
So folg' ich über Wolken ihren Fahrten.

Da macht ein Hauch mich von Verfall erzittern.
Ein Vogel klagt in den entlaubten Zweigen
Es schwankt der rote Wein an rostigen Gittern,

Indess' wie blasser Kinder Todesreigen,
Um dunkle Brunnenränder, die verwittern
Im Wind sich fröstelnd fahle Astern neigen.

Das Grauen

Ich sah mich durch verlass'ne Zimmer gehn.
– Die Sterne tanzten irr auf blauem Grunde,
Und auf den Feldern heulten laut die Hunde,
Und in den Wipfeln wühlte wild der Föhn.

Doch plötzlich: Stille! Dumpfe Fieberglut
Läßt giftige Blumen blühn aus meinem Munde,
Aus dem Geäst fällt wie aus einer Wunde
Blaß schimmernd Tau, und fällt, und fällt wie Blut.

Aus eines Spiegels trügerischer Leere
Hebt langsam sich, und wie in Ungefähre
Aus Graun und Finsternis ein Antlitz: Kain!

Sehr leise rauscht die samtene Portiere,
Durchs Fenster schaut der Mond gleichwie ins Leere,
Da bin mit meinem Mörder ich allein.

Andacht

Das Unverlorne meiner jungen Jahre
Ist stille Andacht an ein Glockenläuten,
An aller Kirchen dämmernde Altare
Und ihrer blauen Kuppeln Himmelweiten.

I dream after their brighter destinies
And hardly feel the motion of the hour hands.
Thus I follow their journey over the clouds.

Then a whiff of decay makes me tremble.
A bird complains in branches stripped of leaves.
The red wine sways on rusty trellises.

While like the death-dances of pale children
Around dark fountain rims that weather,
Shivering blue asters bend in the wind.

The Horror

I saw myself go through abandoned rooms.
—The stars danced crazily on blue ground,
And on the fields the dogs howled loud,
And in the treetops the foehn rummaged wildly.

But suddenly: stillness! Dull fever-glow
Lets poisonous flowers bloom from my mouth,
From the branches like out of a wound
Pale gleaming dew falls, and falls, and falls like blood.

From a mirror's deceitful emptiness
A countenance slowly lifts in the vagueness
Out of horror and sinisterness: Cain!

Very quietly the velvet curtains rustle,
Through the window the moon peers as if into emptiness,
There I am alone with my murderer.

Devotion

Not lost from my young years
Is silent devotion to a sound of bells,
To the dusking altars of all churches
And their blue domes' heavenly expanses.

An einer Orgel abendliche Weise,
An weiter Plätze dunkelndes Verhallen,
Und an ein Brunnenplätschern, sanft und leise
Und süß, wie unverstandnes Kinderlallen.

Ich seh' mich träumend still die Hände falten
Und längst vergessene Gebete flüstern,
Und frühe Schwermut meinen Blick umdüstern.

Da schimmert aus verworrenen Gestalten
Ein Frauenbild, umflort von finstrer Trauer,
Und gießt in mich den Kelch verruchter Schauer.

Sabbath

Ein Hauch von fiebernd giftigen Gewächsen
Macht träumen mich in mondnen Dämmerungen,
Und leise fühl' ich mich umrankt, umschlungen,
Und seh' gleich einem Sabbath toller Hexen

Bundfarbne Blüten in der Spiegel Hellen
Aus meinem Herzen keltern Flammenbrünste,
Und ihre Lippen kundig aller Künste
Aus meiner trunknen Kehle wütend schwellen.

Pestfarbne Blumen tropischer Gestade,
Die reichen meinen Lippen ihre Schalen,
Die trüben Geiferbronnen ekler Qualen.

Und eine schlingt – o rasende Mänade –
Mein Fleisch, ermattet von den schwülen Dünsten,
Und schmerzverzückt von fürchterlichen Brünsten.

To an organ's tune at evening,
To wide squares fading in darkness,
And to a fountain that splashes, gently and quietly
And sweetly, like the babbling of unintelligible children.

I see myself dreaming quietly, folding the hands,
And whispering prayers long forgotten,
And early sadness sombering my gaze.

Because a woman's figure, wreathed
By sinister grief, glimmers from confused shapes
And pours into me the chalice of nefarious shudders.

Sabbath

A whiff of feverish poisonous plants
Makes me dream in lunar dusks,
And quietly I feel entwined, embraced,
And see blood-colored blossoms in the mirrors' brightness

Like a sabbath of insane witches
Pressing flaming prurience from my heart,
And their lips, experienced in all arts,
Swell enraged near my drunken throat.

Pestilence colored flowers from tropical beaches
Offer their chalices to my lips,
Cloudy fountains of drool from nauseating tortures.

And one gobbles—o raving Maenad—
My flesh, weary from the sultry vapors,
And enraptured in pain by terrible prurience.

Gesang zur Nacht

I

Vom Schatten eines Hauchs geboren
Wir wandeln in Verlassenheit
Und sind im Ewigen verloren,
Gleich Opfern unwissend, wozu sie geweiht.

Gleich Bettlern ist uns nichts zu eigen,
Uns Toren am verschloßnen Tor.
Wie Blinde lauschen wir ins Schweigen,
In dem sich unser Flüstern verlor.

Wir sind die Wandrer ohne Ziele,
Die Wolken, die der Wind verweht,
Die Blumen, zitternd in Todeskühle,
Die warten, bis man sie niedermäht.

II

Daß sich die letzte Qual an mir erfülle,
Ich wehr' euch nicht, ihr feindlich dunklen Mächte.
Ihr seid die Straße hin zur großen Stille,
Darauf wir schreiten in die kühlsten Nächte.

Es macht mich euer Atem lauter brennen,
Geduld! Der Stern verglüht, die Träume gleiten
In jene Reiche, die sich uns nicht nennen,
Und die wir traumlos dürfen nur beschreiten.

III

Du dunkle Nacht, du dunkles Herz,
Wer spiegelt eure heiligsten Gründe,
Und eurer Bosheit letzte Schlünde?
Die Maske starrt vor unsrem Schmerz –

Vor unsrem Schmerz, vor unsrer Lust
Der leeren Maske steinern Lachen,
Daran die irdnen Dinge brachen,
Und das uns selber nicht bewußt.

Song in the Night

I

Born from the shadow of a breath
We wander in abandonment
And are lost in the eternal,
Like victims ignorant of why they are consecrated.

Like beggars nothing is our own,
We fools at the locked gate.
As blind people, we listen in the silence
In which our whisper is lost.

We are the wanderers without destinations,
The clouds which the wind blows away,
The flowers shaking in death's coolness
That wait until one mows them down.

II

So that the last torment becomes complete with me,
I do not defend you, you hostile dark powers.
You are the road to great stillness
Upon which we stride in the coolest nights.

Your breath makes me burn louder,
Patience! The star dies down, the dreams glide
In those realms not named to us,
And which we may only walk along dreamlessly.

III

You dark night, you dark heart,
Who mirrors your holiest ground,
And the last abysses of your malice?
The mask stares before our pain—

Before our pain, before our lust
The empty mask's stony laughter,
On it the earthen things broke,
And ourselves unconsciously.

Und steht vor uns ein fremder Feind,
Der höhnt, worum wir sterbend ringen,
Daß trüber unsre Lieder klingen
Und dunkel bleibt, was in uns weint.

IV

Du bist der Wein, der trunken macht,
Nun blüh ich hin in süßen Tänzen
Und muß mein Leid mit Blumen kränzen!
So will's dein tiefster Sinn, o Nacht!

Ich bin die Harfe in deinem Schoß,
Nun ringt um meine letzten Schmerzen
Dein dunkles Lied in meinem Herzen
Und macht mich ewig, wesenlos.

V

Tiefe Ruh – o tiefe Ruh!
Keine fromme Glocke läutet,
Süße Schmerzensmutter du –
Deinen Frieden todgeweitet.

Schließ mit deinen kühlen, guten
Händen alle Wunden zu –
Daß nach innen sie verbluten –
Süße Schmerzensmutter – du!

VI

O laß mein Schweigen sein dein Lied!
Was soll des Armen Flüstern dir,
Der aus des Lebens Gärten schied?
Laß namenlos dich sein in mir –

Die traumlos in mir aufgebaut,
Wie eine Glocke ohne Ton,
Wie meiner Schmerzen süße Braut
Und meiner Schlafe trunkner Mohn.

VII

Blumen hörte ich sterben im Grund

And a strange enemy stands before us,
Who jeers, over which we struggle dying,
So that our songs sound cloudier
And what weeps in us remains dark.

IV

You are the wine that makes drunk,
Now I bleed in sweet dances
And must wreath my suffering with flowers!
So your deepest mind wills, o night!

I am the harp in your womb,
Now your dark song struggles
For the last pains in my heart
And makes me eternal, unreal.

V

Deep rest—o deep rest!
No devout bell rings,
You sweet mother of pain—
Your deathly expanse of peace.

Close all wounds
With your cool, good hands—
So that inward they bleed to death—
Sweet mother of pain—you!

VI

O let my silence be your song!
What should the poor person whisper to you
Who is separated from life's gardens?
Let you be nameless in me—

Who are dreamlessly built up in me,
Like a bell without tone,
Like my pain's sweet bride
And the drunken poppy of my sleepings.

VII

I heard flowers die in the ground

Und der Bronnen trunkne Klage
Und ein Lied aus Glockenmund,
Nacht, und eine geflüsterte Frage;
Und ein Herz – o todeswund,
Jenseits seiner armen Tage.

VIII

Das Dunkel löschte mich schweigend aus,
Ich ward ein toter Schatten im Tag –
Da trat ich aus der Freunde Haus
In die Nacht hinaus.

Nun wohnt ein Schweigen im Herzen mir,
Das fühlt nicht nach den öden Tag –
Und lächelt wie Dornen auf zu dir,
Nacht – für und für!

IX

O Nacht, du stummes Tor vor meinem Leid,
Verbluten sieh dies dunkle Wundenmal
Und ganz geneigt den Taumelkelch der Qual!
O Nacht, ich bin bereit!

O Nacht, du Garten der Vergessenheit
Um meiner Armut weltverschloss'nen Glanz,
Das Weinlaub welkt, es welkt der Dornenkranz.
O komm, du hohe Zeit!

X

Es hat mein Dämon einst gelacht,
Da war ich ein Licht in schimmernden Gärten,
Und hatte Spiel und Tanz zu Gefährten
Und der Liebe Wein, der trunken macht.

Es hat mein Dämon einst geweint,
Da war ich ein Licht in schmerzlichen Gärten
Und hatte die Demut zum Gefährten,
Deren Glanz der Armut Haus bescheint.

Doch nun mein Dämon nicht weint noch lacht,
Bin ich ein Schatten verlorener Gärten

And the wells' drunken lament
And a song from the bell's mouth,
Night, and a whispered question;
And a heart—o death-wound,
Beyond its poor days.

VIII

The darkness extinguished me in silence,
I became a dead shadow in the day—
Then I stepped from the house of joy
Outside in the night.

Now a silence dwells in my heart
That does not feel the dreary day—
And smiles up to you like thorns,
Night—forever and ever!

IX

O night, you mute gate before my suffering,
See this dark stigmata bleeding to death
And the reeling chalice of agony completely bowed!
O night, I am ready!

O night, you garden of oblivion
Around my poverty's closed-to-the-world radiance,
The wine leaves wilt, the wreath of thorns wilts.
O come, you grand time!

X

My demon once laughed
When I was a light in gleaming gardens,
And play and dance were my companions
And the wine of love, which makes drunk.

My demon once wept
When I was a light in painful gardens
And humility, whose radiance shines
On poverty's house, was my companion.

Yet now my demon neither weeps nor laughs,
I am a shadow of lost gardens

Und habe zum todesdunklen Gefährten
Das Schweigen der leeren Mitternacht.

XI

Mein armes Lächeln, das um dich rang,
Mein schluchzendes Lied im Dunkel verklang.
Nun will mein Weg zu Ende gehn.

Laß treten mich in deinen Dom
Wie einst, ein Tor, einfältig, fromm,
Und stumm anbetend vor dir stehn.

XII

Du bis in tiefer Mitternacht
Ein totes Gestade an schweigendem Meer,
Ein totes Gestade: Nimmermehr!
Du bist in tiefer Mitternacht.

Du bist in tiefer Mitternacht
Der Himmel, in dem du als Stern geglüht,
Ein Himmel, aus dem kein Gott mehr blüht.
Du bist in tiefer Mitternacht.

Du bist in tiefer Mitternacht
Ein Unempfangner in süßem Schoß,
Und nie gewesen, wesenlos!
Du bist in tiefer Mitternacht.

Das tiefe Lied

Aus tiefer Nacht ward ich befreit.
Meine Seele staunt in Unsterblichkeit,
Meine Seele lauscht über Raum und Zeit
Der Melodie der Ewigkeit!
Nicht Tag und Lust, nicht Nacht und Leid
Ist Melodie der Ewigkeit,
Und seit ich erlauscht die Ewigkeit,
Fühl nimmermehr ich Lust und Leid!

And my death-dark companion is
The silence of the empty midnight.

XI

My poor smile which struggled for you,
My sobbing song faded away in darkness.
Now my path comes to an end.

Let me tread in your cathedral
Like once, a fool, simple minded, devoutly,
And stand adoring mutely before you.

XII

You are in deep midnight
A dead shore at the silent sea,
A dead shore: Never more!
You are in deep midnight.

You are in deep midnight
The heaven in which you glowed as a star,
A heaven from which no more God blossoms.
You are in deep midnight.

You are in deep midnight
An unbegotten in sweet womb,
And never existing, unreal!
You are in deep midnight.

The Deep Song

From deep night I was released.
My soul is astonished in immortality,
My soul listens over space and time
To the melody of eternity!
Neither day and lust, nor night and suffering
Is the melody of eternity,
And since I listened to eternity
I feel no more lust and suffering!

Ballade

Ein Narre schrieb drei Zeichen in Sand,
Eine bleiche Magd da vor ihm stand.
Laut sang, o sang das Meer.

Sie hielt einen Becher in der Hand,
Der schimmerte bis auf zum Rand,
Wie Blut so rot und schwer.

Kein Wort ward gesprochen – die Sonne schwand,
Da nahm der Narre aus ihrer Hand
Den Becher und trank ihn leer.

Da löschte sein Licht in ihrer Hand,
Der Wind verwehte drei Zeichen im Sand –
Laut sang, o sang das Meer.

Ballade

Es klagt ein Herz: Du findest sie nicht,
Ihre Heimat ist wohl weit von hier,
Und seltsam ist ihr Angesicht!
Es weint die Nacht an einer Tür!

Im Marmorsaal brennt Licht an Licht,
O dumpf, o dumpf! Es stirbt wer hier!
Es flüstert wo: O kommst du nicht?
Es weint die Nacht an einer Tür!

Ein Schluchzen noch: O säh' er das Licht!
Da ward es dunkel dort und hier –
Ein Schluchzen: Bruder, o betest du nicht?
Es weint die Nacht an einer Tür.

Ballad

A fool wrote three signs in the sand,
A pale maiden stood there before him.
Loudly the sea sang, o it sang.

She held a cup in the hand
Which gleamed up to the edge,
Like blood so red and heavy.

No word was spoken—the sun faded away,
Then the fool took the cup
Out of her hand and drank it empty.

Then its light extinguished in her hand,
The wind blew away the three signs in the sand—
Loudly the sea sang, o it sang.

Ballad

A heart laments: you do not find her,
Her native country is probably far from here,
And her face is strange!
The night weeps by a door!

In the marble hall light upon light burns,
O musty, o musty! Somebody dies here!
A whisper somewhere: o do you not come?
The night weeps by a door!

A sobbing still: o that he would see the light!
Then it became dark there and here—
A sobbing: brother, o do you not pray?
The night weeps by a door.

Ballade

Ein schwüler Garten stand die Nacht.
Wir verschwiegen uns, was uns grauend erfaßt.
Davon sind unsre Herzen erwacht
Und erlagen unter des Schweigens Last.

Es blühte kein Stern in jener Nacht
Und niemand war, der für uns bat.
Ein Dämon nur hat im Dunkel gelacht.
Seid alle verflucht! Da ward die Tat.

Melusine

An meinen Fenstern weint die Nacht –
Die Nacht ist stumm, es weint wohl der Wind,
Der Wind, wie ein verlornes Kind –
Was ist's, das ihn so weinen macht?
O arme Melusine!

Wie Feuer ihr Haar im Sturme weht,
Wie Feuer an Wolken vorüber und klagt –
Da spricht für dich, du arme Magd,
Mein Herz ein stilles Nachtgebet!
O arme Melusine!

Verfall

Es weht ein Wind! Hinlöschend singen
Die grünen Lichter – groß und satt
Erfüllt der Mond den hohen Saal,
Den keine Feste mehr durchklingen.

Die Ahnenbilder lächeln leise
Und fern – ihr letzter Schatten fiel,
Der Raum ist von Verwesung schwül,
Den Raben stumm umziehn im Kreise.

Ballad

A sultry garden stood the night.
We kept tight-lipped about what grips us horribly.
From this our hearts awoke
And succumbed under the burden of silence.

No star blossomed in that night
And nobody asked for us.
Only a demon has laughed in the darkness.
Be cursed everyone! Then the deed came into being.

Melusine

At my windows the night weeps—
The night is mute, it's probably the wind that weeps,
The wind, like a lost child—
What is it that makes him weep so?
O poor Melusine!

Like fire her hair blows in the storm,
Like fire in passing clouds, and laments—
There for you, you poor maiden,
My heart speaks a still night prayer!
O poor Melusine!

Decay

A wind is blowing! The green lights
Sing extinguished—large and satiated
The moon fulfills the exulted hall
Where no more celebrations sound.

The ancestral portraits quietly smile
And far-off—their last shadow fell,
The room is sultry with putrefaction
Around which ravens mutely move in circles.

Verlorner Sinn vergangner Zeiten
Blickt aus den steinernen Masken her,
Die schmerzverzerrt und daseinsleer
Hintrauern in Verlassenheiten.

Versunkner Gärten kranke Düfte
Umkosen leise den Verfall –
Wie schluchzender Worte Widerhall
Hinzitternd über off'ne Grüfte.

Gedicht

Ein frommes Lied kam zu mir her:
Du einfach Herz, du heilig Blut,
O nimm von mir so böse Glut!
Da ward's erhört und klagt nicht mehr!

Mein Herz ist jeder Sünde schwer
Und zehrt sich auf in böser Glut,
Und ruft nicht an das heilige Blut,
Und ist so stumm und tränenleer.

Nachtlied

Über nächtlich dunkle Fluten
Sing' ich meine traurigen Lieder,
Lieder, die wie Wunden bluten.
Doch kein Herz trägt sie mir wieder
Durch das Dunkel her.

Nur die nächtlich dunklen Fluten
Rauschen, schluchzen meine Lieder,
Lieder, die von Wunden bluten,
Tragen an mein Herz sie wieder
Durch das Dunkel her.

A lost sense of past times
Looks from the stony masks,
Pain distorted and empty of existence
Mourning in abandonments.

Sick perfumes of sunken gardens
Quietly caress the decay—
Like the echo of sobbing words
Quivering over open crypts.

Poem

A pious song came to me here:
You simple heart, you holy blood,
O take from me such an evil fervor!
There it was heard and laments no more!

My heart is heavy with every sin
And is exhausted in evil fervor,
And does not plead to the holy blood,
And is so mute and empty of tears.

Night Song

Over nocturnal dark floods
I sing my sad songs,
Songs which bleed like wounds.
Yet no heart carries them to me again
Through the darkness.

Only the nocturnal dark waters
Rush, sob my songs,
Songs which bleed from wounds,
They carry them to my heart again
Through the darkness.

An einem Fenster

Über den Dächern das Himmelsblau,
Und Wolken, die vorüberziehn,
Vorm Fenster ein Baum im Frühlingstau,

Und ein Vogel, der trunken himmelan schnellt,
Von Blüten ein verlorener Duft –
Es fühlt ein Herz: Das ist die Welt!

Die Stille wächst und der Mittag glüht!
Mein Gott, wie ist die Welt so reich!
Ich träume und träum' und das Leben flieht,

Das Leben da draußen – irgendwo
Mir fern durch ein Meer von Einsamkeit!
Es fühlt's ein Herz und wird nicht froh!

Farbiger Herbst
[1. Fassung]

Der Brunnen singt, die Wolken stehn
Im klaren Blau, die weißen, zarten;
Bedächtig, stille Menschen gehn
Da drunten im abendblauen Garten.

Der Ahnen Marmor ist ergraut
Ein Vogelflug streift in die Weiten
Ein Faun mit toten Augen schaut
Nach Schatten, die ins Dunkel gleiten.

Das Laub fällt rot vom alten Baum
Und kreist herein durchs offne Fenster,
In dunklen Feuern glüht der Raum,
Darin die Schatten, wie Gespenster.

Opaliger Dunst webt über das Gras,
Eine Wolke von welken, gebleichten Düften,
Im Brunnen leuchtet wie ein grünes Glas

By a Window

Above the sky-blue of roofs
And clouds that pass by,
Before the window a tree in spring dew,

And a bird shoots up skyward drunk,
A lost scent of blossoms—
A heart feels: This is the world!

The stillness increases and the midday glows!
My God, how rich is the world!
I dream and dream and life flees,

Life there outdoors—somewhere
Distant to me because of a sea of loneliness!
A heart feels it and doesn't become glad!

Colorful Autumn
[version 1 of 'Music in Mirabell']

The fountain sings, the clouds stand
In clear blueness, white, delicate;
Silent people wander thoughtfully
Down there in the evening-blue garden.

The ancestors' marble has turned gray.
A line of birds streaks into the distance
A faun with dead eyes gazes
After shadows that glide into darkness.

Leaves fall red from the old tree
And whirl inside through the open window.
The room glows in dark fires,
In it the shadows like ghosts.

Opal smoke weaves over the grass
A cloud of wilted, bleached scents,
In the fountain the sickle moon shines

Die Mondessichel in frierenden Lüften.

Die drei Teiche in Hellbrunn
[1. Fassung]

Der erste

Um die Blumen taumelt das Fliegengeschmeiß,
Um die bleichen Blumen auf dumpfer Flut,
Geh fort! Geh fort! Es brennt die Luft!
In der Tiefe glüht der Verwesung Glut!
Die Weide weint, das Schweigen starrt,
Auf den Wassern braut ein schwüler Dunst.
Geh fort! Geh fort!! Es ist der Ort
Für schwarzer Kröten ekle Brunst.

Der zweite

Bilder von Wolken, Blumen und Menschen –
Singe, singe, freudige Welt!
Lächelnde Unschuld spiegelt dich wider –
Himmlisch wird alles, was ihr gefällt!
Dunkles wandelt sich freundlich in Helle,
Fernes wird nah! O freudiger du!
Sonne, Wolken, Blumen und Menschen
Atmen in dir Gottesruh.

Der dritte

Die Wasser schimmern grünlich-blau
Und ruhig atmen die Zypressen,
Es tönt der Abend glockentief –
Da wächst die Tiefe unermessen.
Der Mond steigt auf, es blaut die Nacht,
Erblüht im Widerschein der Fluten –
Ein rätselvolles Sphinxgesicht,
Daran mein Herz sich will verbluten.

Like a green glass in freezing air.

The Three Ponds in Hellbrunn
[version 1]

The First

Around the flowers the blowflies reel,
Around the pale flowers on murky waters,
Go away! Go away! The air burns!
In the depth the heat of putrefaction glows!
The pasture weeps, the silence stares,
A sultry vapor brews on the waters.
Go away! Go away! It is the place
For black toads' disgusting rut.

The Second

Images of clouds, flowers, and people
Sing, sing, joyful world!
Smiling innocence reflects you—
Everything it likes becomes heavenly!
It amicably transforms darkness into light,
Distant things become near! O joyful you!
Sun, clouds, flowers and people
Breathe the peace of God in you.

The Third

The waters shimmer greenish-blue
And calmly the cypresses breathe,
The evening sounds bell-deep—
Then the depths grow immeasurably.
The moon rises, the night turns blue,
Blossoms in the reflection of the waters—
An enigmatic Sphinx face
On which my heart wants to bleed to death.

Auf den Tod einer alten Frau

Oft lausche ich voll Grauen an der Tür
Und tret' ich ein, deucht mich, daß jemand floh,
Und ihre Augen sehn vorbei an mir
Verträumt, als sähen sie mich anderswo.

So sitzt sie ganz in sich gebeugt und lauscht
Und scheint den Dingen fern, die um sie sind,
Doch bebt sie, wenn Gebüsch ans Fenster rauscht,
Und weint dann still, gleichwie ein banges Kind.

Und kost mit müder Hand ihr weißes Haar
Und fragt mit fahlem Blick: Muß ich schon gehn?
Und fiebert irr: Das Lichtlein am Altar
Erlosch! Wo gehst du hin? Was ist geschehn?

Zigeuner

Die Sehnsucht glüht in ihrem nächtigen Blick
Nach jener Heimat, die sie niemals finden.
So treibt sie ein unseliges Geschick,
Das nur Melancholie mag ganz ergründen.

Die Wolken wandeln ihren Wegen vor,
Ein Vogelzug mag manchmal sie geleiten,
Bis er am Abend ihre Spur verlor,
Und manchmal trägt der Wind ein Aveläuten

In ihres Lagers Sterneneinsamkeit,
Daß sehnsuchtsvoller ihre Lieder schwellen
Und schluchzen von ererbtem Fluch und Leid,
Das keiner Hoffnung Sterne sanft erhellen.

On the Death of an Old Woman

Often I listen full of horror at the door
And when I arrive it seems to me that someone fled,
And her eyes see past me
Dreamily, as if they would see me elsewhere.

So she sits completely hunched over and listens
And seems distant from the things around her,
Yet she trembles when shrubs rustle by the window,
And then cries quietly, just like an anxious child.

And caresses her white hair with tired hand
And asks with paled glance: Must I go already?
And has a crazy fever: The little light in the altar
Went out! Where are you going? What has happened?

Gypsy

The yearning glows in their nightly gaze
Toward that homeland they will never find.
So they drift in an unfortunate fate
That only melancholy may completely comprehend.

The clouds lead their way,
A migration of birds may occasionally escort them
Until their track is lost in the evening,
And sometimes the wind carries an Avé of bells

In their camp's star-loneliness,
So that their songs rise more longingly
And sob from inherited curse and suffering
That no stars of hope gently illuminate.

Naturtheater

Nun tret' ich durch die schlanke Pforte!
Verworrner Schritt in den Alleen
Verweht und leiser Hauch der Worte
Von Menschen, die vorübergehn.

Ich steh' vor einer grünen Bühne!
Fang an, fang wieder an, du Spiel
Verlorner Tage, ohn' Schuld und Sühne,
Gespensterhaft nur, fremd und kühl!

Zur Melodie der frühen Tage
Seh' ich da oben mich wiedergehn,
Ein Kind, des leise, vergessene Klage
Ich weinen seh', fremd meinem Verstehn.

Du staunend Antlitz zum Abend gewendet,
War ich dies einst, das nun weinen mich macht,
Wie deine Gebärden noch ungeendet,
Die stumm und schaudernd deuten zur Nacht.

Ermatten

Verwesung traumgeschaffner Paradiese
Umweht dies trauervolle, müde Herz,
Das Ekel nur sich trank aus aller Süße,
Und das verblutet in gemeinem Schmerz.

Nun schlägt es nach dem Takt verklungner Tänze
Zu der Verzweiflung trüben Melodien,
Indes der alten Hoffnung Sternenkränze
An längst entgöttertem Altar verblühn.

Vom Rausch der Wohlgerüche und der Weine
Blieb dir ein überwach Gefühl der Scham –
Das Gestern in verzerrtem Widerscheine –
Und dich zermalmt des Alltags grauer Gram.

Nature Theater

Now I step through the narrow gate!
Confused footsteps in the avenues
And the quiet breeze of words
Drifts away from people, passersby.

I stand before a green stage!
Begin, begin again, you play
Of lost days, without crime and punishment,
Only ghostly, strange and cool!

I see myself going up there again,
To the melody of the early days,
A child whose quiet, forgotten lament
I see weeping, alien to my understanding.

You wondering face turned to the evening,
Was I once this that now makes me weep,
Like your still unfinished gestures
That point to the night mute and shuddering.

Exhausting

Putrefaction of dream-created paradises
Blows around this mourning-filled, tired heart
That drank only disgust out of all sweetness,
And bleeds to death in vulgar pain.

Now it beats after the rhythm of faded dances
To the cloudy melodies of despair,
While the star-crowns of old hope
Wither on the long ago godless altar.

From the drunkenness of fragrances and wines
A heightened feeling of shame remained with you—
Yesterday in distorted reflection—
And everyday's gray grief crushes you.

Ausklang

Vom Tage ging der letzte, blasse Schein,
Die frühen Leidenschaften sind verrauscht,
Verschüttet meiner Freuden heiliger Wein,
Nun weint mein Herz zur Nacht und lauscht

Nach seiner jungen Feste Widerhall,
Der in dem Dunkel sich verliert so sacht,
So schattengleich, wie welker Blätter Fall
Auf ein verlaßnes Grab in Herbstesnacht.

Einklang

Sehr helle Töne in den dünnen Lüften,
Sie singen dieses Tages fernes Trauern,
Der ganz gefüllt von ungeahnten Düften
Uns träumen macht nach niegefühlten Schauern.

Wie Andacht nach verlorenen Gefährten
Und leiser Nachhall nachtversunkner Wonnen,
Das Laub fällt in den längst verlaßnen Gärten,
Die sich in Paradiesesschweigen sonnen.

Im hellen Spiegel der geklärten Fluten
Sehn wir die tote Zeit sich fremd beleben
Und unsre Leidenschaften im Verbluten,
Zu ferner'n Himmeln unsre Seelen heben.

Wir gehen durch die Tode neugestaltet
Zu tiefern Foltern ein und tiefern Wonnen,
Darin die unbekannte Gottheit waltet –
Und uns vollenden ewig neue Sonnen.

Closing Chord

The last, pale light went from the day,
The early passions have rustled down,
The holy wine of my joys spilled,
Now my heart weeps in the night and listens

After the echo of its young celebrations
Which trails off so softly in the dark,
So shadowy, like wilted leaves falling
On an abandoned grave in autumn night.

Accord

Very bright tones in the thin winds,
They sing the distant mourning of this day,
Completely filled with unimaginable perfumes
That make us dream after never-felt shudders.

Like mementos to lost companions
And quiet echoes of night-immersed delights,
The foliage falls in the long ago abandoned gardens
Which sun themselves in the silence of paradise.

In the bright mirror of the clear waters
We see dead time strangely revive
And our passions in the bleeding
Lift our souls to more distant heavens.

We go through deaths newly transformed
To deeper tortures and deeper delights
Where the unknown deity governs—
And we are consummated by eternally new suns.

Crucifixus

Er ist der Gott, vor dem die Armen knien,
Er ihrer Erdenqualen Schicksalsspiegel,
Ein bleicher Gott, geschändet, angespien,
Verendet auf der Mörderschande Hügel.

Sie knien vor seines Fleisches Folternot,
Daß ihre Demut sich mit ihm vermähle,
Und seines letzten Blickes Nacht und Tod
Ihr Herz im Eis der Todessehnsucht stähle –

Daß öffne – irdenen Gebrests Symbol –
Die Pforte zu der Armut Paradiesen
Sein todesnächtiges Dornenkapitol,
Das bleiche Engel und Verlorene grüßen.

Confiteor

Die bunten Bilder, die das Leben malt
Seh' ich umdüstert nur von Dämmerungen,
Wie kraus verzerrte Schatten, trüb und kalt,
Die kaum geboren schon der Tod bezwungen.

Und da von jedem Ding die Maske fiel,
Seh' ich nur Angst, Verzweiflung, Schmach und Seuchen,
Der Menschheit heldenloses Trauerspiel,
Ein schlechtes Stück, gespielt auf Gräbern, Leichen.

Mich ekelt dieses wüste Traumgesicht.
Doch will ein Machtgebot, daß ich verweile,
Ein Komödiant, der seine Rolle spricht,
Gezwungen, voll Verzweiflung – Langeweile!

Crucifixus

He is the God before whom the poor kneel,
He, fate's mirror of their earthly torments,
A pale God, disgraced, spit at,
Perished on the hill of the murderer's dishonor.

They kneel before His flesh's torture
So that their humility is wedded to Him,
And the night and death of His last glance
Shall toughen their heart in the ice of death's longing—

So that His death-night's crown of thorns—
The symbol of earthly suffering—opens
The gate to poverty's paradises
Greeted by pale angels and the lost.

Confiteor

The colored pictures which life paints,
I see them gloomily only by twilights,
Like muddled distorted shadows, cloudy and cold,
Barely born, already defeated by death.

And since the mask fell from each thing,
I see only fear, desperation, disgrace and plagues,
Mankind's heroless tragedy,
A bad play, staged on graves, corpses.

This terrible dream-view disgusts me.
But a higher authority wants me to stay,
A comedian who speaks his role,
Coerced, full of desperation—boredom!

Schweigen

Über den Wäldern schimmert bleich
Der Mond, der uns träumen macht,
Die Weide am dunklen Teich
Weint lautlos in die Nacht.

Ein Herz erlischt – und sacht
Die Nebel fluten und steigen –
Schweigen, Schweigen!

Vor Sonnenaufgang

Im Dunkel rufen viele Vogelstimmen,
Die Bäume rauschen und die Quellen laut,
In Wolken tönt ein rosenfarbnes Glimmen
Wie frühe Liebesnot. Die Nacht verblaut –

Die Dämmrung glättet sanft, mit scheuen Händen
Der Liebe Lager, fiebernd aufgewühlt,
Und läßt den Rausch erschlaffter Küsse enden
In Träumen, lächelnd und halb wach gefühlt.

Blutschuld

Es dräut die Nacht am Lager unsrer Küsse.
Es flüstert wo: Wer nimmt von euch die Schuld?
Noch bebend von verruchter Wollust Süße
Wir beten: Verzeih uns, Maria, in deiner Huld!

Aus Blumenschalen steigen gierige Düfte,
Umschmeicheln unsere Stirnen bleich von Schuld,
Ermattend unterm Hauch der schwülen Lüfte
Wir träumen: Verzeih uns, Maria, in deiner Huld!

Doch lauter rauscht der Brunnen der Sirenen
Und dunkler ragt die Sphinx vor unsrer Schuld,

Silence

Over the forests the moon
Gleams pale, makes us dream,
The willow by the dark pond
Weeps soundlessly in the night.

A heart expires—and gently
The fogs flood in and rise—
Silence, silence!

Before Sunrise

In the dark many bird voices call,
The trees and the springs murmur noisily,
In the clouds a rose-colored glow sounds
Like early love's distress. The night blues away—

With shy hands the twilight softly polishes
The love lair, feverishly stirred up,
And lets the drunkenness of languished kisses end
In dreams, smiling and felt half-awake.

Blood Guilt

Night threatens at the bed of our kisses.
Somewhere a whisper: who absolves your guilt?
Still trembling from the sweetness of nefarious lust
We pray: forgive us, Mary, in your mercy.

Out of flower vases greedy scents climb,
Wooing our foreheads pale with guilt.
Languishing under the breath of sultry air
We dream: forgive us, Mary, in your mercy.

But the well of the sirens whispers louder,
And the sphinx rises darker before our guilt

Daß unsre Herzen sündiger wieder tönen,
Wir schluchzen: Verzeih uns, Maria, in deiner Huld!

Begegnung

Am Weg der Fremde – wir sehn uns an
Und unsre müden Augen fragen:
Was hast du mit deinem Leben getan?
Sei still! sei still! Laß alle Klagen!

Es wird schon kühler um uns her,
Die Wolken zerfließen in den Weiten.
Mich deucht, wir fragen nicht lange mehr
Und niemand wird uns zur Nacht geleiten.

Vollendung

Mein Bruder, laß uns stiller gehn!
Die Straßen dunkeln sachte ein.
Von ferne schimmern wohl Fahnen und wehn,
Doch Bruder, laß uns einsam sein –

Und uns zum Himmel schauend ruhn,
Im Herzen sanft und ganz bereit,
Und selbstvergessen einstigem Tun.
Mein Bruder, sieh, die Welt ist weit!

Da draußen spielt mit Wolken der Wind,
Die kommen wie wir, von irgendwo.
Laß sein uns, wie die Blumen sind,
So arm, mein Bruder, so schön und froh!

So that our hearts resound again more sinfully,
We sob: forgive us, Mary, in your mercy.

Encounter

On the way, the stranger—we look at each other
And our tired eyes ask:
What have you done with your life?
Be silent! Be silent! Cease all laments!

Already it grows cooler around us,
The clouds dissolve in the vastnesses.
I think we shall ask nothing else
And no one will escort us to the night.

Perfection

My brother, let us go more quietly!
Gently the streets darken.
In the distance flags probably gleam and wave,
However, brother, let us be alone—

And rest looking at heaven,
Softly and wholly prepared in the heart,
And oblivious to past deed.
My brother, see, the world is vast!

Outdoors the wind plays with clouds,
Like us they come from somewhere.
Let us be like the flowers,
So poor, my brother, so beautiful and glad!

Metamorphose

Ein ewiges Licht glüht düsterrot,
Ein Herz so rot, in Sündennot!
Gegrüßt seist du, o Maria!

Dein bleiches Bildnis ist erblüht
Und ein verhüllter Leib erglüht,
O Fraue du, Maria!

In süßen Qualen brennt dein Schoß,
Da lächelt dein Auge schmerzlich und groß,
O Mutter du, Maria!

Abendgang

Ich gehe in den Abend hinein,
Der Wind läuft mit und singt:
Verzauberter du von jedem Schein,
O fühle, was mit dir ringt!

Einer Toten Stimme, die ich geliebt,
Spricht: Arm ist der Toren Herz!
Vergiß, vergiß, was die Seele dir trübt!
Das Werdende sei dein Schmerz!

Der Heilige

Wenn in der Hölle selbstgeschaffener Leiden
Grausam-unzüchtige Bilder ihn bedrängen –
Kein Herz ward je von lasser Geilheit so
Berückt wie seins, und so von Gott gequält
Kein Herz – Hebt er die abgezehrten Hände,
Die unerlösten, betend auf zum Himmel.
Doch formt nur qualvoll-ungestillte Lust
Sein brünstig-fieberndes Gebet, des Glut
Hinströmt durch mystische Unendlichkeiten.

Metamorphosis

An eternal light glows dark red,
A heart so red, in sin's pressure!
Hail, o Mary!

Your pale likeness has blossomed
And your mantled body glows,
O woman, Mary!

In sweet tortures your lap burns,
Then your eye smiles painfully and large,
O mother, Mary!

Evening Walk

I go into the evening,
The wind jogs along and sings:
You are bewitched by every light,
O feel, what struggles with you!

A dead woman's voice that I loved
Speaks: poor is the fools' heart!
Forget, forget what clouds the soul!
The becoming shall be your pain!

The Saint

When in the hell of self-created sufferings
Cruelly indecent images plague him—
No heart was ever so enchanted by lascivious prurience
Like his, and no heart so tormented
By God—he lifts gaunt hands,
Unredeemed, praying to heaven.
But only agonizingly insatiable lust forms
His rutting, feverish prayer, its fervor
Surges there through mystical infinities.

Und nicht so trunken tönt das Evoe
Des Dionys, als wenn in tödlicher,
Wutgeifernder Ekstase Erfüllung sich
Erzwingt sein Qualschrei: Exaudi me, o Maria!

Einer Vorübergehenden

Ich hab' einst im Vorübergehn
Ein schmerzenreiches Antlitz gesehn,
Das schien mir tief und heimlich verwandt,
So gottgesandt –
Und ging vorüber und entschwand.

Ich hab' einst im Vorübergehn
Ein schmerzenreiches Antlitz gesehn,
Das hat mich gebannt,
Als hätte ich eine wiedererkannt,
Die träumend ich einst Geliebte genannt
In einem Dasein, das längst entschwand.

Die tote Kirche

Auf dunklen Bänken sitzen sie gedrängt
Und heben die erloschnen Blicke auf
Zum Kreuz. Die Lichter schimmern wie verhängt,
Und trüb und wie verhängt das Wundenhaupt.
Der Weihrauch steigt aus güldenem Gefäß
Zur Höhe auf, hinsterbender Gesang
Verhaucht, und ungewiß und süß verdämmert
Wie heimgesucht der Raum. Der Priester schreitet
Vor den Altar; doch übt mir müdem Geist er
Die frommen Bräuche – ein jämmerlicher Spieler,
Vor schlechten Betern mit erstarrten Herzen,
In seelenlosem Spiel mit Brot und Wein.
Die Glocke klingt! Die Lichter flackern trüber –
Und bleicher, wie verhängt das Wundenhaupt!
Die Orgel rauscht! In toten Herzen schauert
Erinnerung auf! Ein blutend Schmerzensantlitz

And not so drunkenly the Evoe
Of Dionysus sounds, as if his shout
Of torment forces fulfillment in deadly,
Furiously slobbering ecstasy: Exaudi me, o Mary!

To a Woman Passer-by

I have once seen passing-by
A face rich with pain,
That seemed deeply and clandestinely akin to me,
So god-sent—
And passed and disappeared.

I have once seen passing-by
A face rich with pain
That impressed me,
As if I had recognized one,
Who dreaming, I once called beloved
In an existence that long ago disappeared.

The Dead Church

They sit packed on dark benches
And lift extinguished glances
To the cross. The lights gleam as if covered
And cloudy, and the head of wounds.
Incense rises from a golden vessel
Toward the heights, dying songs
Exhale, and as if afflicted the room darkens with dusk
Uncertain and sweet. The priest strides
Before the altar; but he practices pious rites
With tired spirit—a miserable player
Before bad prayers with numb hearts,
In soulless play with bread and wine.
The bell sounds! The lights flicker more cloudily—
And paler, as if the head of wounds were covered!
The organ hisses! In dead hearts memory
Shudders on! A bleeding countenance of pain

Hüllt sich in Dunkelheit und die Verzweiflung
Starrt ihm aus vielen Augen nach ins Leere.
Und eine, die wie aller Stimmen klang,
Schluchzt auf – indes das Grauen wuchs im Raum,
Das Todesgrauen wuchs: Erbarme dich unser –
Herr!

Wraps itself in darkness and the despair
Stares after him in the emptiness of many eyes.
And one who sounded like all voices
Sobs out—while the horror grew in the room,
The horror of death grew: Have mercy on us—
Lord!

Melusine

Wovon bin ich nur aufgewacht?
Mein Kind, es fielen Blüten zur Nacht!

Wer flüstert so traurig, als wie im Traum?
Mein Kind, der Frühling geht durch den Raum.

O sieh! Sein Gesicht ist tränenbleich!
Mein Kind, er blühte wohl allzu reich.

Wie brennt sein Mund! Warum weine ich?
Mein Kind, ich küsse mein Leben in dich!

Wer faßt mich so hart, wer beugt sich zu mir?
Mein Kind, ich falte die Hände dir.

Wo geh' ich nur hin? Ich träumte so schön!
Mein Kind, wir wollen in Himmel gehn.

Wie gut, wie gut! Wer lächelt so leis'
Da wurden ihre Augen weiß –

Da löschten alle Lichter aus
Und tiefe Nacht durchwehte das Haus.

Die Nacht der Armen

Es dämmert!
Und dumpf o hämmert
Die Nach an unsre Tür!
Es flüstert ein Kind:
Wie zittert ihr
So sehr!
Doch tiefer neigen

Melusine

What just woke me?
My child, blossoms fell in the night!

Who whispers so sadly, as if in dream?
My child, spring goes through the room.

O see! His face pale like tears!
My child, he probably blossomed much too richly.

How his mouth burns! Why do I weep?
My child, I kiss my life into you!

Who grabs me so hard, who bends to me?
My child, I fold your hands.

Only where do I go? I dreamed so beautifully!
My child, we want to go to heaven.

How good, how good! Who smiles so quietly?
Then her eyes turned white—

Then all lights extinguished
And deep night drifted through the house.

The Night of the Poor

Dusk falls!
And o the night hammers
Dully on our door!
A child whispers:
How you tremble
So much!
Yet we poor

Wir Armen uns und schweigen
Und schweigen, als wären wir nicht mehr!

Nachtlied

Triff mich Schmerz! Die Wunde glüht.
Dieser Qual hab' ich nicht acht!
Sieh aus meinen Wunden blüht
Rätselvoll ein Stern zur Nacht!
Triff mich Tod! Ich bin vollbracht.

De profundis

Die Totenkammer ist voll Nacht
Mein Vater schläft, ich halte Wacht.

Des Toten hartes Angesicht
Flimmert weiß im Kerzenlicht.

Die Blumen duften, die Fliege summt
Mein Herz lauscht fühllos und verstummt.

Der Wind pocht leise an die Tür.
Die öffnet sich mit hellem Geklirr.

Und draußen rauscht ein Ährenfeld,
Die Sonne knistert am Himmelszelt.

Von Früchten voll hängt Busch und Baum
Und Vögel und Falter schwirren im Raum.

Im Acker mähen die Bauersleut'
Im tiefen Schweigen der Mittagszeit.

Ich schlag' ein Kreuz auf den Toten hin
Und lautlos verliert sich mein Schritt im Grün.

Bend deeper and keep silent
And keep silent as if we were no more!

Night Song

Strike me pain! The wound glows.
I shall not notice this agony!
Look a riddle-filled star blooms
From my wounds in the night!
Strike me death! I am finished.

De profundis

The chamber of the dead is full of night
My father sleeps, I keep vigil.

The dead one's hard face
Shimmers white in the candlelight.

The flowers smell, the fly hums
My heart listens without feeling and becomes silent.

The wind throbs quietly at the door.
It opens with a light rattling.

And outside a field of corn ears rustles,
The sun crackles in the firmament.

Bush and tree hang full of fruits
And birds and butterflies whir in space.

In the field the peasants mow
In the deep silence of high noon.

I make the sign of the cross on the dead person
And soundlessly my step fades away in the green.

Am Friedhof

Morsch Gestein ragt schwül erwärmt.
Gelbe Weihrauchdünste schweben.
Bienen summen wirr verschwärmt
Und die Blumengitter beben.

Langsam regt sich dort ein Zug
An den sonnenstillen Mauern,
Schwindet flimmernd, wie ein Trug –
Totenlieder tief verschauern.

Lange lauscht es nach im Grün,
Läßt die Büsche heller scheinen;
Braune Mückenschwärme sprühn
Über alten Totensteinen.

Sonniger Nachmittag

Ein Ast wiegt mich im tiefen Blau.
Im tollen, herbstlichen Blattgewirr
Flimmern Falter, berauscht und irr.
Axtschläge hallen in der Au.

In roten Beeren verbeißt sich mein Mund
Und Licht und Schatten schwanken im Laub.
Stundenlang fällt goldener Staub
Knisternd in den braunen Grund.

Die Drossel lacht aus den Büschen her
Und toll und laut schlägt über mir
Zusammen das herbstliche Blattgewirr –
Früchte lösen sich leuchtend und schwer.

At the Cemetery

Rotten stone towers sultrily warmed.
Yellow haze of incense hovers.
Bees hum chaotically swarmed
And the flower trellises shake.

Slowly a breath stirs there
By the sun-still walls,
Dwindles glimmering, like an illusion—
Songs for the dead deeply shiver away.

It listens long after in the green,
Allows the bushes to shine brighter;
Brown swarms of mosquitoes spray
Over old tombstones.

Sunny Afternoon

A branch rocks me in the deep blue.
In the frolicking, autumn leaf-tangle
Moths flicker, intoxicated and crazy.
Ax blows resound in the floodplain.

My mouth bites into red berries
And light and shadows sway in the foliage.
For hours golden dust falls
Crackling in the brown ground.

The thrush laughs from the bushes
And frolicking and loudly the autumn leaf-tangle
Smashes together above me—
Fruits detach bright and heavy.

Zeitalter

Ein Tiergesicht im braunen Grün
Glüht scheu mich an, die Büsche glimmen.
Sehr ferne singt mit Kinderstimmen
Ein alter Brunnen. Ich lausche hin.

Die wilden Dohlen spotten mein
Und rings die Birken sich verschleiern.
Ich stehe still vor Unkrautfeuern
Und leise malen sich Bilder darein,

Auf Goldgrund uralte Liebesmär.
Ihr schweigen breiten die Wolken am Hügel.
Aus geisterhaftem Weiherspiegel
Winken Früchte, leuchtend und schwer.

Der Schatten

Da ich heut morgen im Garten saß –
Die Bäume standen in blauer Blüh,
Voll Drosselruf und Tirili –
Sah ich meinen Schatten im Gras,

Gewaltig verzerrt, ein wunderlich Tier,
Das lag wie ein böser Traum vor mir.

Und ich ging und zitterte sehr,
Indes ein Brunnen ins Blaue sang
Und purpurn eine Knospe sprang
Und das Tier ging nebenher.

Wunderlicher Frühling

Wohl um die tiefe Mittagszeit,
Lag ich auf einem alten Stein,
Vor mir in wunderlichem Kleid

Age

An animal face in the brown green
Glows shyly to me, the bushes smolder.
Very far away an old fountain sings
With children's voices. I listen there.

The wild jackdaws mock me
And all around the birches veil themselves.
I stand silent before a weed fire
And quietly images paint themselves on it,

An ancient fairytale of love on golden ground.
The clouds spread their silence on the hill.
From the ghostly pond-mirror
Fruits beckon, shining and heavy.

The Shadow

Since I sat in the garden this morning—
The trees stood in bluer bloom
Full of thrush calls and trills—
I saw my shadow in the grass,

Immensely distorted, a fantastical animal
That lay before me like a bad dream.

And I left and trembled much,
While a fountain sang in the blueness
And a bud leapt purple
And the animal went alongside.

Quaint Spring

Perhaps around the deep midday,
I lay on an old stone,
Before me in quaint dress

Standen drei Engel im Sonnenschein.

O ahnungsvolles Frühlingsjahr!
Im Acker schmolz der letzte Schnee,
Und zitternd hing der Birke Haar
In den kalten, klaren See.

Vom Himmel wehte ein blaues Band,
Und schön floß eine Wolke herein,
Der lag ich träumend zugewandt –
Die Engel knieten im Sonnenschein.

Laut sang ein Vogel Wundermär,
Und konnt mit einmal ihn verstehn:
Eh' noch gestillt dein erst' Begehr,
Mußt sterben gehn, mußt sterben gehn!

Der Traum eines Nachmittags

Still! der Alte kommt gegangen;
Und sein Schritt verdämmert wieder.
Schatten schweben auf und nieder –
Birken, die ins Fenster hangen.

Und am alten Rebenhügel
Tollt aufs neu der faunische Reigen,
Und die schlanken Nymphen steigen
Leise aus dem Brunnenspiegel.

Hör! da droht ein fern Gewittern.
Weihrauch dampft aus dunklen Kressen,
Falter feiern stille Messen
Vor verfall'nen Blumengittern.

Sommersonate

Täubend duften faule Früchte.
Büsch' und Bäume sonnig klingen,

Three angels stood in the sunshine.

O ominous spring year!
In the acre the last snow melted,
And the birch's hair hung quivering
In the cold, clear lake.

From the sky a blue ribbon blew,
And beautifully a cloud flowed within,
Facing it, I lay dreaming—
The angels kneeled in sunshine.

Loudly a bird sang marvelous stories,
And at once I could understand it:
Still before your first desire is satisfied,
You must go die, must go die!

The Dream of an Afternoon

Silence! the ancestor arrives;
And his step turns to dusk again.
Shadows float up and down—
Birches that dangle in the window.

And on the old hill of vines
The round dance of fauns romps anew,
And the slender nymphs rise
Quietly from the fountain's mirror.

Hear! A distant thunderstorm threatens.
Incense steams from dark cresses,
Moths celebrate silent masses
Before decayed flower trellises.

Summer Sonata

Rotten fruits smell stunning.
Bushes and trees sound sunny,

Schwärme schwarzer Fliegen singen
Auf der braunen Waldeslichte.

In des Tümpels tiefer Bläue
Flammt der Schein von Unkrautbränden.
Hör' aus gelben Blumenwänden
Schwirren jähe Liebesschreie.

Lang sich Schmetterlinge jagen;
Trunken tanzt auf schwülen Matten
Auf dem Thymian mein Schatten.
Hell verzückte Amseln schlagen.

Wolken starre Brüste zeigen,
Und bekränzt von Laub und Beeren
Siehst du unter dunklen Föhren
Grinsend ein Gerippe geigen.

Leuchtende Stunde

Fern am Hügel Flötenklang.
Faune lauern an den Sümpfen,
Wo versteckt in Rohr und Tang
Träge ruhn die schlanken Nymphen.

In des Weihers Spiegelglas
Goldne Falter sich verzücken,
Leise regt im samtnen Gras
Sich ein Tier mit zweien Rücken.

Schluchzend haucht im Birkenhain
Orpheus zartes Liebeslallen,
Sanft und scherzend stimmen ein
In sein Lied die Nachtigallen.

Phöbus eine Flamme glüht
Noch an Aphroditens Munde,
Und von Ambraduft durchsprüht –
Rötet dunkel sich die Stunde.

Swarms of black flies sing
On the brown forest glade.

In the pool's deep blueness
The light of weed-fires blazes.
Hear sudden love cries whirring
From yellow walls of flowers.

Butterflies chase each other for a long time;
Drunkenly my shadow dances
On sultry meadows of thyme.
Radiantly ecstatic blackbirds trill.

Clouds show stiff breasts,
And under dark pines wreathed
By foliage and berries you see
A skeleton play the violin grinning.

Luminous Hour

Far on the hill flute-sounds.
Fauns lurk in the marshes
Where sluggishly slender nymphs
Rest hidden in reed and seaweed.

In the pond's mirror-glass
Golden butterflies are enraptured,
Quietly an animal with two backs
Moves in the velvety grass.

Sobbing in the birch grove
Orpheus breathes tender love-babble,
Gently and jokingly the nightingales
Join in his song.

Phoebus a flame glows
Still on Aphrodite's mouth,
And drizzled with amber perfume—
The hour reddens darkly.

Kindheitserinnerung

Die Sonne scheint einsam am Nachmittag,
Und leise entschwebt der Ton der Immen.
Im Garten flüstern der Schwestern Stimmen –
Da lauscht der Knabe im Holzverschlag,

Noch fiebernd über Buch und Bild.
Müd welken die Linden im Blau versunken.
Ein Reiher hängt reglos im Äther ertrunken,
Am Zaun phantastisches Schattenwerk spielt.

Die Schwestern gehen still ins Haus,
Und ihre weißen Kleider schimmern
Bald ungewiß aus hellen Zimmern,
Und wirr erstirbt der Büsche Gebraus.

Der Knabe streichelt der Katze Haar,
Verzaubert von ihrer Augen Spiegel.
Ein Orgelklang hebt fern am Hügel
Sich auf zum Himmel wunderbar.

Ein Abend

Am Abend war der Himmel verhangen.
Und durch den Hain voll Schweigen und Trauer
Fuhr ein dunkelgoldener Schauer.
Ferne Abendgeläute verklangen.

Die Erde hat eisiges Wasser getrunken,
Am Waldsaum lag ein Brand im Verglimmen,
Der Wind sang leise mit Engelstimmen
Und schaudernd bin ich ins Knie gegangen,

In's Haidekraut, in bittere Kressen.
Weit draußen schwammen in silbernen Lachen
Wolken, verlassene Liebeswachen.
Die Haide war einsam und unermessen.

Childhood Memory

The sun shines alone in the afternoon,
And quietly the tone of the honey-bees wafts away.
In the garden the sisters' voices whisper—
There the boy listens in the wooden shed

Still fevering over book and picture.
Weary the linden trees wilt immersed in the blue.
A heron hangs motionless drowned in the ether,
By the fence fantastic shadow-shapes play.

The sisters go quietly into the house,
And soon their white clothes glimmer
Vaguely from bright rooms,
And woozily the bushes' bluster dies down.

The boy strokes the cat's hair,
Bewitched by the mirror of her eyes.
An organ sound far away on the hill
Lifts wonderfully into heaven.

An Evening

In the evening the sky was overcast.
And through the grove full of silence and grief
A dark-golden shower went.
Distant evening bells faded away.

The earth has drunk icy water,
At the forest's edge a fire lay glowing,
The wind quietly sang with angel's voices
And shivering I have gone to the knee,

In the heather, in bitter cresses.
Far outside clouds swam in silver puddles,
Desolate guards of love.
The heath was lonesome and unmeasured.

Jahreszeit

Rubingeäder kroch ins Laub.
Dann war der Weiher still und weit.
Am Waldsaum lagen bunt verstreut
Bläulich Gefleck und brauner Staub.

Ein Fischer zog sein Netze ein.
Dann kam die Dämmrung übers Feld.
Doch schien ein Hof noch fahl erhellt
Und Mägde brachten Obst und Wein.

Ein Hirtenlied starb ferne nach.
Dann standen Hütten kahl und fremd.
Der Wald im grauen Totenhemd
Rief traurige Erinnerung wach.

Und über Nacht ward leis' die Zeit
Und wie in schwarzen Löchern flog
Im Wald ein Rabenheer und zog
Nach der Stadt sehr fernem Geläut.

Im Weinland

Die Sonne malt herbstlich Hof und Mauern,
Das Obst, zu Haufen rings geschichtet,
Davor armselige Kinder kauern.
Ein Windstoß alte Linden lichtet.

Durchs Tor ein goldener Schauer regnet
Und müde ruhn auf morschen Bänken
Die Frauen, deren Leib gesegnet.
Betrunkne Glas und Krüge schwenken.

Ein Strolch läßt seine Fidel klingen
Und geil im Tanz sich Kittel blähen.
Hart braune Leiber sich umschlingen.
Aus Fenstern leere Augen sehen.

Season

Ruby veins crept into the foliage.
Then the pond was calm and wide.
By the forest's edge bluish speckles
And brown dust lay brightly scattered.

A fisherman drew in his nets.
Then dusk came over the field.
But a yard shined still palely illuminated
And maids brought fruit and wine.

Distantly a shepherd's song died after.
Then huts stood bleak and strange.
The forest in gray shroud
Roused sad memories.

And overnight time became quiet
And an army of ravens flew
As if in black holes in the forest and moved
Toward the town's very distant ringing.

In Wine Country

The sun paints courtyard and walls with autumn,
The fruit stacked in heaps all around,
Before them poor children cower.
A gust thins out old linden trees.

Through the gate a golden shower rains
And the women blessed with child
Tiredly rest on rotten benches.
Drunkards swing glasses and jugs.

A vagabond lets his fiddle sound
And smocks swell lustfully in the dance.
Roughly brown bodies embrace.
From windows empty eyes gaze.

Gestank steigt aus dem Brunnenspiegel.
Und schwarz, verfallen, abgeschieden
Verdämmern rings die Rebenhügel.
Ein Vogelzug streicht rasch gen Süden.

Das dunkle Tal

In Föhren zerflattert ein Krähenzug
Und grüne Abendnebel steigen
Und wie im Traum ein Klang von Geigen
Und Mägde laufen zum Tanz in Krug.

Man hört Betrunkener Lachen und Schrei,
Ein Schauer geht durch alte Eiben.
An leichenfahlen Fensterscheiben
Huschen die Schatten der Tänzer vorbei.

Es riecht nach Wein und Thymian
Und durch den Wald hallt einsam Rufen.
Das Bettelvolk lauscht auf den Stufen
Und hebt sinnlos zu beten an.

Ein Wild verblutet im Haselgesträuch.
Dumpf schwanken riesige Baumarkaden,
Von eisigen Wolken überladen.
Liebende ruhn umschlungen am Teich.

Sommerdämmerung

Im grünen Äther flimmert jäh ein Stern
Und im Spitale wittern sie den Morgen.
Die Drossel trällert irr im Busch verborgen
Und Klosterglocken gehn traumhaft und fern.

Ein Standbild ragt am Platz, einsam und schlank
Und in den Höfen dämmern rote Blumenpfühle.
Die Luft um Holzbalkone bebt von Schwüle

Stench rises from the fountain's mirror.
And black, decayed, isolated
The hills of vines dusk all around.
A migration of birds glides swiftly southwards.

The Dark Valley

In pines a migration of crows flutters away
And green evening fogs rise
And like in dream a sound of violins
And maids run to the dance in the inn.

One hears laughter and shouts of drunkards,
A shudder goes through old yews.
In deathly pale window panes
The shadows of the dancers scurry past.

It smells of wine and thyme
And lonely calling resounds through the forest.
The beggars listen on the steps
And begin to pray senselessly.

A deer bleeds to death in the hazel bushes.
Muffled gigantic tree arcades sway,
Overloaded by icy clouds.
Lovers rest embraced by the pond.

Summer Dawn

In the green ether suddenly a star flickers
And in the hospital they smell the morning.
Hidden in the bush the thrush trills crazily
And cloister bells go dreamlike and far.

A statue towers in the square, lonely and slender
And in the courtyard red flowerbeds dawn.
The air around wooden balconies shakes with sultriness

Und Fliegen taumeln leise um Gestank.

Der Silbervorhang dort vor'm Fenster hehlt
Verschlungene Glieder, Lippen, zarte Brüste.
Ein hart' Gehämmer hallt vom Turmgerüste
Und weiß verfällt der Mond am Himmelszelt.

Ein geisterhafter Traumakkord verschwebt
Und Mönche tauchen aus den Kirchentoren
Und schreiten im Unendlichen verloren.
Ein heller Gipfel sich am Himmel hebt.

Im Mondschein

Ein Heer von Ungeziefer, Mäusen, Ratten
Tollt auf der Diele, die im Mondschein schimmert.
Der Wind schreit wie im Traume auf und wimmert.
Am Fenster zittern kleiner Blätter Schatten.

Bisweilen zwitschern Vögel in den Zweigen
Und Spinnen kriechen an den kahlen Mauern.
Durch leere Gänge bleiche Flecken schauern.
Es wohnt im Haus ein wunderliches Schweigen.

Im Hofe scheinen Lichter hinzugleiten
Auf faulem Holz, verfallenem Gerümpel.
Dann gleißt ein Stern in einem schwarzen Tümpel.
Figuren stehn noch da aus alten Zeiten.

Man sieht Konturen noch von anderen Dingen
Und eine Schrift, verblaßt auf morschen Schildern,
Vielleicht die Farben auch von heitreren Bildern:
Engel, die vor Mariens Throne singen.

Märchen

Raketen sprühn im gelben Sonnenschein;
Im alten Park welch maskenhaft Gewimmel.

And flies quietly reel around the stench.

The silver curtain there before the window hides
Entwined limbs, lips, tender breasts.
A hard hammering echoes from the tower scaffold
And the moon decays white in the firmament.

A ghostly dream-chord floats away
And monks plunge from the church gates
And stride lost in the infinite.
In the sky a bright summit rises.

In the Moonlight

An army of vermin, mice, rats
Romps in the hallway which shimmers in the moonlight.
The wind cries out as if in dream and whimpers.
At the window the shadows of small leaves quiver.

Occasionally birds twitter in the branches
And spiders creep on the bleak walls.
Through empty hallways pale specks shudder.
A quaint silence dwells in the house.

In the courtyard lights seem to float
On putrid wood, decayed junk.
Then a star glistens in a black pool.
Statues still stand there from old times.

One still sees contours from other things
And a writing, faded on rotten signs,
Also perhaps the colors of cheerful pictures:
Angels singing before Mary's throne.

Fairy Tale

Rockets sparkle in the yellow sunshine;
What a mask-like throng in the old park.

Landschaften spiegeln sich am grauen Himmel
Und manchmal hört den Faun man gräßlich schrein.

Sein goldnes Grinsen zeigt sich grell im Hain.
In Kressen tobt der Hummeln Schlachtgetümmel,
Ein Reiter trabt vorbei auf fahlem Schimmel.
Die Pappeln glühn in ungewissen Reihn.

Die Kleine, die im Weiher heut ertrank,
Ruht eine Heilige im kahlen Zimmer
Und öfter blendet sie ein Wolkenschimmer.

Die Alten gehn im Treibhaus stumpf und krank
Und gießen ihre Blumen, die verdorren.
Am Tore flüstern Stimmen traumverworren.

Ein Frühlingsabend

Komm' Abend, Freund, der mir die Stirn umdüstert,
Auf Pfaden gleitend durch sanftgrüne Saat.
Auch winken Weiden feierlich und stad;
Geliebte Stimme in den Zweigen flüstert.

Der heitere Wind spült Holdes her von wannen,
Narzissenduft, der silbern dich berührt.
Im Haselstrauch die Amsel musiziert –
Ein Hirtenlied gibt Antwort aus den Tannen.

Wie lange ist das kleine Haus entschwunden,
Wo nun ein Birkenwäldchen niederquillt;
Der Weiher trägt ein einsam Sternenbild –
Und Schatten, die sich still ins Goldne runden!

Und also wundertätig ist die Zeit,
Daß man die Engel sucht in Menschenblicken,
Die sich in unschuldsvollem Spiel entzücken.
Ja! Also wundertätig ist die Zeit.

Landscapes are mirrored in the gray sky
And sometimes one hears the faun scream dreadfully.

Its golden grin appears garishly in the grove.
In cresses the rampage of bumblebees in the thick of battle,
A rider trots past on a pale white horse.
The poplars glow in vague rows.

The little girl who drowned in the pond today
Rests as a saint in the bleak room
And a glimmer of clouds often blinds her.

The old people go into the hothouse dulled and ill
And water their flowers which wither.
At the gate voices whisper dream-confused.

A Spring Evening

Come evening, friend that surrounds my forehead with darkness
Gliding on paths through soft-green sowing.
Also willows beckon solemn and calm;
A beloved voice whispers in the branches.

The tranquil wind floats beautiful things here from somewhere,
Daffodil fragrance which silverly touches you.
In the hazel bush the blackbird plays music—
A shepherd's song answers from the firs.

How long the small house has disappeared
Where now a birch grove swells;
The pond bears a lonely constellation—
And shadows rounding silently in the goldenness!

And time is so miraculous
That one looks for angels in human glances
Which delight in innocent play.
Yes! Time is so miraculous.

Klagelied

Die Freundin, die mit grünen Blumen gaukelnd
Spielt in mondenen Gärten –
O! Was glüht hinter Taxushecken!
Goldener Mund, der meine Lippen rührt,
Und sie erklingen wie die Sterne
Über dem Bache Kidron.
Aber die Sternennebel sinken über der Ebene,
Tänze wild und unsagbar.
O! Meine Freundin deine Lippen
Granatapfellippen
Reifen an meinem kristallenen Muschelmund.
Schwer ruht auf uns
Das goldene Schweigen der Ebene.
Zum Himmel dampft das Blut
Der von Herodes
Gemordeten Kinder.

Frühling der Seele

Blumen blau und weiß verstreut
Streben heiter auf im Grund.
Silbern webt die Abendstund',
Laue Öde, Einsamkeit.

Leben blüht nun voll Gefahr,
Süße Ruh um Kreuz und Grab.
Eine Glocke läutet ab,
Alles scheinet wunderbar.

Weide sanft im Äther schwebt,
Hier und dort als flackernd Licht.
Frühling flüstert und verspricht
Und der feuchte Efeu bebt.

Saftig grünen Brot und Wein,
Orgel tönt voll Wunderkraft.
Und um Kreuz und Leidenschaft
Glänzt ein geisterhafter Schein.

Elegy

The girlfriend juggling with green flowers
Plays in lunar gardens—
O! what glows behind yew hedges!
Golden mouth which stirs my lips,
And they ring out like the stars
Over the brook Kidron.
But the starry nebulas sink over the plain,
Dance wild and nameless.
O! my girlfriend your lips
Pomegranate lips
Ripen on my crystalline mouth of shells.
Heavily the golden silence
Of the plain rests on us.
The blood of the children
Murdered by Herod
Steams to heaven.

Springtime of the Soul

Flowers scattered blue and white
Strive cheerfully upon the ground.
Silverly the evening hour weaves,
Balmy wasteland, loneliness.

Life blooms dangerously now,
Sweet rest around cross and grave.
A bell rings away,
Everything seems marvelous.

A willow softly hovers in the ether,
Here and there a flickering light.
Spring whispers and promises
And the damp ivy trembles.

Lushly bread and wine flourish,
The organ sounds full of miraculous power.
And around cross and passion
A ghostly light gleams.

O! Wie schön sind diese Tag'.
Kinder durch die Dämmerung gehn;
Blauer schon die Winde wehn.
Ferne spottet Drosselschlag.

Westliche Dämmerung

Ein Faungeschrei durch Funken tollt,
In Parken schäumen Lichtkaskaden,
Metallischer Brodem um Stahlarkaden
Der Stadt, die um die Sonne rollt.

Ein Gott jagt schimmernd im Tigergespann
Vorbei an Frauen und hellen Bazaren,
Erfüllt von fließenden Golden und Waren.
Und Sklavenvolk heult dann und wann.

Ein trunknes Schiff dreht am Kanal
Sich träg in grünen Sonnengarben.
Ein heiteres Konzert von Farben
Hebt leise an vorm Hospital.

Ein Quirinal zeigt finstere Pracht.
In Spiegeln bunte Mengen kreisen
Auf Brückenbögen und Geleisen.
Vor Banken bleich ein Dämon wacht.

Ein Träumender sieht schwangere Fraun
In schleimigem Glanz vorübergleiten,
Ein Sterbender hört Glocken läuten –
Ein goldner Hort glüht leis' im Graun.

Die Kirche

Gemalte Engel hüten die Altäre;
Und Ruh und Schatten; Strahl aus blauen Augen.
In Weihrauchdünsten schimmern schmutzige Laugen.

O! How beautiful are these days.
Children go through the dusk;
Already the wind blows bluer.
Far away thrushes mock.

Western Dusk

A faun-cry romps through sparks,
In the parks cascades of light foam,
Metallic vapors at the steel arcades
Of the city that rolls around the sun.

A god races shimmering in a harness of tigers
Past women and bright bazaars
Filled with flowing gold and wares.
And slave people howl now and then.

In the canal a drunken ship turns
Sluggishly in green sheaves of sun.
A cheerful concert of colors
Rises quietly before the hospital.

A Quirinal exhibits sinister splendor.
In mirrors colorful crowds circulate
On bridge arches and tracks.
Before benches a demon wakes palely.

A dreamer sees pregnant women
Glide past in slimy brilliance,
A dying man hears bells ringing—
A golden hoard glows quietly in the horror.

The Church

Painted angels guard the altars;
And rest and shadows; radiance from blue eyes.
In incense fumes dirty lyes swim.

Gestalten schwanken jammervoll ins Leere.

Im Schwarzen Betstuhl gleichet der Madonne
Ein kleines Hürlein mit verblichnen Wangen.
An goldnen Strahlen Wachsfiguren hangen;
Weißbärtigen Gott umkreisen Mond und Sonne.

Ein Schein von weichen Säulen und Gerippen.
Am Chor der Knaben süße Stimmen starben.
Sehr leise regen sich versunkene Farben,
Ein strömend Rot von Magdalenens Lippen.

Ein schwangeres Weib geht irr in schweren Träumen
Durch diese Dämmerung voll Masken, Fahnen.
Ihr Schatten kreuzt der Heiligen stille Bahnen,
Der Engel Ruh in kalkgetünchten Räumen.

An Angela
[1. Fassung]

1

Ein einsam Schicksal in verlaßnen Zimmern
Ein sanfter Wahnsinn tastet an Tapeten.
An Fenstern fließen Pelagonienbeeten,
Narzissen auch und keuscher im Verkümmern
Als Alabaster, die im Garten schimmern.

In blauen Schleiern lächeln Indiens Morgen.

Ihr süßer Weihrauch scheucht des Fremdlings Sorgen,
Schlaflose Nacht am Weiher um Angelen.
In leerer Maske ruht sein Schmerz verborgen,
Gedanken, die sich schwarz ins Dunkel stehlen.

Die Drosseln lachen rings aus sanften Kehlen.

2

Die Früchte, die sich rot in Zweigen runden, –

Figures stagger woebegone in the emptiness.

In the black kneeler a smallish whore
With faded cheeks resembles the Madonna.
In golden beams wax figures hang;
Moon and sun circle the white-bearded God.

A shine of smooth columns and skeletons.
The sweet voices of boys died at the chancel.
Very quietly enraptured colors move,
A flowing red from Magdalene's lips.

A pregnant woman goes astray in grave dreams
Through this twilight full of masks, flags.
Her shadow crosses the saints' still ways,
The repose of angel's in lime-washed rooms.

To Angela
[version 1]

1

A lonely destiny in abandoned rooms
A gentle insanity gropes along wallpapers.
Beds of geraniums flow by windows,
Daffodils also and more chaste in the wasting away
As alabaster gleams in the garden.

In blue veils India's mornings smile.

Their sweet incense scares away the stranger's worries,
Sleepless night by the pond because of Angela.
His pain rests hidden in an empty mask,
Thoughts which steal away blackly in the darkness.

The thrushes laugh all around from gentle throats.

2

The fruits which round redly in branches,—

Angelens Lippen, die ihr Süßes zeigen,
Wie Nymphen, die sich über Quellen neigen
In ruhevollem Anblick lange Stunden,
Des Nachmittags grüngoldne, lange Stunden.

Doch manchmal kehrt der Geist zu Kampf und Spiele.

In goldnen Wolken wogt ein Schlachtgewühle
Und Hyazinthnes treibt aus wirren Kressen.
Ein Dämon sinnt Gewitter in der Schwüle,
Im Grabesschatten trauriger Zypressen.

Da fällt der erste Blitz aus schwarzen Essen.

3

Der Juniweiden abendlich Geflüster;
Lang klingt ein Regen nach in Flötenklängen.
Wie regungslos im Grau die Vögel hängen!
Und hier Angelens Ruh im Zweiggedüster;
Es ist der Dichter dieser Schönheit Priester.

Von dunkler Kühle ist sein Mund umflossen.

Im Tal ruhn weiche Nebel hingegossen.
Am Saum des Waldes und der Schwermut Schatten
Schwebt Goldenes von seinem Mund geflossen
Am Saum des Waldes und der Schwermut Schatten.

Die Nacht umfängt sein trunkenes Ermatten.

An Angela
[2. Fassung]

1

Ein einsam Schicksal in verlaßnen Zimmern.
Ein sanfter Wahnsinn tastet an Tapeten,
An Fenstern, rötlichen Geranienbeeten,
Narzissen auch und keuscher im Verkümmern

Angela's lips which show her sweetness,
Like nymphs who bend over springs
In restful viewing for long hours,
The afternoon's green-gold, long hours.

Yet sometimes the spirit returns to fight and game.

In golden clouds a battle melee surges
And a hyacinthlike shape floats from tangled cresses.
A demon ponders thunderstorms in the sultriness,
In the grave's shadow of sad cypresses.

Then the first lightning falls from black flues.

3

The June willows whisper in the evening;
A rain resounds for a long time in flute sounds.
How motionless the birds hang in the gray!
And here Angela's rest in the gloomy branches;
The poet is this beauty's priest.

His mouth is surrounded by dark coolness.

In the valley fog rests softy poured out.
By the edge of the forest and sorrow's shadow
A golden shape floats flowing from his mouth
By the edge of the forest and sorrow's shadow.

Night embraces his drunken exhaustion.

To Angela
[version 2]

1

A lonely destiny in abandoned rooms.
A gentle insanity gropes along wallpapers,
Along windows, reddish beds of geraniums,
Daffodils also and more chaste in the wasting away

Als Alabaster, die im Garten schimmern.

In blauen Schleiern lächeln Indiens Morgen.

Ihr süßer Weihrauch scheucht des Fremdlings Sorgen,
Schlaflose Nacht am Weiher um Angelen.
In leerer Maske ruht sein Schmerz verborgen,
Gedanken, die sich schwarz ins Dunkel stehlen.

Die Drosseln lachen rings aus sanften Kehlen.

2

Den spitzes Gras umsäumt, am Kreuzweg hocken
Die Mäher müde und von Mohne trunken,
Der Himmel ist sehr schwer auf sie gesunken,
Die Milch und Öde langer Mittagsglocken.
Und manchmal flattern Krähen auf im Roggen.

Von Frucht und Greueln wächst die heiße Erde

In goldnem Glanz, o kindliche Geberde
Der Wollust und ihr hyazinthnes Schweigen,
So Brot und Wein, genährt am Fleisch der Erde,
Sebastian im Traum ihr Geistiges zeigen.

Angelens Geist ist weichen Wolken eigen.

3

Die Früchte, die sich rot in Zweigen runden,
Des Engels Lippen, die ihr Süßes zeigen,
Wie Nymphen, die sich über Quellen neigen
In ruhevollem Anblick lange Stunden,
Des Nachmittags grüngoldne, lange Stunden.

Doch manchmal kehrt der Geist zu Kampf und Spiele.

In goldnen Wolken wogt ein Schlachtgewühle
Von Fliegen über Fäulnis und Abszessen.
Ein Dämon sinnt Gewitter in der Schwüle,
Im Grabesschatten trauriger Zypressen.

As alabaster gleams in the garden.

In blue veils India's mornings smile.

Their sweet incense scares away the stranger's worries,
Sleepless night by the pond because of Angela.
His pain rests hidden in an empty mask,
Thoughts which steal away blackly in the darkness.

The thrushes laugh all around from gentle throats.

2

At the crossroads surrounded by spikes of grass
The mowers crouch tired and drunk with poppy,
The sky has sunk very heavy on them,
The milk and desolation of long midday bells.
And sometimes crows flutter up in the rye.

With fruit and horrors the hot earth grows.

In golden brilliance, o childish gesture
Of lust and its hyacinthine silence
When bread and wine nurtured by the flesh of the earth
Show Sebastian in dream their spirituality.

Angela's spirit belongs to soft clouds.

3

The fruits which round redly in branches,
The angel's lips which show her sweetness,
Like nymphs who bend over springs
In restful viewing for long hours,
The afternoon's green-gold, long hours.

However, sometimes the spirit returns to fight and game.

In golden clouds a battle melee of flies
Surges over putrefaction and abscesses.
A demon ponders thunderstorms in the sultriness,
In the grave's shadow of sad cypresses.

Da fällt der erste Blitz aus schwarzen Essen.

4

Des Weidenwäldchens silbernes Geflüster;
Lang klingt ein Regen nach in Flötenklängen.
Im Abend regungslose Vögel hängen!
Ein blaues Wasser schläft im Zweiggedüster.
Es ist der Dichter dieser Schönheit Priester.

Schmerzvolles Sinnen in der dunklen Kühle.

Von Mohn und Weihrauch duften milde Pfühle
Am Saum des Waldes und der Schwermut Schatten
Angelens Freude und der Sterne Spiele
Die Nacht umfängt der Liebenden Ermatten.

Der Saum des Waldes und der Schwermut Schatten.

. . .
. . .
In Milch und Öde; – dunkle Plage
Saturn lenkt finster deine Stund.

Im Schatten schwarzer Thujen irrt
Eva entstellt von Blut und Wunden,
Der süße Leib zerfetzt von Hunden –
O Mund, der herzzerreißend girrt.

Der Arme starr erhobnes Flehn
Ragt wild ins weiße Zelt der Sterne.
Im Ahorn dampft die Mondlaterne,
Am Weiher glühn die Azaleen.

O still! Die blinde Drossel singt
Im Käfig ihre trunkne Weise
Dem goldnen Helios zum Preise –
Ein Kerzenflämmchen zuckt und klingt.

Then the first lightning falls from black flues.

4

Silver whispering of the willow grove;
A rain resounds long after in flute sounds.
In the evening birds hang motionless!
And here Angela's rest in the gloomy branches;
The poet is this beauty's priest.

Painful pondering in the dark coolness.

Balmy puddles fragrant with poppy and incense
By the edge of the forest and gloom's shadow
Angela's joy and the games of the stars
The night embraces the exhaustion of lovers.

The edge of the forest and gloom's shadow.

. . .
. . .

In milk and desolation;—dark plague
Saturn sinisterly steers your hour.

In the shadow of black thujas
Eve strays disfigured with blood and wounds,
The sweet body shredded by dogs—
O mouth which coos heartbreakingly.

The rigidly upraised entreaty of arms
Juts wildly into the white tent of stars.
In the maple the lunar lantern steams,
By the pond the azaleas glow.

O hush! In the cage the blind thrush
Sings her drunken melody
For the price of golden Helios—
A little candle flame twitches and sounds.

O Lied voll Schmerz und Ewigkeit!
Gestirn und Schatten grau erbleichen
Und sind bald nur verlorne Zeichen.
Ein Hahn kräht um die Dämmerzeit.

Träumerei am Abend

Wo einer abends geht, ist nicht des Engels Schatten
Und Schönes! es wechseln Gram und sanfteres Vergessen;
Des Fremdlings Hände tasten Kühles und Zypressen
Und seine Seele faßt ein staunendes Ermatten.

Der Markt ist leer von roten Früchten und Gewinden.
Einträchtig stimmt der Kirche schwärzliches Gepränge,
In einem Garten tönen sanften Spieles Klänge,
Wo Müde nach dem Mahle sich zusammenfinden.

Ein Wagen rauscht, ein Quell sehr fern durch grüne Pfühle.
Da zeigt sich eine Kindheit traumhaft und verflossen,
Angelens Sterne, fromm zum mystischen Bild geschlossen,
Und ruhig rundet sich die abendliche Kühle.

Dem einsam Sinnenden löst weißer Mohn die Glieder,
Daß er Gerechtes schaut und Gottes tiefe Freude.
Vom Garten irrt sein Schatten her in weißer Seide
Und neigt sich über trauervolle Wasser nieder.

Gezweige stießen flüsternd ins verlaßne Zimmer
Und Liebendes und kleiner Abendblumen Beben.
Der Menschen Stätte gürten Korn und goldne Reben,
Den Toten aber sinnet nach ein mondner Schimmer.

Wintergang in a-Moll

Oft tauchen rote Kugeln aus Geästen,
Die langer Schneefall sanft und schwarz verschneit.
Der Priester gibt dem Toten das Geleit.

O song full of pain and eternity!
Stars and shadows pale into gray
And are soon only lost signs.
A cock crows around dawn-time.

Daydreaming in the Evening

Where one goes in the evening is not the angel's shadow
And beauty! grief and gentler forgetting alternate;
The stranger's hands grope coolness and cypresses
And his soul is gripped by an astonishing exhaustion.

The market is emptied of red fruits and garlands.
Harmoniously the church's blackish pageantry attunes
In a garden the tones of soft play sound
Where tired ones find each other after the meal.

A carriage rushes, a spring very far away through green puddles.
There a childhood appears dreamlike and bygone,
Angela's stars, closed devoutly into a mystical constellation,
And calmly the evening coolness becomes full.

White poppy loosens the limbs of the lonely ponderer,
So that he views righteousness and God's deep joy.
From the garden his shadow strays here in white silk
And bends down over mournful waters.

Branches knocked whispering into the abandoned room
And lovers and trembling of small evening flowers.
Corn and golden vines gird the site of man,
But a lunar shimmer ponders after the dead.

Winter Walk in A-Minor

Often red spheres emerge from branches,
Snowed under soft and black by a long snowfall.
The priest escorts the dead person.

Die Nächte sind erfüllt von Maskenfesten.

Dann streichen übers Dorf zerzauste Krähen;
In Büchern stehen Märchen wunderbar.
Ans Fenster flattert eines Greisen Haar.
Dämonen durch die kranke Seele gehen.

Der Brunnen friert im Hof. Im Dunkel stürzen
Verfallne Stiegen und es weht ein Wind
Durch alte Schächte, die verschüttet sind.
Der Gaumen schmeckt des Frostes starke Würzen.

Immer dunkler

Der Wind, der purpurne Wipfel bewegt,
Ist Gottes Odem, der kommt und geht.
Das schwarze Dorf vorm Wald aufsteht;
Drei Schatten sind über den Acker gelegt.

Kärglich dämmert unten und still
Den Bescheidenen das Tal.
Grüßt ein Ernstes in Garten und Saal,
Das den Tag beenden will,

Fromm und dunkel ein Orgelklang.
Marie thront dort im blauen Gewand
Und wiegt ihr Kindlein in der Hand.
Die Nacht ist sternenklar und lang.

Unterwegs
[1. Fassung]

Ein Duft von Myrrhen, der im Zwielicht irrt.
Im Qualm versingen Plätze rot und wüst.
Bazare kreisen und ein Goldstrahl fließt
In alte Läden seltsam und verwirrt.

Im Spülicht glüht Verfallnes; und der Wind

The nights are fulfilled by celebrations of masks.

Then tousled crows glide over the village;
In books fairy tales are written miraculously.
At the window an old man's hair flutters.
Demons go through the sick soul.

The well freezes in the courtyard. Decayed stairs fall
In the darkness and a wind blows
Through old shafts which are buried.
The palate tastes the frost's strong spices.

Always Darker

The wind, which moves purple treetops,
Is God's breath that comes and goes.
The black village rises before the forest;
Three shadows are laid over the field.

Meagerly the valley dusks
Below and silent for the humble.
In garden and hall an earnestness greets
Which wants to complete the day,

An organ-sound pious and dark.
Marie is enthroned there in blue vestment
And cradles her babe in hand.
The night is starlit and long.

On the Way
[version 1]

A scent of myrrh which roams in the twilight.
Plazas red and desolate sink in dense smoke.
Bazaars gyrate and a golden ray flows
Into old shops odd and confused.

In the dishwater decay glows; and the wind

Ruft dumpf die Qual verbrannter Gärten wach.
Beseßne jagen goldnen Träumen nach.
An Fenstern ruhn Dryaden schlank und lind.

Traumsüchtige wandeln, die ein Wunsch verzehrt.
Arbeiter strömen schimmernd durch ein Tor.
Stahltürme glühn am Himmelsrand empor.
O Märchen in Fabriken grau versperrt!

Im Finstern trippelt puppenhaft ein Greis
Und lüstern lacht ein Klimperklang von Geld.
Ein Heiligenschein auf jene Kleine fällt,
Die vorm Kaffeehaus wartet, sanft und weiß.

O goldner Glanz, den sie in Scheiben weckt!
Durchsonnter Lärm dröhnt ferne und verzückt.
Ein krummer Schreiber lächelt wie verrückt
Zum Horizont, den grün ein Aufruhr schreckt.

Auf Brücken von Kristall Karossen ziehn,
Obstkarren, Leichenwägen schwarz und fahl,
Von hellen Dampfern wimmelt der Kanal,
Konzerte klingen. Grüne Kuppeln sprühn.

Volksbäder flimmern in Magie von Licht,
Verwunschne Straßen, die man niederreißt.
Ein Herd von Seuchen wirr im Äther kreist,
Ein Schein von Wäldern durch Rubinstaub bricht.

Verzaubert glänzt im Grau ein Opernhaus.
Aus Gassen fluten Masken ungeahnt,
Und irgendwo loht wütend noch ein Brand.
Ein kleiner Falter tanzt im Windgebraus.

Quartiere dräun voll Elend und Gestank.
Violenfarben und Akkorde ziehn
Vor Hungrigen an Kellerlöchern hin.
Ein süßes Kind sitzt tot auf einer Bank.

Evokes dully the agony of burnt gardens.
The possessed pursue golden dreams.
By windows dryads rest slender and dulcet.

The dream-addicted wander who are consumed by a wish.
Workers surge shimmering through a gate.
Steel towers glow upward at the edge of the sky.
O fairy tale shut gray in factories!

In the sinisterness an old man dollishly trips
And a jingling sound of money laughs lasciviously.
A halo falls on that little girl
Who waits before the coffee house, gentle and white.

O golden brilliance which she wakes in panes!
Sun-filled noise roars distant and ecstatic.
A crooked writer smiles as if crazy
To the horizon which is frightened green by an uproar.

State coaches of crystal move on bridges,
Fruit carts, hearse black and pale,
The canal swarms with bright steamboats,
Concerts sound. Green domes sparkle.

Public baths flicker in magic of light,
Enchanted streets that one demolishes.
A source of epidemics chaotically circles in ether,
A light from forests breaks through ruby-dust.

Spellbound an opera house shines in the gray.
From alleys masks flood unimagined,
And somewhere a fire still blazes furiously.
A small moth dances in the wind-roar.

Lodgings threaten full of squalor and stench.
Viola colors and chords move
Along cellar holes before the hungry.
A sweet child sits dead on a bank.

Unterwegs
[2. Fassung]

Ein Duft von Myrrhen, der durchs Zwielicht irrt,
Ein Fastnachtsspiel, auf Plätzen schwarz und wüst.
Gewölk durchbricht ein goldner Strahl und fließt
In kleine Läden traumhaft und verwirrt.

Im Spülicht glüht Verfallnes und der Wind
Ruft dumpf die Qual verbrannter Gärten wach.
Beseßne jagen dunklen Dingen nach;
An Fenstern ruhn Dryaden schlank und lind.

Ein Knabenlächeln, das ein Wunsch verzehrt.
Verschlossen starrt ein altes Kirchentor.
Sonaten lauscht ein wohlgeneigtes Ohr;
Ein Reiter jagt vorbei auf weißem Pferd.

Im Finstern trippelt puppenhaft ein Greis
Und lüstern lacht ein Klimperklang von Geld.
Ein Heiligenschein auf jene Kleine fällt,
Die vorm Kaffeehaus wartet, sanft und weiß.

O goldner Glanz, den sie in Scheiben weckt!
Der Sonne Lärm dröhnt ferne und verzückt.
Ein krummer Schreiber lächelt wie verrückt
Zum Horizont, den grün ein Aufruhr schreckt.

Karossen abends durch Gewitter ziehn.
Durchs Dunkel stürzt ein Leichnam, leer und fahl.
Ein heller Dampfer landet am Kanal,
Ein Mohrenmädchen ruft im wilden Grün.

Schlafwandler treten vor ein Kerzenlicht,
In eine Spinne fährt des Bösen Geist.
Ein Herd von Seuchen Trinkende umkreist;
Ein Eichenwald in kahle Stuben bricht.

Im Plan erscheint ein altes Opernhaus,
Aus Gassen fluten Masken ungeahnt
Und irgendwo loht wütend noch ein Brand.
Die Fledermäuse schrein im Windgebraus.

On the Way

[version 2]

A scent of myrrh which roams in the twilight.
A carnival play on plazas black and desolate.
A golden ray breaks through clouds and flows
In small shops dreamlike and confused.

In the dishwater decay glows and the wind
Evokes dully the agony of burnt gardens.
The possessed pursue dark things;
By windows dryads rest slender and dulcet.

A boy's smile consumed by a wish.
Locked an old church gate stares.
The benevolent ear listens to sonatas;
A rider trots past on a white horse.

In the sinisterness an old man dollishly trips
And a jingling sound of money laughs lasciviously.
A halo falls on that little girl
Who waits before the coffee house, gentle and white.

O golden brilliance which she wakes in panes!
The sun's noise roars distant and ecstatic.
A crooked writer smiles as if crazy
To the horizon which is frightened green by an uproar.

In the evening state coaches move through thunderstorms.
Through darkness a corpse falls, empty and pale.
A bright steamboat disembarks in the canal,
A young negress calls in the wild green.

Sleep walkers step before a candle light,
The spirit of evil goes into a spider.
A source of epidemics circles the drinkers;
An oak forest breaks into bleak rooms.

In the plan an old opera house appears.
From alleys masks flood unimagined,
And somewhere a fire still blazes furiously.
The bats cry in the wind-roar.

Quartiere dräun voll Elend und Gestank.
Violenfarben und Akkorde ziehn
Vor Hungrigen an Kellerlöchern hin.
Ein süßes Kind sitzt tot auf einer Bank.

Dezember
[1. Fassung]

Am Abend ziehen Gaukler durch den Wald
Auf wunderlichen Wägen, kleinen Rossen.
In Wolken scheint ein goldner Hort verschlossen.
Im weißen Plan sind Dörfer eingemalt.

Der Wind schwingt Schild und Knüppel schwarz und kalt.
Ein Rabe folgt den mürrischen Genossen.
Vom Himmel fällt ein Strahl auf blutige Gossen
Und sacht ein Leichenzug zum Friedhof wallt.

Des Schäfers Hütte schwindet nah im Grau,
Im Weiher gleißt ein Glanz von alten Schätzen;
Die Bauern sich im Krug zum Weine setzen.

Ein Knabe gleitet scheu zu einer Frau.
Man sieht noch in der Sakristei den Küster
Und rötliches Geräte, schön und düster.

Dezembersonett
[2. Fassung]

Am Abend ziehen Gaukler durch den Wald,
Auf wunderlichen Wägen, kleinen Rossen.
In Wolken scheint ein goldner Hort verschlossen,
Im dunklen Plan sind Dörfer eingemalt.

Der rote Wind bläht Linnen schwarz und kalt.
Ein Hund verfault, ein Strauch raucht blutbegossen.
Von gelben Schrecken ist das Rohr durchflossen
Und sacht ein Leichenzug zum Friedhof wallt.

Lodgings threaten full of squalor and stench.
Viola colors and chords move
Along cellar holes before the hungry.
A sweet child sits dead on a bank.

December
[version 1]

At evening jugglers travel through the forest
On quaint wagons, small steeds.
A golden hoard seems locked in clouds.
In the white plain villages are painted.

The wind swings sign and billet black and cold.
A raven follows the morose comrades.
From the sky a ray falls on bloody gutters
And gently a funeral procession floats to the cemetery.

The shepherd's hut dwindles nearby in the gray,
In the pond a brilliance of old treasures glistens;
The farmers sit down in the tavern for wine.

A boy glides shyly to a woman.
One still sees the sexton in the vestry
And reddish utensils, beautiful and dark.

December Sonnet
[version 2]

At evening jugglers travel through the forest
On quaint wagons, small steeds.
A golden hoard seems locked in clouds.
In the dark plain villages are painted.

The red wind billows linen black and cold.
A dog rots, a shrub smokes doused in blood.
A yellow horror flows through the reed
And gently a funeral procession floats to the cemetery.

Des Greisen Hütte schwindet nah im Grau.
Im Weiher gleißt ein Schein von alten Schätzen.
Die Bauern sich im Krug zum Weine setzen.

Ein Knabe gleitet scheu zu einer Frau.
Ein Mönch verblaßt im Dunkel sanft und düster.
Ein kahler Baum ist eines Schläfers Küster.

Grüngolden geht der Tag hervor
Am Hügel über der Kapelle
Marie schaut blütenweiß hervor
So schön erglänzt die alte Schwelle.
Dort wiegen Weiden sanft im Blau
Von Himmelschlüsselchen fällt Tau!
Freu dich! Freu dich!

Dort sing' ich wohl den lieben Tag
Vor dir, Marie, im weißen Kleide
Mein töricht wunderliches Leide
So fröhlich lacht der Drosselschlag
Und grün die Birken aufergehn
Und über stille Gräber wehn –
Freu dich! Freu dich!

Hölderlin

Der Wald liegt herbstlich ausgebreitet
Die Winde ruhn, ihn nicht zu wecken
Das Wild schläft friedlich in Verstecken,
Indes der Bach ganz leise gleitet.

So ward ein edles Haupt verdüstert
In seiner Schönheit Glanz und Trauer
Von Wahnsinnn, den ein frommer Schauer
Am Abend durch die Kräuter flüstert.

The old man's hut dwindles nearby in the gray,
In the pond a brilliance of old treasures glistens;
The farmers sit down in the tavern for wine.

A boy glides shyly to a woman.
A monk fades in the darkness gentle and dark.
A bare tree is a sleeper's sexton.

Green-golden the day arises
By the hill over the chapel
Marie looks out bloom-white
So beautifully the old threshold gleams.
There willows rock softly in the blue
From primrose dew falls!
Be happy! Be happy!

There I will probably sing all the dear day
Before you, Marie, in the white dress
My foolish whimsical suffering
So cheerfully the thrush-trill laughs
And the birches rise green
And blow about still graves—
Be happy! Be happy!

Hölderlin

The forest lies spread out in an autumnal beauty,
The winds are at rest, so as not to awaken it,
The wild animals sleep peacefully in hiding,
While the brook flows ever so gently.

Thus was a noble mind darkened
In the splendor and sorrow of its beauty,
By madness, which a pious shudder
Whispers through the herbs in the evening.

Gedichte 1912–1914

Ein Teppich, darein die leidende Landschaft verblat
Vielleicht Genezareth, im Sturm ein Nachen
Aus Wetterwolken stürzen goldene Sachen
Der Wahnsinn, der den sanften Menschen faßt.
Die alten Wasser gurgeln ein blaues Lachen.

Und manchmal öffnet sich ein dunkler Schacht.
Besessene spiegeln sich in kalten Metallen
Tropfen Blutes auf glühende Platten fallen
Und ein Antlitz zerfällt in schwarzer Nacht.
Fahnen, die in finstern Gewölben lallen.

Andres erinnert an der Vögel Flug
Über dem Galgen der Krähen mystische Zeichen
In spitzen Gräsern versinken kupferne Schleichen
In Weihrauchkissen ein Lächeln verhurt und klug.

Charfreitagskinder blind an Zäunen stehen
Im Spiegel dunkler volle Verwesung
Der Sterbenden hinseufzende Genesung
Und Engel die durch weiße Augen gehen
Von Lidern düstert goldene Erlösung.

Rosiger Spiegel: ein häßliches Bild,
Das im schwarzen Rücken erscheint,
Blut aus brochenen Augen weint
Lästernd mit toten Schlangen spielt.

Schnee rinnt durch das starrende Hemd
Purpurn über das schwarze Gesicht,
Das in schwere Stücken zerbricht
Von Planeten, verstorben und fremd.

Spinne im schwarzen Rücken erscheint
Wollust, dein Antlitz verstorben und fremd.

Poems 1912–1914

A carpet, into which the suffering landscape pales
Perhaps the Sea of Galilee, a boat in the gale
Golden things fall out of storm clouds
Insanity that seizes the gentle human.
The old waters gurgle a blue laughter.

And sometimes a dark pit opens.
The possessed are reflected in cold metals
Drops of blood fall on glowing plates
And a countenance decays in black night.
Flags which babble in sinister vaults.

Other things remind on the birds' flight
Over the gallows the crows' mystical signs
Coppery snakes sink in spiky grasses
In pillows of incense a smile whore-like and clever.

Good Friday's children stand blindly at fences
In the mirror of dark gutters full of rot
The sighing recovery of the dying
And angels who go through white eyes
From lids dimming golden redemption.

Rosy mirror: an ugly image
That appears in the black background,
Blood weeps from broken eyes
Blaspheming plays with dead snakes.

Snow runs through the staring shirt
Purple over the black face
That breaks in heavy pieces
From planets, deceased and strange.

A spider appears in the black background
Lust, your countenance deceased and strange.

Blut rinnt durch das starrende Hemd
Schnee aus brochenen Augen weint.

Dunkel ist das Lied des Frühlingsregens in der Nacht,
Unter den Wolken die Schauer rosiger Birnenblüten
Gaukelei des Herzens, Gesang und Wahnsinn der Nacht.
Feurige Engel, die aus verstorbenen Augen treten.

Gestalt die lange in Kühle finstern Steins gewohnt
Öffnet tönend den bleichen Mund
Runde Eulenaugen – Tönendes Gold.

Verfallen und leer fanden jene die Höhle des Walds
Den Schatten einer Hirschkuh im morschen Geäst
Am Saum der Quelle die Finsternis seiner Kindheit.

Lange singt ein Vogel am Waldsaum deinen Untergang
Die bangen Schauer deines braunen Mantels;
Erscheint der Schatten der Eule im morschen Geäst.

Lange singt ein Vogel am Waldsaum deinen Untergang
Die bangen Schauer deines blauen Mantels
Erscheint der Schatten der Mutter im spitzen Gras.

Lange singt ein Vogel am Waldsaum deinen Untergang
Die bangen Schauer deines schwarzen Mantels
Erscheint der Schatten des Rappens im Spiegel des Quells.

Blood runs through the staring shirt
Snow weeps from broken eyes.

Dark is the song of the spring rain in the night,
Under the clouds the showers of rosy pear blossoms
Trickery of the heart, chant and insanity of the night.
Fiery angels who step from deceased eyes.

Figure which has long dwelt in the coolness of sinister stone
Opens the pale mouth sounding
Round owl's eyes—sounding gold.

Those found the cave of the forest decayed and empty
The shadow of a doe in the rotten branches
At the border of the spring the darkness of his childhood.

Long at the forest border a bird sings your decline
The anxious shudders of your brown coat;
The shadow of the owl appears in the rotten branches.

Long at the forest border a bird sings your decline
The anxious shudders of your blue coat
The shadow of the mother appears in the spiky grass.

Long at the forest border a bird sings your decline
The anxious shudders of your black coat
The shadow of the black horse appears in the mirror of the spring.

[Delirien]

[1 fehlt]

2

Dunkle Deutung des Wassers: Stirne im Mund der Nacht,
Seufzend in schwarzen Kissen des Menschen rosiger Schatten,
Röte des Herbstes, das Rauschen des Ahorns im alten Park,
Kammerkonzerte, die auf verfallenen Treppen verklingen.

3

Der schwarze Kot, der von den Dächern rinnt.
Ein roter Finger taucht in deine Stirne
In die Mansarde sinken blaue Firne,
Die Liebender erstorbene Spiegel sind.

Delirium

Der schwarze Schnee, der von den Dächern rinnt;
Ein roter Finger taucht in deine Stirne
Ins kahle Zimmer sinken blaue Firne,
Die Liebender erstorbene Spiegel sind.
In schwere Stücke bricht das Haupt und sinnt
Den Schatten nach im Spiegel blauer Firne,
Dem kahlen Lächeln einer toten Dirne.
In Nelkendüften weint der Abendwind.

Am Rand eines alten Wassers
[1. Fassung]

Dunkle Deutung des Wassers: Stirne im Mund der Nacht,
Seufzend in schwarzen Kissen des Menschen rosiger Schatten,

[Deliriums]

[1 missing]

2

Dark interpretation of the water: forehead in the mouth of the night,
Sighing in black pillows the rosy shadow of man,
Redness of autumn, the rustle of the maple in the old park,
Chamber concerts which fade on decayed stairs.

3

The black excrement which runs off the roofs.
A red finger dips into your forehead
Blue snow sinks in the attic,
The deceased mirror of lovers.

Delirium

The black snow which runs off the roofs;
A red finger dips into your forehead
Blue snow sinks in the bleak room,
The deceased mirror of lovers.
The head breaks in heavy pieces and ponders
After the shadows in the mirror of blue snow,
The cold smile of a dead strumpet.
In carnation perfume the evening wind weeps.

On the Edge of an Old Water
[version 1]

Dark interpretation of the water: stars in the mouth of the night,
Sighing in black pillows the rosy shadow of man,

Röte des Herbstes, das Rauschen des Ahorns im alten Park,
Kammerkonzerte, die auf verfallenen Treppen verklingen.

Am Rand eines alten Wassers
[2. Fassung]

Dunkle Deutung des Wassers: Zerbrochene Stirne im Munde der Nacht,
Seufzend in schwarzen Kissen des Knaben bläulicher Schatten,
Das Rauschen des Ahorns, Schritte im alten Park,
Kammerkonzerte, die auf einer Wendeltreppe verklingen,
Vielleicht ein Mond, der leise die Stufen hinaufsteigt.
Die sanften Stimme der Nonnen in der verfallenen Kirche,
Ein blaues Tabernakel, das sich langsam auftut,
Sterne, die auf deine knöchernen Hände fallen,
Vielleicht ein Gang durch verlassene Zimmer,
Der blaue Ton der Flöte im Haselgebüsch – sehr leise.

An Mauern hin

Es geht ein alter Weg entlang
An wilden Gärten und einsamen Mauern.
Tausendjährige Eiben schauern
Im steigenden fallenden Windgesang.

Die Falter tanzen, als stürben sie bald,
Mein Blick trinkt weinend die Schatten und Lichter.
Ferne schweben Frauengesichter
Geisterhaft ins Blau gemalt.

Ein Lächeln zittert im Sonnenschein,
Indes ich langsam weiterschreite;
Unendliche Liebe gibt das Geleite.
Leise ergrünt das harte Gestein.

Redness of autumn, the rustling of the maple in the old park,
Chamber concerts which fade on decayed stairs.

On the Edge of an Old Well
[version 2]

Dark interpretation of the water: broken forehead in the mouth
    of the night,
The boy's bluish shadow sighing in black pillows,
The rustling of the maple, steps in the old park,
Chamber concerts which fade on a spiral staircase,
Perhaps a moon which quietly climbs the steps.
The gentle voices of the nuns in the decayed church,
A blue tabernacle which slowly opens,
Stars which fall on your bony hands,
Perhaps a walk through abandoned rooms,
The blue tone of the flute in the hazel bushes—very quietly.

Along Walls

An old path goes along
Near wild gardens and lonesome walls.
Thousand-year-old yews shudder
In the rising falling chant of the wind.

The moths dance as if they would die soon,
My glance drinks weeping the shadows and lights.
Far away women's faces float
Ghostly painted in the blue.

A smile trembles in the sunshine
While I slowly stride on;
Unending love gives escort.
Quietly the hard rock turns green.

I

Ein Blasses, ruhend im Schatten verfallener Stiegen –
Jenes erhebt sich nachts in silberner Gestalt
Und wandelt unterm Kreuzgang hin.

In Kühle eines Baums und ohne Schmerz
Atmet das Vollkommene
Und bedarf der herbstlichen Sterne nicht –

Dornen, darüber jener fällt.
Seinem traurigen Fall
Sinnen lange Liebende nach.

Die Stille der Verstorbenen liebt den alten Garten
Die Irre die in blauen Zimmern gewohnt,
Am Abend erscheint die stille Gestalt am Fenster

Sie aber ließ den vergilbten Vorhang herab –
Das Rinnen der Glasperlen erinnerte an unsere Kindheit,
Nachts fanden wir einen schwarzen Mond im Wald

In eines Spiegels Bläue tönt die sanfte Sonate
Lange Umarmungen
Gleitet ihr Lächeln über des Sterbenden Mund.

Mit rosigen Stufen sinkt ins Moor der Stein
Gesang von Gleitendem und schwarzes Lachen
Gestalten gehn in Zimmern aus und ein
Und knöchern grinst der Tod in schwarzem Nachen.

Pirat auf dem Kanal im roten Wein
Dess Mast und Segel oft im Sturm zerbrachen.
Ertränkte stoßen purpurn aus Gestein
Der Brücken. Stählern klirrt der Ruf der Wachen.

I

A paleness resting in the shadow of decayed staircases—
That one rises at night in silver guise
And wanders under the cloister.

In coolness of a tree and without pain
The perfect breathes
And does not need the autumn stars—

Thorns over which the other falls.
Lovers ponder long after
His sad fall.

The stillness of the deceased loves the old garden,
The madwoman who dwelled in blue rooms,
In the evening the still shape appears in the window

But she draws the yellowed curtain—
The trickling of the glass beads reminded of our childhood,
At night we found a black moon in the forest

The gentle sonata sounds in a mirror's blueness
Long embraces
Her smile glides over the dying one's mouth.

With rosy steps the stone sinks in the moor
Song of gliding and black laughter
Figures go in and out of rooms
And death grins bony in black boat.

Pirate on the canal in the red wine
Whose mast and sail often broke in the storm.
The drowned bump purple against the rock
Of the bridges. Steely the call of the guards clashes.

Doch manchmal lauscht der Blick ins Kerzenlicht
Und folgt den Schatten an verfallnen Wänden
Und Tänzer sind mit schlafverschlungnen Händen.

Die Nacht, die schwarz an deinem Haupt zerbricht
Und Tote, die sich in den Betten wenden
Den Marmor greifen mit zerbrochnen Händen.

Die blaue Nacht ist sanft auf unsren Stirnen aufgegangen.
Leise berühren sich unsere verwesten Hände
Süße Braut!

Bleich ward unser Antlitz, mondene Perlen
Verschmolzen in grünem Weihergrund.
Versteinerte schauen wie unsre Sterne.

O Schmerzliches! Schuldige wandeln im Garten
In wilder Umarmung die Schatten,
Daß in gewaltigem Zorn Baum und Tier über sie sank.

Sanfte Harmonien, da wir in kristallnen Wogen
Fahren durch die stille Nacht
Ein rosiger Engel aus den Gräbern der Liebenden tritt.

O das Wohnen in der Stille des dämmernden Gartens,
Da die Augen der Schwester sich rund und dunkel im Bruder aufgetan,
Der Purpur ihrer zerbrochenen Münder
In der Kühle des Abends hinschmolz.
Herzzerreißende Stunde.

September reifte die goldene Birne. Süße von Weihrauch
Und die Georgine brennt am alten Zaun
Sag! wo waren wir, da wir auf schwarzem Kahn
Im Abend vorüberzogen,

But sometimes the gaze listens in the candlelight
And follows the shadows on decayed walls
And dancers with sleep-devoured hands.

The night that breaks blackly on your head
And dead people who turn over in beds
Grasp the marble with broken hands.

The blue night has gently risen on our foreheads.
Quietly our putrid hands touch
Sweet bride!

Our countenance became pale, lunar pearls
Melted in green pond-ground.
Petrified we contemplate our stars.

O painful! The guilty wander in the garden
The shadows in wild embrace
So that tree and animal sank about them in immense anger.

Gentle harmonies when we ride
Through the still night in crystalline waves
A rosy angel steps from the graves of the lovers.

O the dwelling in the stillness of the dusking garden,
When the eyes of the sister round and dark opened in the brother,
The purple of their broken mouths
Melted in the coolness of the evening.
Heartbreaking hour.

September ripened the golden pear. Sweetness of incense
And the dahlia burns at the old fence
Say! where we were when we passed by on small black boat
In the evening,

Darüberzog der Kranich. Die frierenden Arme
Hielten Schwarzes umschlungen, und innen rann Blut.
Und feuchtes Blau um unsere Schläfen. Arm Kindlein.
Tief sinnt aus wissenden Augen ein dunkles Geschlecht.

Am Abend

Ein blauer Bach, Pfad und Abend an verfallenen Hütten hin.
Hinter dunklen Gebüschen spielen Kinder mit blau und roten Kugeln;
Manche wechseln die Stirne und die Hände verwesen im braunen Laub.

In knöcherner Stille glänzt das Herz des Einsamen,
Schaukelt ein Kahn auf schwärzlichen Wassern.
Durch dunkles Gehölz flattert Haar und Lachen brauner Mägde.

Die Schatten der Alten kreuzen den Flug eines kleinen Vogels;
Geheimnis blauer Blumen auf ihren Schläfen.
Andere schwanken auf schwarzen Bänken im Abendwind.

Goldene Seufzer erlöschen leise in den kahlen Zweigen
Der Kastanie; ein Klang von dunklen Zymbeln des Sommers,
Wenn die Fremde auf der verfallenen Stiege erscheint.

Gericht

Hütten der Kindheit im Herbste sind,
Verfallener Weiler; dunkle Gestalten,
Singende Mütter im Abendwind;
An Fenstern Angelus und Händefalten.

Tote Geburt; auf grünem Grund
Blauer Blumen Geheimnis und Stille.
Wahnsinn öffnet den purpurnen Mund:
Dies irae – Grab und Stille.

Tasten an grünen Dornen hin;
Im Schlaf: Blutspeien, Hunger und Lachen;
Feuer im Dorf, Erwachen im Grün;

The crane passed over. The freezing arms
Held black embraced, and inside blood ran.
And around our temples moist blue. Poor little child.
Deeply a dark race ponders out of knowing eyes.

In the Evening

A blue brook, path and evening along decayed huts.
Behind dark shrubbery children play with blue and red balls;
Some swap the forehead and the hands rot in the brown foliage.

In bony stillness the heart of the lonely one shines,
A small boat rocks on blackish waters.
Through dark woods hair and laughter of brown maids flutters.

The shadows of the old people cross the flight of a small bird;
Mystery of blue flowers on their temples.
Others sway on black benches in the evening wind.

Golden sighs quietly expire in the bleak branches
Of the chestnut; a sound of dark cymbals of summer,
When the strangeress appears on the decayed staircase.

Justice

Huts of childhood in autumn,
Decayed hamlet; dark shapes,
Singing mothers in the evening wind;
At windows Angelus and hands fold.

Still birth; on green ground
Mystery and stillness of blue flowers.
Insanity opens the purple mouth:
Dies irae—grave and stillness.

Groping along green thorns;
In sleep: blood-vomit, hunger and laughter;
Fire in the village, awakening in the green;

Angst und Schaukeln auf gurgelndem Nachen.

Oder an hölzerner Stiege lehnt
Wieder der fremden weißer Schatten. –
Armer Sünder ins Blaue versehnt
Ließ seine Fäulnis Lilien und Ratten.

Schwesters Garten
[1. Fassung]

Es wird schon kühl, es wird schon spat,
Es ist schon Herbst geworden
In Schwesters Garten, still und stad;
Ihr Schritt ist weiß geworden.
Ein Amselruf verirrt und spat,
Es ist schon Herbst geworden
In Schwesters Garten, still und stad;
Ein Engel ist geworden.

Schwesters Garten
[2. Fassung]

In Schwesters Garten still und stad
Ein Blau ein Rot von Blumen spat
Ihr Schritt ist weiß geworden.
Ein Amselruf verirrt und spat,
In Schwesters Garten still und stad;
Ein Engel ist geworden.

[1. Fassung]

Wind, weiße Stimme, die an des Schläfers Schläfe flüstert
In morschem Geäst hockt das Dunkle in seinem purpurnen Haar
Lange Abendglocke, versunken im Schlamm des Teichs
Und darüber neigen sich die gelben Blumen des Sommers.

Fear and swaying on gurgling boat.

Or in wooden staircase again
The white shadow of the strange woman leans.—
Poor sinner longing away in the blueness
Left his putrefaction behind for lilies and rats.

Sister's Garden
[version 1]

It's already become cool, it's already become late,
It already became autumn
In sister's garden, still and quiet;
Her step has turned white.
A blackbird call lost and late,
It already became autumn
In sister's garden, still and quiet;
An angel became.

Sister's Garden
[version 2]

In sister's garden still and quiet
A blue a red from flowers late
Her step has turned white.
A blackbird call lost and late,
In sister's garden still and quiet;
An angel became.

[version 1]

Wind, white voice that whispers near the temple of the sleeper
In rotten branches the darkness crouches in his purple hair
Long evening bell, sunk in the mud of the pond
And over it the yellow flowers of the summer bend.

Konzert von Hummeln und blauen Fliegen in Wildgras und Einsamkeit,
Wo mit rührenden Schritten ehdem Ophelia ging
Sanftes Gehaben des Wahnsinns. Ängstlich wogt das Grün im Rohr
Und die gelben Blätter der Wasserrosen, zerfällt ein Aas in heißen Nesseln
Erwachend umflattern den Schläfer kindliche Sonnenblumen.

Septemberabend, oder die dunklen Rufe der Hirten,
Geruch von Thymian. Glühendes Eisen sprüht in der Schmiede
Gewaltig bäumt sich ein schwarzes Pferd; die hyazinthene Locke der Magd
Hascht nach der Inbrunst seiner purpurnen Nüstern.
Zu gelber Mauer erstarrt der Schrei des Rebhuhns verrostet in faulender
    Jauche ein Pflug
Leise rinnt roter Wein, die sanfte Guitarre im Wirtshaus.
O Tod! Der kranken Seele verfallener Bogen Schweigen und Kindheit.

Aufflattern mit irren Gesichtern die Fledermäuse.

[2. Fassung]

Wind, weiße Stimme, die an des Trunknen Schläfe flüstert;
Verwester Pfad. Lange Abendglocken versanken im Schlamme des Teichs
Und darüber neigen sich die gelben Blumen des Herbstes, flackern
    mit irren Gesichtern
Die Fledermäuse.

Heimat! Abendrosiges Gebirg! Ruh! Reinheit!
Der Schrei des Geiers! Einsam dunkelt der Himmel,
Sinkt gewaltig das Haupt am Waldsaum hin.
Steigt aus finsteren Schluchten die Nacht.

Erwachend umflattern den Schläfer kindliche Sonnenblumen.

So leise läuten
Am Abend die blauen Schatten
An der weißen Mauer.
Stille neigt sich das herbstliche Jahr.

Concert of bumblebees and blue flies in wild grass and loneliness,
Where once Ophelia went with stirring steps
Gentle demeanor of insanity. Anxiously the green surges in the reeds
And the yellow leaves of the water lilies, a carcass molders in hot nettles
Awaking childish sunflowers flutter around the sleeper.

September evening, or the dark calls of the shepherds,
Smell of thyme. Glowing iron sprays in the smithy
Enormously a black horse rears up; the hyacinthine lock of the maid
Snatches after the fervor of its purple nostrils.
The cry of the partridge stiffens to yellow walls a plow rusting
    in rotting manure
Quietly red wine trickles, the gentle guitar in the inn.
O death! The ill soul's decayed arch silence and childhood.

With mad faces the bats flutter up

[version 2]

Wind, white voice that whispers near the temple of the drunken one;
Rotten path. Long evening bells sunk in the mud of the pond
And over it the yellow flowers of the summer bend, the bats flicker
With mad faces.

Homeland! Mountains rosy with evening! Rest! Purity!
The cry of the vulture! Lonely the sky darkens,
By the forest's edge the head sinks enormously.
The night rises from dark ravines.

Awaking childish sunflowers flutter around the sleeper.

So quietly in the evening
The blue shadows ring
By the white wall.
The autumn year ends silently.

Stunde unendlicher Schwermut,
Als erlitt' ich den Tod um dich.
Es weht von Gestirnen
Ein schneeiger Wind durch dein Haar.

Dunkle Lieder
Singt dein purpurner Mund in mir,
Die schweigsame Hütte unserer Kindheit,
Vergessene Sagen;

Als wohnt' ich ein sanftes Wild
In der kristallnen Woge
Des kühlen Quells
Und es blühten die Veilchen rings

Der Tau des Frühlings, der von dunklen Zweigen
Niederfällt, es kommt die Nacht
Mit Sternenstrahlen, da des Lichtes du vergessen.

Unter dem Dornenbogen lagst du und es grub der Stachel
Sich tief in den kristallenen Leib
Daß feuriger sich die Seele der Nacht vermähle.

Es hat mit Sternen sich die Braut geziert,
Die reine Myrthe
Die sich über des Toten anbetendes Antlitz neigt.

Blühender Schauer voll
Umfängt dich endlich der blaue Mantel der Herrin.

O die entlaubten Buchen und der schwärzliche Schnee.
Leise der Nord weht. Hier den braunen Pfad
Ist vor Monden ein Dunkles gegangen.

Allein im Herbst. Immer fallen die Flocken
In das kahle Geäst

Hour of unending sorrow,
As if I perished for you.
From stars a snowy wind
Blows through your hair.

Dark songs
Your purple mouth sings in me,
The taciturn hut of our childhood,
Forgotten legends;

As if I dwell a gentle deer
In the crystalline wave
Of the cool well
And the violets bloomed all around

The dew of spring, which falls down
From dark branches, the night comes
With star beams, because of the light you forgot.

You lay under the arch of thorns and the barb dug
Deeply in the crystal body
So that fierier the soul weds the night.

The bride has adorned herself with stars,
The pure myrtle
Which bends over the adoring countenance of the dead.

Full of blossoming shiver
The blue coat of the mistress finally embraces you.

O the beeches stripped of leaves and the blackish snow.
Quietly the north blows. Here a darkness walked
The brown path months ago.

Alone in autumn. Always the flakes fall
In the bleak branches

Ins dürre Rohr; grünes Kristall singt im Weiher

Leer die Hütte von Stroh; ein Kindliches
Sind die wehenden Birken im Nachtwind.
O der Weg der leise ins Dunkel friert.
Und das Wohnen in rosigem Schnee

An Novalis
[1. Fassung]

Ruhend in kristallner Erde, heiliger Fremdling,
Vom dunklen Munde nahm ein Gott ihm die Klage,
Da er in seiner Blüte hinsank
Friedlich erstarb ihm das Saitenspiel
In der Brust,
Und es streute der Frühling seine Palmen vor ihn,
Da er mit zögernden Schritten
Schweigend das nächtige Haus verließ.

[An Novalis]
[2a. Fassung]

In dunkler Erde ruht der heilige Fremdling.
Es nahm von sanftem Munde ihm die Klage der Gott,
Da er in seiner Blüte hinsank.
Eine blaue Blume
Fortlebt sein Lied im nächtlichen Haus der Schmerzen.

An Novalis
[2b. Fassung]

In dunkler Erde ruht der heilige Fremdling
In zarter Knospe
Wuchs dem Jüngling der göttliche Geist,
Das trunkene Saitenspiel

In the dry reeds; green crystal sings in the pond

The hut of straw empty; the blowing birches
Are a childish shape in the night wind.
O the way which quietly freezes in the darkness.
And the dwelling in rosy snow

To Novalis
[version 1]

Resting in crystalline earth, holy stranger,
A God took his lament from the dark mouth,
When he sank into his bloom
Peacefully the string music died down
In his breast,
And spring scattered its palms before him,
When with halting steps
He silently left the nocturnal house.

[To Novalis]
[version 2a]

In dark earth the holy stranger rests.
God took the lament from his gentle mouth
When he sank into his bloom.
A blue flower
His song lives on in the nocturnal house of pain.

To Novalis
[version 2b]

In dark earth the holy stranger rests
In tender bud
The divine spirit grew in the youth,
The drunken string music

Und verstummte in rosiger Blüte.

Stunde des Grams

Schwärzlich folgt im herbstlichen Garten der Schritt
Dem glänzenden Mond,
Sinkt an frierender Mauer die gewaltige Nacht.
O, die dornige Stunde des Grams.

Silbern flackert im dämmernden Zimmer der Leuchter des Einsamen,
Hinsterbend, da jener ein Dunkles denkt
Und das steinerne Haupt über Vergängliches neigt,

Trunken von Wein und nächtigem Wohllaut.
Immer folgt das Ohr
Der sanften Klage der Amsel im Haselgebüsch.

Dunkle Rosenkranzstunde. Wer bis du
Einsame Flöte,
Stirne, frierend über finstere Zeiten geneigt.

[Nächtliche Klage]
[1. Fassung]

Die Nacht ist über der zerwühlten Stirne aufgegangen
Mit schönen Sternen
Am Hügel, da du von Schmerz versteinert lagst,

Ein wildes Tier im Garten dein Herz fraß.
Ein feuriger Engel
Liegst du mit zerbrochener Brust auf steinigem Acker,

Oder ein nächtlicher Vogel im Wald
Unendliche Klage
Immer wiederholend in dornigem Nachtgezweig.

And fell silent in rosy bloom.

Hour of Grief

Blackish the step follows the gleaming moon
In the autumn garden,
The immense night sinks by the freezing wall.
O, the thorny hour of grief.

Silverly the candlestick of the lonely one flickers in the dusking room,
Dying away, when that one thinks a dark thing
And bends the stony head over the perishing,

Drunk with wine and nightly harmonies.
The ear always follows
The gentle lament of the blackbird in the hazel bushes.

Dark rosary hour. Who are you
Lonesome flute,
Forehead bent freezing over sinister times.

[Nocturnal Lament]
   [version 1]

The night has risen over the wrinkled forehead
With beautiful stars
By the hill where you lay petrified with pain,

A wild animal in the garden feeds on your heart.
A fiery angel
You lie with broken breast on stony field,

Or in the forest a nocturnal bird's
Unending lament
Always repeating in thorny night branches.

Nächtliche Klage

[2. Fassung]

Die Nacht ist über der zerwühlten Stirne aufgegangen
Mit schönen Sternen
Über dem schmerzversteinerten Antlitz,
Ein wildes Tier fraß des Liebenden Herz
Ein feuriger Engel
Stürzt mit zerbrochener Brust auf steinigen Acker,
Wiederaufflatternd ein Geier.
Weh in unendlicher Klage
Mischt sich Feuer, Erde und blauer Quell

An Johanna

Oft hör' ich deine Schritte
Durch die Gasse läuten.
Im braunen Gärtchen
Die Bläue deines Schattens.

In der dämmernden Laube
Saß ich schweigend beim Wein.
Ein Tropfen Blutes
Sank von deiner Schläfe

In das singende Glas
Stunde unendlicher Schwermut.
Es weht von Gestirnen
Ein schneeiger Wind durch das Laub.

Jeglichen Tod erleidet,
Die Nacht der bleiche Mensch.
Dein purpurner Mund
Wohnt eine Wunde in mir.

Als käm' ich von den grünen
Tannenhügeln und Sagen
Unserer Heimat,
Die wir lange vergaßen –

Nocturnal Lament
[version 2]

The night has risen over the wrinkled forehead
With beautiful stars
Over the pain-petrified countenance.
A wild animal feeds on the loving heart
A fiery angel
Falls with broken breast on stony field,
Again a vulture flutters up.
Woe in unending lament
Fire, earth and blue well mingle

To Johanna

Often I hear your steps
Ring through the alley.
In the small brown garden
The blueness of your shadow.

In the dawning bower
I sat in silence with wine.
A drop of blood
Sank from your temple

Into the singing glass
Hour of unending gloom.
From stars a snowy wind
Blows through the foliage.

Any death suffers,
The night of the pale man.
Your purple mouth
Dwells in me like a wound.

As if I came from the green
Fir hills and legends
Of our homeland,
Which we long forgot—

Wer sind wir? Blaue Klage
Eines moosigen Waldquells,
Wo die Veilchen
Heimlich im Frühling duften.

Ein friedliches Dorf im Sommer
Beschirmte die Kindheit einst
Unsres Geschlechts,
Hinsterbend nun am Abend–

Hügel die weißen Enkel
Träumen wir die Schrecken
Unseres nächtigen Blutes
Schatten in steinerner Stadt.

Melancholie

Die blaue Seele hat sich stumm verschlossen,
Ins offne Fenster sinkt der braune Wald,
Die Stille dunkler Tiere; im Grunde mahlt
Die Mühle, am Steg ruhn Wolken hingegossen,

Die goldnen Fremdlinge. Ein Zug von Rossen
Sprengt rot ins Dorf. Der Garten braun und kalt.
Die Aster friert, am Zaun so zart gemalt
Der Sonnenblume Gold schon fast zerflossen.

Der Dirnen Stimmen; Tau ist ausgegossen
Ins harte Gras und Sterne weiß und kalt.
Im teuren Schatten sieh den Tod gemalt,
Voll Tränen jedes Antlitz und verschlossen.

Bitte
[1. Fassung]

Dem Geist schick' deine Flammen, so er duldet,
Gefangen seufzt in schwarzer Mitternacht,
Am Frühlingshügel, so sich dargebracht

Who are we? Blue lament
Of a mossy forest spring
Where the violets
Secretly become fragrant in spring.

A peaceful village in summer
Once sheltered the childhood
Of our race,
Dying off now at the evening—

Hill the white grandchildren
We dream the terror
Of our nightly blood
Shadows in stony city.

Melancholy

The blue soul has mutely closed,
In the open window the brown forest sinks,
The stillness of dark animals; in the valley
The mill grinds, by the footbridge clouds rest poured out,

The golden strangers. A procession of steeds
Gallops red in the village. The garden brown and cold.
The aster freezes so delicately painted on the fence
The sunflower's gold almost flown away.

The stumpets' voices; dew is poured out
On the hard grass and stars white and cold.
See death painted in the dear shadow,
Every countenance full of tears and closed.

Please
[version 1]

Send your flames to the spirit so it endures
Imprisoned sighs in black midnight,
Near the spring hill, when the gentle lamb

Das sanfte Lamm, der Schmerzen tiefsten duldet;
O Liebe, die gleich einem runden Licht
Aufgeht im Herzen und ein Sanftes duldet,
Daß dieses irdene Gefäß zerbricht.

Bitte

[2. Fassung]

Dem Geist schick' deine Flammen, so er duldet,
Gefangen liegt in schwarzer Nacht,
Bis einst er fromm sich dargebracht
Der Welt, der er der Schmerzen tiefsten schuldet;
Die Liebe, die gleich einem Licht
Entbrennt im Herzen und ein Sanftes duldet,
Daß dies Gefäß der Tod zerbricht;
Gemordet Lamm, des Blut die Welt entschuldet.

An Luzifer

[3. Fassung]

Dem Geist leih deine Flamme, glühende Schwermut;
Seufzend ragt das Haupt in die Mitternacht,
Am grünenden Frühlingshügel; wo vor Zeiten
Verblutet ein sanftes Lamm, der Schmerzen tiefsten
Erduldet; aber es folgt der Dunkle dem Schatten
Des Bösen, oder er hebt die feuchten Schwingen
Zur goldenen Scheibe der Sonne und es erschüttert
Ein Glockenton die schmerzzerrissene Brust ihm,
Wilde Hoffnung; die Finsternis flammenden Sturzes.

Nimm blauer Abend eines Schläfe, leise ein Schlummerndes
Unter herbstlichen Bäumen, unter goldener Wolke.
Anschaut der Wald; als wohnte der Knabe ein blaues Wild
In der kristallnen Woge des kühlen Quells

Offers itself, the deepest pain endures;
O love that rises in the heart
Like a round light and endures a gentle shape,
So that this earthen vessel breaks.

Please
[version 2]

Send your flames to the spirit so it endures,
Imprisoned lies in black midnight,
Until once it piously offers itself
For the world, for which he owes the deepest pain.
Love that flames up in the heart
Like a light and endures a gentle shape
So that death breaks this vessel;
Murdered lamb whose blood absolves the world.

To Lucifer
[version 3]

Lend your flame to the spirit, glowing gloom;
Sighing the head rises into midnight,
At the greening spring hill; where before
A gentle lamb bled, endured the deepest
Pain; but the dark one follows the shadow
Of evil, or he lifts the moist wings
To the golden disk of the sun and a sound of bells
Convulses his pain-torn breast,
Wild hope; the sinisterness of flaming downfall.

Blue evening take someone's temple, quietly a slumberer
Under autumn trees, under golden cloud.
The forest beholds; as if the boy a blue deer dwelled
In the crystalline wave of the cool well

So leise schlägt sein Herz in hyazinthener Dämmerung,
Trauert der Schatten der Schwester, ihr purpurnes Haar;
Dieses flackert im Nachtwind. Versunkene Pfade
Nachtwandelt jener und es träumt sein roter Mund
Unter verwesenden Bäumen; schweigend umfängt
Des Weihers Kühle den Schläfer, gleitet
Der verfallene Mond über seine schwärzlichen Augen.
Sterne versinkend im braunen Eichengeäst.

[Am Abend]
[1. Fassung]

Noch ist gelb das Gras, grau und schwarz der Baum
Aber mit ergrünendem Schritt gehst du am Wald hin,
Knabe, der mit großen Augen in die Sonne schaut.
O wie schön sind die entzückten Schrei der Vögelchen.

Der Fluß kommt von den Bergen kalt und klar
Tönt im grünen Versteck; also tönt es,
Wenn du trunken die Beine bewegst. Wilder Spaziergang

Im Blau; Geist der aus Bäumen tritt und bittrem Kraut
Siehe deine Gestalt. O Rasendes! Liebe neigt sich zu Weiblichem,
Bläulichen Wassern. Ruh und Reinheit!

Knospe viel bewahrt, Grünes! Die schon sehr dunkel
Entsühne die Stirn mit dem feuchten Abendzweig,
Schritt und Schwermut tönt einträchtig in purpurner Sonne.

Am Abend
[2. Fassung]

Noch ist gelb das Gras, grau und schwarz der Wald;
Aber am Abend dämmert ein Grün auf.
Der Fluß kommt von den Bergen kalt und klar,
Tönt im Felsenversteck; also tönt es,
Wenn du trunken die Beine bewegst; wilder Spaziergang
Im Blau; und die entzückten Schreie der Vögelchen.

His heart beats so quietly in hyacinthine dusk,
The shadow of the sister mourns, her purple hair;
This flickers in the night wind. Someone
Sleepwalks sunken paths and his red mouth dreams
Under rotting trees; the pond's coolness
Embraces the sleeper silently,
The decayed moon glides over his blackish eyes.
Stars sinking in the brown oak branches.

[In the Evening]
[version 1]

The grass is still yellow, the tree gray and black
But with greening step you go past the forest,
Boy, who with large eyes looks at the sun.
O how beautiful are the enraptured cries of the little birds.

The river comes from the mountains cold and clear
Sounds in the green hiding place; so it sounds,
When you drunkenly move the legs. Wild walk

In the blue; ghost who steps from trees and bitter herb
See your figure. O raving! Love bows towards feminine,
To bluish waters. Rest and purity!

Bud saves many, verdancy! Absolve the forehead
Which is already very dark with the moist evening branches,
Step and gloom resound harmoniously in the purple sun.

In the Evening
[version 2]

The grass is still yellow, the forest gray and black
But in the evening a green dawns,
The river comes from the mountains cold and clear,
Sounds in the rock hiding place; so it sounds,
When you drunkenly move the legs; wild walk
In the blue; and the ecstatic cries of the small birds.

Die schon sehr dunkel, tiefer neigt
Die Stirne sich über bläuliche Wasser, Weibliches;
Untergehend wieder in grünem Abendgezweig.
Schritt und Schwermut tönt einträchtig in purpurner Sonne.

Beim jungen Wein
[1. Fassung]

Sonne purpurn untergeht,
Schwalbe ist schon ferngezogen.
Unter abendlichen Bogen
Junger Wein die Runde geht;
Kind dein wildes Lachen.

Schmerz, darin die Welt vergeht.
Bleib der Augenblick gewogen,
Da im Abend hölzner Bogen
Junger Wein die Runde geht;
Kind dein wildes Lachen.

Flackerstern ans Fenster weht,
Kommt die schwarze Nacht gezogen,
Wenn im Schatten dunkler Bogen
Junger Wein die Runde geht;
Kind dein wildes Lachen.

Beim jungen Wein
[2. Fassung]

Sonne purpurn untergeht,
Schwalbe ist schon ferngezogen.
Unter abendlichen Bogen
Junger Wein die Runde geht;
Schnee fällt hinterm Berge.

Sommers letztes Grün verweht,
Jäger kommt vom Wald gezogen.
Unter abendlichen Bogen

The forehead, which is already very dark,
Bends deeper over bluish waters, feminine;
Declining again in green evening branches.
Step and gloom resound harmoniously in the purple sun.

With the Young Wine
[version 1]

Sun sets purple,
Swallow has already flown far off.
Under arches in the evening
New wine goes round;
Child your wild laughter.

Pain in which the world passes.
Remain attached to the moment
When in the evening of wooden arches
New wine goes round;
Child your wild laughter.

Flickering star blows at the window,
The black night comes,
When in the shadow of dark arches
New wine goes round;
Child your wild laughter.

With the Young Wine
[version 2]

Sun sets purple,
Swallow has already flown far off.
Under arches in the evening
New wine goes round;
Snow falls behind the mountain.

Summer's last green drifts away,
Hunter comes from the forest.
Under arches in the evening

Junger Wein die Runde geht;
Schnee fällt hinterm Berge.

Fledermaus die Stirn umweht,
Kommt ein Fremdling still gezogen.
Unter abendlichen Bogen
Junger Wein die Runde geht;
Schnee fällt hinterm Berge.

Rote Gesichter verschlang die Nacht,
An härener Mauer
Tastet ein kindlich Gerippe im Schatten
Des Trunkenen, zerbrochenes Lachen
Im Wein, glühende Schwermut,
Geistesfolter – ein Stein verstummt
Die blaue Stimme des Engels
Im Ohr des Schläfers. Verfallenes Licht.

Heimkehr

Wenn goldne Ruh der Abend odmet
Wald und dunkle Wiese davor
Ein Schauendes ist der Mensch,
Ein Hirt, wohnend in der Herden dämmernder Stille,
Der Geduld der roten Buchen;
So klar da es Herbst geworden. Am Hügel
Lauscht der Einsame dem Flug der Vögel,
Dunkler Bedeutung und die Schatten der Toten
Haben sich ernster um ihn versammelt;
Mit Schauern erfüllt ihn kühler Resedenduft,
Die Hütten der Dörfler der Hollunder,
Wo vor Zeiten das Kind gewohnt.

Erinnerung, begrabene Hoffnung
Bewahrt dies braune Gebälk,
Darüber Georginen hangen
Daß darnach er die Hände ringe,

New wine goes round;
Snow falls behind the mountain.

Bat blows around the forehead,
A stranger comes silently.
Under arches in the evening
New wine goes round;
Snow falls behind the mountain.

The night devoured red faces,
By a hairy wall
A childish skeleton gropes in the shadow
Of the drunkard, broken laughter
In the wine, glowing gloom,
Spirit's torture—a stone falls silent
The blue voice of the angel
In the ear of the sleeper. Decayed light.

Homecoming

When the evening breathes golden rest
Forest and dark meadow before which
Man is an onlooker,
A shepherd dwelling in the flocks' dusking stillness,
The patience of the red beeches;
So clear since it has become autumn. By the hill
The lonely one listens to the flight of birds,
To dark meaning and the shadows of the dead
Have gathered more earnestly around him;
Cool mignonette fragrance fulfills him with shudders,
The huts of the villagers the elder tree
Where in former times the child dwelled.

Memory, buried hope
Is preserved by these brown rafters,
Over which dahlias hang
So that the hands strive after them,

Im braunen Gärtchen den schimmernden Schritt
Verboten Lieben, dunkles Jahr,
Daß von blauen Lidern die Tränen stürzten
Dem Fremdling unaufhaltsam.

Von braunen Wipfeln tropft der Tau,
Da jener ein blaues Wild am Hügel erwacht,
Lauschend den lauten Rufen der Fischer
Am Abendweiher
Dem ungestalten Schrei der Fledermäuse;
Aber in goldener Stille
Wohnt das trunkene Herz
Seines erhabenen Todes voll.

Träumerei
[1. Fassung]

Sanftes Leben wächst im Stillen
Schritt und Herz durchs Grüne eilt
Liebendes an Hecken weilt,
Die sich schwer mit Düften füllen.

Buche sinnt; die feuchten Glocken
Sind verstummt, der Bursche singt
Feuer Dunkeles umschlingt
O Geduld und stumm Frohlocken.

Frohen Mut gib noch zum Ende
Schön beseelte, stille Nacht,
Goldnen Wein, den dargebracht
Einer Schwester blaue Hände.

Träumerei
[2. Fassung]

Sanftes Leben wächst rings im Stillen
Durchs Grüne eilt Schritt und Herz.
Liebendes weilt an Hecken,

In the brown garden the shimmering step
Forbidden love, dark year,
So that from blue eyelids the tears
Of the stranger fell irresistibly.

From brown treetops dew drips,
When that one a blue deer awakes on the hill,
Listening to the loud calls of the fishermen
By the evening pond
To the amorphous cry of the bats;
But in golden stillness
The drunken heart dwells
Full of its noble death.

Daydreaming
[version 1]

Gentle life grows in the stillness
Step and heart hurries through the green
Love stays by hedges
That fill up heavily with fragrances.

Beech ponders; the moist bells
Fell silent, the fellow sings
Fire embraces darkness
O patience and mute rejoicing.

Beautifully animated, silent night
Still gives glad courage to the end.
Golden wine, offered by
A sister's blue hands.

Daydreaming
[version 2]

Gentle life grows all around in the stillness
Step and heart hurries through the green
Love stays by hedges

Die sich mit Düften füllen.

Tiefsinnige Buche im Wirtshausgarten. Die feuchten Glocken
Sind verstummt; ein Bursche singt
– Feuer das Dunkles sucht –
O blaue Stille, Geduld!

Frohen Mut auch gib
Grünende Nacht dem Einsamen,
Dem sein Stern erlosch,
Lachen in purpurnem Wein.

Träumerei
[3. Fassung]

Verliebte gehn an Hecken,
Die sich mit Düften füllen.
Am Abend kommen frohe Gäste
Von der dämmernden Straße.

Sinnige Kastanie im Wirtshausgarten.
Die feuchten Glocken sind verstummt.
Ein Bursche singt am Fluß
– Feuer, das Dunkeles sucht –

O blaue Stille! Geduld!
Wenn jegliches blüht.

Sanften Mut auch gib
Nacht dem Heimatlosen,
Unergründliches Dunkel
Goldne Stunde im Wein.

Psalm

Stille; als sänken Blinde an herbstlicher Mauer hin,
Lauschend mit morschen Schläfen dem Flug des Raben;
Goldne Stille des Herbstes, das Antlitz des Vaters in flackernder Sonne

That fill up with fragrance.

Profound beech in the inn garden; the moist bells
Fell silent; a fellow sings
—Fire that searches darkness—
O blue stillness, patience!

Greening night, give
the lonely one glad courage,
Whose star expired,
Laughter in purple wine.

Daydreaming
[version 3]

Lovers go by hedges
That fill up with fragrance.
In the evening glad guests come
From the dusking road.

Pondering chestnut in the inn garden.
The moist bells fell silent.
A fellow sings by the river
—Fire that searches darkness—

O blue stillness! Patience!
When anything blooms.

Night, also give
The homeless one gentle courage,
Unfathomable darkness
Golden hour in vine.

Psalm

Stillness; as if blind people sank down by autumn wall,
Listening with rotten temples to the flight of the ravens;
Golden silence of autumn, the countenance of the father

Am Abend verfällt im Frieden brauner Eichen das alte Dorf,
Das rote Gehämmer der Schmiede, ein pochendes Herz.
Stille; in langsamen Händen verbirgt die hyazinthene Stirne die Magd
Unter flatternden Sonnenblumen. Angst und Schweigen
Brechender Augen erfüllt das dämmernde Zimmer, die zögernden Schritte
Der alten Frauen, die Flucht des purpurnen Munds, der langsam
    im Dunkel erlischt.

Schweigsamer Abend in Wein. Vom niedern Dachgebälk
Fiel ein nächtlicher Falter, Nymphe vergraben in bläulichen Schlaf.
Im Hof schlachtet der Knecht ein Lamm, der süße Geruch des Blutes
Umwölkt unsre Stirnen, die dunkle Kühle des Brunnens.
Nachtrauert die Schwermut sterbender Astern, goldne Stimmen im Wind.
Wenn es Nacht wird siehst du mich aus vermoderten Augen an,
In blauer Stille verfielen deine Wangen zu Staub.
So leise erlöscht ein Unkrautbrand, verstummt der schwarze Weiler
    im Grund
Als stiege das Kreuz den blauen Kalvarienhügel herab,
Würfe die schweigende Erde ihre Toten aus.

[Herbstliche Heimkehr]
[1b. Fassung]

Erinnerung, begrabene Hoffnung
Bewahrt dies braune Gebälk,
Darüber Georginen hangen
Immer stillere Heimkehr,
Der verfallne Garten den dunklen Abglanz
Vergangener Jahre,
Daß von blauen Lidern die Tränen stürzen
Dem Fremdling unaufhaltsam.

Herbstliche Heimkehr
[2. Fassung]

Erinnerung, begrabene Hoffnung
Bewahrt dies braune Gebälk

in the flickering sun
At evening the old village decays in the peace of brown oaks,
The red hammering of the smithy, a pounding heart.
Stillness; in slow hands the maid hides the hyacinthine forehead
Under fluttering sunflowers. Fear and silence
Of extinguishing eyes fulfills the dusking room, the halting steps
Of old women, the escape of the purple mouth which slowly expires
in the darkness.

Taciturn evening in vine. From the low rafters
A nocturnal moth fell, nymph buried in bluish sleep.
In the courtyard the farm boy slaughters a lamb, the sweet smell
of the blood
Clouds our foreheads, the dark coolness of the fountain.
The gloom of dying asters regrets, golden voices in the wind.
When it becomes night you look at me from moldered eyes,
In blue stillness your cheeks decayed to dust.
So quietly a weed's fire expires, the black hamlet in the ground falls silent
As if the cross climbed down the blue hill of Calvary,
The silent earth ejected its dead.

[Autumn Homecoming]
[version 1b]

Memory, buried hope
Is preserved by this brown timber,
Dahlias hang over it
Ever silenter homecoming,
The dark reflection of past years
By the decayed garden,
So that from blue eyelids the tears
Of the stranger fall irresistibly.

Autumn Homecoming
[version 2]

Memory, buried hope
Is preserved by this brown timber,

Darüber Georginen hangen,
Immer stillere Heimkehr,
Der verfallne Garten dunklen Abglanz
Vergangner Jahre,
Daß von blauen Lidern Tränen stürzen
Unaufhaltsam.
O Geliebtes!
Schon tropft vom rostigen Ahorn
Laub, hinüberschimmern der Schwermut
Kristallne Minuten
Zur Nacht.

Herbstliche Heimkehr
[3. Fassung]

Erinnerung, begrabene Hoffnung
Bewahrt dies braune Gebälk
Darüber Georginen hangen,
Immer stillere Heimkehr,
Der verfallne Garten dunklen Abglanz
Kindlicher Jahre,
Daß von blauen Lidern Tränen stürzen
Unaufhaltsam;
Hinüberschimmern der Schwermut
Kristallne Minuten
Zur Nacht.

[Neige]
[1. Fassung]

O geistlich Wiedersehn
Im alten Herbst!
So stille entblättern gelbe Rosen
Am Gartenzaun,
Schmolz in Tränen
Ein großer Schmerz.
So endet der goldne Tag.
Reich' deine Hand mir liebe Schwester

Dahlias hang over it
Ever silenter homecoming,
The dark reflection of past years
By the decayed garden,
So that tears fall from blue eyelids
Irresistibly.
O beloved!
Already foliage drips from the rusty maple,
Gloom's crystalline minutes
Gleam across
To the night.

Autumn Homecoming
[version 3]

Memory, buried hope
Is preserved by this brown timber,
Dahlias hang over it
Ever silenter homecoming,
The dark reflection of childish years
By the decayed garden,
That tears fall from blue eyelids
Irresistibly;
Gloom's crystalline minutes
Gleam across
To the night.

[Remnant]
[version 1]

O spiritual reunion
In old autumn!
So still yellow roses shed
Their leaves by the garden fence,
A great pain
Melted in tears.
So the golden day ends.
Reach your hand to me dear sister

In der Abendkühle.

[Neige]
[2. Fassung]

O geistlich Wiedersehn
In altem Herbst.
Gelbe Rosen
Entblättern am Gartenzaun,
Zu dunkler Träne
Schmolz ein großer Schmerz,
O Schwester!
So stille endet der goldne Tag.

Lebensalter

Geistiger leuchten die wilden
Rosen am Gartenzaun;
O stille Seele!

Im kühlen Weinlaub weidet
Die kristallne Sonne;
O heilige Reinheit!

Es reicht ein Greis mit edlen
Händen gereifte Früchte.
O Blick der Liebe!

Die Sonnenblumen

Ihr goldenen Sonnenblumen,
Innig zum Sterben geneigt,
Ihr demutsvollen Schwestern
In solcher Stille
Endet Helians Jahr

In the evening coolness.

[Remnant]
[version 2]

O spiritual reunion
In old autumn.
Yellow roses
Shed their leaves by the garden fence,
A great pain melted
To a dark tear,
O sister!
So still the golden day ends.

Age

More spiritually the wild roses
Shine by the garden fence;
O silent soul!

In the cool wine leaves
The crystalline sun grazes;
O holy purity!

An old man with noble
Hands offers ripened fruits.
O look of love!

The Sunflowers

You golden sunflowers,
Tenderly bowed toward death,
You sisters full of humility
In such stillness
Helian's year

Gebirgiger Kühle.

Da erbleicht von Küssen
Die trunkne Stirne ihm
Inmitten jener goldenen
Blumen der Schwermut
Bestimmt den Geist
Die schweigende Finsternis.

So ernst o Sommerdämmerung.
Von müdem Munde
Sank dein goldner Odem ins Tal
Zu den Stätten der Hirten,
Versinkt im Laub.
Ein Geier hebt am Waldsaum
Das versteinerte Haupt –
Ein Adlerblick
Erstrahlt im grauen Gewölk
Der Nacht.

Wild erglühen
Die roten Rosen am Zaun
Erglühend stirbt
In grüner Woge Liebendes hin
Eine erblichene Rose

Of mountainous coolness ends.

Then his drunken forehead
Pales from kisses
Amid those golden
Flowers of gloom
The spirit is determined
By silent sinisterness.

So earnestly o summer dusk.
From tired mouth
Your golden breath sank in the valley
To the places of the shepherds,
Sinks into the foliage.
A vulture lifts at the forest's edge
The petrified head—
An eagle's view
Shines in the gray clouds
The night.

The red roses
Glow wildly by the fence
What loves
Dies away glowing in the green wave
A pale rose

Doppelfassungen

der zu Lebzeiten publizierten Gedichte

Farbiger Herbst
[2. Fassung]

Ein Brunnen singt. Die Wolken stehn
Im klaren Blau die weißen zarten.
Bedächtig stille Menschen gehn
Am Abend durch den alten Garten.

Der Ahnen Marmor ist ergraut
Ein Vogelzug streift in die Weiten.
Ein Faun mit toten Augen schaut
Nach Schatten, die ins Dunkel gleiten.

Das Laub fällt rot vom alten Baum
Und kreist herein durchs offene Fenster.
Ein Feuerschein glüht auf im Raum
Und malet trübe Angstgespenster.

Opaliger Dunst webt über das Gras
Ein Teppich von verwelkten Düften.
Im Brunnen schimmert wie grünes Glas
Die Mondessichel in frierenden Lüften.

Traum des Bösen
[2. Fassung]

O diese kalkgetünchten, kahlen Gänge;
Ein alter Platz; die Sonn' in schwarzen Trümmern.
Gebein und Schatten durch ein Durchhaus schimmern
Im Hafen blinken Segel, Masten, Stränge.

Ein Mönch, ein schwangres Weib dort im Gedränge.
Guitarren klimpern; Flucht aus leeren Zimmern.
Kastanien schwül in goldnem Glanz verkümmern;

Double Versions

of the poems published during Trakl's lifetime

Colorful Autumn
[version 2 of 'Music in Mirabell']

A fountain sings. The clouds stand
In clear blueness, white, delicate.
Silent people wander thoughtfully
Through the old garden in the evening.

The ancestors' marble has turned gray.
A line of birds streaks into the distance.
A faun with dead eyes gazes
After shadows that glide into darkness.

The leaves fall red from the old tree
And whirl inside through the open window.
A firelight glows in the room
And paints dim specters of anxiety.

Opal smoke weaves over the grass,
A carpet of wilted smells.
In the fountain the sickle moon shimmers
Like green glass in freezing air.

Dream of Evil
[version 2]

O these lime-whitewashed, bleak alleys;
An old square; the sun in black ruins.
Bones and shadows shimmer through a passageway
In the harbor sails, masts, and ropes flash.

A monk, a pregnant woman there in the crowd.
Guitars strum; escape from empty rooms.
Chestnuts shrivel sultry in golden radiance;

Schwarz ragt der Kirchen trauriges Gepränge.

Aus bleichen Masken schaut der Geist des Bösen.
Paläste dämmern grauenvoll und düster;
Am Abend regt auf Inseln sich Geflüster.

Des Vogelfluges wirre Zeichen lesen
Aussätzige, die zur Nacht vielleicht verwesen.
Im Park erblicken zitternd sich Geschwister.

Traum des Bösen
[3. Fassung]

Verhallend eines Sterbeglöckchens Klänge –
Ein Liebender erwacht in schwarzen Zimmern,
Die Wang' an Sternen, die am Fenster flimmern.
Am Strome blitzen Segel, Masten, Stränge.

Ein Mönch, ein schwangres Weib dort im Gedränge.
Guitarren klimpern, rote Kittel schimmern.
Kastanien schwül in goldnem Glanz verkümmern;
Schwarz ragt der Kirchen trauriges Gepränge.

Aus bleichen Masken schaut der Geist des Bösen.
Ein Platz verdämmert grauenvoll und düster;
Am Abend regt auf Inseln sich Geflüster.

Des Vogelfluges wirre Zeichen lesen
Aussätzige, die zur Nacht vielleicht verwesen.
Im Park erblicken zitternd sich Geschwister.

Leise
[1. Fassung]

Im Stoppelfeld ein schwarzer Wind gewittert.
Aufblühn der Traurigkeit Violenfarben,
Gedankenkreis, der trüb das Hirn umwittert.
Am Zaune lehnen Astern, die verstarben

The churches' sad pageantry towers black.

The spirit of evil watches from pale masks.
Palaces dusk gruesome and somber.
In the evening whispers stir on the islands.

Lepers, perhaps decaying during the night,
Read confused signs from the flight of birds.
In the park siblings behold each other trembling.

Dream of Evil
[version 3]

Fading away of a death-bell's sounds—
A lover awakens in black rooms,
The cheek near stars that flicker at the window.
In the river sails, masts, and ropes flash.

A monk, a pregnant woman there in the crowd.
Guitars strum, red smocks gleam.
Chestnuts shrivel sultry in golden shine;
The churches' sad pageantry towers black.

The spirit of evil watches from pale masks.
A square dusks gruesome and somber.
In the evening whispers stir on the islands.

Lepers, perhaps decaying during the night,
Read confused signs from the flight of birds.
In the park siblings behold each other trembling.

Quietly
[version 1 of 'Melancholy']

In the stubble field a black wind thunders.
Sadness' violet colors burst into bloom,
Thought-circle that cloudily shrouds the brain.
By the fence asters lean, deceased,

Und Sonnenblumen schwärzlich und verwittert,
Gelöst in Schminken und Zyanenfarben.
Ein wunderlicher Glockenklang durchzittert
Reseden, die in schwarzem Flor verstarben
Und unsere Stirnen schattenhaft vergittert
Versinken leise in Zyanenfarben
Mit Sonnenblumen schwärzlich und verwittert
Und braunen Astern, die am Zaun verstarben.

Melancholia
[2. Fassung]

Bläuliche Schatten. O ihr dunklen Augen
Die lang mich anschaun im Vorübergleiten.
Guitarrenklänge sanft den Herbst begleiten
Im Garten aufgelöst in braunen Laugen.
Des Todes ernste Düsternis bereiten
Nymphische Hände, an Purpurbrüsten saugen
Verfallne Lippen und in braunen Laugen
Des Sonnenjünglings feuchte Locken gleiten.

Ein Stoppelfeld. Ein schwarzer Wind gewittert.
Aufblühn der Traurigkeit Violenfarben,
Gedankenkreis, der trüb das Hirn umwittert.
An Zäunen lehnen Astern, die verstarben
Und Sonnenblumen schwärzlich und verwittert;
Da schweigt die Seele grauenvoll erschüttert
Entlang an Zimmern, leer und dunkelfarben.

[Verwandlung]
[1. Fassung]

Des Herbstes Kühle: Ein Zimmer grau verhängt.
Hier zeigt sich Heiterkeit, ein tüchtig Leben
Des Menschen Hände tragen goldne Reben
In sanfte Augen Gott sich stille senkt.

Am Abend wandelt jener über Land.

And sunflowers blackish and weathered
Dissolve in paints and cyan colors.
A quaint bell-sound quivers through
Mignonettes that are deceased in black rows
And our foreheads, shadowy trellised,
Sink quietly into cyan colors
With sunflowers blackish and weathered
And brown asters deceased by the fence.

Melancholia
[version 2 of 'Melancholy']

Bluish shadows. O you dark eyes,
That gaze long at me gliding past.
Guitar chords softly accompany autumn
In the garden, dissolved in brown lyes.
Nymph-like hands prepare
Death's earnest somberness, decayed lips
Suck at red breasts, and in brown lyes
The moist curls of the sun-youth glide.

A stubble field. A black wind thunders.
Sadness' violet colors burst into bloom,
Thought-circle that cloudily shrouds the brain.
By the fences asters lean, deceased,
And sunflowers blackish and weathered;
There the soul silences grimly shaken
Along rooms empty and dark colored.

[Transformation]
[version 1]

The coolness of autumn: a room imposes gray.
Here cheerfulness appears, a hard life
The hands of man carrying golden vines
In gentle eyes God silently descends.

In the evening the other one wanders over land.

Den Weg erfüllt der Eichen braunes Schweigen
Und immer sinken Blätter von den Zweigen
Die Seele friert im schwärzlichen Gewand.

Geruhiges vor einer Schenke spielt
Vom Munde ist die Bitternis gesunken
Holunderfrüchte, Klänge, weich und trunken
Dem Einsamen folgt leise nach ein Wild.

Heiterer Frühling
[1. Fassung]

Wenn neu ergrünt der Bach in Abend fließt,
In Rohr und Weide rauscht das Frühlingsjahr;
Die blaue Luft ist wunderbar
Von Blühendem, das sich zur Nacht ergießt.

An stillen Dämmerhecken läuft der Wind
Und sucht des Einsamen gestirnten Pfad.
In Gottes Schoß erglänzt die junge Saat,
Der Wald mit seinen Tieren weich und lind.

Die Birken dort, der schwarze Dornenstrauch
Stehn sanft in Schmerz und Wollust aufgelöst.
Hell Grünes blüht, ein dunkles Grün verwest
Und Kröten schliefen durch den jungen Lauch.

Dich lieb' ich treu, du derbe Wäscherin.
Noch trägt die Flut des Himmels rosige Last.
Ein Fischlein blitzt vorüber und verblaßt;
Der Wind läuft silbern durch die Erlen hin,

Entlang an Dämmerhecken schwer und leis';
Ein kleiner Vogel trällert wie verrückt.
Das junge Korn schwillt leise und verzückt
Und Bienen sammeln noch mit ernstem Fleiß.

Komm Liebe nun zum müden Arbeitsmann;
In seine Hütte fällt ein lauer Strahl.
Der Wald strömt durch das Dunkel herb und fahl
Und Knospen flüstern heiter dann und wann.

The oaks' brown silence fulfills the way
And always leaves sink from the branches
The soul freezes in the blackish vestment.

Peacefulness plays before an inn,
From the mouth the bitterness sank
Fruits of the elder, sounds soft and drunk,
A deer quietly follows the lonely one.

Cheerful Spring
[version 1]

When newly greened the brook flows into evening,
The spring-year rustles in reed and willow.
The blue air is glorious
With blossoming which pours forth into the night.

Past silent dusking hedges the wind runs
And seeks the starry path of the lonely one.
In God's womb the young sowing gleams,
The forest with its animals gentle and dulcet.

The birches there, the black thorn bush,
Stand softly dissolved in pain and lust.
Brightly green blooms, a dark green rots
And toads slept among the young leeks.

I love you truly, sturdy laundress,
Still the waters bear the sky's rosy burden.
A small fish flashes past and fades;
The wind runs silverly along through the alders.

Along by dusking hedges heavy and quiet,
A small bird warbles like crazy.
The young corn swells quietly and ecstatically
And bees still collect with earnest diligence.

Come now, love, to the weary laborer;
Into his hut a mild beam falls.
The forest streams through the evening austere and pale
And now and then buds whisper cheerfully.

Wie scheint doch alles Werdende so krank!
Ein Fieberhauch um einen Weiler kreist;
Doch aus Gezweigen winkt ein sanfter Geist
Und öffnet das Gemüte weit und bang.

Ein blühender Erguß verrinnt sehr sacht
Und Ungebornes pflegt der eignen Ruh.
Die Liebenden blühn ihren Sternen zu
Und süßer fließt ihr Odem durch die Nacht.

So schmerzlich gut und wahrhaft ist, was lebt;
Und leise rührt dich an ein alter Stein:
Wahrlich! Ich werde immer bei euch sein.
O Mund! der durch die Silberweide bebt.

[Trübsinn]
[2. Fassung]

In Schenken träumend oft am Nachmittag,
In Gärten früh vom Herbst verbrannt und wüst
Der trunkene Tod geht stumm vorbei und grüßt
In dunklem Käfig tönt ein Drosselschlag.

Aus solcher Bläue tritt ein rosig Kind
Und spielt mit seinen Augen schwarz und glatt.
Ein Goldnes tropft aus Zweigen mild und matt
In rotem Laubwerk aber spielt der Wind.

Schon glänzt Saturn. Im Dunkel rauscht der Bach
Und leise rührt des Freundes blaue Hand
Und glättet stille Stirne und Gewand.
Ein Licht ruft Schatten in Hollunder wach.

How all that is being born seems so ill!
A whiff of fever encircles a hamlet.
Yet from branches a gentle spirit beckons,
And opens the mind wide and frightened.

A blooming outpour trickles away very gradually
And the unborn tends to its own repose.
The lovers bloom toward their stars
And sweeter their breath flows through the night.

So painfully good and true is, what lives;
And quietly an old stone touches you:
Truly! I will always be with you.
O mouth! that trembles through the white willow.

[Doldrums]
[version 2]

In inns dreaming often in the afternoon,
In gardens burnt early by autumn and desolate
The drunken death goes mutely past and greets
In dark cage a thrush-flapping resounds.

From such blueness a rosy child steps
And plays with his eyes black and smooth.
A goldenness drips from branches bland and dull
But in red foliage the wind plays.

Already Saturn shines. In darkness the brook rushes
And quietly the friend's blue hand stirs
And silently smoothes forehead and robe.
A light rouses shadows in the elders.

Psalm
[1. Fassung]

Es ist ein Licht, das der Wind ausgelöscht hat.
Es ist ein Heidekrug, den am Nachmittag ein Betrunkener verläßt.
Es ist ein Weinberg verbrannt und schwarz mit Löchern voll Spinnen.
Es ist ein Raum, den sie mit Milch getüncht haben.
Der Wahnsinnige ist gestorben. Es ist eine Insel der Südsee,
Den Sonnengott zu empfangen. Man rührt die Trommeln.
Die Männer führen kriegerische Tänze auf.
Die Frauen wiegen die Hüften in Schlinggewächsen und Feuerblumen,
Wenn das Meer singt. O! unser verlorenes Paradies.

Die Nymphen haben die goldenen Wälder verlassen.
Man begräbt den Fremden; dann hebt ein Flimmerregen an.
Der Sohn des Pan erscheint in Gestalt eines Erdarbeiters,
Der den Mittag am glühenden Asphalt verschläft.
Es sind kleine Mädchen in einem Hof mit Kleidchen
        voll herzzerreißender Armut.
Es sind Zimmer erfüllt von Akkorden und Sonaten.
Es sind Schatten, die sich vor einem erblindeten Spiegel umarmen.
An den Fenstern des Spitals wärmen sich Genesende.
Ein weißer Dampfer am Kanal trägt blutige Seuchen herauf.

Die fremde Schwester erscheint in Jemands bösen Träumen.
Ruhend im Haselgebüsch spielt sie mit seinen Sternen.
Der Student, vielleicht ein Doppelgänger schaut ihr lange
        vom Fenster nach.
Hinter ihm steht sein toter Bruder. Im Dunkel des Zimmers mögen
        seltsame Dinge vor sich gehen.
In roten Hyazinthen verblaßt die Erscheinung der jungen Krankenwärterin.
Der Garten ist im Abend. Im Kreuzgang flattern die Fledermäuse umher.
Die Kinder des Hausmeisters hören zu spielen auf und suchen das Gold
        des Himmels.
Es ist eine Wolke die sich auflöst. In der Laube hat sich der Gärtner erhängt.
Im Glashaus verschwimmen braune und blaue Farben. Es ist
        der Untergang, dem wir zutreiben.

Wo die Toten von gestern lagen, trauern Engel mit weißen
        zerbrochenen Flügeln.
Unter Eichen irren Dämonen mit brennenden Stirnen.
Im Moorland schweigen vergangene Vegetationen.
Es ist ein Flüsterwind – Gott der traurige Stätten verläßt.

Psalm

[version 1]

It is a light, which the wind has extinguished.
It is a village inn, which a drunkard abandons in the afternoon.
It is a vineyard, burned and black with holes full of spiders.
It is a room, which they have whitewashed with milk.
The lunatic is dead. It is an island of the South Pacific
To receive the sun god. One beats the drums.
The men perform warlike dances.
When the sea sings, the women sway the hips
Between climbing plants and fire flowers. O our lost paradise.

The nymphs have left the golden forests.
One buries the stranger; then a shimmering rain begins.
The son of Pan appears in the guise of an excavator
Who sleeps away the midday near the glowing asphalt.
There are small girls in a courtyard in little dresses full of heartbreaking
  poverty.
There are rooms fulfilled with chords and sonatas.
There are shadows that embrace before a blind mirror.
By the windows of the hospital convalescents warm themselves.
A white steamboat in the canal bears bloody epidemics along.

The strange sister appears again in someone's evil dreams.
Resting in the hazel bush she plays with his stars.
The student, possibly a double, looks after her from the window for a long
  time.
His dead brother stands behind him. In the darkness of the room strange
  things may take place.
In red hyacinths the guise of the young attendant of the sick fades.
The garden is in evening. In the cloister the bats flutter about.
The caretaker's children stop to play and search the gold of heaven.
It is a cloud that dissolves. In the bower the gardener has hanged himself.
In the greenhouse brown and blue colors blur. It is the decline, toward
  which we drift.

Where the dead of yesterday lay, angels with white broken wings mourn.
Under oaks daemons with burning foreheads stray.
In the moorland bygone vegetation grows silent.
It is a whispering wind—God who leaves sad places.
The churches are deceased, worms nest in the niches.
The summer has burned the corn. The shepherds have migrated.

Die Kirchen sind verstorben, Würmer nisten sich in den Nischen ein.
Der Sommer hat das Korn verbrannt. Die Hirten sind fortgezogen.
Wo immer man geht rührt man ein früheres Leben.
Die Mühlen und Bäume gehen leer im Abendwind.
In der zerstörten Stadt richtet die Nacht schwarze Zelte auf.

Wie eitel ist alles!

[Nähe des Todes]
[1. Fassung]

Lange lauscht der Mönch dem sterbenden Vogel am Waldsaum
O die Nähe des Todes, die beinerne Stätte am Hügel
Der Angstschweiß der auf die wächserne Stirn tritt.
Der weiße Schatten des Bruders, der den Hohlweg herabläuft.

Der Abend ist in die dunklen Dörfer der Kindheit gegangen
Der Weiher unter den Weiden
Füllt sich mit den roten Gulden trauriger Herbste.

O die dicken Ratten im Stroh!
Der Blinde, der abends wieder am Weg steht
Die Stille grauer Wolken ist auf den Acker gesunken.

Spinnen verhangen die weißen Höhlen der Schwermut
Da aus des Einsamen knöchernen Händen
Der Purpur seiner nächtlichen Tage hinsinkt –
Leise des Bruders mondene Augen.

O schon lösen in kühleren Küssen
Vergilbt von Weihrauch sich der Liebenden schmächtige Glieder.

Im Spital
[1. Fassung]

Die Uhr, die tief im Grünen zwölfe schlägt –
Die Fieberkranken packt ein helles Grausen.
Der Himmel glitzert und die Gärten brausen.

Always one touches an earlier life where one goes.
The mills and trees go empty in the evening wind.
In the destroyed city the night raises black tents.

How vain is everything!

[Nearness of Death]
[version 1]

The monk listens long to the dying bird by the forest edge
O the nearness of the death, the bony place at the hill
The sweat of fear which appears on the waxy forehead.
The white shadow of the brother, which runs down the narrow path.

The evening has gone into the dark villages of childhood
The pond under the willows
Fills with the red florins of sad autumns.

O the large rats in the straw!
The blind one, who in the evening stands again at the way
The stillness of gray clouds has sunk on the acre.

Spiders conceal the white caves of gloom
When from the lonely one's bony hands
The purple of his nightly days sinks down—
Quietly the brother's lunar eyes.

O already in cooler pillows
Yellowed by incense, the slender limbs of lovers' release.

In the Hospital
[version 1 of 'Human Misery']

The clock that strikes twelve deep in the green—
A bright horror grips the feverish sick.
The sky glistens and the gardens roar.

Ein wächsern Antlitz sich am Fenster regt.

Vielleicht, daß diese Stunde stille steht.
Vor trüben Augen bunte Bilder gaukeln
Im Takt der Schiffe, die im Strome schaukeln.
Am Gang ein Schwesternzug vorüberweht.

Und Wolken regen sich im blauen Wind,
Wie Liebende die sich im Schlaf umschlingen.
Vielleicht, daß um ein Aas dort Fliegen schwingen,
Vielleicht auch weint im Mutterschoß ein Kind.

Am Fenster welken Blumen warm und rot,
Die man dem schönen Knaben heute brachte.
Wie er die Hände hob und leise lachte.
Man betet dort. Vielleicht liegt einer tot.

Es scheint, man hört auch gräßliches Geschrei
Und sieht in schwülem Brodem Fratzen flimmern.
Klavierspiel tönt gedämpft aus hellen Zimmern.
Die Uhr im tiefen Grün schlägt plötzlich drei.

Ein schwarzer Zug schwebt wieder dort davon.
Dann hört man ferne noch Choräle klingen.
Vielleicht, daß auch im Saale Engel singen.
Im Garten flattert traumhaft weißer Mohn.

Menschliche Trauer

[2. Fassung]

Die Uhr, die vor der Sonne fünfe schlägt –
Einsame Menschen packt ein dunkles Grausen.
Im Abendgarten morsche Bäume sausen;
Des Toten Antlitz sich am Fenster regt.

Vielleicht daß diese Stunde stillesteht.
Vor trüben Augen nächtige Bilder gaukeln
Im Takt der Schiffe, die am Flusse schaukeln;
Am Kai ein Schwesternzug vorüberweht.

Es scheint, man hört der Fledermäuse Schrei,

A waxen countenance stirs at the window.

Perhaps that this hour stands still.
Before dull eyes blue images flutter
To the rhythm of the ships which rock in the river.
At the alleyway a row of nuns blows by.

And clouds stir in the blue wind
Like lovers who embrace in sleep.
Perhaps flies linger around a carcass there,
Perhaps also a child weeps in the mother's lap.

At the window flowers wither warm and red
Which one brought to the beautiful boy today.
How he lifted the hands and quietly laughed.
One prays there. Perhaps one lies dead.

It seems one also hears horrible screaming
And sees grimaces flickering in sultry vapor.
Piano-play sounds muted from bright rooms.
The clock in the deep green suddenly strikes three.

A black procession floats out of there again.
Then one hears chorales still sounding far away.
Perhaps also in the hall angels sing.
In the garden white poppy flutters dreamlike.

Human Mourning
[version 2 of 'Human Misery']

The clock that strikes five before the sun—
A dark terror grips lonely people,
In the evening garden rotten trees swish,
The dead one's countenance stirs at the window.

Perhaps this hour stands still.
Before dull eyes blue images flutter
To the rhythm of the ships which rock in the river.
At the wharf a row of nuns blows by.

It seems one hears the bats' scream;

Im Garten einen Sarg zusammenzimmern.
Gebeine durch verfallne Mauern schimmern
Und schwärzlich schwankt ein Irrer dort vorbei.

Ein blauer Strahl im Herbstgewölk erfriert.
Die Liebenden im Schlafe sich umschlingen,
Gelehnet an der Engel Sternenschwingen,
Des Edlen bleiche Schläfe Lorbeer ziert.

[Landschaft]
[1. Fassung]

Septemberabend, oder die dunklen Rufe der Hirten,
Geruch von Thymian. Glühendes Eisen sprüht in der Schmiede
Gewaltig bäumt sich ein schwarzes Pferd; die hyazinthene Locke der Magd
Hascht nach der Inbrunst seiner purpurnen Nüstern.
Zu gelber Mauer erstarrt der Schrei des Rebhuhns verrostet
 in faulender Jauche ein Pflug
Leise rinnt roter Wein, die sanfte Guitarre im Wirtshaus.
O Tod! Der kranken Seele verfallener Bogen Schweigen und Kindheit.

Aufflattern mit irren Gesichtern die Fledermäuse

Elis
[1. Fassung]

Vollkommen ist die Stille dieses goldenen Tags.
Unter alten Eichen
Erscheinst du, Elis, ein Ruhender mit runden Augen.

Ihre Bläue spiegelt den Schlummer der Liebenden.
An deinem Mund
Verstummten ihre rosigen Seufzer.

Am Abend zog der Fischer die leeren Netze ein.
Ein guter Hirt
Führt seine Herde am Waldsaum hin.
O wie gerecht sind, Elis, alle deine Tage.

In the garden a coffin is cobbled together.
Bones shimmer through decayed walls
And blackish a madman staggers past.

A blue beam freezes to death in the autumn clouds.
The lovers embrace in sleep,
Leaning on the angels' star-wings,
Laurel adorns the noble one's pale temple.

[Landscape]
[version 1]

September evening, or the dark calls of the shepherds,
Smell of thyme. Red-hot iron sprays in the smithy
Enormously a black horse rears up; the hyacinthine lock of the maid
Snatches after the fervor of its crimson nostrils.
The cry of the partridge stiffens to yellow walls a plow rusting
    in rotting manure
Quietly red wine flows, the gentle guitar in the inn.
O death! The sick soul's decayed arch silence and childhood.

With mad faces the bats flutter up

Elis
[version 1]

Perfect is the stillness of this golden day.
Under ancient oaks
You appear, Elis, as one at rest with round eyes.

Their blue mirrors the slumber of lovers.
By your mouth
Their rosy sighs fell silent.

In the evening the fisherman hauled in heavy nets.
A good shepherd
Leads his flock along the forest's edge.
O how righteous, Elis, are all your days.

Ein heiterer Sinn
Wohnt in der Winzer dunklem Gesang,
Der blauen Stille des Ölbaums.
Bereitet fanden im Haus die Hungernden Brot und Wein.

Elis

[2. Fassung]

1

Elis, wenn die Amsel im schwarzen Wald ruft,
Dieses ist dein Untergang.
Deine Lippen trinken die Kühle des blauen Felsenquells.

Laß wenn deine Stirne leise blutet,
Uralte Legenden
Und dunkle Deutung des Vogelflugs.

Du aber gehst mit weichen Schritten in die Nacht,
Die voll purpurner Trauben hängt
Und du regst die Arme schöner im Blau.

Ein Dornenbusch tönt,
Wo deine mondenen Augen sind.
O! wie lange bist Elis du verstorben.

Dein Leib ist eine Hyazinthe,
In die ein Mönch die wächsernen Finger taucht.
Eine schwarze Höhle ist unser Schweigen;

Daraus bisweilen ein sanftes Tier tritt
Und langsam die schweren Lider sinkt;
Auf deine Schläfen tropft schwarzer Tau,

Das letzte Gold verfallener Sterne.

2

Vollkommen ist die Stille dieses goldenen Tags.

A cheerful meaning
Dwells in the winegrowers' dark singing,
The blue stillness of the olive tree.
The starving found bread and wine prepared in the house.

Elis
[version 2]

1

Elis, when the blackbird calls in the black woods,
This is your decline.
Your lips drink the coolness of the blue rock-spring.

Cease, when your forehead bleeds quietly
Ancient legends
And dark interpretations of the flight of birds.

But with tender steps you walk into the night
That hangs full of purple grapes,
And you move the arms more beautifully in the blueness.

A thorn bush tinges,
Where your moon-like eyes are.
O! how long, Elis, have you been dead.

Your body is a hyacinth,
Into which a monk dips his waxy fingers.
Our silence is a black cavern;

From which a soft animal steps at times
And slowly lowers heavy eyelids.
On your temples black dew drips,

The last gold of expired stars.

2

Perfect is the stillness of this golden day.

Unter alten Eichen
Erscheinst du, Elis, ein Ruhender mit runden Augen.

Die Bläue spiegelt den Schlummer der Liebenden.
An deinem Mund
Verstummten ihre rosigen Seufzer.

Am Abend zog der Fischer die schweren Netze ein.
Ein guter Hirt
Führt seine Herde am Waldsaum hin.
O! wie gerecht sind, Elis, alle deine Tage.

Ein heiterer Sinn
Wohnt in der Winzer dunklem Gesang,
Der blauen Stille des Ölbaums.

Bereitet fanden im Haus die Hungernden Brot und Wein.

3

Ein sanftes Glockenspiel tönt in Elis' Brust
Am Abend
Da sein Haupt ins schwarze Kissen sinkt.

Ein blaues Wild
Blutet leise im Dornengestrüpp.

Ein brauner Baum steht einsam da;
Seine blauen Früchte fielen von ihm.

Zeichen und Sterne
Versinken leise im Abendweiher.

Hinter dem Hügel ist es Winter geworden.

Blaue Tauben
Trinken nachts den goldenen Schweiß,
Der von Elis' kristallener Stirne rinnt.

Immer tönt
An schwarzen Mauern Gottes eisiger Odem.

Under ancient oaks
You appear, Elis, as one at rest with round eyes.

Their blue mirrors the slumber of lovers.
By your mouth
Their rosy sighs fell silent.

In the evening the fisherman hauled in heavy nets.
A good shepherd
Leads his flock along the forest's edge.
O! how righteous, Elis, are all your days.

A cheerful meaning
Dwells in the winegrowers' dark singing,
The blue stillness of the olive tree.

The starving found bread and wine prepared in the house.

3

A gentle glockenspiel sounds in Elis' breast
In the evening,
When his head sinks into the black pillow.

A blue animal
Quietly bleeds in the thorn bushes.

A brown tree stands alone there;
Its blue fruits have fallen away.

Signs and stars
Sink quietly in the evening pond.

Behind the hill it has become winter.

Blue doves
Drink at night the gold sweat
That runs down Elis' crystal forehead.

Always
God's icy breath sounds along black walls.

[Hohenburg]
[1. Fassung]

Leer und erstorben des Vaters Haus,
Dunkle Stunde
Und Erwachen im dämmernden Garten.

Immer denkst du das weiße Antlitz des Menschen,
Fern dem Getümmel der Zeit.
Über ein Träumendes neigt sich gerne grünes Gezweig;

Kreuz und Abend,
Umfängt den Tönenden mit purpurnen Armen sein Stern
Und das Läuten bläulicher Blumen.

Dezember
[1. Fassung]

Der Mantel im schwarzen Wind; leise flüstert das dürre Rohr
In der Stille des Moors. Am grauen Himmel
Folgt ein Zug von wilden Vögeln –
Quere über finsteren Wassern.

Durch kahle Birken gleiten die knöchernen Hände.
Knickt der Schritt in braunes Gehölz
Wo zu sterben ein einsames Tier wohnt.

Alte Weiblein kreuzten den Weg
Ins Dorf. Spinnen fielen aus ihren Augen
Und roter Schnee. Krähen und langes Glockengeläut

Geleitet den schwarzen Pfad, Endymions Lächeln
Und mondener Schlummer
Und die metallene Stirne tastet frierend durchs Haselgebüsch

Laß in der Schenke den Abend erwarten
Wohnen in purpurner Höhle des Weins,
Von der Tapete lautlos der trunkene Schatten sinkt.

Stundenlang fällt härener Schnee ans Fenster

[Hohenburg]
[version 1]

The father's house empty and dead,
Dark hour
And the awakening in the dusking garden.

You always imagine the white countenance of man
Far from the turmoil of time.
Over a dreaming shape green branches bend with pleasure;

Cross and evening,
The sounding one is embraced with purple arms by his star
And the ringing of bluish flowers.

December
[version 1 of 'At the Moor']

The coat in the black wind; quietly the dry reeds whisper
In the stillness of the moor. In the gray sky
A flock of wild birds follows—
Slanting over sinister waters.

Through bleak birches the bony hands glide.
The step cracks in brown woods
Where a lonesome animal dwells to die.

Old women crossed the path
Into the village. Spiders fell from their eyes
And red snow. Crows and long bell-ringing

Accompany the black path, Endymion's smile
And lunar slumber
And the metal forehead gropes freezing through the hazel bushes

Anticipate the evening in the inn
Dwelling in purple cave of wine,
From the wallpaper the drunkard's shadow soundlessly sinks.

For hours hairy snow falls against the window,

Jagt den Himmel mit schwarzen Flaggen und zerbrochenen
Masten die Nacht.

[Am Moor]
[2. Fassung]

Mantel im schwarzen Wind. Leise flüstert das stille Rohr
In der Stille des Moors; am grauen Himmel
Ein Zug von wilden Vögeln folgt;
Quere über finsteren Wassern.

Knöchern gleiten die Hände durch kahle Birken,
Knickt der Schritt in braunes Gehölz,
Wo zu sterben ein einsames Tier wohnt.

Aufruhr. In verfallener Hütte
Flattert mit schwarzen Flügeln ein gefallener Engel,
Schatten der Wolke; und der Wahnsinn des Baums;

Schrei der Elster. Altes Weiblein kreuzt den Weg
Ins Dorf. Unter schwarzem Geäst
O was bannt mit Fluch und Feuer den Schritt
Stummes Nachtgeläut; Nähe des Schnees.

Sturm. Der dunkle Geist der Fäulnis im Moor
Und die Schwermut grasender Herden.
Schweigend jagt
Den Himmel mit zerbrochnen Masten die Nacht.

Am Moor
[4. Fassung]

Wanderer im schwarzen Wind; leise flüstert das dürre Rohr
In der Stille des Moors. Am grauen Himmel
Ein Zug von wilden Vögeln folgt;
Quere über finsteren Wassern.

Aufruhr. In verfallener Hütte

The night hunts the sky with black flags and broken masts.

[At the Moor]
[version 2]

Coat in the black wind. Quietly the still reeds whisper
In the stillness of the moor; in the gray sky
A flock of wild birds follows;
Slanting over sinister waters.

Bony the hands glide through bleak birches,
The step cracks in brown grove,
Where a lonely animal dwells to die.

Turmoil. In decayed hut
A fallen angel flutters with black wings,
Shadow of the cloud; and the insanity of the tree;

Cry of the magpie. Old woman crosses the path
Into the village. Under black branches
O what banishes the step with curse and fire
Mute bell-ringing; nearness of the snow.

Storm. The dark spirit of putrescence in the moor
And the gloom of grazing herds.
Silently the night hunts
The sky with broken masts.

At the Moor
[version 4]

Wanderer in the black wind; quietly the dry reeds whisper
In the stillness of the moor. In the gray sky
A flock of wild birds follows;
Slanting over sinister waters.

Turmoil. In decayed hut

Flattert mit schwarzen Flügeln der Geist der Fäulnis;
Verkrüppelte Birken im Herbstwind.

Abend in verödeter Schenke. Den Heimweg umwittert
Die sanfte Schwermut grasender Herden;
Erscheinung der Nacht; Kröten tauchen aus braunen Wassern.

Sommer
[1. Fassung]

Sommer unter kalkgetünchten Bogen,
Vergilbtes Korn, ein Vogel der ein und aus fliegt
Abend und die dunklen Gerüche des Grüns.
Roter Mensch, auf dämmerndem Weg, wohin?
Über einsamen Hügel, vorbei am knöchernen Haus
Über die Stufen des Walds tanzt das silberne Herz.

Am Mönchsberg
[1. Fassung]

Für Adolf Loos

Wo im Schatten herbstlicher Ulmen der verfallne Pfad hinabsinkt,
Ferne den Hütten von Laub, schlafenden Hirten,
Immer folgt dem Wandrer die dunkle Gestalt der Kühle

Übern knöchernen Steg, die hyazinthene Stimme des Knaben,
Leise sagend die vergessene Legende des Walds;
Sanfter ein Krankes nun lauschend im Wahnsinn.

Weich umschmeichelt ein spärliches Grün das Knie des Fremdlings,
Ein milder Gott die sehr ermüdete Stirn,
Tastet silbern der Schritt in die Stille zurück.

The spirit of putrescence flutters with black wings.
Crippled birches in the autumn wind.

Evening in deserted tavern. The way home is scented all around
By the gentle gloom of grazing herds;
Apparition of the night; toads plunge out of brown waters.

Summer
[version 1 of 'Evening in Lans']

Summer under lime-whitewashed arches,
Yellowed corn, a bird which flies in and out
Evening and the dark smells of green.
Red person, on the dusking way, where to?
Over lonely hill, past the bony house
Over the steps of the forest the silver heart dances.

At the Mönchsberg
[version 1]

For Adolf Loos

Where in the shadow of autumn elms the ruined path sinks downward,
Far from the huts of foliage, sleeping shepherds,
Always the dark figure of coolness follows the wanderer

Over the bony footbridge, the hyacinthine voice of the boy,
Quietly telling the forgotten legend of the forest;
A sick shape gentler now and listening in the insanity.

Gently a scanty green caresses the knee of the stranger,
A mild God the very exhausted forehead,
Silverly the step fumbles back into the stillness.

Erinnerung

(Fragment)

[1. Fassung]

Stille wohnte in nächtiger Höhle das Kind lauschend in der blauen Woge des Quells dem Geläute einer strahlenden Blume. Und es trat aus verfallener Mauer die bleiche Gestalt der Mutter und sie trug in schlummernden Händen das Schmerzgeborne nachtwandelnd im Garten. Und es waren die Sterne Tropfen Blutes schimmernd im kahlen Geäst des alten Baumes und sie fielen in der Nächtigen härenes Haar, und es hob die purpurnen Lider leise der Knabe, seufzend die silberne Stirne im Nachtwind.

Wachend im Abendgarten im stillen Schatten des Vaters, o wie ängstigt dies strahlende Haupt duldend in blauer Kühle und das Schweigen in herbstlichen Zimmern. Ein goldener Kahn sank die Sonne am einsamen Hügel und es verstummten zu Häupten die ernsten Wipfel. Stille begegnet in feuchter Bläue das schlummernde Antlitz der Schwester, vergraben in ihr scharlachfarbenes Haar. Schwärzlich folgte jenem die Nacht.

Was zwingt so stille zu stehen auf verfallener Wendeltreppe im Haus der Väter und es erlöscht in schmächtigen Händen der flackernde Leuchter. Stunde einsamer Finsternis, stummes Erwachen im Hausflur im fahlen Gespinst des Mondes. O das Lächeln des Bösen traurig und kalt, daß der Schläferin rosige Wange erbleicht. In Schauern verhüllte ein schwarzes Linnen das Fenster. Und es sprang eine Flamme aus jenes Herzen und sie brannte silbern im Dunkel, ein singender Stern. Schweigend versanken der Kindheit kristallene Pfade im Garten

Im Winter

[1. Fassung]

Wenn der Schnee ans Fenster fällt,
Lang die Abendglocke läutet,
Vielen ist der Tisch bereitet
Und das Haus ist wohlbestellt.

Mancher auf der Wanderschaft
Kommt ans Tor auf dunklen Pfaden.
Seine Wunde voller Gnaden
Pflegt der Liebe sanfte Kraft.

O! des Menschen bloße Pein.
Der mit Engeln stumm gerungen,

Memory

(Fragment)

[version 1 of 'Metamorphosis of Evil']

Silently the child dwelled in nocturnal cave listening in the blue wave of the spring to the ringing of a radiant flower. And the pale figure of the mother stepped out of the decayed wall and sleepwalking she carried the one born into pain in slumbering hands to the garden. And the stars were drops of blood shimmering in the bleak branches of the old tree and they fell in the nocturnal one's course cloth of hair, and the boy quietly lifted the purple eyelids, the silver forehead sighing in the night wind.

Wakening in the evening garden in the quiet shadow of the father, o how frightened this radiant head suffering in blue coolness and the silence in autumn rooms. A golden boat the sun sank at the lonely hill and the earnest treetops fall quiet overhead. Silently the slumbering countenance of the sister encounters in moist blueness, buried in her scarlet-colored hair. Blackish the night followed the other one.

What forces to stand so silently on the decayed spiral staircase in the house of the fathers and the flickering candlestick dies in slender hands. Hour of lonely sinisterness, mute awakening in the hallway in the sallow web of the moon. O the smile of evil sad and cold, so that the sleeping woman's rosy cheek pales. In showers a black linen veiled the window. And a flame jumped out of the other one's heart and it burned silverly in darkness, a singing star. Silently childhood's crystalline paths sank in the garden

In Winter

[version 1 of 'A Winter Evening']

When the snow falls against the window,
The evening bell rings long,
The table is prepared for many,
And the house is well appointed.

Some in their wanderings
Come to the gate on dark paths.
Love's gentle power tends
His wound full of grace.

O! the pure agony of man.
Who mutely struggled with angels,

Langt von heiligem Schmerz bezwungen
Still nach Gottes Brot und Wein.

[Herbstseele]
[1. Fassung]

Tief in Grünes die Sense mäht
Blaue Luft, vergilbte Garben.
Stimmen flogen auf, verstarben
Nur ein altes Wasser geht.

Abends geht die dunkle Fahrt
Über braune Herbsteshügel
Silbern grüßt ein Weiherspiegel
Schreit der Habicht hell und hart.

Abendspiegel
[1. Fassung]

Ein Kind mit braunem Haar. Schwärzliche Flammen
Verscheucht ein Schritt in feuchter Abendkühle
In dunkelgoldner Sonnenblumen Rahmen;
Ein weiches Tier versinkt auf rote Pfühle.

Ein Schatten gleitet beinern übern Spiegel
Und leise taucht aus blauer Astern Schweigen
Ein roter Mund, ein rätselvolles Siegel,
Und schwarze Augen strahlen aus den Zweigen

Des Ahorns, dessen tolle Röte blendet.
Die Mauer hat ein sanfter Leib verlassen,
Ein blauer Glanz, der in der Dämmerung endet.
Der Wind klirrt leise in den leeren Gassen.

Am offenen Fenster welken still die Stunden
Des Liebenden. Der Wolken kühne Fahrten
Sind mit dem Pfad des Einsamen verbunden.
Ein Blick sinkt silbern in den braunen Garten.

Defeated by holy pain,
Reaches silently for God's bread and wine.

[Autumn Soul]
[version 1]

Deeply in green the scythe mows
Blue air, yellowed sheaves.
Voices flew up, deceased
Only an old water moves.

In the evening the dark journey moves
Over brown autumn hills
Silverly a pond-mirror greets
The hawk cries bright and hard.

Evening Mirror
[version 1 of 'Afra']

A child with brown hair. In moist evening coolness
A step frightens away blackish flames
Into the dark gold frame of sunflowers;
A gentle animal sinks on a red puddle.

A shadow glides bony over the mirror
And quietly a red mouth emerges
From blue asters' silence, an enigmatic seal,
And black eyes shine from the branches

Of the maple, whose mad redness dazzles.
A gentle body has left the wall,
A blue brightness which ends in dusk.
The wind quietly rattles in the empty lanes.

At the open window the hours of the loving
Wither silently. The clouds' bold journeys
Are joined with the path of the lonely one.
A gaze sinks silverly in the brown garden.

Die Hände rührt des Wassers düstre Regung.
Ein frommer Geist reift ins Kristallne, Klare.
Unsäglich ist der Vögel Flug, Begegnung
Mit Sterbenden; dem folgen dunkle Jahre.

[Untergang]
[1. Fassung]

Am Abend, wenn wir durch goldene Sommer nach Hause gehn
Sind die Schatten froher Heiliger mit uns.
Sanfter grünen die Reben rings, vergilbt das Korn
O mein Bruder, welche Ruh ist in der Welt.
Umschlungen tauchen wir in braune Wasser,
Die dunkle Grotte männlicher Schwermut
Auf dürren Pfaden kreuzen die Wege Verwester sich,
Wir aber ruhn Beseligte im Sonnenuntergang.
Friede, wo die Farben des Herbstes leuchten
Zu Häupten rauscht der Nußbaum unsre alten Vergangenheiten

[Untergang]
[2. Fassung]

Wenn wir durch goldene Sommer nach Hause gehn
Sind die Schatten froher Heiliger um uns.
Sanfter grünen die Reben rings, vergilbt das Korn
O mein Bruder, welche Stille ist in der Welt

Zu Häupten rauscht der Ahorn unsere alten Vergangenheiten
Weht uns die Kühle blauer Wasser an,
Die dunklen Spiegel männlicher Schwermut
O mein Bruder, reift die Süße des Abends heran

Leise tönen die Lüfte am einsamen Hügel
Starb vor Zeiten
Dädalus' Geist in rosigen Seufzern hin
O mein Bruder, verwandelt sich dunkel die Landschaft der Seele

The water's somber moving stirs the hands.
A pious spirit ripens in the crystal, clear.
Unspeakable is the flight of birds, encounter
With the dying; after this dark years follow.

[Decline]
[version 1]

In the evening, when we go home through golden summers
The shadows of glad saints are with us.
Gentler the vine greens all around, the grain yellows
O my brother what rest is in the world.
Embraced we plunge in blue waters,
The dark grotto of manly gloom
The ways of the putrefied cross on meager paths,
But we blissful ones rest in the sunset.
Peace, where the colors of the autumn shine
Overhead the walnut tree of our old yesteryears rustles

[Decline]
[version 2]

When we go home through golden summers
The shadows of glad saints are with us.
Gentler the vines green all around, the grain yellows
O my brother, what stillness is in the world.

Overhead the maple rustles our old yesteryears
The coolness of blue waters blows on us,
The dark mirrors of male gloom
O my brother, the sweetness of the evening is ripening

Quietly the air sounds by the lonely hill
In former times Daedalus' spirit
Died off in rosy sighs
O my brother, the landscape of the soul transforms darkly

[Untergang]
[3. Fassung]

Wenn wir durch unserer Sommer purpurnes Dunkel gehn
Treten die Schatten trauriger Mönche vor uns.
Schmächtiger glühen die Reben rings, vergilbt das Korn.
O mein Bruder, welche Stille ist in der Welt.

Zu Häupten rauscht die Eiche unsre alten Vergangenheiten
Weht uns das Antlitz steinerner Wasser an,
Die runde Grotte männlicher Schwermut,
O mein Bruder reifen schwarze Rosenkranznächte herein.

Vergangener tönen die Lüfte am einsamen Hügel,
Eines Liebenden trunkenes Saitenspiel.
Unter Dornenbogen
O mein Bruder steigen wir blinde Zeiger gen Mitternacht

Untergang
[4. Fassung]

Unter den dunklen Bogen unserer Schwermut
Spielen am Abend die Schatten verstorbener Engel.
Über den weißen Weiher
Sind die wilden Vögel fortgezogen.

Träumend unter Silberweiden
Kosen unsere Wangen vergilbte Sterne,
Beugt sich die Stirne vergangener Nächte herein.
Immer starrt uns das Antlitz unserer weißen Gräber an.

Leise verfallen die Lüfte am einsamen Hügel,
Die kahlen Mauern des herbstlichen Hains.
Unter Dornenbogen
O mein Bruder steigen wir blinde Zeiger gen Mitternacht.

[Decline]
[version 3]

When we go through our summers' purple darkness
The shadows of sad monks step before us.
More slenderly the vines glow all around, the grain yellows
O my brother, what stillness is in the world.

Overhead the oak rustles our old yesteryears
The countenance of stony waters blows on us,
The round grottos of manly gloom,
O my brother the black nights of rosaries ripen inside.

More bygone the air sounds by a lonely hill,
A lover's drunken string-play.
Under arches of thorns
O my brother we climb blind clock-hands toward midnight.

Decline
[version 4]

Under the dark arches of our gloom
The shadows of deceased angels play in the evening.
Over the white pond
The wild birds have migrated.

Dreaming under white willows
Our cheeks caress yellowed stars,
The forehead of past nights bends in here.
Always the countenance of our white grave stares at us.

Quietly the air decays by a lonely hill,
The bleak walls of the autumnal grove.
Under arches of thorns
O my brother we climb blind clock-hands toward midnight.

Am Hügel

[1. Fassung]

Still vergeht am Saum des Waldes
Ein dunkles Wild
Am Hügel endet leise der Abendwind,

Balde verstummt die Klage der Amsel
Und die Flöten des Herbstes
Schweigen im Rohr.

Mit silbernen Dornen
Schlägt uns der Frost,
Sterbende wir über Gräber geneigt

Oben löst sich blaues Gewölk;
Aus schwarzem Verfall
Treten Gottes strahlende Engel

Wanderers Schlaf

[1. Fassung]

Immer lehnt am Felsen die weiße Nacht
Wo in Silbertönen die Föhre ragt
Stein und Sterne sind.

Über den Gießbach wölbt sich der knöcherne Steg
Folgt dem Schläfer die dunkle Gestalt der Kühle,
Sichelmond in rosiger Schlucht.

Ferne schlummernden Hirten. In altem Gestein
Schaut aus kristallenen Augen die Kröte
Erwacht der blühende Wind, die Silberstimme
Des Totengleichen.

Leise sagend die vergessene Legende des Walds
Das weiße Antlitz des Engels
Leise umschmeichelt sein Knie der [...] Schaum des Wassers

Rosige Knospe

At the Hill

[version 1 of 'Spiritual Dusk']

Silently a dark deer passed by at the edge
Of the forest
The evening wind dies quietly on the hill,

Soon the blackbird's lament grows mute
And autumn flutes
Silence in the reeds.

With silver thorns
The frost strikes us,
Dying we bend over graves

Blue clouds separate above;
Out of black decay
God's radiant angels step

Wanderer's Sleep

[version 1 of 'The Wanderer']

Always the white night leans on the rock
Where the pine rises in silver tones
Are stone and stars.

Over the flooding brook the bony footbridge arches
The dark figure of coolness follows the sleeper,
Sickle moon in rosy ravine.

Far away slumbering shepherd. In old rock
The toad looks from crystal eyes
The flowering wind awakens the silver-voice
Of the deathlike man.

Quietly telling the forgotten legend of the forest
The white face of the angel
Quietly the [...] foam of the water caresses his knee

Rosy bud

Des Singenden trauriger Vogelmund.
Ein schöner Glanz erwacht auf seiner Stirne

Stein und Stern
Darin der weiße Fremdling ehdem gewohnt.

Passion
[1. Fassung]

Wenn silbern Orpheus die Laute rührt,
Beklagend ein Totes im Abendgarten –
Wer bist du Ruhendes unter hohen Bäumen?
Es rauscht die Klage das herbstliche Rohr,
Der blaue Teich.

Weh, der schmalen Gestalt des Knaben,
Die purpurn erglüht,
Schmerzlicher Mutter, in blauem Mantel
Verhüllend ihre heilige Schmach.

Weh, des Geborenen, daß er stürbe,
Eh er die glühende Frucht,
Die bittere der Schuld genossen.

Wen weinst du unter dämmernden Bäumen?
Die Schwester, dunkle Liebe
Eines wilden Geschlechts,
Dem auf goldenen Rädern der Tag davonrauscht.

O, daß frömmer die Nacht käme,
Kristus.

Was schweigst du unter schwarzen Bäumen?
Den Sternenfrost des Winters,
Gottes Geburt
Und die Hirten an der Krippe aus Stroh.

Blaue Monde
Versanken die Augen des Blinden in härener Höhle.

Ein Leichnam suchest du unter grünenden Bäumen

The singing one's sad bird-mouth.
A beautiful brilliance awakes on his forehead

Stone and star
In which the white stranger anciently dwelled.

Passion
[version 1]

When Orpheus silverly stirs the lyre,
Lamenting the dead in the evening garden—
Who are you resting under tall trees?
The lament rustles the autumn reeds,
The blue pond.

Woe over the slender figure of the boy
Which glows purple,
Over the hurtful mother, in blue coat
Cloaking her holy dishonor.

Woe over the born that he would die
Before he enjoyed the glowing fruit
Which is bitter with guilt.

Who do you weep under dusking trees?
The sister, dark love
Of a wild race,
Which the day rushes away from on golden wheels.

O, that more piously the night would come,
Kristus.

What do you silence under black trees?
The star-frost of winter,
God's birth
And the shepherds by the manger of straw.

Blue moons,
The eyes of the blind sank into hairy cave.

A corpse you search for your bride

Deine Braut,
Die silberne Rose
Schwebend über dem nächtlichen Hügel.

Wandelnd an den schwarzen Ufern
Des Todes,
Purpurn erblüht im Herzen die Höllenblume.

Über seufzende Wasser geneigt
Sieh dein Gemahl: Antlitz starrend von Aussatz
Und ihr Haar flattert wild in der Nacht.

Zwei Wölfe im finsteren Wald
Mischten wir unser Blut in steinerner Umarmung
Und die Sterne unseres Geschlechts fielen auf uns.

O, der Stachel des Todes.
Verblichene schauen wir uns am Kreuzweg
Und in silbernen Augen
Spiegeln sich die schwarzen Schatten unserer Wildnis,
Gräßliches Lachen, das unsere Münder zerbrach.

Dornige Stufen sinken ins Dunkel,
Daß röter von kühlen Füßen
Das Blut hinströme auf den steinigen Acker.

Auf purpurner Flut
Schaukelt wachend die silberne Schläferin.

Jener aber ward ein schneeiger Baum
Am Beinerhügel,
Ein Wild äugend aus eiternder Wunde,
Wieder ein schweigender Stein.

O, die sanfte Sternenstunde
Dieser kristallnen Ruh,
Da in dorniger Kammer
Das aussätzige Antlitz von dir fiel.

Nächtlich tönt der Seele einsames Saitenspiel

Under greening trees,
The silver rose
Hovering over the nocturnal hill.

Wandering by the black shores
Of death,
Hell's flower blossoms purple in the heart.

Bent over sighing waters
See your spouse: countenance staring with leprosy
And her hair flutters wildly in the night.

Two wolves in the sinister forest,
We mixed our blood in stony embrace
And the stars of our race fell on us.

O, the sting of death.
Deceased we look on ourselves at the crossroad
And in silver eyes
The black shadows of our wilderness are mirrored,
Gruesome laughter which broke our mouths.

Thorny steps sink into darkness,
So that the blood pours
More red from cool feet on the stony acre.

On purple tides
The silver woman asleep sways waking.

But the other one became a snowy tree
By the hill of bones,
A deer eying from ulcerating wound,
Again a silent stone.

O, the gentle star-hour
Of this crystalline rest,
When in thorny chamber
The leprous countenance fell from you.

Nightly the soul's lonely string-play sounds

Dunkler Verzückung
Voll zu den silbernen Füßen der Büßerin
Im verlorenen Garten;
Und an dorniger Hecke knospt der blaue Frühling.

Unter dunklen Olivenbäumen
Tritt der rosige Engel
Des Morgens aus dem Grab der Liebenden.

Passion
[2. Fassung]

Wenn silbern Orpheus die Laute rührt,
Beklagend ein Totes im Abendgarten –
Wer bist du Ruhendes unter hohen Bäumen?
Es rauscht die Klage das herbstliche Rohr,
Der blaue Teich.

Weh, der schmalen Gestalt des Knaben,
Die purpurn erglüht,
Schmerzlicher Mutter, in blauem Mantel
Verhüllend ihre heilige Schmach.

Weh, des Geborenen, daß er stürbe,
Eh er die glühende Frucht,
Die bittere der Schuld genossen.

Wen weinst du unter dämmernden Bäumen?
Die Schwester, dunkle Liebe
Eines wilden Geschlechts,
Dem auf goldenen Rädern der Tag davonrauscht.

O, daß frömmer die Nacht käme,
Kristus.

Ein Leichnam suchest du unter grünenden Bäumen
Deine Braut,
Die silberne Rose
Schwebend über dem nächtlichen Hügel.

Wandelnd an den schwarzen Ufern

Full of dark ecstasy
To the silver feet of the penitent women
In the lost garden;
And by thorny hedges the blue spring buds.

Under dark olive trees
The rosy angel
Of morning steps from the grave of the lovers.

Passion

[version 2]

When Orpheus silverly stirs the lyre,
Lamenting the dead in the evening garden—
Who are you resting under high trees?
The lament rustles the autumn reeds,
The blue pond.

Woe over the slender figure of the boy,
Which glows purple,
Over the hurtful mother, in blue coat
Cloaking her holy dishonor.

Woe over the born that he would die
Before he enjoyed the glowing fruit,
Which is bitter with guilt.

Who do you weep under dusking trees?
The sister, dark love
Of a wild race,
Which the day rushes away from on golden wheels.

O, that more piously the night would come,
Kristus.

A corpse you search for your bride
Under greening trees,
The silver rose
Hovering over the nocturnal hill.

Wandering by the black shores

Des Todes,
Purpurn erblüht im Herzen die Höllenblume.

Über seufzende Wasser geneigt
Sieh dein Gemahl: Antlitz starrend von Aussatz
Und ihr Haar flattert wild in der Nacht.

Zwei Wölfe im finsteren Wald
Mischten wir unser Blut in steinerner Umarmung
Und die Sterne unseres Geschlechts fielen auf uns.

O, der Stachel des Todes.
Verblichene schauen wir uns am Kreuzweg
Und in silbernen Augen
Spiegeln sich die schwarzen Schatten unserer Wildnis,
Gräßliches Lachen, das unsere Münder zerbrach.

Dornige Stufen sinken ins Dunkel,
Daß röter von kühlen Füßen
Das Blut hinströme auf den steinigen Acker.

Auf purpurner Flut
Schaukelt wachend die silberne Schläferin.

Jener aber ward ein schneeiger Baum
Am Beinerhügel,
Ein Wild äugend aus eiternder Wunde,
Wieder ein schweigender Stein.

O, die sanfte Sternenstunde
Dieser kristallnen Ruh,
Da in dorniger Kammer
Das aussätzige Antlitz von dir fiel.

Nächtlich tönt der Seele einsames Saitenspiel
Dunkler Verzückung
Voll zu den silbernen Füßen der Büßerin
In der blauen Stille
Und Versühnung des Ölbaums.

Of death,
Hell's flower blossoms purple in the heart.

Bent over sighing waters
See your spouse: countenance staring with leprosy
And her hair flutters wildly in the night.

Two wolves in the gloomy forest,
We mixed our blood in stony embrace
And the stars of our race fell on us.

O, the sting of death.
Deceased we look on ourselves at the crossroad
And in silver eyes
The black shadows of our wilderness are mirrored,
Gruesome laughter which broke our mouths.

Thorny steps sink into darkness
So that the blood pours
More red from cool feet on the stony field.

On purple tides
The silver woman asleep sways waking.

But the other one became a snowy tree
By the hill of bones,
A deer eying from ulcerating wound,
Again a silent stone.

O, the soft star-hours
Of this crystalline rest,
When in thorny chamber
The leprous countenance fell from you.

Nightly the soul's lonely string-play sounds
Full of dark ecstasy
To the silver feet of the penitent women
In the blue stillness
And atonement of the olive tree.

[Vorhölle]
[1. Fassung]

Am Saum des Waldes – es wohnen dort die Schatten der Toten –
Am Hügel sinkt ein goldener Kahn, der Wolken blaue Ruh
Weidend in der braunen Stille der Eichen. Härene Angst
Odmet das Herz, Kelch überfließend von purpurner Abendröte,
Dunkle Schwermut. Den Lauscher im Laub, ein Geistliches
Geleitet der Schritt den verfallenen Pfad hinab.
Nachweht Kühle aus klagendem Mund, als folgte ein schmächtiger
    Leichnam.

Abendland
[1a. Fassung]

Verfallene Weiler versanken
Im braunen November,
Die dunklen Pfade der Dörfler
Unter verkrüppelten
Apfelbäumchen, die Klage
Der Frauen im silbernen Flor.

Hinstirbt der Väter Geschlecht.
Es ist von Seufzern
Erfüllt der Abendwind
Dem Geist der Wälder.
Stille führet der Steg
Zu wolkigen Rosen
Ein frommes Wild am Hügel
Und es tönen
Die blauen Quellen im Dunkel
Daß ein Sanftes
Ein Kind geboren werde.

Leise verließ am Kreuzweg
Der Schatten den Fremdling
Und steinern erblinden
Dem die schauenden Augen,
Daß von der Lippe
Süßer fließe das Lied.

[Limbo]

[version 1]

By the edge of the forest—the shadows of the dead dwell there—
By the hill a golden boat sinks, the clouds' blue repose
Grazing in the brown stillness of the oaks. The heart
Breathes hairy fear, chalice overflowing with purple glow of sunset,
Dark gloom. The eavesdropper in the leaves, a clergyman
Escorts the step down the decayed path.
Coolness blows after from lamenting mouth, as if a delicate corpse followed.

Occident

[version 1a]

Decayed hamlets sank
In the brown November,
The dark paths of the villagers
Under crippled
Apple trees, the laments
Of the women in the silver veil.

The race of the fathers dies off.
The evening wind is fulfilled
With sighs
For the spirit of the forests.
Silently the footbridge leads
To cloudy roses
A pious deer at the hill
And the blue springs
Sound in the dark
So that a gentle shape,
A child will be born.

Quietly the shadow left the stranger
At the crossroad
And stonily his watching eyes
Go blind
So that the song flows
More sweetly from the lip.

Denn es ist Nacht
Die Wohnung des Liebenden,
Ist sprachlos das blaue Antlitz
Über ein Totes
Die Schläfe aufgetan;
Kristallner Anblick.
Dem folgt auf dunklen Pfaden
An Mauern hin
Ein Abgestorbenes nach.

Wanderschaft
[1b. Fassung]

So leise sind die grünen Wälder
Unserer Heimat
Die Sonne sinkt am Hügel
Und wir haben im Schlaf geweint;
Wandern wir mit weißen Schritten
An der dornigen Hecke hin
Singende im Ährensommer
Und Schmerzgeborne.

Schon reift dem Menschen das Korn
Und die heilige Rebe
Und in steinernem Zimmer,
Im kühlen ist bereitet das Mahl.
Auch ist dem Guten
Das Herz versöhnt in grüner Stille
Und Kühle hoher Bäume
Speise teilt er mit sanften Händen aus.

Vieles ist ein Wachendes
In der sternigen Nacht
Und schön die Bläue,
Schreitend ein Bleiches, Odmendes,
Ein Saitenspiel.

Gelehnt an den Hügel der Bruder
Und Fremdling,
Der menschenverlassene, ihm sanken
Die feuchten Lider

Since the night is
The dwelling of the lover,
The blue countenance is speechless
Over a dead person
The temple opened up;
Crystalline sight;
After this on dark paths
Along walls
A dead shape follows.

Wanderings
[version 1b of 'Occident']

So quiet are the green forests
Of our homeland
The sun sinks at the hill
And we have wept in sleep;
We wander with white steps
Along the thorny hedge
Singers in the summer ears of corn
And ones born into pain.

Already the grain ripens for man
And the holy vine
And in stony room,
In the cool the meal is prepared.
Also for the good
The heart is reconciled in green silence
And coolness of tall trees
He distributes the food with gentle hands.

Many things are a waking shape
In the starry night
And beautiful in the blueness,
A pale, breathing shape striding,
A string-play.

The brother and stranger
Leaned on the hill,
Abandoned by man, his moist
Eyelids sank

In unsäglicher Schwermut.
Aus schwärzlicher Wolke
Träufelt bitterer Mohn.

Mondesweiß schweiget der Pfad
An jenen Pappeln hin
Und balde
Endet des Menschen Wanderschaft,
Gerechte Duldung.
Auch freuet die Stille der Kinder,
Die Nähe der Engel
Auf kristallener Wiese.

Abendland
[2. Fassung]

1

Verfallene Weiler versanken
Im braunen November,
Die dunklen Pfade der Dörfler
Unter verkrüppelten
Apfelbäumchen, die Klagen
Der Frauen im silbernen Flor.

Hinstirbt der Väter Geschlecht.
Es ist von Seufzern
Erfüllt der Abendwind,
Dem Geist der Wälder.

Stille führt der Steg
Zu wolkigen Rosen
Ein frommes Wild am Hügel;
Und es tönen
Die blauen Quellen im Dunkel,
Daß ein Sanftes,
Ein Kind geboren werde.

Leise verließ am Kreuzweg
Der Schatten den Fremdling
Und steinern erblinden

In unspeakable gloom.
From blackish clouds
Bitter poppy trickles.

Lunar-white the path silences
By those poplars
And soon
The wanderings of man end,
Righteous tolerance.
Also the stillness of the children rejoices,
The nearness of the angels
On crystal meadow.

Occident
[version 2]

1

Decayed hamlets sank
In the brown November,
The dark paths of the villagers
Under crippled
Apple trees, the complaints
Of the women in the silver veil.

The race of the fathers dies off.
The evening wind is fulfilled
With sighs
For the spirit of the forests.

Silently the footbridge leads
To cloudy roses
A pious deer at the hill
And the blue springs
Sound in the dark
So that a gentle shape,
A child will be born.

Quietly the shadow left the stranger
At the crossroad
And stonily his watching eyes

Dem die schauenden Augen,
Daß von der Lippe
Süßer fließe das Lied;

Denn es ist die Nacht
Die Wohnung des Liebenden,
Ist sprachlos das blaue Antlitz,
Über ein Totes
Die Schläfe aufgetan;
Kristallener Anblick;

Dem folgt auf dunklen Pfaden
An Mauern hin
Ein Abgestorbenes nach.

2

Wenn es Nacht geworden ist
Erscheinen unsre Sterne am Himmel
Unter alten Olivenbäumen,
Oder an dunklen Zypressen hin
Wandern wir weiße Wege;
Schwerttragender Engel:
Mein Bruder.
Es schweigt der versteinerte Mund
Das dunkle Lied der Schmerzen.

Wieder begegnet ein Totes
Im weißen Linnen
Und es fallen der Blüten
Viele über den Felsenpfad.

Silbern weinet ein Krankes,
Aussätziges am Weiher,
Wo vor Zeiten
Froh im Nachmittag Liebende geruht.

Oder es läuten die Schritte
Elis' durch den Hain,
Den hyazinthenen,
Wieder verhallend unter Eichen.
O des Knaben Gestalt
Geformt aus kristallenen Tränen

Go blind
So that the song flows
More sweetly from the lip;

Since the night is
The dwelling of the lover,
The blue countenance is speechless
Over a dead person
The temple opened up;
Crystalline sight;

After this on dark paths
Along walls
A dead shape follows.

2

When it has become night
Our stars appear in the sky
Under old olive trees,
Or along dark cypresses
We wander white paths;
Sword-bearing angel:
My brother.
The petrified mouth silences
The dark song of pain.

Again a dead shape encounters
In white linen
And many blossoms fall
Across the rock path.

Silverly a sick shape weeps,
Leper by the pond
Where in former times
Lovers rested gladly in the afternoon.

Or the steps of Elis
Ring through the grove,
The hyacinthine,
Again fading under oaks.
O the boy's figure
Formed from crystalline tears

Und nächtigen Schatten.

Anders ahnt die Stille Vollkommenes,
Die kühle, kindliche,
Wenn über grünendem Hügel
Frühlingsgewitter ertönt.

3

So leise sind die grünen Wälder
Unserer Heimat,
Die Sonne sinkt am Hügel
Und wir haben im Schlaf geweint;
Wandern mit weißen Schritten
An der dornigen Hecke hin
Singende im Ährensommer
Und Schmerzgeborene.

Schon reift dem Menschen das Korn,
Die heilige Rebe.
Und in steinernem Zimmer,
Im kühlen, ist bereitet das Mahl.
Auch ist dem Guten
Das Herz versöhnt in grüner Stille
Und Kühle hoher Bäume.
Speise teilt er mit sanften Händen aus.

Vieles ist ein Wachendes
In der sternigen Nacht
Und schön die Bläue,
Schreitend ein Bleiches, Odmendes,
Ein Saitenspiel.

Gelehnt an den Hügel der Bruder
Und Fremdling,
Der menschenverlassene, ihm sanken
Die feuchten Lider
In unsäglicher Schwermut.
Aus schwärzlicher Wolke
Träufelt bitterer Mohn.

Mondesweiß schweigt der Pfad
An jenen Pappeln hin

And nocturnal shadows.

The forehead, cool, childlike,
Anticipates perfect shapes differently
When over greening hill
Spring thunderstorm resounds.

3

So quiet are the green forests
Of our homeland,
The sun sinks by the hill
And we have wept in sleep;
Wandering with white steps
By the thorny hedge
Singers in the summer ears of corn
And ones born into pain.

Already the grain ripens for man
And the holy vine.
And in stony room,
In the cool the meal is prepared.
Also for the good
The heart is reconciled in green silence
And coolness of high trees.
He distributes the food with gentle hands.

Many things are a waking shape
In the starry night
And beautiful in the blueness,
A pale, breathing shape striding,
A string-play.

The brother and stranger
Leaned at the hill,
Abandoned by man, his moist
Eyelids sank
In unspeakable gloom.
From blackish clouds
Bitter poppy trickles.

Lunar-white the path silences
By those poplars

Und balde
Endet des Menschen Wanderschaft,
Gerechte Duldung.
Auch freut die Stille der Kinder
Die Nähe der Engel
Auf kristallener Wiese.

4

Ein Knabe mit zerbrochener Brust
Hinstirbt Gesang in der Nacht.
Laß nur stille am Hügel gehn
Unter den Bäumen
Gefolgt vom Schatten des Wilds.
Süß duften die Veilchen im Wiesengrund.

Oder laß treten ins steinerne Haus,
Im gramvollen Schatten der Mutter
Neigen das Haupt.
In feuchter Bläue leuchtet das Lämpchen
Die Nacht lang;
Denn es ruht der Schmerz nicht mehr;

Auch sind die weißen Gestalten
Der Odmenden, die Freunde ferne gegangen;
Gewaltig schweigen die Mauern rings.

5

Wenn es auf der Straße dunkelt
Und es begegnet in blauem Linnen
Ein lange Abgeschiedenes,
O, wie schwanken die tönenden Schritte
Und es schweigt das grünende Haupt.

Groß sind Städte aufgebaut
Und steinern in der Ebene;
Aber es folgt der Heimatlose
Mit offener Stirne dem Wind,
Den Bäumen am Hügel;
Auch ängstet öfter die Abendröte.

And soon
The wanderings of man end,
Righteous tolerance.
Also the stillness of the children rejoices,
The nearness of the angels
On crystal meadow.

4

A boy with broken chest
Chanting dies away in the night.
Only let go silently by the hill
Under the trees
Followed by the shadow of the deer.
The violets smell sweet in the meadow-valley.

Or take step into the stony house,
In the grief-filled shadow of the mother
Bend the head.
In moist blueness the lamp shines
The entire night;
Because pain rests no more;

Also the white figures are
The breathing, the friends gone far away;
Enormously the walls all around grow silent.

5

When it is dusk in the street
And a long departed shape
Encounters in blue linen,
O, how the resounding steps falter
And the greening head grows silent.

Mighty are the cities constructed
And stony on the plain;
But the homeless one follows
The wind with open forehead,
The trees at the hill;
Also often fears the glow of sunset.

Balde rauschen die Wasser
Laut in der Nacht,
Rührt die kristallenen Wangen
Eines Mädchens der Engel,
Ihr blondes Haar,
Beschwert von der Schwester Tränen.

Dieses ist oft Liebe: es rührt
Ein blühender Dornenbusch
Die kalten Finger des Fremdlings
Im Vorübergehn;
Und es schwinden die Hütten der Dörfler
In der blauen Nacht.

In kindlicher Stille,
Im Korn, wo sprachlos ein Kreuz ragt,
Erscheint dem Schauenden
Seufzend sein Schatten und Hingang.

Abendland
[3. Fassung]

1

Mond, als träte ein Totes
Aus blauer Höhle
Und es fallen der Blüten
Viele über den Felsenpfad.
Silbern weint ein Krankes
Am Abendweiher,
Auf schwarzem Kahn
Hinüberstarben Liebende.

Oder es läuten die Schritte
Elis' durch den Hain
Den hyazinthenen
Wieder verhallend unter Eichen.
O des Knaben Gestalt
Geformt aus kristallenen Tränen,
Nächtigen Schatten.
Zackige Blitze erhellen die Schläfe

Soon the waters rush
Loud in the night,
The angel stirs
The crystal cheeks of a girl,
Her blond hair
Burdened by the sister's tears.

Often this is love:
A blossoming thorn bush
Stirs the cold fingers of the stranger
In the passing by;
And the huts of the villagers recede
In the blue night.

In childlike stillness,
In corn where speechless a cross rises,
His shadow and demise
Appears sighing to the onlooker.

Occident
[version 3]

1

Moon, as if a dead thing would step
From a blue cave,
And many blossoms fall
Across the rock path.
Silverly a sick shape weeps
By the evening pond,
In a black boat
Lovers have died crossing over.

Or Elis' footsteps
Ring through the grove,
The hyacinthine
Again fading under oaks.
O the boy's figure
Formed from crystalline tears,
Nocturnal shadows.
Jagged lightning illuminates the temple

Die immerkühle,
Wenn am grünenden Hügel
Frühlingsgewitter ertönt.

2

So leise sind die grünen Wälder
Unsrer Heimat,
Die kristallen Woge
Hinsterbend an verfallner Mauer
Und wir haben im Schlaf geweint;
Wandern mit zögernden Schritten
An der dornigen Hecke hin
Singende im Abendsommer,
In heiliger Ruh
Des fern verstrahlenden Weinbergs
Schatten nun im kühlen Schoß
Der Nacht, trauernde Adler.
So leise schließt ein mondener Strahl
Die purpurnen Male der Schwermut.

3

Strahlend nachtet die steinerne Stadt
In der Ebene.
Ein schwarzer Schatten
Folgt der Fremdling
Mit dunkler Stirne dem Wind,
Kahlen Bäumen am Hügel;
Auch ängstet im Herzen
Einsame Abendröte
Als stürzten silberne Wasser
Ins kühle Dunkel –
O Liebe, es rührt
Ein blauer Dornenbusch
Die kalte Schläfe,
Mit fallenden Sternen
Schneeige Nacht.

That is always cool,
When by the greening hill
Spring thunderstorm resounds.

2

So quiet are the green forests
Of our homeland,
The crystalline wave
Dying on a decayed wall
And we have wept in sleep;
Wander with hesitant steps
Along the thorny hedge,
Singers in the summer evening,
In holy peace
Of the far away radiant vineyard
Shadows now in the cool lap
Of night, mourning eagles.
So quietly a moonbeam closes
The purple stigmata of gloom.

3

Radiantly the stony city falls into night
On the plain.
A black shadow,
The stranger follows
The wind with dark forehead,
Bleak trees by the hill;
Also lonely glow of sunset
Strikes fear in the heart
As if silver waters fell
Into the cool darkness—
O love, a blue
Thorn bush stirs
The cold temple,
Snowy night
With falling stars.

An Mauern hin
[1. Fassung]

Nimmer das goldene Antlitz des Frühlings;
Dunkles Lachen im Haselgebüsch. Abendspaziergang im Wald
Und der inbrünstige Schrei der Amsel.
Taglang rauscht in der Seele des Fremdlings das glühende Grün.

Metallne Minute: Mittag, Verzweiflung des Sommers;
Die Schatten der Buchen und das gelbliche Korn.
Taufe in keuschen Wassern. O der purpurne Mensch.
Ihm aber gleichen Wald, Weiher und weißes Wild.

Kreuz und Kirche im Dorf. In dunklem Gespräch
Erkannten sich Mann und Weib
Und an kahler Mauer wandelt mit seinen Gestirnen der Einsame.

Leise über den mondbeglänzten Weg des Walds
Sank die Wildnis vergessener Jagden.
Blick der Bläue aus verfallenen Felsen bricht.

[Der Schlaf]
[1. Fassung]

Getrost ihr dunklen Gifte
Erzeugend weißen Schlaf
Einen höchst seltsamen Garten
Dämmernder Bäume
Erfüllt von Schlangen, Nachtfaltern,
Fledermäusen;
Fremdling dein jammervoller Schatten
Schwankt, bittere Trübsal
Im Abendrot!
Uralt einsame Wasser
Versanken im Sand.

Weiße Hirsche am Nachtsaum
Sterne vielleicht!
Gehüllt in Spinnenschleier
Schimmert toter Auswurf.

Along Walls
[version 1 of 'In Darkness']

Never the golden countenance of spring;
Dark laughter in the hazel bushes. Evening walk in the forest
And the ardent cry of the blackbird.
Daylong the glowing green rushes in the soul of the stranger.

Metallic minute: midday, desperation of summer;
The shadows of the beeches and the yellowish corn.
Baptism in chaste waters. O the purple man.
But he resembles forest, pond and white deer.

Cross and church in the village. In dark conversation
Man and woman know each other
And along a bleak wall the lonely one wanders with his stars.

Quietly over the moon-brightened ways of the forest
The wilderness of forgotten hunts sank.
Glimpse of blue breaks from mouldered rocks.

[Sleep]
[version 1]

Confidently you dark poisons
Producing white sleep
A most strange garden
Of dusking trees
Fulfilled with snakes, moths,
Bats;
Stranger your woebegone shadow
Sways, bitter misery
In the glow of sunset!
Ancient lonely waters
Sank in the sand.

White stags at the border of night
Stars perhaps!
Wrapped in spider webs
Dead phlegm shimmers.

Eisernes Anschaun.
Dornen umschweben
Den blauen Pfad ins Dorf,
Ein purpurnes Lachen
Den Lauscher in leerer Schenke.
Über die Diele
Tanzt mondesweiß
Des Bösen gewaltiger Schatten.

An
[1. Fassung]

Die Kühle dunkler Jahre, Schmerz und Hoffnung
Bewahrt dies braune Gebälk
Darüber flammend Georginen hangen.
Als sänke ein goldner Helm von blutender Stirne
Stille endet der Tag,
Schaut Kindheit sanft aus den schwärzlichen Augen an.
Leise verstrahlen im Abend die roten Buchen,
Liebe, Hoffnung, daß von blauen Lidern
Tau tropft unaufhaltsam.
Einsame Heimkehr! Die dunklen Rufe der Fischer
Tönen immer am dämmernden Fluß;
Liebe, Nacht, der Schwermut kristallne Minuten
Hinüberschimmernd, Sterne, schon stilleres Anschaun

Im Schnee
[1. Fassung]

Der Wahrheit nachsinnen –
Viel Schmerz!
Endlich Begeisterung
Bis zum Tod.
Winternacht
Du reine Mönchin!

Iron gazing.
Thorns hover around
The blue path into the village,
A purple laughter
The eavesdropper in the empty inn.
Over the floorboard
Evil's enormous shadow
Dances lunar-white.

To
[version 1 of 'The Homecoming']

The coolness of dark years, pain and hope,
Is preserved by these brown rafters
Over which dahlias hang flamingly.
As if a golden helmet sank from bleeding forehead
The day ends silently,
Childhood watches gently from blackish eyes.
Quietly the red beeches shine in the evening.
Love, hope so that dew drops
From blue eyelids irresistibly.
Lonely homecoming! The dark calls of the fishermen
Sound always by the dusking river.
Love, night, gloom's crystalline minutes
Shimmering beyond, stars, already quieter beholding

In Snow
[version 1 of 'The Homecoming']

Contemplate the truth—
Much pain!
Finally enthusiasm
Up to death.
Winter night
You pure monkess!

Anblick
[2. Fassung]

Da so rot der Herbst und leise
Unter Ulmen dunkle Qual
Dämmernd Dorf und Liebesmahl
Falke winkt auf goldner Reise.

Stirne blutet sanft und dunkel
Sonnenblume welkt am Zaun
Schwermut blaut im Schoß der Fraun;
Gottes Wort im Sterngefunkel!

Purpurn flackert Mund und Lüge.
In verfallnem Zimmer kühl,
Scheint nur Lachen, golden Spiel,
Daß ein Sturm dies Haupt zerschlüge

Nachts mit Blitzen; schwärzlich fallen
Faule Früchte nachts vom Baum.
Kind an deinem blauen Saum
Muß ich stumm vorüberwallen.

An die Nacht
[3. Fassung]

Mönchin schließ mich in dein Dunkel,
Kreuz im kühlen Sterngefunkel.
Purpurn brachen Mund und Lüge
Einer Glocke letzte Züge.
Nacht dein lüstern Wolkendunkel
Rote Frucht, verfluchte Lüge
Einer Glocke letzte Züge –
Blutend Kreuz im Sterngefunkel.

Sight

[version 2 of 'Surrender at Night']

There the autumn so red and quiet
Under elm trees dark agony
Dusking village and love feast
Hawk beckons on golden journey.

Forehead bleeds soft and dark
Sunflower withers by the fence
Gloom blues in the womb of the women;
God's word in star-glitter!

Purply mouth and lies flicker.
Cool in decayed room,
Only laughter shines, golden play,
That a storm would smash this head

At night with lightnings; blackish
Foul fruits fall at night from the tree.
Child at your blue hemline
I must mutely wander past.

To the Night

[version 3 of 'Surrender at Night']

Monkess enclose me in your darkness,
Cross in cool star-glitter.
Purply mouth and lies broke
A bell's final knells.
Night your lecherous cloud-darkness
Red fruit, cursed lie
A bell's final knells—
Bleeding cross in the star-glitter.

An die Nacht
[4. Fassung]

Nymphe zieh mich in dein Dunkel;
Aster friert und schwankt am Zaun,
Schwermut blüht im Schoß der Fraun,
Blutend Kreuz im Sterngefunkel.

Purpurn brachen Mund und Lüge
In verfallner Kammer kühl;
Scheint noch Lachen, golden Spiel;
Einer Glocke letzte Züge.

Blaue Wolke! Schwärzlich fallen
Faule Früchte dumpf vom Baum
Und zum Grabe wird der Raum
Und zum Traum trüb' Erdenwallen.

To the Night

[version 4 of 'Surrender at Night']

Nymph draw me into your darkness;
Aster freezes and sways by the fence,
Gloom blossoms in the womb of the women,
Bleeding cross in the star-glitter.

Purply mouth and lies broke
Cool in the decayed chamber;
Laughter still shines, golden play,
A bell's final knells.

Blue cloud! Blackish
Foul fruits fall dully from the tree
And the room becomes the grave,
And dreary wandering on earth the dream.

Gedichtkomplexe und Fragmente

Lange lauscht der Mönch dem sterbenden Vogel am Waldsaum
O die Nähe des Todes, verfallender Kreuze am Hügel
Der Angstschweiß der auf die wächserne Stirne tritt.
O das Wohnen in blauen Höhlen der Schwermut.
O blutbefleckte Erscheinung, die den Hohlweg herabsteigt
Daß der Besessene leblos in die silbernen Kniee bricht.

Mit Schnee und Aussatz füllt sich die kranke Seele
Da sie am Abend dem Wahnsinn der Nymphe lauscht,
Den dunklen Flöten des [...] im dürren Rohr;
Finster ihr Bild im Sternenweiher beschaut;

Stille verwest die Magd im Dornenbusch
Und die verödeten Pfade und leeren Dörfer
Bedecken sich mit gelbem Gras.
Über verschüttete Stiegen hinab – purpurner Abgrund.

Wo an schwarzen Mauern Besessene stehn
Steigt der bleiche Wanderer im Herbst hinab
Wo vordem ein Baum war, ein blaues Wild im Busch
Öffnen sich, zu lauschen, die weichen Augen
Helians.
Wo in finstern Zimmern einst die Liebenden schliefen
Spielt der Blinde mit silbernen Schlangen,
Der herbstlichen Wehmut des Mondes.

Grau verdorren im braunen Gewand die Glieder
Ein steinerner Bogen
Der sich im Spiegel faulender Wasser verzückt.
Knöcherne Maske, die einst Gesang war.
Wie schweigsam die Stätte.

Ein verpestetes Antlitz, das zu den Schatten sinkt,
Ein Dornenbusch der den roten Mantel des Büßenden sucht;
Leise folgt der magische Finger des Blinden
Seinen erloschenen Sternen

Complexes of Poems and Fragments

The monk listens long to the dying bird by the forest's edge
O the nearness of death, decaying crosses at the hill
The sweat of fear that arises on the waxen forehead.
O the dwelling in blue caves of gloom.
O blood-stained apparition who climbs down the narrow pass
So that the possessed breaks lifeless in the silver knees.

The sick soul fills itself with snow and leprosy
When it listens to the insanity of the nymph in the evening,
The dark flutes [...] in the meager reeds;
Sinisterly its image contemplates in the starry pond;

Silently the maid decomposes in the thorn bush
And the desolate paths and empty villages
Cover themselves with yellow grass.
Down over buried stairs—purple abyss.

Where the possessed stand by black walls
In autumn the pale wanderer climbs down
Where a tree was before, a blue deer in the bush
The gentle eyes of Helian open
To listen.
Where in sinister rooms the lovers once slept
The blind one plays with silver snakes,
The autumn melancholy of the moon.

Gray the limbs dry up in brown garb
A stony arch
That enraptures in the mirror of putrescent water.
Bony mask which once was singing.
How taciturn the site.

A mephitic countenance that sinks to the shadows,
A thorn bush that seeks the red coat of the penitent;
Quietly the magic finger of the blind one follows
His extinct stars

Ein weißes Geschöpf ist der einsame Mensch
Das staunend Arme und Beine bewegt,
Purpurne Höhlen darin verblichene Augen rollen.

Über verschüttete Stiegen hinab wo Böse stehn
Ein Klang von herbstlichen Zymbeln verklingt
Öffnet sich wieder ein weißer Abgrund.

Durch schwarze Stirne geht schief die tote Stadt
Der trübe Fluß darüber Möven flattern
Dachrinnen kreuzen sich an vergangenen Mauern
Ein roter Turm und Dohlen. Darüber
Wintergewölk, das aufsteigt.

Jene singen den Untergang der finsteren Stadt;
Traurige Kindheit, die nachmittags im Haselgebüsch spielt,
Abends unter braunen Kastanien blauer Musik lauscht,
Der Brunnen erfüllt von goldenen Fischen.

Über das Antlitz des Schläfers neigt sich der greise Vater
Des Guten bärtiges Antlitz, das ferne gegangen
Ins Dunkel

O Fröhlichkeit wieder, ein weißes Kind
Hingleitend an erloschenen Fenstern.
Wo vordem ein Baum war, ein blaues Wild im Busch
Öffnen sich zu sterben die weichen Augen
Helians.

Wo an Mauern die Schatten der Ahnen stehn,
Vordem ein einsamer Baum war, ein blaues Wild im Busch

A white creature is the lonely man
That marveling moves arms and legs,
Purple sockets in which faded eyes roll.

Down over buried stairs where demons stand
A sound of autumn cymbals fades away
Again a white abyss opens.

Through black forehead the dead city goes awry
The cloudy river over which gulls flutter
Gutters cross at bygone walls
A red tower and jackdaws. Over there
Winter clouds that ascend.

Those sing the decline of the sinister city;
Sad childhood that plays in the hazel bush in the afternoon,
Listens to blue music in the evening under brown chestnuts,
The fountain fulfilled by golden fish.

Over the countenance of the sleeper the aged father bends
The good one's bearded countenance that has gone far
In the darkness
O cheerfulness again, a white child

Gliding away by extinct windows.
Where a tree was before, a blue deer in the bush
The gentle eyes of Helian open
To die.

Where by walls the shadows of the ancestors stand,
A lonely tree was before, a blue deer in the bush

Steigt der weiße Mensch auf goldenen Stiegen,
Helian ins seufzende Dunkel hinab.

Finster blutet ein braunes Wild im Busch;
Einsam der Blinde, der über verfallene Stufen herabsteigt.
Im Zimmer die dunklen Flöten des Wahnsinns.

Mit Schnee und Aussatz füllt sich die kranke Seele,
Da sie am Abend ihr Bild im rosigen Weiher beschaut.
Verfallene Lider öffnen sich weinend im Haselgebüsch.
O der Blinde,
Der schweigend über verfallene Stufen hinabsteigt im Dunkel.
Im Dunkel sinken Helians Augen.

Sommer. In Sonnenblumen gelb klapperte morsches Gebein,
Sank zu jungen Mönchen der Abend des verfallenen Gartens hinab
Duft und Schwermut des alten Hollunders,
Da aus Sebastians Schatten die verstorbene Schwester trat,
Purpurn des Schlafenden Mund zerbrach.
Und die Silberstimme des Engels

Spielende Knaben am Hügel. O wie leise die Zeit,
Des Septembers und jener, da er in schwarzem Kahn
Am Sternenweiher vorbeizog, am dürren Rohr.
In wilder Vögel Flug und Schrei.

Ferne ging in Schatten und Stille des Herbstes
Ein Haupt,
Stieg der Schatten des Schläfers verfallene Stufen hinab.

Ferne saß die Mutter im Schatten des Herbstes
Ein weißes Haupt. Über verfallene Stufen

The white human climbs on golden stairs,
Helian down in the sighing darkness.

Sinisterly a brown deer bleeds in the bush;
Lonely the blind one that climbs down over decayed stairs.
In the room the dark flutes of insanity.

The sick soul fills with snow and leprosy
When in the evening it contemplates its image in the rosy pond.
Decayed eyelids open weeping in the hazel bush.
O the blind one
Who silently climbs down over decayed stages in the darkness.
In darkness Helian's eyes sink.

Summer. In sunflowers yellow rotten bones rattled,
The evening of the decayed garden sank to young monks
Scent and gloom of the old elder tree,
Since the deceased sister stepped out of Sebastian's shadow,
Purple the sleeping one's mouth broke.
And the silver voice of the angel

Playing boys at the hill. O how quiet the time
Of September and one who moved along in black boat
On the starry pond by dry reed.
Into wild bird's flight and cry.

Far away a head went in shadow and stillness
Of autumn,
The shadow of the sleeper climbed down decayed stairs.

Far away the mother sat in the shadow of autumn
A white head. Over decayed steps

Stieg im Garten der dunkle Schläfer hinab.
Klage der Drossel.

O die härene Stadt; Stern und frostig Erwachen.

Ferne ging im braunen Schatten des Herbstes
Der weiße Schläfer.
Über verfallenen Stufen glänzte ein Mond sein Herz,
Klangen leise ihm blaue Blumen nach,
Leise ein Stern.

Oder wenn er ein sanfter Novize
Abends in Sankt Ursulas dämmernde Kirche trat,
Eine silberne Blume sein Antlitz barg in Locken
Und in Schatten ihn der blaue Mantel des Vaters umfing
Die dunkle Kühle der Mutter

Oder wenn er ein sanfter Novize
Abends in Sankt Ursulas dämmernde Kirche trat,
Eine silberne Stimme das Antlitz barg in härenen Locken,
Und in Schauern ihn die

Fragmente

1
Kindheit

Was leise gehet unter Herbstesbäumen
Am grünen Fluß, darüber Möven gleiten –
Es fällt das Laub; Einfalt dunkeler Zeiten.
's ist Gottes Ruh. Die Abendschatten säumen
Ein schwarzer Vogel singt in Herbstesbäumen.

Ein Händefalten müde und einträchtig
Am Abend folgen ihren Vogelzeichen
Die Augen, ehe sie dem Schlummer weichen –
Erinnerung des Knaben sanft und schmächtig.

In the garden the dark sleeper climbed down.
Complaint of the thrush.

O the hairy city; star and rosy awaking.

Far away the white sleeper went in the brown shadow
Of autumn.
Over decayed steps his heart shined, a moon,
Blue flowers resounded quietly after him,
Quietly a star.

Or when he a gentle novice
In the evening stepped into Saint Ursula's dusking church,
A silver flower his countenance rescued in curls
And in showers the blue coat of the father surrounded him
The dark coolness of the mother

Or when he a gentle novice
Stepped in the evening into Saint Ursula's dusking church,
A silver voice rescued the countenance in hairy curls,
And in showers the

Fragments

1
Childhood

What quietly walks under autumn's trees
By the green river, over which gulls glide—
The leaves fall; simple-mindedness of dark times.
It's God's rest. The evening shadows border
A black bird sings in autumn trees.

A hand-folding tired and peaceful
In the evening the eyes follow
Their bird-signs, before they give way to the slumber—
Memory of the boy gentle and slender.

Ein schwarzer Vogel singt in Herbstesbäumen
Den Frieden dieser Tage süß und mächtig
Auch will die Seele stille sich bereiten.

2
Ein Kreuz ragt Elis
Dein Leib auf dämmernden Pfaden

3
Geburt

Gang mit dem Vater, Gang mit der Mutter

4
Im Frühling

Abend ist im alten Garten worden.

5
Nachtwandlung, Tod und Seele

Da ich hinsank am schwarzen Hügel des Schlafs müde der Wildnis und Verzweiflung finsterer Wintertage, kam auf glühendem Flügel ein Traum zu mir:

6
Da der Tag dahinsank fuhr K

7
Es kehret der Heimatlose
Zurück zu moosigen Wäldern

8
Gegen Abend erwachte Münch am Saum des Waldes. Eine goldene Wolke erlosch über ihm und die dunkle Stille des Herbstes erfüllte ihn mit Angst, die Einsamkeit der Hügel rings.

9
Im Frühling; ein zarter Leichnam
Erstrahlend in seinem Grab
Unter den wilden
Hollunderbüschen der Kindheit.

A black bird sings in autumn trees
The peace of these days sweet and powerful
Also the soul silently wants to prepare.

2

A cross towers Elis
Your body on dusking paths

3
Birth

Walk with the father, walk with the mother

4
In Spring

Evening has been in the old garden.

5
Night Transformation, Death and Soul

When I sank at the black hill of sleep tired of the wilderness and despair of sinister winter days, a dream came to me on glowing wing:

6
When the day sank K drove

7
The homeless one turns
Back to mossy forests

8
At evening Münch awaked at the border of the forest. A golden cloud expired over him and the dark stillness of autumn filled him with fear, the loneliness of the hills all around.

9
In spring; a delicate corpse
Shining in its grave
Under the wild
Elder bushes of childhood.

10

Nächtliche Buchen; es wohnt im Herzen
Dunkler Landschaft ein roter Wurm.

11

Schneeige Nacht!
Ihr dunklen Schläfer
Unter der Brücke
Von zerbrochener Stirne
Tropft kristallner Schweiß euch

10

Nocturnal beeches; in the heart
Of a dark landscape dwells a red worm.

11

Snowy night!
You dark sleepers
Under the bridge
Crystalline sweat drips
From your broken forehead

Dramatic Fragments

Blaubart
[**Ein Puppenspiel**; Fragment]

Prologue

Vorausnahme
Beklagst du, Gerechter dies wirre Bild,
Das von Gelächter und Irrsinn zerwühlt
Glaub mir, bis wir uns wiedersehn
Wird mein Helde auf sittsameren Wegen gehn!
Amen!

Personen:
Bluebeard
The Old Man
Herbert
Elisabeth

1. Szene *[1. Fassung]*

Zimmer im Schloß. Es ist Nacht. Orgelspiel verklingt.
DER ALTE *(am Fenster)*:
Gott sei ihm gnädig! Die Mess ist aus –
Nun treten sie aus der Kirche heraus!
Gott sei ihr gnädig!
HERBERT *(kniend)*:
Gott sei ihr gnädig – der bleichen Braut!
(angstvoll) Mir ist, ich hört einen seufzenden Laut
Der Nacht entsteigen! Gütiger Gott!
Hilf den Sündern aus ihrer Höllennot!
Ich halts nicht aus!
DER ALTE:
In den Wipfeln wühlt das Frühlingsgebraus!
Sei still! Mein Knabe, sie nahn!
HERBERT *(wie verzückt)*:
Die alle
Nach dieser Nacht den Tag nicht sahn
Nun sind sie da unten wieder erwacht

Dramatic Fragments

Bluebeard
[**A Puppet Play**; fragment]

Prologue

Anticipation
If you bemoan, righteous one, this confused picture
That is disheveled by laughter and madness
Believe me, until we meet again
My hero will go on more modest paths!
Amen!

Persons:
Bluebeard
The Old Man
Herbert
Elisabeth

Scene 1 [version 1]

Room in the palace. It is night. Organ-play fades away.
THE OLD MAN *(by the window)*:
God be merciful to him! The Mass is over—
Now they step outside the church!
God be merciful to her!
HERBERT *(kneeling)*:
God be merciful to her—the pale bride!
(fearfully) Seems to me, I heard a sighing sound
Emerge from the night! Kindest God!
Help the sinners out of their infernal need!
I won't endure it!
THE OLD MAN:
In the treetops spring's roar rummages!
Be still! My boy, they approach!
HERBERT *(as if ecstatic)*:
All who
Did not see the day after this night
Now they are awakened again down there

Und seufzen in die Blutbrautnacht!
Nimm mir Ohr und Aug! Ich bin verflucht!
Die Nacht ist voll Wahnsinn – und verrucht!
Hilf! Alter hörst du das Schrein!

DER ALTE *(still)*:
Nein!

HERBERT:
Laß mich fort! Ins Dorf hin!
Auf offnem Platz will ich niederknien
Und will bekennen – was hier geschah –
Und heute geschieht – daß sie fern und nah
Sturmglocken läuten in die Nacht –
Eh noch das Namenlose vollbracht!

DER ALTE:
Ich halt dich nicht! Ward dir zu tun
Dies auferlegt, dann magst dus tun!
Du dauerst mich!

HERBERT:
Vater! Bet, für mich!
Daß ich den leibeignen Herrn verrat!
Wir sehn uns nimmer! Ich hör er naht!
Fort! Fort! Leb wohl!

DER ALTE:
Leb wohl!
(Herbert ab)

1. Szene *[2. Fassung]*

Zimmer im Schloß. Es ist Nacht. Orgelspiel verklingt.

DER ALTE *(am Fenster)*:
Gott sei ihm gnädig! Die Mess ist aus –
Nun treten sie aus der Kirche heraus!
Gott sei ihr gnädig!

HERBERT *(kniend)*:
Gott sei ihr gnädig – der bleichen Braut!
(angstvoll) Mir ist, ich hört einen seufzenden Laut
Der Nacht entsteigen! Gütiger Gott!
Hilf den Sündern aus ihrer Höllennot!
Ich halts nicht aus!

DER ALTE:
In den Wipfeln wühlt das Frühlingsgebraus!
Sei still! Mein Knabe, sie nahn!

And sigh into the blood bride's night!
Take from me ear and eye! I am cursed!
The night is full of insanity—and nefarious!
Help! Old man do you hear the scream!
THE OLD MAN *(still)*:
No!
HERBERT:
Let me go! Into the village!
I want to kneel down in an open place
And want to confess—what happened here—
And today happens—that far and near they
Ring alarm bells in the night—
Still before the nameless is done!
THE OLD MAN:
I won't stop you! If you were enjoined
To do this, then you may do it!
I pity you!
HERBERT:
Father! Pray, for me!
That I betray the master to whom I am slave!
We never see for ourselves! I hear he approaches!
Away! Away! Goodbye!
THE OLD MAN:
Goodbye!
(Herbert exits)

Scene 1 *[version 2]*

Room in the palace. It is night. Organ-play fades away.
THE OLD MAN *(by the window)*:
God be merciful to him! The Mass is over—
Now they step outside the church!
God be merciful to her!
HERBERT *(kneeling)*:
God be merciful to her—the pale bride!
(fearfully) Seems to me, I heard a sighing sound
Emerge from the night! Kindest God!
Help the sinners out of their infernal need!
I won't endure it!
THE OLD MAN:
In the treetops spring's roar rummages!
Be still! My boy, they approach!

HERBERT *(wie verzückt)*:
Die alle
Nach dieser Nacht den Tag nicht sahn
Nun sind sie da unten wieder erwacht
Und seufzen in die Blutbrautnacht!
Nimm mir Ohr und Aug! Ich bin verflucht!
Die Nacht ist voll Wahnsinn – und verrucht!
Hilf! Alter hörst du das Schrein!
DER ALTE *(still)*:
Nein!
HERBERT:
Ich sah sie gehn, wie verlöschend Licht
Durch meinen Traum, und faßt es nicht
Fühlt ihre Näh, wie im Fieberglühn –
Und mußte schrein und vor ihnen fliehn!
Ein böser Traum hat mich krank gemacht
Nun weine ich die ganze Nacht
Ich vergaß – warum!
DER ALTE:
Deine Kindertage sind um –
HERBERT:
Laß mich fort, Greis, laß mich fort.
Aasgeier umflattern wieder den Ort!
Sie gießen Blut auf die Schwelle hin –
Dort wo die Braut muß niederknien
Sieh Alter – siehst du das Blut?
DER ALTE:
Der Fackeln flackernde Glut!
HERBERT:
Die Schatten winken der bleichen Braut
Was heißt mich tun – davor mir so graut!
Kehr um – du Magd! Ein Schritt noch vom Tor!
Ihr geliebten Frauen tretet doch vor!
Der Tod vor der Schwelle! Bete für mich!
Der Tod vor der Schwelle: Laß mich sterben für dich.
Maria – Jungfrau o bitt für mich!
(Er stürzt sich zum Fenster hinaus)
DER ALTE *(fällt in die Knie)*:
Läßt du darum Frühling werden
Gott auf dieser dunklen Erden?

HERBERT (*as if ecstatic*):
All who
Did not see the day after this night
Now they are awakened again down there
And sigh into the blood bride's night!
Take from me ear and eye! I am cursed!
The night is full of insanity—and nefarious!
Help! Old man do you hear the scream!
THE OLD MAN (*still*):
No!
HERBERT:
I saw her move, like an extinguishing light
Through my dream, and could not believe it
Felt her nearness, like in fever-glow—
And had to weep and flee before them!
A bad dream made me ill
Now I weep the whole night
I forgot—why!
THE OLD MAN:
Your childhood days are over—
HERBERT:
Let me go, old man, let me go.
Vultures flutter around the place again!
They pour blood on the threshold—
There where the bride must kneel down
See old man—do you see the blood?
THE OLD MAN:
The torches' flickering glow!
HERBERT:
The shadows beckon to the pale bride
What calls me to act—I dread it so!
Turn around—you maid! Still a step from the gate!
Yet, you beloved women step forward!
Death before the threshold! Pray for me!
Death before the threshold: Let me die for you.
Maria—virgin o please for me!
(*He jumps out of the window*)
THE OLD MAN (*falls to the knees*):
God, that's why you let spring come
To this dark earth?

1. Szene *[3. Fassung; Fragment]*

DER DIENER:
Gott sei ihr gnädig!
Wie sie geht – gleich einem verlöschenden Licht
Wie ein ferner Traum – o fühlst du sie nicht!
Und seh ich sie an, fühl ich Fieberglühn –!
Und möchte vor ihr niederknien
Was ists, das mein Herze so brennen macht,
Und tausend Stimmen leiht der Nacht!
DER ALTE:
Du sollst sie nicht ansehn, mein armes Kind
DER JUNGE:
Gott sei ihr gnädig der bleichen Braut

2. Szene

Blaubart und Elisabeth
ELISABETH:
Mein Herr! Als wie gingen durch dies Haus
Da löschten alle Fackeln aus!
BLAUBART:
Meine Taube, fühlst gar darin einen Sinn?
ELISABETH:
Ich weiß nicht Herr! Meine Hände glühn!
Mich däucht es weint wo immerzu!
BLAUBART:
Geh! Alter! Leg dich zur Ruh!
DER ALTE *(kniet vor ihm nieder)*:
Gott sei Euch gut!
BLAUBART:
Was weinst du?
DER ALTE:
Kreist hundert Jahr nun schon mein Blut –
Hab nie Herr einen gesehn in der Welt –
Der so wie Ihr von Gott gequält!
Gäb gern dies bißchen Leben für Euch –
Und kann nur weinen und knien vor Euch!
BLAUBART:
Du redest irr! Geh altes Kind!
DER ALTE *(küßt seine Hände)*:
Erbarm dich dieser Hände so bleich –

Scene 1 *[version 3; fragment]*

THE SERVANT:
God be merciful to her!
How she moves—like an extinguishing light
Like a distant dream—o don't you feel her!
And if I look at her, I feel fever-glow—!
And would like to kneel down before her
What is it that makes my heart burn so
And lends the night a thousand voices!
THE OLD MAN:
You should not look at her, my poor child
THE BOY:
God be merciful to her the pale bride

Scene 2

Bluebeard and Elisabeth
ELISABETH:
My master! Just as we went through this house
All torches extinguished here!
BLUEBEARD:
My dove, do you feel even in this a meaning?
ELISABETH:
I do not know master! My hands glow!
I would think it weeps incessantly somewhere.
BLUEBEARD:
Go! Old man! Lie down to rest!
THE OLD MAN *(kneels down before him)*:
God be good to you!
BLUEBEARD:
Why do you weep?
THE OLD MAN:
Already one hundred years now my blood circles—
Have never seen a master in the world—
Who was tormented by God like you!
Would give gladly this bit of life for you—
And can only weep and kneel before you!
BLUEBEARD:
You talk crazy! Go old child!
THE OLD MAN *(kisses his hands)*:
Have mercy on these hands so pale—

O Jesus! dieser Hände so bleich
Gut Nacht! *(ab)*
BLAUBART *(am Fenster)*:
Der Mond
Wie eine besoffene Dirne stiert –
ELISABETH:
Mich friert!
BLAUBART *(tritt zurück)*:
Hier zitterndes Kindlein – trink Wein!
Daß die Augen dir glühn! Wie sehn sie rein!
Hei! Bist du torig! Ich trink dir zu!
Vergaß ich es? Wie alt bist du?
ELISABETH:
Fünfzehn Jahre Herr! In dieser Nacht!
Was ist Euch Herr?
BLAUBART:
Hab ich gelacht?
Hei trink! Du zartliche Braut!
Sieh nur, wie der Mond dich brünstig anschaut!
ELISASBETH:
Versteh Euch nicht, hab Angst vor Euch!
BLAUBART:
Wahrhaftig! Deine Wangen sind bleich!
Ich sing die ein Lied, das dich lachen macht.
ELISABETH:
Das sänget Ihr?
BLAUBART:
Der Tausend ich weiß ein Liedlein dir,
Das oft ich vernommen in solcher Nacht.
(Er singt)
Wer sagt, daß ihr Licht erloschen war,
Als ich zur Feier löste ihr Haar.
Was klagt ihr mich an ihr Glocken
Möchtet lieber frohlocken.

Wer sagt, daß ihr stummer Mund verwest,
Als ich zur Nacht bei ihr gewest.
O schweige, schweige, du leise
Unendliche traurige Weise.

Wer sagt, daß offen stünd ein Grab,
Und daß ich im Blick was Böses hab!
Wenn das meine Herze wüßte!
Erbarm dich, o Jesus Christe!

O Jesus! these hands so pale
Good night! *(exit)*
BLUEBEARD *(at the window)*:
The moon
Ogles like a drunken strumpet—
ELISABETH:
I'm freezing!
BLUEBEARD *(steps back)*:
Here shivering child—drink some wine!
So that your eyes glow! How purely they see!
Hey! You are foolish! I drink to you!
Did I forget? How old are you?
ELISABETH:
Fifteen years master! On this night!
What's the matter with you, master?
BLUEBEARD:
Did I laugh?
Hey drink! You delicate bride!
Just look how the moon watches you in heat!
ELISABETH:
I do not understand you, am afraid of you!
BLUEBEARD:
Really! Your cheeks are pale!
I'll sing you a song that will make you laugh.
ELISABETH:
Would you sing that?
BLUEBEARD:
I know thousands of little songs for you
That I often heard on such a night.
(He sings)
Who says that her light had extinguished,
As I loosened her hair for the celebration.
What do you accuse me of, you bells
Should rather rejoice.

Who says that her mute mouth decomposes,
When I was by you through the night.
O be silent, be silent, you quiet
Endless sad melody.

Who says that a grave would stand open,
And that in the glance I have something evil!
If my heart would know this!
Have mercy, o Jesus Christ!

ELISABETH *schluchzt auf*

BLAUBART:
Wie stehn dir die schimmernden Tränen gut!
Trink Wein!

ELISABETH:
Ich hab ihn verschüttet – er leuchtet wie Blut!

BLAUBART:
Sagtest du Blut! Des Mondes trübe Glut
Nichts weiter! Hörst du, wie der Maien rauscht!

ELISABETH:
Mich däucht, daß im Dunkel zitternd wer lauscht
…
Träumt gestern unter dem Lindenbaum
An Vaters Haus einen bösen Traum.
(träumerisch) Heinrich, mein Knabe! Hilf!

BLAUBART *(flüsternd)*:
Du Hur!
Ists ein Affe oder ists ein Stier –
Ein Wolf oder sonstig reißend Getier!
Hei lustig geschnäbelt zur Nacht,
Bis zweie nur mehr eines macht –
Und das ist drei!
So hört ichs die Spatzen pfeifen im Mai!

ELISABETH *(wie verzaubert)*:
Komm Lieber! Feuer fließt mir im Haar
Weiß nimmer, nimmer, was gestern war
Blut stickt und würgt mir die Kehle zu
Nun hab ich keine Nacht mehr Ruh!
Möchte nackend in der Sonne gehn,
Vor aller Augen mich lassen sehn,
Und tausend Schmerzen auf mich flehn
Und Schmerzen dir tun, zu rasender Wut!
Mein Knabe komm! Trink meine Glut,
Bist du nicht durstig nach meinem Blut,
Nach meiner brennenden Haare Flut?
Hörst nicht, wie die Vögel im Walde schrien
Nimm alles, alles was ich bin –
Du Starker – mein Leben – du nimm hin!
Was stehst du fern –

BLAUBART:
Ist erst erloschen der letzte Stern – –

ELISABETH *(wie verzaubert)*:
Trägst du nicht am Hals ein Schlüsselein?

ELISABETH *sobs*
BLUEBEARD:
How the shimmering tears suit you!
Drink some wine!
ELISABETH:
I have spilled it—it shines like blood!
BLUEBEARD:
Did you say blood! The moon's cloudy glow
Nothing else! Do you hear how May roars!
ELISABETH:
It seems to me someone listens trembling in the darkness
…
Dreamed yesterday an evil dream
Under the linden tree at father's house.
(dreamy) Heinrich, my boy! Help!
BLUEBEARD *(whispering)*:
You whore!
Is it a monkey or is it a bull—
Wolf or other clawing creatures!
Hey merrily pecked by the night,
Until two only makes one more—
And that is three!
So I heard the sparrows whistle in May!
ELISABETH *(as if bewitched)*:
Come dear! Fire flows in my hair
Never knowing, never, what yesterday was
Blood shuts and chokes my throat
Now I have no more nights of rest!
I'd like to walk naked in the sun,
Let myself be seen by all eyes,
And pray a thousand pains on me
And inflict pain on you with raging fury!
Come my boy! Drink in my fervor,
Are you not thirsty after my blood,
After the flood of my burning hair?
Don't you hear how the birds cried in the forest
Take everything, everything that I am—
You strong man—my life—you shall take!
What makes you so distant—
BLUEBEARD:
When the last star will be extinguished—
ELISABETH *(as if bewitched)*:
Do you not carry a small key around your neck?

Es leuchtet – möchts ein goldenes sein?
Was öffnets mir?

BLAUBART:

Es öffnet zum Brautgemach die Tür!
Sein Geheimnis ist Verwesung und Tod,
Erblüht aus des Fleisches tiefster Not.
(Es schlägt Mitternacht! Alles Licht erlischt)
In Mitternacht du brünstige Braut
Zur Todesblume greifend erblaut –
Sei dir dies süße Geheimnis vertraut.
Starb Gott einst für des Fleisches Not
Muß der Teufel feiern zur Lust den Tod.
(Er sperrt eine Türe auf)
Hörst du des Asrael Flügelschlag –
Wie die Vögel du schreien hörtest im Hag.
Lust peitschen Haß, Verwesung und Tod
Entsprungen dem Blute, gellend und rot
Komm zitternde Braut! *(Er fällt über sie her)*

ELISABETH:

Hu! Hu! Wies mich schüttelt und graut!
Nicht du! Nicht du! O rette mich!
Lieber!

BLAUBART:

Wie dein Knabe – so keusch, o lieb ich dich!
Doch soll ich dich Kindlein ganz besitzen –
Muß ich, Gott wills den Hals dir schlitzen!
Du Taube, und trinken dein Blut so rot
Und deinen zuckenden, schäumenden Tod!
Und saugen aus deinem Eingeweid
Deine Scham und deine Jungfräulichkeit

ELISABETH:

Erbarmen! Was zerrst du mich am Haar!

BLAUBART:

Keusch blühende Rose auf meinem Altar –

ELISABETH:

Gott steh mir bei! Du geifernd Tier!

BLAUBART:

Ists ein Affe oder ists ein Stier
Ein Wolf oder ander reißend Getier
Hei lustig geschnäbelt zur Nacht –
Bis zweie nur mehr eines macht!
Und eins ist der Tod!

ELISABETH:

Neigt niemand sich meiner grausen Not?

It shines—could it be a golden one?
What does it open for me?
BLUEBEARD:
It opens the door to the bridal room!
Its mystery is decay and death,
Blooming out of the flesh's deepest need.
(It strikes midnight! All light extinguishes)
At midnight you bride in heat
Turning blue when you grasp death's flower—
This sweet mystery shall be confided to you.
Because God died once for the flesh's need
The devil must celebrate death for his lust.
(He unlocks a door)
Do you hear Azrael's wing beat—
Like you heard the birds crying in the hedge.
Hatred, decay and death whip lust
Arisen out of the blood, screaming and red
The trembling bride comes! *(He pounces on her)*
ELISABETH:
O no! O no! How it shakes me and terrifies!
Not you! Not you! O save me!
Dear!
BLUEBEARD:
Like your boy—so chaste, o I love you!
But to possess you completely little child—
By God's will I must slit your throat!
You dove, and drink your blood so red
And your twitching, foaming death!
And suck out your bowels
Your shame and your virginity
ELISABETH:
Mercy! Why do you drag me by the hair!
BLUEBEARD:
Chastely blooming rose on my altar—
ELISABETH:
God stand by me! You drooling animal!
BLUEBEARD:
It is a monkey or it is a bull
Wolf or other clawing creatures
Hey merrily pecked by the night,
Until two only makes one more—
And one is death!
ELISABETH:
Will no one end my dreaded need?

BLAUBART *(schreit)*:
Gott!
(Er zerrt sie in die Tiefe. Man hört einen gellenden Schrei. Dann tiefe Stille. Nach einiger Zeit erscheint Blaubart, bluttriefend, und trunken außer sich und stürzt wie niedergemäht vor einem Crucifix nieder)
BLAUBART *(verlöschend)*:
Gott!

Fragmentarische Szene

BLAUBART:
Ist ein spaßhafter wieder milder Gast.
Was macht dir so heiß – du fieberst ja fast!
(Er streichelt ihre Finger)
Atmest du diese mondene Nacht –
Die Molche und Lilien geile macht.
Hei, wies aus bebenden Kelchen schäumt,
Und schwärend sich Leib an Leib aufbäumt –
Und geifernd sich voll Wut umschlingt –
Und ringt – und ringt!
So heiß und schwer

BLUEBEARD *(shouts)*:
God!
(He drags her into the depths. One hears a screaming shout. Then deep stillness. After some time Bluebeard appears, dripping with blood, and drunkenly beside himself and falls as if mowed down before a Crucifix)
BLUEBEARD *(expiring)*:
God!

Fragmentary Scene

BLUEBEARD:
Is a funny mild guest again.
What makes you so hot—you almost have a fever!
(He strokes her fingers)
You breathe this moon-filled night—
Makes newts and lilies lustful.
Hey, how it foams out of quivering cups,
And rears up festering body pressed against body—
And droolingly embraces full of rage—
And struggles—and struggles!
So hot and hard

Don Juans Tod
[**Eine Tragödie in 3 Akten**; Fragment]

Prolog

… festlich hohe Träume …
…
… dionysisch Antlitz,
In dem die Freuden einer Götterwelt,
Die einst dahinsank, auferstanden schienen
Ein Enkel derer, die die Götter liebten
Und die das Leben segnet und befreit.
Weh!
Aus dir starrt mich des Erdendaseins hohle
Und schmerz… Maske steinern an,
Dahinter Tod und heißer Wahnsinn lauern.
…
… das qualentlohte Schicksal …
…
Durch finstere Tat, im Zwiespalt deines Wesens –
Ein Fremdgeborener und ein Qualbestimmter
Ein überwundner Sieger, Selbstverlorner,
Auf eisigen Gipfeln, die den Menschen fremd,
Ein Jäger, der die Pfeile schickt nach Gott.

Der Tragödie dritter Akt
[1. Fassung]

Szene: Ein Saal im Schloß des Don Juan.
CATALINON *(vor sich hinmurmelnd)*:
Was scharrt dort an der Tür! Nur immer zu!
Ich rühr' mich nicht! – Es scheint geduldig wie
Ein Tier, das selbst dem Schweigen eine Antwort
Entlocken möchte – scharrt und scharrt! He du,
Gib acht! Hier ist die Hölle – sagt' ich Hölle?
Vielleicht des Himmels Eingang auch. Wer weiß!
Dem Unfaßbaren hascht das träge Wort
Vergeblich nach, das nur in dunklem Schweigen
An unsres Geistes letzte Grenzen rührt.
Nur nicht so laut, ich komme schon und öffne!
(Er geht zur Tür und schiebt den Riegel zurück)
Tritt ein, du Unermüdlicher! Bist du

Don Juan's Death

[**A Tragedy in Three Acts**; Fragment]

Prologue

... festive exulted dreams ...

...

... Dionysian countenance
In which the joys of a gods' world,
That sank away once, seemed revived
A grandson of those who loved the gods
And who life blesses and frees.
Woe!
From you the hollow and painful[...] mask
Of mundane existence stares stony at me,
Behind it death and fervent insanity lurk.

...

destiny... flaming out of agony

...

With a sinister act, in the duality of your being—
One strangely born and directed by agony
A beaten winner, self-doomed,
On icy summits that are strange for man,
A hunter who sends arrows against God.

The Tragedy's Third Act

[version 1]

Scene: *A hall in the castle of Don Juan.*
CATALINON (*murmuring to himself*):
What scratches there at the door! Keep at it!
I won't get up!—It seems patient like
An animal that wants to entice an answer
Even from silence—scratches and scratches! Hey you,
Pay attention! Hell is here—did I say hell?
Perhaps the entrance to heaven also. Who knows!
The idle word grasps in vain
After the incomprehensible that only in dark silence
Touches our mind's final frontiers .
Just not so loud, I'm coming already and will open!
(*He goes to the door and pushes back the bolt*)
Enter, you relentless one! If you are

Ein Mensch, laß deine Sprache draußen,
Daß du vorwitzig sie nicht brauchst.

FIORELLO (*am ganzen Körper bebend, tritt ein*)

CATALINON:
Dacht' ich's doch gleich!

FIORELLO:
Daß du nur da bist!
Leer steht das Haus, die Diener sind geflohn
Laut schreiend in die Nach die Greueltat
Die hier in dieser Stunde sich bereitet.

CATALINON:
Schweig alter Mensch!

FIORELLO:
O namenloser Frevel!

CATALINON:
Schenk' dir den Schluß der Rede, weiß ich doch
Wonach der Witz dir steht. Schweig du, wie ich
Gesagt.

FIORELLO:
Ich schweige schon, du fürchterlicher Mensch.

CATALINON:
Wenn's dir beliebt, kannst du auch wieder gehn!
Dir wäre besser – –

FIORELLO:
Ich, meinen Herrn verlassen!
Ich bleibe hier, wenn auch die Angst mich tötet,
Und die Erwartung dessen, was da kommen
Wird.

(*Er setzt sich nieder*)

CATALINON (*vor sich hinsummend*):
In deine erloschenen Augen
Pflanz ich ein loderndes Licht
Ich entreiß dich dem Todesdunkel
Und Gott und Teufel, sie hindern es nicht!

FIORELLO:
Der Entsetzliche!

CATALINON (*horcht auf*):
Er naht – er kommt!

(*Don Juan erscheint in der Tür zur rechten Seite, durch die man in einem fahl erleuchteten Zimmer die Leiche der Donna Anna auf einem Ruhebett liegen sieht.*)

DON JUAN:
Weg, schreckliches Gesicht!
Was scheuchst du mich von meinem Lager auf
Da dieser Stunde tiefster Wonneschauer

A person, leave your way of speaking outside,
So you do not use it meddlesomely.

FIORELLO *(his whole body shaking, enters)*

CATALINON:
I thought that right away!

FIORELLO:
That only you are here!
The house is empty, the servants have fled,
Loudly shouting out into the night the atrocities
That are prepared here in this hour.

CATALINON:
Be silent old man!

FIORELLO:
O nameless sacrilege!

CATALINON:
Forgo the end of the speech, after all, I know
Whereof your wit is made up. Be silent, as I
Said.

FIORELLO:
I'm already silent, you dreadful person.

CATALINON:
If you like, you can also go again!
You would feel better—

FIORELLO:
I should leave my master!
I will stay here, even if the fear kills me,
And the expectation of what will
Come.

(He sits down)

CATALINON *(humming to himself)*:
In your expired eyes
I plant a blazing light
I snatch you from death's darkness
And God and the devil, they do not hinder it!

FIORELLO:
The horrible one!

CATALINON *(listening attentively)*:
He approaches—he comes!

(Don Juan appears in the door to the right side through which one sees the corpse of Donna Anna lying on a daybed in a sickly illuminated room.)

DON JUAN:
Away, terrible face!
What makes you rouse me from my bed
When this hour's deepest thrill of ecstasy

Mir noch im Blute bebt und mich erfüllt
Mit übermenschlichen Gesichten. Weg, weg!
Du Fratze, die ein geiler Schreck gebar,
Mich ekelt, sehe ich dich an – ich möcht'
Es nicht und muß. So fass' ich dich verfluchtes
Gebilde, du Auswurf meiner heißen Sinne
Erwürge dich mit diesen Händen, versenge
Mit meines Atem Glut, dich, Tiergesicht!
Ah! Schwebst du mir noch vor und blickst mich an
Aus toderstarrten Augenhöhlen, worin
Die Finsternis, die noch kein Lichtstrahl je
Erhellte, weint. Und füllst den Raum mit Schweigen,
Das blaß, grufttief sich schleicht in meines Herzens
Aufschäumend Pulsen und schlangengleich sich windet
Um meiner Sinne trunkene Entzückung,
Daß ferner immer ferner mir des Lebens
Vielstimmiges Geräusch verklingt, sich brechend
An ekler Öde. Es engt der Raum sich und
Verschlingt, der nahen Dinge sichere
Gestalt. Es steigt an mir empor und schon
Droht es mich zu umfassen. Weg Wesenloses!
Noch widertönt mein Blut von dieser Welt
Die Erde hält mich und ich lache dein.
(Er taumelt ans Fenster, und stößt es auf)
Hier öffne ich dem Leben weit die Pforten,
Und tönend braut's herein, mich zu umfassen,
Mit seinen Schwingen hüllt's mich ein – und ich –
Bin sein!
Und atme ein die Welt, bin wieder Welt
Bin Wohllaut, farbenheißer Abglanz – bin
Unendliche Bewegung – bin.

Still shakes in my blood and fulfills me
With superhuman visions. Away, away!
You grimace born by a lustily fright,
I'm nauseated when I look at you—I don't want to
And must. So I catch you cursed
Shape, you phlegm of my hot senses,
Strangle you with these hands, scorch
You with my breath's fervor, animal face!
Ah! Do you float before me and look on me
From death-numbed eye sockets, wherein
The sinisterness, which no beam of light ever
Illuminated, weeps. And you fill the room with silence,
Which pale, grave-deep creeps into my heart's
Foaming pulses and squirms serpent-like
Around the drunken delight of my senses,
So that farther always farther life's
Many-voiced noise fades away from me, refracting
With nauseating dreariness. The room constricts and
Devours the certain form of things
Nearby. It climbs upon me and already
Threatens to envelop me. Away apparition!
Still my blood resounds of this world
The earth holds me and I laugh at you.
(He lurches to the window and pushes open it)
Here I open the gates to life widely,
And sounding it concocts herein to envelop me,
It wraps me with its wings—and I—
Belong to it!
And inhale the world, am world again
Am harmony, reflection of hot colors—am
Infinite movement—am.

Der Tragödie dritter Akt

[2. Fassung]

Szene: Ein Saal im Schloß des Don Juan. Don Juan erscheint in der Tür zur rechten Seite, durch die man in einem hellerleuchteten Zimmer die Leiche der Donna Anna auf einem Ruhebett liegen sieht.

DON JUAN:
Weg, schreckliches Gesicht!
Was scheuchst du mich von meinem Lager auf,
Da dieser Stunde tiefster Wonneschauer
Mir noch im Blute bebt, und mich erfüllt
Mit übermenschlichen Gesichten. Weg – weg!
Du Fratze, die ein geiler Schreck gebar!
Ich schaudere, seh' ich dich an – ich möcht'
Es nicht und muß. *(Mit den Händen ins Leere fassend)*
So fass' ich dich verfluchtes
Gebilde, du Auswurf meiner heißen Sinne,
Erwürge dich, mit diesen Händen, versenge
Mit meines Atem Glut – dich, Tiergesicht!
Ah! Schwebst du mir noch vor, und blickst mich an
Aus toderstarrten Augenhöhlen, worin
Die Finsternis, die noch kein Lichtstrahl je
Erhellte, weint. Und füllst den Raum mit Schweigen,
Das blaß, grufttief, sich schleicht in meines Blutes
Aufschäumend Pulsen und schlangengleich sich windet
Um meiner Sinne trunkene Entzückung,
Daß ferner, immer ferner mir des Lebens
Vielstimmiges Geräusch verklingt, sich brechend
An ekler Öde. Es engt der Raum sich und
Verschlingt der nahen Dinge sichere
Gestalt. Es steigt an mir empor und schon
Droht es mich zu umfassen. Weg – Wesenloses!
Noch widertönt mein Blut von dieser Welt
Die Erde hält mich und ich lache dein!
(Er taumelt ans Fenster und stößt es auf)
Hier öffne ich dem Leben weit die Pforten,
Und atme ein die Welt, bin wieder Welt
Bin Wohllaut, farbenheißer Abglanz – bin
Unendliche Bewegung! – Bin!
(Er sinkt mit einem lauten Schrei zu den Stufen nieder)

II. Auftritt
Es treten auf: Der Hausverwalter Fiorello, und Catalinon.

The Tragedy's Third Act
[version 2]

*Scene: A hall in the castle of Don Juan. Don Juan appears in the door to the
right side through which one sees the corpse of Donna Anna lying in a brightly
illuminated room on a daybed.*

DON JUAN:
Away, terrible face!
What makes you rouse me from my bed
When this hour's deepest thrill of ecstasy
Still shakes in my blood and fulfills me
With superhuman visions. Away, away!
You grimace born by a lustily fright!
I shudder, when I look at you—I don't want to
And must. *(With hands grabbing at the emptiness)*
So I catch you cursed
Shape, you phlegm of my hot senses,
Strangle you with these hands, scorch
You with my breath's fervor, animal face!
Ah! Do you float before me and look on me
From death-numbed eye sockets, wherein
The sinisterness, which no beam of light ever
Illuminated, weeps. And you fill the room with silence,
Which pale, grave-deep creeps into my heart's
Foaming pulses and squirms serpent-like
Around the drunken delight of my heart,
So that farther always farther life's
Many-voiced noise fades away from me, refracting
With nauseating dreariness. The room constricts and
Devours the certain form of things
Nearby. It climbs upon me and already
Threatens to envelop me. Away—apparition!
Still my blood resounds of this world
The earth holds me and I laugh at you.
(He lurches to the window and pushes open it)
Here I open the gates to life widely,
And inhale the world, am world again
Am harmony, reflection of hot colors—am
Infinite movement!—Am!
(He sinks to the steps with a loud shout)

II. Appearance
Appearing: the house caretaker Fiorello and Catalinon.

Dramenfragment
[1. Fassung]

1

Hütte am Saum eines Waldes. Im Hintergrund ein Schloß. Es ist Abend.

DER PÄCHTER:
Unser Tagwerk ist getan. Die Sonne ist untergegangen. Laß uns ins Haus gehen.

PETER:
Bei der Mühle hat man heute die Leiche eines Knaben gefunden. Die Waisen des Dorfes sangen seine schwarze Verwesung. Die roten Fische haben seine Augen gefressen und ein Tier den silbernen Leib zerfleischt; das blaue Wasser einen Kranz von Nesseln und wildem Dorn in seine dunklen Locken geflochten.

DER PÄCHTER:
Rotes Gestern, da ein Wolf mein Erstgebornes zerriß. Fluch, Fluch durch finstere Jahre. Woran erinnerst du mich: Leise tönen die Glocken, langsam wölbt sich der schwarze Steg über den Bach und die roten Jagden verhallen in den Wäldern. Dunkel singt der Wahnsinn im Dorf; morgen heben wir vielleicht das Bahrtuch von einem teueren Toten. Laß uns gehn. O die läutenden Herden am Waldsaum, das Rauschen des Korns –

PETER:
Euere Tochter –

DER PÄCHTER:
Sprichst du von deiner Schwester! Ihr Antlitz sah ich heut' nacht im Sternenweiher, gehüllt in blutende Schleier. Das Vaters Fremdlingin –

PETER:
Die Schwester singend im Dornbusch und das Blut rann von ihren silbernen Fingern, Schweiß von der wächsernen Stirne. Wer trank ihr Blut?

DER PÄCHTER:
Gott mein Haus hast du heimgesucht. In dämmernden Zimmern steh ich geneigten Haupts, vor der Flamme meines Herdes; darin ist Ruß und Reines, und im Schatten weiß ich einen knöchernen Gast; glühend Erblinden. Wo bist du Peter?

PETER:
Grüne Schlangen flüstern im Haselbusch – Schritt in englischer Flamme –

DER PÄCHTER:
O die Wege voll Stacheln und Stein. Wer ruft euch; daß ihr in Schlummer das Haus und das weiße Haupt verlasset eh' am Morgen der Hahn kräht.

PETER:
O die Pforte des Klosters, die sich leise schließt. Gewitter ziehn über das Schloß. Höllenfratzen und die flammenden Schwerter der Engel. Fort! Fort! Lebt wohl.

DER PÄCHTER:
O die Ernte di[e ...] Schon rauscht das wilde Gras auf den Stufen des Hauses, nistet im Gemäuer der Skorpion. O meine Kinder. Maria sprichst du ein kleines

Drama Fragment

[version 1]

1

Hut at the edge of a forest. In the background a castle. It is evening.
THE TENANT:
Our day's work is done. The sun has set. Let's go in the house.
PETER:
They found the body of a boy today at the mill. The orphans of the village sang
his black decay. The red fish ate his eyes and an animal mauled the silver body;
the blue water braided a wreath of nettles and wild thorns in his dark locks.
THE TENANT:
Red yesterday, when a wolf tore my first-born. Curse, curse through sinister years.
Of which you remind me: quietly the bells sound, slowly the black footbridge
arches over the brook and the red hunts fade away in the forests. Darkly the insan-
ity sings in the village; tomorrow we may lift the pall of a beloved dead person.
Let us go. O the ringing herds along the forest's edge, the murmur of the corn—
PETER:
Your daughter—
THE TENANT:
You speak of your sister! I saw her countenance tonight in the pond of stars,
wrapped in bleeding veils. The father's strangeress—
PETER:
The sister singing in the thorn bush and the blood ran from her silver fingers, sweat
from the waxy forehead. Who drank her blood?
THE TENANT:
God, you have afflicted my house. In the dawning room I stand with bent head,
before the flame of my hearth; in it is soot and purity, and in the shadow I know a
bony guest; go blind from the glowing. Where are you Peter?
PETER:
Green snakes whisper in the hazel bush—step in angelic flame—
THE TENANT:
O the paths full of barb and stone. Who calls you; so that you leave the house and
the white head in slumber before the cock crows in the morning.
PETER:
O the gate of the cloister which quietly shuts. Thunderstorms move about the
palace. Hellish grimaces and the flaming swords of the angels. Away! Away!
Goodbye.
THE TENANT:
O the harvest [...] Already the wild grass murmurs on the steps of the house, the
scorpion nests in the walls. O my children. Maria you speak a small ghost light
to me, gone away child, a blue spring my deceased wife and the old trees fall on

Irrlicht zu mir, hingegangenes Kind, ein blauer Quell mein verstorbenes Weib und die alten Bäume fallen auf uns. Wer spricht? Johanna, Tochter weiße Stimme im Nachtwind, von welch traurigen Pilgerschaften kehrst du heim. O du, Blut von meinem Blute, Weg und Träumende in mondener Nacht – wer bist du? Peter, dunkelster Sohn, ein Bettler sitzest du am Saum des steinigen Ackers, hungernd, daß du die Stille deines Vaters erfülltest. O die Sommerschwere des Korns; Schweiß und Schuld und endlich sinkt in leeren Zimmern das müde Haupt auch. O das Rauschen der Linde von Kindheit an, vergebliche Hoffnung des Lebens, das versteinerte Brot! Neige dich stille Nacht nun. *(Er verbirgt das Haupt in den Händen)*

2

Dornige Wildnis, Felsen, ein Quell. Es ist Nacht.
JOHANNA:
Stich schwarzer Dorn. Ach noch tönen von wildem Gewitter die silbernen Arme. Fließe Blut von den rasenden Füßen. Wie weiß sind sie geworden von nächtigen Wegen! O das Schreien der Ratten im Hof, der Duft der Narzissen. Rosiger Frühling nistet in den schmerzenden Brauen. Was spielt ihr verwesten Träume der Kindheit in meinen zerbrochenen Augen. Fort! Fort! Rinnt nicht Scharlach vom Munde mir. Weiße Tänze im Mond. Tier brach ins Haus mit keuchendem Rachen. Tod! Tod! O wie süß ist das Leben! In kahlem Baum wohnt die Mutter, sieht mich mit meinen traurigen Augen an. Weiße Locke des Vaters sank ins Hollundergebüsch – Liebes es ist mein brennendes Haar. Rühre nicht dran, Schwester mit deinen kalten Fingern.
DIE ERSCHEINUNG:
Leises Schweben erglühender Blüte –
JOHANNA:
Weh, die Wunde die dir am Herzen klafft, liebe Schwester.
DIE ERSCHEINUNG:
Brennende Lust; Qual ohne Ende. Fühl' meines Schoßes schwärzliche Wehen.
JOHANNA:
In deinem Schatten wes Antlitz erscheint; gefügt aus Metall und feurige Engel im Blick; zerbrochne Schwerter im Herzen.
DIE ERSCHEINUNG:
Weh! Mein Mörder! *(Die Erscheinung versinkt)*
JOHANNA:
Glühende Schmach, die mich tötet; Elai! Schneeiges Feuer im Mond!
(Sie stürzt besinnungslos in den Dornenbusch, der sich über ihr schließt)
DER WANDERER:
Was schrie in der Nacht, stört das süße Vergessen in schwarzer Wolke mir? Weg und Hügel, wo ich in glühenden Tränen geruht – laß Gott nur Traum sein, den Schritt im moosigen Wald, Hütte die ich im Abendrot verließ, Frau und Kind. Weg aus diesen furchtbaren Schatten.

us. Who speaks? Johanna, daughter white voice in the night wind, from what sad pilgrimages do you come home. O you, blood of my blood, path and dreaming woman in lunar night—who you are? Peter, darkest son, a beggar you sit at the edge of the stony field, starving to fulfill the stillness of your father. O the summer gravity of the corn; sweat and guilt and, finally, the tired head also sinks in empty rooms. O the murmur of the linden tree from childhood on, vain hope of the life, the petrified bread! End now silent night. *(He hides the head in the hands)*

2

Thorny wilderness, rocks, a spring. It is night.

JOHANNA:

Sting black thorn. Alas the silver arms still sound from the wild thunderstorm. Flow blood from the raving feet. How white they have become from nocturnal ways! O the screams of the rats in the courtyard, the smell of the daffodils. Rosy spring nests in the aching brows. What do you putrid dreams of childhood play in my broken eyes. Away! Away! Does not scarlet fever run from my mouth. White dances in the moon. Animal broke into the house with wheezy throat. Death! Death! O how sweet is life! The mother dwells in the bleak tree, looks at me with my sad eyes. White lock of the father sank in the elder bush beloved it is my burning hair. Do not touch it, sister with your cold fingers.

THE APPARITION:

Quiet floating of glowing blossom—

JOHANNA:

Woe, the wound which gapes near your heart, dear sister.

THE APPARITION:

Burning lust; agony without end. Feel my lap's blackish labor pains.

JOHANNA:

In your shadow whose countenance appears; joined from metal and fiery angels in the glance; broken swords in the heart.

THE APPARITION:

Woe! My murderer! *(The apparition sinks)*

JOHANNA:

The glowing dishonor which kills me; Elai! Snowy fire in the moon!

(She falls unconsciously into the thorn bush which closes about her)

THE TRAVELLER:

Who screamed at night, disturbs my sweet forgetfulness in black cloud? Path and hill where I rested in glowing tears—let God only be dream, the step in the mossy forest, hut I left in the sunset, wife and child. Way out of these dreadful shadows.

THE MURDERER:

Leaden steps in nothingness. Who tore me out of sleep; called me to go on desolate

DER MÖRDER:
Bleierne Stufe ins Nichts. Wer riß aus dem Schlaf mich; hieß mich verödete Pfade gehn. Wer hat mein Antlitz genommen, das Herz in Kalk verwandelt. Verflucht dein Name! Wer hat die Lampe aus meinen Händen genommen. Wildes Vergessen. Wer drückt das Messer in meine rote Rechte. Lachendes Gold! Verflucht! Verflucht! *(Er starrt in die Luft)*

DER WANDERER:
Wie dunkel ist es um mich geworden; Stimme im Innern verkündet Unheil, heilige Mutter trockne den Schweiß auf meiner Stirne, das Blut; trauriger Amselruf, Nachmittagssonne im Wald – wo träumte ich das?

DER MÖRDER *(über ihn herfallend)*:
Hund, dein Gebein! *(Er ersticht ihn)*

DER WANDERER *(sterbend)*:
Weg von meiner Kehle die schwarze Hand – weg von den Augen nächtige Wunde – purpurner Alb der Kindheit. *(Er sinkt zurück)*

DER MÖRDER: Lachendes Gold, Blut – o verflucht! *(Er durchsucht den Ranzen des Toten)*

Dramenfragment
[2. Fassung]

I. Akt

In der Hütte des Pächters. Es ist Nacht. Der Pächter, Peter, sein Sohn. Es klopft.
PETER:
Wer da?

STIMME DRAUSSEN:
Öffne! *(Peter öffnet, Kermor tritt ein)*

KERMOR:
Meinem Rappen brach ich im Wald das Genick, da der Wahnsinn aus seinen purpurnen Augen brach. Der Schatten der Ulmen fiel auf mich, das blaue Lachen des Wassers. Nacht und Mond! Wo bin ich. Einbrech ich in süßen Schlummer, umflattert mich silbernes Hexenhaar! Fremde Nähe nachtet um mich. *(Er sinkt am Herd nieder)*

PETER:
Seine Schläfe blutet. Sein Antlitz ist schwarz von Hochmut und Trauer, Vater!

DER PÄCHTER:
Getan ist das Tagwerk, die Sonne untergegangen. Stille unser Leben.

PETER:
Bei der Mühle hat man heute die Leiche des Mönchs gefunden. Die Waisen des Dorfes sangen seine schwarze Verwesung. Rote Fische haben seine Augen gefres-

paths. Who has taken my countenance, transformed the heart into lime. Cursed be your name! Who has taken the lamp from my hands. Wild forgetfulness. Who presses the knife in my red right hand. Laughing gold! Cursed! Cursed! *(He stares in the air)*

THE TRAVELLER:
How dark it has become around me; voice inside heralds calamity, holy mother dry the sweat on my forehead, the blood; sad blackbird call, afternoon sun in the forest—where did I dream this?

THE MURDERER *(attacking him)*:
Dog, your skeleton! *(He stabs him)*

THE TRAVELLER *(dying)*:
The black hand away from my throat—the nocturnal wound away from the eyes—purple nightmare of childhood. *(He sinks back)*

THE MURDERER: Laughing gold, blood—o cursed! *(He searches the satchel of the dead person)*

Drama Fragment
[version 2]

Act I

In the hut of the tenant. It is night. The tenant, Peter, his son. A knocking.
PETER:
Who is there?
VOICE OUTDOORS:
Open! *(Peter opens, Kermor enters)*
KERMOR:
In the forest I broke the neck of my black horse, when insanity broke from his purple eyes. The shadow of the elms fell on me, the blue laughter of the water. Night and moon! Where am I. I break into sweet slumber, the silver hair of witches flutters about me! Strange vicinities darken around me. *(He sinks down by the stove)*
PETER:
His temple bleeds. His countenance is black from arrogance and grief, father!
THE TENANT:
The day's work is done, the sun has set. Silence our life.
PETER:
Today at the mill they found the body of the monk. The orphans of the village sang his black decay. Red fish ate his eyes and an animal mauled the silver body; the blue water braided a wreath of nettles and wild thorns in his dark locks.

sen und ein Tier den silbernen Leib zerfleischt; das blaue Wasser einen Kranz aus Nesseln und wildem Dorn ins dunkle Haar im geflochten.

DER PÄCHTER:
Rotes Gestern, grünender Morgen. Mein Weib ist gestorben, das Erstgeborene verdorben erblindet des Greisen Gesicht. Fluch durch finstere Jahre. Wer kam als Fremdling zu uns?

KERMOR *(im Schlaf)*:
Verhallt ihr roten Jagden. Schwarzer Steg, langsam gewölbt über den Bach. Wälder und Glocken. Leise hebt die silberne Hand das Bahrtuch von der finsteren Schläferin, beut in Dornen das metallene Herz. Mondnes Antlitz –

DER PÄCHTER:
Erlosch die Flamme im Herd! Wer verläßt mich!

PETER:
O die Schwester singend im Dornenbusch und das Blut rinnt von ihren silbernen Fingern, Schweiß von ihrer wächsernen Stirne. Wer trinkt ihr Blut?

KERMOR *(im Schlaf)*:
O ihr Wege in Stein. Sternenantlitz gehüllt in eisige Schleier; singende Fremdlingin – – Finsternis wogt im Herzen mir.

DER PÄCHTER:
Furchtbarer Gott, der eingekehrt in mein Haus. Geerntet ist das Korn, gekeltert die Traube. O die finsteren Zimmer!

PETER:
Schweiß und Schuld! Vater, hör, die Pforte des Klosters, die sich leise auftut. Stürzende Sterne! Gewitter ziehen über das Schloß, Höllenfratzen und die flammenden Schwerter der Engel – –

KERMOR *(im Schlaf)*:
Mädchen dein glühender Schoß im Sternenweiher – –

PETER:
O die Rosen, grollend in Donnern! Fort! Fort! Lebt wohl. *(Er stürzt fort)*

KERMOR *(im Schlaf)*:
Laß ab, schwarzer Wurm, der purpurn am Herz bohrt! Verfallener Mond, folgend durch morsches Geröll – –

DER PÄCHTER:
Peter, dunkelster Sohn, ein Bettler sitzest du am Saum des steinigsten Ackers, hungernd, daß du die Stille deines Vaters erfülltest. O die Herbstschwere des Weizens, Sichel und harter Gang und endlich sinkt in kahlen Zimmern das weiße Haupt hin. *(In diesem Augenblick tritt Johanna aus ihrer Schlafkammer)* Johanna, ein kleines Irrlicht sprichst du zu uns, stilleres Kind, mit der blauen Stimme des Quells mein verstorbenes Weib und die alten Bäume, die ein Toter gepflanzt, fallen auf uns. Wer spricht. Johanna, Tochter, weiße Stimme im Nachtwind, gerüstet zu purpurner Pilgerschaft; o du Blut, von meinem Blute, Pfad und Träumende in mondener Nacht. Wer sind wir? O vergebliche Hoffnung des Lebens; o das versteinerte Brot! *(Sein Haupt sinkt hin)*

JOHANNA *(traumwandelnd)*:

THE TENANT:
Red yesterday, greening morning. My wife has died, the first-born twistedly blinded the old man's face. A curse through sinister years. Who came as a stranger to us?
KERMOR *(in sleep)*:
Fade away you red hunts. Black footbridge, genty arched over the brook. Forests and bells. Quietly the silver hand lifts the pall of the sinister sleeping woman, offers the metal heart in thorns. Lunar countenance—
THE TENANT:
Did the flame in the stove extinguish! Who leaves me!
PETER:
O the sister singing in the thorn bush and the blood runs from her silver fingers, sweat from her waxy forehead. Who drinks her blood?
KERMOR *(in sleep)*:
O her ways in stone. Star countenance wrapped in icy veils; singing strangeress—
—Sinisterness surges in my heart.
THE TENANT:
Dreadful God who came in my house. The grain is harvested, the grape pressed. O the sinister rooms!
PETER:
Sweat and guilt! Father, hear, the gate of the cloister which quietly opens. Falling stars! Thunderstorms move about the palace, hellish grimaces and the flaming swords of the angels— —
KERMOR *(in sleep)*:
Girls your glowing womb in the pond of stars—
PETER:
O the roses, rumbling in thunders! Away! Away! Goodbye. *(He rushes forth)*
KERMOR *(in sleep)*:
Cease, black worm which bores purpley at the heart! Decayed moon, pursuing through rotten boulders—
THE TENANT:
Peter, darkest son, you sit a beggar at the edge of the stoniest field, starving so that you fulfilled the silence of your father. O the autumn weight of the wheat, sickle and hard walk and, finally, the white head sinks in the bleak room. *(At this moment Johanna steps out of her sleeping chamber)* Johanna, a small ghost light you speak to us, stiller child, with the blue voice of the well my deceased wife, and the old trees that someone dead planted fall on us. Who speaks. Johanna, daughter, white voice in the night wind, prepared for purple pilgrimage; o you blood of my blood, path and dreaming woman in lunar night. Who are we? O vain hope of life; o the petrified bread! *(His head sinks down)*
JOHANNA *(sleepwalking)*:
O the wild grass on the steps which lacerates the freezing soles, picture in hard crystal, you dig with silver nails—o sweet blood.
KERMOR *(awaking)*:
Awakening out of brown poppy! Quietly the gentle voices of the angels fall silent.

O das wilde Gras auf den Stufen, das die frierenden Sohlen zerfleischt, Bild in hartem Kristall, laß dich mit silbernen Nägeln graben – o süßes Blut.

KERMOR *(erwachend)*:
Erwachen aus braunem Mohn! Leise verstummen die sanften Stimmen der Engel. Heule Herbststurm! Falle auf mich, schwarzes Gebirge, Wolke von Stahl; schuldiger Pfad, der mich hergeführt

JOHANNA:
Lachende Stimme im Nachtwind – –

KERMOR *(erblickt sie)*:
Dornige Stufen in Verwesung und Dunkel; purpurne Höllenflamme flamme! *(Er erhebt sich und flieht ins Dunkel)*

JOHANNA *(hoch aufgerichtet)*:
Mein Blut über dich – da du brachest in meinen Schlaf.

Howl autumn storm! Drop over me, black mountains, cloud of steel; guilty path which led me here.

JOHANNA:

Laughing voice in the night wind—

KERMOR *(catching sight of her)*:

Thorny steps in rot and darkness; purple hellfire flame! *(He rises and flees in the darkness)*

JOHANNA *(very erect)*:

My blood is upon you—since you burst into my sleep.

Die Briefe

An Karl vom Kalmár (In Wien)

Salzburg, August / erste Hälfte September 1905 (?)

Lieber Freund Kalmár

Besten Dank für Deinen letzten Brief. Die Ferien haben für mich so schlecht als es nur möglich ist, begonnen. Seit acht Tagen bin ich krank - in verzweifelter Stimmung. Ich habe anfangs viel, ja sehr viel gearbeitet. Um über die nachträgliche Abspannung der Nerven hinwegzukommen habe ich leider wieder zum Chloroform meine Zuflucht genommen. Die Wirkung war furchtbar. Seit acht Tagen leide ich daran - meine Nerven sind zum Zerreißen. Aber ich widerstehe der Versuchung, mich durch solche Mittel wieder zu beruhigen, denn ich sehe die Katastrophe zu nahe. Was Deine liebenswürdige Einladung nach Wien anbetrifft, so ist das nicht so einfach. Ich habe gleich zu Anfang der Ferien eine Partie von 5 Tagen nach Gastein und Umgebung gemacht. Dort ist alles rasend teuer gewesen - es war ja auch Mitte der Saison. In Wien werden die Hotels auch nicht billig sein - und die Verpflegungsfrage für längere Zeit ist für mich ein ?. Denn ich will meinem Vater nicht solche Ausgaben bereiten. Ich weiß mir nicht zu raten - da ich ja mit den Großstadtverhältnissen nicht vertraut bin - so gern ich Deine Einladung annehmen möchte.

Empfiehl mich Deinen werten Eltern. Es grüßt Dich herzlich

Dein Jörg Trakl

4. An Hermine Von Rauterberg

Wien, 5. X. 1908

Liebe Minna!

Mögest Du ein gütiges Verzeihen dafür gewähren, daß ich es versäumt habe, bis heute an Dich zu schreiben. In der Lage der veränderten Verhältnisse, in der ich mich befinde, mag es wohl leicht geschehen, daß man für kurze Zeit die wenigen Dinge und Menschen, die einem besonders angelegen und wert sind, vernachlässigt, um sonach nur lebhafter ihrer zu gedenken, wenn man wieder zu sich gebracht ist.

Was mir in diesen Tagen geschah, das zu beobachten hat mich genugsam interessiert, denn es schien mir nicht gewöhnlich und trotzdem wieder nicht so außergewöhnlich, wenn ich all meine Veranlagungen in Betracht nehme. Als ich hier ankam, war es mir, als sähe ich zum ersten Male das Leben so klar wie es ist, ohne alle persönliche Deutung, nackt, voraussetzungslos, als vernähme ich alle jene Stimmen, die die Wirklichkeit spricht, die grausamen, peinlich vernehmbar. Und

Selected Letters

1. To Karl von Kalmár (in Vienna)

Salzburg, August / first half of September 1905 (?)
Dear friend Kalmár,

Thank you very much for your last letter. The holidays have begun for me as poorly as it is humanly possible. For eight days now, I have been sick, in a desperate mood. At first, I worked a lot, indeed very much. To overcome the subsequent exhaustion of my nerves, unfortunately, I resorted to chloroform again. The effect was terrible. For eight days, I have been suffering from it - my nerves are on the verge of breaking. But I resist the temptation to calm myself through such means because I see the catastrophe too closely.

As for your kind invitation to Vienna, it's not that simple. At the beginning of the holidays, I took a 5 day trip to Gastein and its surroundings. Everything there was outrageously expensive - it was the middle of the season, after all. Hotels in Vienna won't be cheap either, and the question of sustenance for an extended period is a concern for me. I don't want to burden my father with such expenses. I don't know what to do - since I'm not familiar with big city conditions - as much as I would like to accept your invitation.

Please give my regards to your esteemed parents. Hertfelt greetings from
Your Jörg Trakl

4. To Hermine von Rauterberg

Vienna, X.5.1908
Dear Minna!

May you grant me your good-natured forgiveness that I neglected to write until today. In the state of changed circumstances I find myself in, it can easily happen that for a short time one neglects the few things and people who are especially close and worthy, only to think about them more vividly when one is again brought back to oneself.

What's happened to me these days is interesting enough to observe, because it seemed uncommon and yet again not so remarkable, if I take all my idiosyncrasies into consideration. When I arrived here it was as if for the first time I could see life as it is so clearly, without personal interpretation, naked, conditionless, as if I could hear all those voices, which reality speaks, the cruel, keenly audible. And for an instant I felt something of the pressure that usually weighs on people, and the force of destiny.

einen Augenblick spürte ich etwas von dem Druck, der auf den Menschen für gewöhnlich lastet, und das Treibende des Schicksals.

Ich glaube, es müßte furchtbar sein, immer so zu leben, im Vollgefühl all der animalischen Triebe, die das Leben durch die Zeiten wälzen. Ich habe die fürchterlichsten Möglichkeiten in mir gefühlt, gerochen, getastet und im Blute die Dämonen heulen hören, die tausend Teufel mit ihren Stacheln, die das Fleisch wahnsinnig machen. Welch entsetzlicher Alp!

Vorbei! Heute ist diese Vision der Wirklichkeit wieder In Nichts versunken, ferne sind mir die Dinge, ferner noch ihre Stimme und ich lausche, ganz beseeltes Ohr, wieder auf die Melodien, die in mir sind, und mein beschwingtes Auge träumt wieder seine Bilder, die schöner sind als alle Wirklichkeit! Ich bin bei mir, bin meine Welt! Meine ganze, schöne Welt, voll unendlichen Wohllauts. Und also bist auch Du mir wieder nahe und kommst zu mir, daß ich Dich recht ernst und aus tiefstem Herzensgrund grüße und Dir sage, daß, Dich glücklich zu sehen, mein bester Wunsch ist.

Ganz Dein Georg.

5. An Maria Geipel (In Salzburg)

Wien, Ende Oktober 1908
Liebes Schwesterlein!
Daß mein Brief so bald eine Erwiederung fand, ist mir zwiefache Freude gewesen. Eine jede Zeile, jedes Blatt, das von Salzburg kommt, ist eine meinem Herzen teuere Erinnerung an eine Stadt, die ich über alles liebe, eine Erinnerung an die wenigen, denen meine Liebe gehört.

Ich denke, der Kapuzinerberg ist schon im flammenden Rot des Herbstes aufgegangen, und der Gaisberg hat sich in ein sanft' Gewand gekleidet, das zu seinen so sanften Linien am besten steht. Das Glockenspiel spielt die "letzte Rose" in den ernsten freundlichen Abend hinein, so süß-bewegt, daß der Himmel sich ins Unendliche wölbt! Und der Brunnen singt so melodisch hin über den Residenzplatz, und der Dom wirft majestätische Schatten. Und die Stille steigt und geht über Plätze und Straßen. Könnt' ich doch inmitten all' dieser Herrlichkeit bei euch weilen, mir wäre besser. Ich weiß nicht ob jemand den Zauber dieser Stadt so wie ich empfinden kann, ein Zauber, der einem das Herz traurig von übergroßem Glücke macht! Ich bin immer traurig, wenn ich glücklich bin! Ist das nicht merkwürdig! Die Wiener gefallen mir gar nicht. Es ist ein Volk, das eine Unsumme, dummer, alberner, und auch gemeiner Eigenschaften hinter einer unangenehmen Bonhomie verbirgt. Mir ist nichts widerlicher, als ein forciertes Betonen der Gemütlichkeit! Auf der Elektrischen biedert sich einem der Kondukteur an, im Gasthaus ebenso der Kellner u.s.w. Man wird allerorten in der schamlosesten Weise angestrudelt. Und der Endzweck all' dieser Attentate ist – das Trinkgeld! Die Erfahrung mußte ich schon machen, daß in Wien alles seine Trinkgeldtaxe hat. Der Teufel hole diese

I believe it must be dreadful to live continually in full consciousness of all the animal instincts that constantly whirl life through the ages. I felt, smelled, and touched the most frightening possibilities within me and heard the daemons howl in the blood, the thousand devils with their barbs that drive the flesh insane. What a horrible nightmare!

Gone! Today, this vision has once again sunk into nothingness, distant are the things, even more distant their voices, and I listen, with a completely animated ear, once again to the melodies that are within me, and my uplifted eye dreams its images again, which are more beautiful than all reality! I am with myself, I am my world! My entire, beautiful world, full of infinite harmony. And so, you are also near to me again and come to me, that I may greet you with genuine seriousness and from the depths of my heart and tell you that my dearest wish is to see you happy.

Completely your Georg

5. To Maria Geipel (In Salzburg)

Vienna, end of October 1908
Dear little sister!

That my letter found an answer so soon was a twofold joy for me. Each line, each page that comes from Salzburg is a precious memory to my heart of a city I adore, a memory of the few to whom my love belongs.

I think the Kapuzinerberg has already gone up in the flaming red of autumn and the Gaisberg has dressed itself in a soft garment that best shows off its such gentle lines. The glockenspiel plays the "Last Rose" into the solemnly friendly evening so sweetly moved that the sky curves into the infinite! And the fountain sings so melodiously over the Residenzplatz and the cathedral casts a majestic shadow. And the stillness rises and moves over plazas and streets. It would be better for me if I could still dwell with you in the midst of all this glory. I don't know whether anyone else can feel the charm of this city as I do, a charm that makes the heart sad with its oversized happiness! I am always sad when I've been happy. Isn't that strange!

The Viennese don't please me at all. They are a people who hide an enormous sum of stupid, ridiculous, and also vulgar characteristics behind an unpleasant bonhomie. To me nothing is more obnoxious than a forced emphasis on congeniality. On the electric train, the conductor curries favor with you, and likewise the waiter in the inn, etc. You are harassed everywhere in this most shameless way. And the final aim of these assaults is—the tip. I've already had the experience that in Vienna everything has its tip tax. The devil take these impudent bugs!

It makes me very happy that Streicher will come to Vienna soon! Hopefully he

unverschämten Wanzen!

Daß Streicher bald nach Wien kommt, freut mich sehr! Hoffentlich hat er in München seine Zwecke erreicht! Daß Ihr durch Produkte Euerer Kochkunst meinen Gaumen sehr erfreuen würdet, brauche ich wohl nicht lange zu betonen! Schickt nur Manna! Es wünscht Dir und Minna ganz besonders
gesegnete Reise
Euer ganz getreuer Georg.

14. An Erhard Buschbeck (In Salzburg)

Wien, zweite Hälfte Juli 1910
Lieber Buschbek!

Du würdest mir aus einer unsäglich peinlichen Verlegenheit helfen, wenn Du mir dieser Tage den Betrag von 30 K vorstrecken möchtest, da ich mich aus guten Gründen nicht an meinen Bruder wenden will. Ich kann Dir allerdings dieses Geld erst am I. Oktober zurückerstatten. Hoffentlich kannst Du es bis dorthin entbehren. Du würdest mir wahrhaftig einen großen Gefallen erweisen.

Ich muß Dir auch über ein Vorkommnis berichten, das mich mehr als peinlich berührt hat.

Gestern hat mir Herr Ullmann ein Gedicht vorgelesen, vorher des längeren ausgeführt, daß seine Sachen den meinigen verwandt wären, etc, und siehe da, was zum Vorschein kam hatte mehr als Verwandschaft mit einem meiner Gedichte "Der Gewitterabend." Nicht nur, daß einzelne Bilder und Redewendungen beinahe wörtlich übernommen wurden (der Staub, der in den Gossen tanzt, Wolken ein Zug von wilden Rossen, Klirrend stößt der Wind in Scheiben, Glitzernd braust mit einemmale, etc. etc.) sind auch die Reime einzelner Strophen und ihre Wertigkeit den meinigen vollkommen gleich, vollkommen gleich meine bildhafte Manier, die in vier Strophenzeilen vier einzelne Bildteile zu einem einzigen Eindruck zusammenschmiedet, mit einem Wort bis ins kleinste Detail ist das Gewand, die heiß errungene Manier meiner Arbeiten nachgebildet worden. Wenn auch diesem "verwandten" Gedicht das lebendige Fieber fehlt, das sich eben gerade diese Form schaffen mußte, und das ganze mir als ein Machwerk ohne Seele erscheint, so kann es mir doch als gänzlich Unbekanntem und Ungehörtem nicht gleichgiltig sein, vielleicht demnächst irgendwo das Zerrbild meines eigenen Antlitzes als Maske vor eines Fremden Gesicht auftauchen zu sehn -! Wahrhaftig mich ekelt der Gedanke, bereits vor Eintritt in diese papierene Welt, von einem Beflissenen journalistisch ausgebeutet zu werden, mich ekelt diese Gosse voll Verlogenheit und Gemeinheit und mir bleibt nichts übrig, als Tür und Haus zu sperren vor allem Nebelgezücht. Im übrigen will ich schweigen.

Alles Gute von Deinem

G. Trakl

has achieved his purposes in Munich! I don't need to emphasize for long that your culinary creations would delight my palate greatly! Just send manna! Wish you and Minna a particularly blessed journey

your completely faithful Georg

14. To Erhard Buschbeck (In Salzburg)

Vienna, second half July 1910
Dear Buschbeck!

You would help me out of an awkward situation if today you could advance me the amount of 30 K, since I do not want to turn to my brother for good reasons. I can, however, only reimburse you this money on the 1st of October. Hopefully you can do without it until then.

You would be doing me a truly great favor.

I must also report to you on an incident that more than embarrassed me.

Yesterday Mr. Ullmann read a poem to me, explained long in advance that its subject would be related to mine, etc., and lo and behold what emerged had more than a kinship with one of my poems "The Thunderstorm Evening." Not only were the individual images and expressions taken almost literally (the dust which dances in the gutters, clouds racing like wild horses, wind banging against the window panes, glittering booms of lightning flashes, etc., etc.) also the rhymes of individual strophes and their significance are completely identical to mine, completely identical to my figurative style, which in four stanzas the four individual picture-parts fuse together into a single impression, in sum, right down to the last detail, the guise, the ardently won style of my work has been reproduced. Even if this "kindred" poem lacks the fever of life, which this form precisely created, it still cannot be a matter of indifference to me as a complete unknown and unheard of person to perhaps see somewhere in the near future the caricature of my own countenance as mask looming before a strange face—! Truthfully the thought disgusts me, to be journalistically exploited by a zealot already before entering this paper world, these gutters of hypocrisy and dirty tricks disgust me and nothing remains than to close door and house against all the fogs of riffraff. Apart from that, I will remain silent.

All the best from your
G. Trakl

In order to guard against any confusion: This letter is intended for you alone! I had to blow off some steam.

Um jedem Irrtum vorzubeugen: Dieser Brief ist allein für Dich bestimmt! Ich mußte mir Luft machen.

p.s. Ich bitte Dich von Herrn Ullmann unter irgend einem Vorwand die Abschriften die er von meinen Gedichten besitzt, zurückzufordern, und in D e i n e Verwahrung zu nehmen.

18. An Friedrich Trakl in Rovereto

Wien, Herbst 1910
Lieber Fritz!
Nach hartnäckig anhaltender Schreib und Redefaulheit, will ich mich doch endlich aufraffen, um Dich vor allem um Entschuldigung zu bitten, daß ich Deinen Brief, der mich so erfreut hat, unentschuldbar lang nicht beantwortet habe; zugleich hoffe ich, von Deinen Angelegenheiten, die mich lebhaft interessieren, bald wieder etliches zu erfahren. Ich hoffe auch, daß es Dir in Deiner Garnison unverändert gut geht, und bin überzeugt, daß Du unter Deinen dortigen Kameraden alle Sympathien für Dich hast. Wie bekommt Dir wohl diese militärische Touristik? Anstrengend wirds schon genug sein - aber ich glaube es verlohnt des Schweißes.
Was mich anbelangt - so sitze ich mein Jahr ab - und finde es bedauerlich, daß bei dieser Angelegenheit mein Popo das einzige ist, was strapaziert wird. Zu Weihnachten komme ich auf Urlaub nach Hause, und erwarte, Dich bestimmt daheim anzutreffen. Mitzi scheint sich in der Schweiz sehr wohl zu befinden, und Gretl, soweit es ihr nur gegeben ist, desgleichen, was sie nicht hindert, mir bisweilen exzentrische Episteln zu schicken.
Von daheim selbst, wie je, keine Nachrichten. Ich habe kürzlich meine Wohnung gewechselt, und hause derzeit in einem Zimmerchen in der Josef Städterstraße, (Nr. 7. III. St. Tür 19) das die Größe eines Klosetts ausmacht. Im geheimen befürchte ich, darin idiotisch zu werden. Aussicht nehme ich auf einen finsteren, kleinen Lichthof - Wenn man zum Fenster hinaussieht, versteinert man vor Trostlosigkeit. Möge sich in dieser beschaulichen Klause dieses Jahr abrollen - und ich wills zufrieden sein, wenn es vorüber ist. Dir aber, lieber Fritz allen Bergsegen und herzlichste Grüße von Deinem Georg

Falls Du mir schreiben magst, vergiß nicht zu erwähnen wann Du zu Weihnachten Urlaub bekommst. Also auf Wiedersehn!

VIII. Josefstädterstraße N°. 7. in. St. Tür 19.

p.s. I beg you to reclaim under any pretext the transcripts of my poems from Mr. Ullmann which he possesses and to place them in y o u r safekeeping.

18. To Friedrich Trakl in Rovereto

Vienna, Autumn 1910
Dear Fritz!

After persistent laziness in writing and talking, I finally want to pull myself together to first of all ask you for your forgiveness that I have not answered your letter which delighted me so much for an inexcusably long time; at the same time, I hope to hear again soon about your affairs, which interest me very much. I also hope that you are still doing well in your garrison, and I am convinced that you have all the sympathies among your comrades there. How do you like this military tourism? It will be exhausting enough - but I think it will be worth the sweat.

As for me, I am serving out my year and regret that, in this matter, the only thing that's strained is my backside. I will be on leave for Christmas and expect to find you at home without a doubt.

Mitzi seems to be enjoying herself in Switzerland, and Gretl, to the extent she can, too, although that doesn't stop her from sending me eccentric letters from time to time.

No news from home itself, as usual. I recently changed my apartment and currently reside in a tiny room on Josef Städterstraße (No. 7, III. St. Door 19), which is the size of a closet. In secret, I fear going insane in it. The view is of a dark, small courtyard - when you look out the window, you turn to stone from desolation.

May this year roll by in this contemplative cell, and I will be content when it's over. But to you, dear Fritz, all the blessings of the mountains and warmest greetings from your Georg

If you decide to write to me, don't forget to mention when you'll be on leave for Christmas. So, until we meet again!

VIII. Josefstädterstraße No. 7, 3rd floor, Door 19.

29. An Erhard Buschbeck In Wein

Innsbruck, vor dem 21. IV. 1912
Ich hätte mir nie gedacht daß ich diese für sich schon schwere Zeit in der brutalsten
und gemeinsten Stadt würde verleben müssen, die auf dieser beladenen u. verfluch-
ten Welt existiert. Und wenn ich dazudenke, daß mich ein fremder Wille vielleicht
ein Jahrzent hier leiden lassen wird, kann ich in einen Tränenkrampf trostlosester
Hoffnungslosigkeit verfallen.
Wozu die Plage. Ich werde endlich doch immer ein armer Kaspar Hauser bleiben.
Laß mir bald ein paar Zeilen von Dir zukommen
Dein G. T.
Apotheke d. Garnisonsspitals Nr 10

35. An Erhard Buschbeck In Wein

Innsbruck, Ende Oktober / Anfang November 1912
Lieber Freund!
Vielen Dank für die Übersendung der Bilder. Die Gedichte kann ich Dir leider
nicht per Urlaub schicken, da ich sehr viel Arbeit zu erledigen habe, Du wirst sie
nächster Woche per Post erhalten.
Daß es Winter und kalt wird, spüre ich an der abendlichen Weinheizung. Vorge-
stern habe ich 10 (sage! Zehn) Viertel Roten getrunken. Um vier Uhr morgens
habe ich auf meinem Balkon ein Mond und Frostbad genommen und am Morgen
endlich ein herrliches Gedicht geschrieben, das vor Kälte schebbert.
In Wien aber "strahlt" die Sonne am "heiteren" Himmel und die "weiche Melan-
cholie" des Wienerwaldes ist auch nicht "ohne". Beim Heurigen freut sich das
"goldene" Herz und wenn dort die "schmachtenden Weisen" erklingen, so denke
o Mensch daran, daß es bei den "wackeren Älplern" schneit und grimmig kalt ist.
O! wie weh ist die Welt, wie wahnig das Weh, wie weltlich der Wahn. Mit Zähne-
klappern und dampfenden Grüßen
Dein G.

50. An Erhard Buschbeck In Salzburg

Innsbruck, 4. I. 1913
Lieber, lieber Freund!
Ich bin wie ein Toter an Hall vorbeigefahren, an einer schwarzen Stadt, die durch
mich durchgestürzt ist, wie ein Inferno durch einen Verfluchten.
Ich geh in Mühlau durch lauter schöne Sonne und bin noch sehr taumelnd Das
Veronal hat mir einigen Schlaf vergönnt unter der Franziska Kokoschkas.

29. To Erhard Buschbeck in Vienna

Innsbruck, before April 21, 1912

I never thought that I would have to endure this already difficult period in the most brutal and meanest city that exists on this burdened and cursed world. And when I consider that a foreign will may force me to suffer here for perhaps a decade, I can fall into a tearful fit of the most hopeless despair.

What's the point of this torment? I will, in the end, always remain a poor Kaspar Hauser.

Please send me a few lines soon.

Yours, G. T.

Pharmacy of the Garrison Hospital No. 10

35. To Erhard Buschbeck in Vienna

Innsbruck, end of October / beginning of November 1912
Dear friend!

Thank you very much for sending the pictures. Unfortunately, I can't send you the poems right now because I have a lot of work to do. You will receive them by mail next week.

I can feel that winter is approaching and it's getting cold from the evening wine heating. The day before yesterday, I drank 10 (yes, ten!) quarters of red wine. At four in the morning, I took a moon and frost bath on my balcony, and finally, in the morning, I wrote a magnificent poem that shivers with cold.

In Vienna, however, the sun "shines" in the "cheerful" sky, and the "soft melancholy" of the Vienna Woods is not "absent" either. At the wine tavern, the "golden" heart rejoices, and when the "yearning tunes" play there, remember, O human, that it's snowing and bitterly cold among the "brave Alpine people." Oh! How painful the world is, how delusional the pain, how worldly the delusion. With chattering teeth and steaming greetings

Your G.

50. To Erhard Buschbeck in Salzburg

Innsbruck, January 4, 1913
Dear, dear friend!

I passed Hall like a dead man, a black city that rushed through me as if it were an inferno through a cursed soul.

Here in Mühlau, I walk in the midst of beautiful sunshine, still feeling quite dizzy. Veronal has granted me some sleep, under the care of Franziska Kokoschka.

Ich will so lange es geht weilen. Schicke mir bitte meine Reisetasche, da ich notwendig Wäsche benötige.

Schreibe mir, Lieber, ob meine Mutter sehr viel Kummer durch mich hat.

Mit vielen, vielen Grüßen

Dein Georg

meine Adresse: Innsbruck-Mühlau 102

53. An Erhard Buschbeck (In Wein)

Innsbruck, zweite Hälfte Januar 1913

Lieber Freund!

Vielen Dank für die Übersendung von Ullmanns Kritik, die mich außerordentlich gefreut hat und für die ich Dich bitte, Ullmann meinen herzlichsten Dank zu übermitteln.

Mit mir steht es noch immer nicht am besten, obwohl ich es hier so gut habe, wie nirgends. Vielleicht wäre es doch besser gewesen, es in Wien zu einer Krisis kommen zu lassen.

Ich lasse Schwab recht sehr bitten, sich im Allgemeinen Krankenhaus über die dortigen Apothekerverhältnisse zu erkundigen, ob ich Aussicht hätte dort unterzukommen, wie und an wen das bezügliche Gesuch abgefaßt werden müßte, welcher Art auch die Dienstesverhältnisse sind und dergleichen.

Vielleicht könntest Du mir dann so bald als möglich darüber etwas mitteilen.

Einen Abzug des Helian werde ich Dir in den nächsten Tagen schicken. Er ist mir das teuerste und schmerzlichste, was ich je geschrieben.

Mit vielen, herzlichsten Grüßen

Dein G.

61. An Erhard Buschbeck (In Wein)

Salzburg, zweite Hälfte März 1913

Lieber Freund!

Zu beiliegenden Gedichten die Bitte: Statt "Heiterer Frühling" "Im Dorf" zu wählen. Die drei Gedichte: 1 "An die Schwester"', 2 "Nähe d. Todes" und 3 "Amen" unter dem Titel "Rosenkranz-(lieder)" zusammenzuschließen.

Wenn Du einige Minuten Zeit findest, schreibe mir, bitte, ob die Vorlesung definitiv am 2. April stattfindet. Ich werde zwar kaum nach Wien kommen können, da ich von den 30 K, die ich für den Apothekendienst erhalten habe 5 K für Dringliches verausgabt habe, und für denselben Zweck in Bälde nocheinmal denselben Betrag verausgaben werde.

Mit den schönsten Grüßen

I intend to stay here as long as possible. Please send me my travel bag, as I urgently need some clean clothes.

Write me, my dear friend, whether my mother is very distressed because of me. With many, many regards

Your Georg

My address: Innsbruck-Mühlau 102

53. To Erhard Buschbeck (in Vienna)

Innsbruck, Second Half of January 1913

Dear friend!

Thank you very much for sending Ullmann's critique, which delighted me immensely. Please convey my warmest thanks to Ullmann.

Things are still not going well for me, although I have it as good here as anywhere else. Perhaps it would have been better to let it come to a crisis in Vienna.

I kindly ask Schwab to inquire at the General Hospital about the pharmacy conditions there, whether there is a chance for me to get in, how to draft the relevant application, what the employment terms are, and so on.

Perhaps you could inform me about this as soon as possible.

I will send you a copy of "Helian" in the next few days. It is the dearest and most painful thing I have ever written.

With many, warmest regards

Your G.

61. To Erhard Buschbeck (in Vienna)

Salzburg, Second Half of March 1913

Dear friend!

With the enclosed poems, I have a request: Instead of "Cheerful Spring," please choose "In the Village." The three poems: 1 "To the Sister," 2 "Nearness of Death," and 3 "Amen" should be combined under the title "Rosary Songs."

If you find a few minutes, please write to me if the reading is definitively scheduled for April 2nd. I will hardly be able to come to Vienna, as I have already spent 5 K out of the 30 K I received for the pharmacy service on urgent matters, and I will soon spend the same amount again for the same purpose.

With the warmest regards

Your G.

Dein G.

66. An Erhard Buschbeck In Wein

Innsbruck, 2. IV. 1913
Lieber Freund!
Ich bitte Dich dringend mir noch 50 K zu leihen. Ich wollte Herrn von Ficker darum angehen. Es fällt mir aber wahrhaftig zu schwer. Ich wäre Dir überaus dankbar, wenn Du mir diesen Betrag in den nächsten Tagen nach Innsbruck schicken würdest. Ich glaube bestimmt, bis zum Sommer und Eintritt einigermaßen geordneter Verhältnisse Dir dieses Geld zurückerstatten zu können. Herr von F. sagte mir heute, daß er Dir in Angelegenheit meiner Gedichte geschrieben. Ich glaube, es ist das Beste, wenn das Buch im Brennerverlag erscheint.
In den heutigen Innsbr. Zeitungen las ich von dem pöbelhaften Skandal während des Schönberg Konzerts. Welch eine trostlose Schmach für einen Künstler, den die Gemeinheit des Gesindels nicht abhält, noch vor das Werk seiner Schüler zu treten. In längstens 10 Tagen bin ich wieder in Salzburg. Bis dahin wirst wohl auch Du dort eintreffen. Indes ich Dich nochmals bitte, mich nicht in Stich zu lassen verbleibe ich mit den herzlichsten Grüßen
Dein Georg T.

77. An den Kurt Wolff Verlag (in Leipzig)

Salzburg, etwa 8. V. 1913
Sehr geehrter Herr!
Den gegengezeichneten Vertrag habe ich gestern erhalten. Wollen Sie, bitte, das Gedicht "Drei Blicke in einen Opal" an seiner ursprünglichen Stelle eingereiht belassen; dagegen "An den Knaben Elis" nach "In einem verlassenen Zimmer" einreihen.
Beiliegend übersende ich Ihnen einen Aufsatz, den Dr. Borromaeus Heinrich über mich geschrieben. Vielleicht kann er für das Buch von Wert sein. Dr. Heinrich schrieb mir, daß er in der Frankfurter Zeitung nach dem Erscheinen der Gedichte einen neuen, ausführlichen Aufsatz folgen lassen wird.
Nehmen Sie, sehr geehrter Herr, die Ausdrücke vorzüglichster Hochachtung entgegen
Ihres ergebenen Georg Trakl

p. s. Ich hoffe, daß Sie die Subskriptionsbögen bereits erhalten haben, da ich sie vor einer Woche für Ihren Verlag reklamiert habe.

66. To Erhard Buschbeck in Vienna

Innsbruck, April 2, 1913
Dear friend,

I urgently request you to lend me another 50 K. I intended to approach Mr. von Ficker about it, but it truly weighs heavily on me. I would be extremely grateful if you could send me this amount to Innsbruck in the next few days. I firmly believe that I will be able to repay you this money by summer, once some semblance of order is restored.

Mr. von F. told me today that he wrote to you regarding my poems. I think it's best if the book is published by the Brenner Publishing House.

In today's Innsbruck newspapers, I read about the scandalous incident during the Schönberg concert. What a dismal disgrace for an artist, whom the meanness of the mob doesn't deter from presenting the work of his students.

I will be back in Salzburg in no more than 10 days. By then, you will probably have arrived there as well. While I ask you once again not to abandon me, I remain with the warmest regards
Your Georg T.

77. To the Kurt Wolff Publishing House (in Leipzig)

Salzburg, around May 8, 1913
Dear Sir,

I received the countersigned contract yesterday. Would you please leave the poem "Three Gazes into an Opal" in its original position, but include "To the Boy Ellis" after "In a Deserted Room."

Enclosed, I am sending you an essay that Dr. Borromaeus Heinrich has written about me. Perhaps it may be of value for the book. Dr. Heinrich wrote to me that he will follow up with a new and comprehensive essay in the Frankfurter Newspaper after the publication of the poems.

Please accept, dear Sir, the expressions of my utmost respect.
Yours faithfully Georg Trakl

p.s. I hope you have already received the subscription forms, as I requested them for your publishing house a week ago.

85. An Ludwig von Ficker (In Innsbruck)

Lieber Herr von Ficker!

Besten Dank für Ihr Telegramm. Herrn Loos habe ich leider nicht am Bahnhof angetroffen; ich erwartete, ihn in dem Zug um 1h 40 zu treffen, der als einziger einen Speisewagen bis Salzburg führt. Leider war meine Annahme irrig und ich habe es sehr bedauert, Herrn Loos nicht gesprochen zu haben.

Hier ist ein Tag trüber und kälter als der andere und es regnet ununterbrochen. Bisweilen fällt dann ein Strahl der letzten sonnigen Innsbrucker Tage in diese Düsterniß und erfüllt mich mit tiefster Dankbarkeit für Sie und all' die edlen Menschen, deren Güte ich in Wahrheit so gar nicht verdiene. Zu wenig Liebe, zu wenig Gerechtigkeit und Erbarmen, und immer zu wenig Liebe; allzuviel Härte, Hochmut und allerlei Verbrechertum - das bin ich. Ich bin gewiß, daß ich das Böse nur aus Schwäche und Feigheit unterlasse und damit meine Bosheit noch schände. Ich sehne den Tag herbei, an dem die Seele in diesem unseeligen von Schwermut verpesteten Körper nicht mehr wird wohnen wollen und können, an dem sie diese Spottgestalt aus Kot und Fäulnis verlassen wird, die ein nur allzugetreues Spiegelbild eines gottlosen, verfluchten Jahrhunderts ist.

Gott, nur einen kleinen Funken reiner Freude - und man wäre gerettet; Liebe - und man wäre erlöst.

Lassen Sie mich verbleiben

Ihr dankbar ergebener Georg T.

100. An Ludwig von Ficker (In Innsbruck)

Wien, II. XI. 1913

Lieber Herr Ficker!

Ich bin seit einer Woche in Wien. Meine Angelegenheiten sind ganz ungeklärt. Ich habe jetzt 2 Tage und 2 Nächte geschlafen und habe heute noch eine recht arge Veronalvergiftung. In meiner Wirrnis und all' der Verzweiflung der letzten Zeit weiß ich nun gar nicht mehr, wie ich noch leben soll. Ich habe hier wohl hilfsbereite Menschen getroffen; aber mir will es erscheinen, jene können mir nicht helfen und es wird alles im Dunklen enden.

Wollen Sie, lieber Freund, im Kaspar Hauser Lied folgende Änderung machen

1. Zeile: Er liebte die Sonne, die purpurn den Hügel hinabging

2. Strophe. 1. Zeile statt "ernsthaft" "wahrhaft"

Letzte Zeile: Silbern sank des Ungeborenen Haupt hin.

p. s Bitte verständigen Sie mich, ob Sie die Korrekturen angebracht haben. Kraus läßt vielmals grüßen, ebenso Loos. Handkuß an Ihre liebe Frau.

85. To Ludwig von Ficker (In Innsbruck)

Dear Mr. von Ficker!

Many thanks for your telegram. Unfortunately I did not run across Mr. Loos in the railway station; I expected to meet him around 1:40 in the train, which is the only one that pulls a dining car to Salzburg. I'm afraid my assumption was wrong and I have very much regretted not having spoken to Mr. Loos.

Here each day is murkier and colder than the next and it rains continuously. Then sometimes a ray of the last sunny Innsbruck days falls into this somberness and fulfills me with the deepest gratitude for you and all noble people whose goodness in truth I did not earn at all. Too little love, too little justice and compassion, and always too little love; too much callousness, arrogance and all kinds of criminality— that is me. I am certain that I omit the evil only out of weakness and cowardice and for this reason my wickedness still disgraces. At this juncture, I long for the day on which the soul will no longer want and be able to dwell in this contaminated body, ill-fated with melancholy, on which it will forsake this mocking shape made of excrement and rot, which is merely an all too faithful mirror-image of this godless, cursed century.

God, only a small spark of pure joy—and one would be saved; Love—and one would be redeemed.
I remain
Your thankfully devoted Georg T.

100. To Ludwig von Ficker (In Innsbruck)

Vienna, November 2, 1913
Dear Mr. Ficker!

I've been here in Vienna for a week. My affairs are completely unsettled. I have slept now for 2 days and 2 nights and today still have a quite bad case of veronal poisoning. In my confusion and all the despair of recent times, I don't know anymore how I am still alive. I have doubtlessly met helpful people here; but it seems to me that they cannot help and everything will end in darkness. Will you, dear friend, make the following changes in Kaspar Hauser Song:
1st line "He loved the sun which descended crimson behind the hill;"
2nd strophe, line 1, instead of "wholehearted" "truthful;"
last line: "Silver the head of the unborn sank down"

p. s. Please notify me whether you made the corrections. Kraus sends his regards, also Loos. Kiss the hand of your dear wife.

102a. An Rudolf von Ficker In Wien

Wien, 12. XI. 1913
Lieber Herr Ficker!
Ich bitte Sie dringlich mir 40 K zu leihen, da ich mich augenblicklich hier in einer sehr armseligen Lage befinde. Ich bin seit einer Woche in Wien um meine Angelegenheiten endgültig zu ordnen. Ich weiß nicht, ob es mir gelingen wird, aber ich will jedenfalls alles versuchen. Deshalb möchte ich nicht früher Wien verlassen, als bis alle diese Dinge klargestellt sind. Ich wäre sehr erfreut, Sie morgen, Donnerstag, um 2 Uhr nachmittags im Kaffee "Museum" treffen zu können. Falls es Ihnen unmöglich sein wird zu kommen, bitte ich Sie mir einige Zeilen zu schreiben.
Ihr ergebener Georg Trakl
VII. Stiftgasse 27, Tür 25

103. An Ludwig von Ficker In Innsbruck

Wien, 17. XI. 1913
Lieber Herr von Ficker!
Vielen Dank für Ihre Einladung zu einer Vorlesung in Innsbruck. Ich kann sie bestimmt annehmen, da ich ebenso bestimmt nicht in Wien, dieser Dreckstadt bleibe. Ich kehre vorbehaltlos wieder zum Militär zurück, d. h. wenn man mich noch nimmt.
Hoffentlich konnten Sie die Widmung noch anbringen. Ich hatte Loos bereits eine Abschrift gegeben, die diese Widmung trug und Loos hat sie bei vielen herumgezeigt. Deshalb wäre es mir peinlich, wenn das Gedicht ohne Widm. erschiene, besonders als Loos mich darum bat.
Mit den herzlichsten Grüßen
Ihr sehr ergebener G. T.

104. An Ludwig von Ficker (In Innsbruck)

Wien, (19.) XI. 1913
Lieber Herr Ficker
Ich bin mit der Zusammenstellung der vorzulesenden Gedichte sehr einverstanden; ich finde sie ausgezeichnet. Vielleicht könnte man noch die "Elis" gedichte einfügen.

102a. To Rudolf von Ficker in Vienna

Vienna, November 12, 1913
Dear Mr. Ficker,
I urgently request a loan of 40 K from you, as I am currently in a very dire situation here. I have been in Vienna for a week to finally settle my affairs. I'm not sure if I will succeed, but I will certainly try my best. Therefore, I don't want to leave Vienna until all these matters are resolved. I would be very pleased to meet you tomorrow, Thursday, at 2 o'clock in the afternoon at the "Museum" café. If it is impossible for you to come, please write me a few lines.
Your faithful Georg Trakl
VII. Stiftgasse 27, Door 25

103. To Ludwig von Ficker in Innsbruck

Vienna, November 17, 1913
Dear Mr. von Ficker,
Thank you very much for your invitation to give a reading in Innsbruck. I can definitely accept it since I am equally determined not to stay in Vienna, this wretched city. I am returning to the military without reservation, that is if they will still take me.
Hopefully, you were able to include the dedication. I had already given Loos a copy that had this dedication, and Loos had shown it to many people. Therefore, it would be embarrassing for me if the poem were published without the dedication, especially since Loos asked me for it.
With the warmest regards
Your very devoted G. T.

104. To Ludwig von Ficker (In Innsbruck)

Vienna, November 19, 1913
Dear Mr. Ficker,
I am very much in agreement with the selection of poems for the reading; I find them excellent. Perhaps the "Elis" poems could be included as well.
I will be coming to Innsbruck on Saturday or Sunday to initiate my activation

Ich komme Samstag oder Sonntag nach Innsbruck um von dort meine Aktivierung beim Milit in die Wege zu leiten und bitte Sie, mich 2 oder 3 Wochen bei sich zu behalten.

Die Aufsätze von Loos werde ich Ihnen mitbringen. Heute Abend ist Kraus Vorlesung und an der Universität wird ebenfalls heute eine Schauspielerin eine Auswahl meiner Gedichte lesen. Ich selber gehe in Kraus' Vorlesung.

Wollen Sie Ihrer Frau die respektvollsten Grüße sagen. Dr. Heinrichs Karte hat mich sehr überrascht. Ich finde seinen Entschluß sehr respektabel.

Mit den herzlichsten Grüßen

Ihr sehr ergebener Georg Trakl

106. An Ludwig von Ficker (In Innsbruck)

Wien, Ende (?) November 1913

Lieber Herr von Ficker!

Vielen Dank für Ihr Telegramm. Kraus läßt vielmals grüßen. Dr. Heinrich ist hier wieder ernstlich erkrankt und es haben sich sonst in den letzten Tagen für mich so furchtbare Dinge ereignet, daß ich deren Schatten mein Lebtag nicht mehr loswerden kann. Ja, verehrter Freund, mein Leben ist in wenigen Tagen unsäglich zerbrochen worden und es bleibt nur mehr ein sprachloser Schmerz, dem selbst die Bitternis versagt ist.

Wollen Sie bitte, um von meinen nächsten Angelegenheiten zu sprechen, die Güte und Liebe mir erweisen, an Hauptmann Robert Michel zu schreiben (vielleicht ist es wichtig, daß es gleich geschieht) und in meinem Namen um seine freundliche Fürsprache im Kriegsministerium bitten.

Vielleicht schreiben Sie mir zwei Worte; ich weiß nicht mehr ein und aus. Es [ist] ein so namenloses Unglück, wenn einem die Welt entzweibricht. O mein Gott, welch ein Gericht ist über mich hereingebrochen. Sagen Sie mir, daß ich die Kraft haben muß noch zu leben und das Wahre zu tun. Sagen Sie mir, daß ich nicht irre bin. Es ist steinernes Dunkel hereingebrochen. O mein Freund, wie klein und unglücklich bin ich geworden.

Es umarmt Sie innig

Ihr Georg Trakl

110. An Karl Borromaeus Heinrich (In Paris?)

Innsbruck, Anfang (?) Januar 1914

Lieber Freund Borromaeus!

Schönen Dank für Ihre Karte. Gott gebe Ihnen Freude und Gesundheit wieder und segne Ihre Arbeit. O, wie hat es mich gefreut, von Ihnen zu hören, daß Sie ein

with the military from there, and I kindly request to stay with you for 2 or 3 weeks.

I will bring Loos's essays with me. Kraus's lecture is this evening, and at the university an actress will also be reading a selection of my poems tonight. I will attend Kraus's lecture myself.

Please convey my respectful greetings to your wife. Dr. Heinrich's postcard surprised me greatly. I find his decision very commendable.
With the warmest regards
Your very devoted Georg Trakl

106. To Ludwig von Ficker (In Innsbruck)

Vienna, at the end (?) of November, 1913
Dear Mr. von Ficker!

Many thanks for your telegram. Kraus says to send his regards. Dr. Heinrich has seriously fallen ill here again and besides so many dreadful things have happened to me during recent days that I can no longer rid their shadow from my life. Yes, dear friend, my life has become unspeakably broken in a few days and there remains only more of a speechless pain that the bitterness has failed me.

You who bestow goodness and love on me, would you please, in order to see about my next affairs, write to Captain Robert Michael (it is probably vital that it happen immediately) and ask in my name about his friendly intercession in the War Ministry.

Perhaps you could write a couple of words to me; I do not know in from out anymore. It [will be] such a nameless misfortune if the world breaks in two. O my God, what a judgment has befallen me. Tell me that I still have the power to live and to do what's real. Tell me I am not crazy. Stony darkness has befallen me. O my friend, how small and miserable I have become.
I embrace you tenderly
Your Georg Trakl

110. To To Karl Borromaeus Heinrich (in Paris?)

Innsbruck, early (?) January 1914
Dear friend Borromaeus,

Many thanks for your postcard. May God grant you joy and good health and bless your work. Oh, how delighted I was to hear from you that you are planning

neues Werk planen. Ich bin so gewiß, daß es vortrefflich, vielleicht das Beste sein wird. Wie könnte es auch anders sein.

Mir geht es nicht am besten. Zwischen Trübsinn und Trunkenheit verloren, fehlt mir Kraft und Lust eine Lage zu verändern, die sich täglich unheilvoller gestaltet, bleibt nur mehr der Wunsch, ein Gewitter möchte hereinbrechen und mich reinigen oder zerstören. O Gott, durch welche Schuld und Finsterniß müssen wir doch gehn. Möchten wir am Ende nicht unterliegen.

Es umarmt Sie innigst

Ihr G. T.

112. An Karl Borromaeus Heinrich (In Innsbruck)

Berlin, Wilmersdorf, 19. 3. 14

Lieber Freund!

Meine Schwester hat vor wenigen Tagen eine Fehlgeburt gehabt, die mit außerordentlich vehementen Blutungen verbunden war. Ihr Zustand ist ein so besorgniserregender, um so mehr, als sie seit fünf Tagen keine Nahrung zu sich genommen hat, daß vorläufig nicht daran zu denken ist, daß sie nach Innsbruck kommt.

Ich gedenke noch bis Montag oder Dienstag hier zu bleiben und hoffe bestimmt, Dich in Innsbruck noch wiederzusehen.

Teile mir, bitte, mit, ob Herr von Ficker sich in meiner Militär-Angelegenheit erkundigt hat und ob von K. Wolff Nachricht eingelangt ist.

Die respektvollsten Grüße an Deine Frau und alles Gute für Peter. Hoffentlich geht es ihm schon wieder gut. Grüße Ficker herzlichst von mir und sei umarmt von Deinem

G. T.

113. An Ludwig von Ficker (In Innsbruck)

Berlin-Wilmersdorf, 21. III. 1914

Lieber Herr von Ficker!

Meine arme Schwester ist noch immer sehr leidend. Ihr Leben ist von einer so herzzerreißenden Traurigkeit und zugleich braven Tapferkeit, daß ich mir bisweilen sehr gering davor erscheine; und sie verdiente es wohl tausendmal mehr als ich, im Kreise guter und edler Menschen zu leben, wie es mir in solch übergroßem Maß in schwerer Zeit vergönnt war.

Ich gedenke wohl noch etliche Tage in Berlin zu bleiben, denn meine Schwester ist den ganzen Tag allein und meine Gegenwart für sie doch von einigem Nutzen.

Für die Übersendung des Geldes danke ich Ihnen recht von Herzen. Wollen Sie bitte Ihrer Frau die respektvollsten Grüße übermitteln, ebenso alles Gute Ihren

a new work. I am so certain that it will be excellent, perhaps the best. How could it be otherwise?   I am not in the best of spirits. Lost between melancholy and drunkenness, I lack the strength and desire to change a situation that becomes more ominous with each passing day. All that remains is the wish that a storm might break out and cleanse or destroy me. Oh God, through what guilt and darkness must we go? May we not ultimately succumb.

I embrace you most sincerely

Your G. T.

112. To To Karl Borromaeus Heinrich (in Innsbruck)

Berlin, Wilmersdorf, March 19, 1914

Dear friend,

My sister had a miscarriage a few days ago, accompanied by extraordinarily severe bleeding. Her condition is very concerning, especially since she hasn't eaten anything for five days, so it's not currently possible for her to come to Innsbruck.

I plan to stay here until Monday or Tuesday and hope to see you again in Innsbruck. Please inform me if Mr. von Ficker has inquired about my military matter and if there is any news from K. Wolff.

Give my warmest regards to your wife and all the best to Peter. Hopefully, he's feeling better already. Please send my heartfelt greetings to Ficker, and receive an embrace from your

G. T.

113. To Ludwig von Ficker (In Innsbruck)

Berlin-Wilmersdorf, March 21, 1914

Dear Mr. von Ficker!

My poor sister is still very ill. Her life is one of heart-rending sadness and at the same time brave fortitude, so that sometimes I appear very small before it; and she's probably earned it a thousand times more than I, to live in the circles of good and noble humans, as was granted to me in such large measure in difficult times.

I intend to perhaps still remain several days longer in Berlin because my sister is alone the entire day and my presence is nevertheless of some use to her.

I sincerely thank you for the transmittal of money. Please convey to your wife my most respectful regards, and likewise to your children, and to you my expression of devotion and gratitude

Kindern und nehmen Sie die Ausdrücke der Ergebenheit und Dankbarkeit entgegen

gen

Ihres G. T.

Viele Grüße an Dr. Heinrich und seine Frau

115. An den Kurt Wolff Verlag (In Leipzig)

Innsbruck, 10. IV. 1914

Sehr geehrter Herr Wolff!

Besten Dank für Ihre freundliche Verständigung! Als Vertragsbasis würde ich eine einmalige Honorierung einer prozentualen Beteiligung am Erträgnis des Buches vorziehen, da ich gegenwärtig ohne Stellung und ohne eigene Mittel bin, was ich Sie bei Bemessung des Honorars gütigst zu berücksichtigen bitte. Ich erwarte also Ihren diesbezüglichen Vorschlag, den ich möglichst bald erbitte, und bemerke noch, daß der Herausgeber des "Brenner" auch diesmal gerne bereit ist, den Absatz des Buches durch Beilage von Subskriptionskarten im "Brenner" im vorhinein fördern zu helfen. Auch hoffe ich, daß Sie gesonnen sind, meinen neuen Gedichtband als selbständige Publikation (nicht im Rahmen einer numerierten Bücher-Serie) erscheinen zu lassen; in dieser und in Erwartung Ihres sonstigen, recht baldigen Bescheids begrüßt Sie für heute in hochachtungsvoller Ergebenheit

Ihr Georg Trakl

117. An den Kurt Wolff Verlag (In Leipzig)

Innsbruck, Mitte Mai 1914

Sehr geehrter Herr!

Beiliegend retourniere ich Ihnen den unterschriebenen Vertrag. Sie hatten die Freundlichkeit mir einige Druckproben zur Auswahl zu schicken; nach deren Einsicht erscheint es mir besser, eine Antiqua Type zu wählen, die ein ruhiges und wie ich glaube dem Wesen der Gedichte angemessenes Schriftbild gibt. Ich schicke Ihnen als Probe einen Teil der Korrekturbögen von Alb. Ehrensteins Gedichten ein. Vielleicht wäre der nächst kleinere Schriftgrad entsprechend. Wollen Sie, bitte, dieses selbst entscheiden und die Güte haben, mir Bescheid zu geben.

Genehmigen Sie, sehr geehrter Herr, die Ausdrücke vorzüglichster Hochachtung

Ihres sehr ergebenen Georg Trakl

Your G. T.
Give my regards to Dr. Heinrich and his wife

115. To the Kurt Wolff Publishing House (in Leipzig)

Innsbruck, April 10, 1914
Dear Mr. Wolff!

Thank you very much for your kind communication. As a basis for the contract, I would prefer a one-time fee to a percentage share in the proceeds of the book, since I am currently without a position and without my own means, which I would kindly ask you to take into account when assessing the fee. I therefore await your proposal in this regard, which I would like to receive as soon as possible, and I would like to add that the publisher of the "Brenner" is also willing to help promote the sale of the book in advance by enclosing subscription cards in the "Brenner." I also hope that you will be willing to publish my new book of poems as an independent publication (not as part of a numbered series of books); in this respect, and in anticipation of your other, very early decision, I greet you today with great respect

Your Georg Trakl

117. To the Kurt Wolff Publishing House (in Leipzig)

Innsbruck, mid-May 1914
Dear Sir!

Enclosed I am returning the signed contract to you. You had the kindness to send me some print samples to choose from; after looking at them, it seems better to me to choose an antiqua typeface, which provides a calm and, as I believe, appropriate typeface to the essence of the poems. I am sending you as a sample a part of the proof sheets of Alb. Ehrenstein's poems.

Perhaps the next smaller type size would be appropriate. Will you, please, decide this yourself and have the goodness to let me know.

Please accept, dear sir, the expressions of the highest esteem

Your very devoted Georg Trakl

118. An Maria Geipel in Salzburg

Innsbruck, 26. V. 1914
Liebe Mitzi!
Bitte teile mir mit, ob Gretl nach Salzburg kommen wird, oder bereits dort ein-
getroffen ist; und wie lange sie bleiben kann. Herr v. Ficker würde sie herzlich
gerne bei sich aufnehmen. Leider ist seine Frau sehr ernstlich erkrankt und muß
vielleicht noch 4 Wochen das Bett hüten. Unter diesen Umständen ist es natürlich
sehr schwer, Gretl nach Innsbruck zu bringen.
Ich selber bin auf die Hohenburg übersiedelt.
Gretl, bitte ich Dich, die schönsten Grüße zu sagen.
Ich werde vielleicht schon demnächst wieder nach Salzburg kommen.
Mit den herzlichsten Grüßen
Dein Georg
p. Adr: Rud. v. Ficker. Igls bei Innsbruck Hohenburg

122. An den Kurt Wolff Verlag in Leipzig

Innsbruck, Mitte Juli 1914
Sehr geehrter Herr!
Bei der Durchsicht des erhaltenen Bürsten Abzugs habe ich bemerkt, daß auf Seite
12, vorletzte Zeile, der Setzer eine willkürliche Umänderung des von mir korrigier-
ten 1. u. 2 Bürstenabzuges vorgenommen hat. Die Stelle lautete daselbst:
"Die Glocke lang im Abendnovember"
Diese Ausdrucksweise schien vermutlich dem Setzer nicht verständlich und er
machte aus dem "lang" ein "klang" Wollen Sie, bitte, die Güte haben, zu veranlas-
sen, daß die betreffende Stelle nach dem von mir korrigierten Abzug wiederherge-
stellt werde. In vorzüglichster Hochachtung
Ihr sehr ergebener Georg Trakl
p. s. Auf Seite 4, Zeile 5 muß es richtig heißen: "des Frühlingnachmittags" statt
"Frühlings-Nachmittags"
Seite 19 entfallen die Verbindungsstriche im Titel d. Gedichts.

127. An Ludwig Von Ficker In Innsbruck

etwa Anfang September 1914
Verehrter Freund!
Heute geht es nach Galizien. In unsrer ursprünglichen Bestimmungsstation hatten
wir kaum 1 Stunde Aufenthalt. Die Fahrt war außerordentlich schön. Wir werden
wahrscheinlich noch drei Tage auf der Bahn verbringen müssen. Recht herzliche

118. To Maria Geipel in Salzburg

Innsbruck, May 26, 1914
Dear Mitzi!

Please let me know whether Gretl will be coming to Salzburg or has already arrived there; and how long she can stay. Mr. v. Ficker would be very happy to take her in. Unfortunately, his wife is very seriously ill and may have to stay in bed for another 4 weeks. Under these circumstances it is of course very difficult to bring Gretl to Innsbruck.

I myself have moved to the Hohenburg.

Gretl, please convey to her my warmest regards.

Perhaps I will come to Salzburg again soon.

With the warmest greetings

your Georg

Postal address: Rudolf von Ficker. Igls near Innsbruck Hohenburg

122. To the Kurt Wolff Publishing House (in Leipzig)

Innsbruck, mid-July 1914
Dear Sir!

While reviewing the received proof copy, I noticed that on page 12, the penultimate line, the typesetter made an arbitrary change to the first and second proof copies that I had corrected. The passage there originally read:

"The bell long in the November evening"

Apparently, this expression didn't seem clear to the typesetter, and he changed "long" to "rang."

Could you, please, have the goodness to arrange that the passage in question be restored according to the proof I have corrected. With the highest esteem

Your very devoted Georg Trakl

p. s. On page 4, line 5, it should correctly read: "of the spring afternoon" instead of "spring afternoon."

On page 19, the hyphen in the title of the poem should be omitted.

127. To Ludwig von Ficker in Innsbruck

Around early September 1914
Respected friend,

Today, we are heading to Galicia. We had barely an hour stopover at our original destination. The journey has been exceptionally beautiful. We will probably have to spend another three days on the train. Warm regards from your devoted

Grüße von Ihrem ergebenen
Georg Trakl

129. An Ludwig Von Ficker (In Innsbruck)

Limanowa (?), Anfang Oktober 1914
Verehrter Freund!
Wir haben vier Wochen angestrengtester Märsche durch ganz Galizien hinter uns.
Seit zwei Tagen rasten wir in einer kleinen Stadt Westgaliziens inmitten eines sanften und heiteren Hügellandes und lassen es uns nach all' den großen Ereignissen der jüngsten Zeit in Frieden wohl sein. Morgen oder übermorgen marschieren wir weiter. Es scheint sich eine neue große Schlacht vorzubereiten. Wolle der Himmel uns diesmal gnädig sein. Herzliche Grüße an Ihre Frau und Ihre lieben Kinder.
Ihr ergebener Georg Trakl

130. An Karl Röck in Innsbruck

Limanowa (?), Anfang Oktober 1914
Lieber Freund!
Nach wochenlangen Kreuzfahrten durch ganz Galizien die besten Grüße. Ich hoffe daß wir in den nächsten Tagen nach Norden marschieren werden. Ich war einige Tage krank und ganz niedergedrückt von Traurigkeit. Alles Gute von Ihrem
Georg Trakl
Vielleicht schreiben Sie mir einige Zeilen.

131. An Adolf Loos (In Wein)

Limanowa (?), Anfang Oktober 1914
Lieber Herr Loos!
Nach monatelanger Kreuzfahrt durch ganz Galizien sende ich Ihnen die herzlichsten Grüße. Ich war einige Tage recht krank, ich glaube vor unsäglicher Trauer. Heute bin ich froh, weil wir beinahe sicher nach Norden marschieren werden und in einigen Tagen vielleicht schon in Rußland einrücken werden. Die herzlichsten Grüße an Herrn Kraus.
Ihr sehr ergebener Georg Trakl

129. To Ludwig von Ficker (In Innsbruck)

Liminowa (?), beginning October 1914
Esteemed friend!

We have four weeks of strenuous marches through the whole of Galicia behind us. For two days we rested in a small town in Western Galicia amid gentle and cheerful hill-country and after all the great events of recent times it lets us indeed be at peace. Tomorrow or the day after, we march further. It appears a great new battle is being prepared. Would that the heavens be merciful to us this time. Kind regards to your wife and your children

Your devoted Georg Trakl

130. To Karl Röck in Innsbruck

Limanowa (?), beginning of October 1914
Dear friend!

After weeks of cruising all over Galicia the best greetings. I hope that we will be marching north in the next few days. I have been ill for several days and quite depressed with sadness. All the best from your

Georg Trakl

Perhaps you can write me a few lines.

131. To Adolf Loos (In Vienna)

Limanowa (?), beginning of October 1914
Dear Mr. Loos,

After a month-long tour through all of Galicia I send you the most kind regards. I was quite ill for some days, I believe from inexpressible sorrow. Today I am glad because most certainly we will march to the north and will perhaps invade Russia in as soon as a few days. The most cordial greetings to Mr. Kraus.

Your devoted Georg Trakl

132. An Ludwig von Ficker in Innsbruck

Krakau, um dm 11. Oktober 1914
Verehrter Freund!
Ich bin seit fünf Tagen hier im Garns. Spital zur Beobachtung meines Geisteszustandes. Meine Gesundheit ist wohl etwas angegriffen und ich verfalle recht oft in eine unsägliche Traurigkeit. Hoffentlich sind diese Tage der Niedergeschlagenheit bald vorüber. Die schönsten Grüße an Ihre Frau und Ihre Kinder. Bitte telegraphieren Sie mir einige Worte. Ich wäre so froh, von Ihnen Nachricht zu bekommen.
Herzliche Grüße
Ihr ergebener Georg Trakl
Viele Grüße an Röck

133. An Ludwig von Ficker in Innsbruck

Krakau, um den 21. Oktober 1914
Verehrter Freund!
Da ich bis heute noch kein Lebenszeichen erhalten habe nehme ich an, daß Sie meine Feldpostkarten nicht erhalten haben. Ich verlasse nach 14tägigem Aufenthalt im hiesigen Garns. Spital Krakau. Wohin ich komme weiß ich noch nicht. Meine neue Adresse will ich Ihnen baldmöglichst mitteilen.
Herzlichste Grüße
Ihr ergebener Georg Trakl

Praha, 9. XI. (1914)

Herr Trakl ist im Garnisonsspital Krakow eines plötzlichen Todes (Lähmung?) gestorben. Ich war sein Zimmernachbar.
{Unterschrift}

133a. An Cäcile von Ficker in Innsbruck

Krakau, 24. X. 1914
Dir und den Kindern herzlichste Grüße! Onkel Trakl wird in den nächsten Tagen wieder zu seiner Truppe entlassen. Die Stadt ist sehr interessant.
Euer Papa {Ludwig von Ficker}
Die herzlichsten Grüße Ihres ergebenen
Georg Trakl

132. To Ludwig von Ficker in Innsbruck

Krakow, around October 11, 1914
Dear friend,
I've been here at the garrison hospital for the past five days for observation of my mental state. My health is somewhat compromised, and I often fall into an indescribable sadness. Hopefully, these days of despondency will pass soon. Warm regards to your wife and your children. Please telegraph me a few words. I would be so glad to hear from you.
Sincerely
Your devoted Georg Trakl
Many regards to Röck

133. To Ludwig von Ficker in Innsbruck

Krakow, around October 21, 1914
Dear friend,
Since I have not received any sign of life from you until today, I assume that you haven't received my field postcards. I am leaving Krakow after a 14-day stay at the local military hospital. I do not yet know where I am headed next. I will provide you with my new address as soon as possible.
Warmest regards
Your devoted Georg Trakl

Praha, November 9, 1914

Mr. Trakl passed away suddenly (paralysis?) at the Garrison Hospital in Krakow. I was his roommate.
{Signature}

133a. To Cäcile von Ficker in Innsbruck

Krakow, October, 24, 1914
Warmest regards to you and the children! Uncle Trakl will be released to his troops in the next few days. The city is very interesting.
Your Papa {Ludwig von Ficker}
The warmest greetings from your devoted
Georg Trakl

136. An den Kurt Wolff Verlag in Leipzig

Krakow, 25. X. 1914
sie wuerden mir grosse freude bereiten, wenn sie mir ein exemplar meines neuen buches sebastian im traum schickten. liege krank im hiesigen garnisonspital krakau = georg trakl

137. An Ludwig Von Ficker (In Innsbruck)

Krakau, am 27. Oktober 1914.
Lieber, verehrter Freund!
Anbei übersende ich Ihnen die Abschriften der beiden Gedichte, die ich Ihnen versprochen. Seit Ihrem Besuch im Spital ist mir doppelt traurig zu Mute. Ich fühle mich fast schon jenseits der Welt.
Zum Schlusse will ich noch beifügen, daß im Fall meines Ablebens, es mein Wunsch und Wille ist, daß meine liebe Schwester Grete, alles was ich an Geld und sonstigen Gegenständen besitze, zu eigen haben soll. Es umarmt Sie, lieber Freund innigst Ihr Georg Trakl

139. An Gustav Streicher in Wein

Wien, Wintersemester 1908/09 (?)
Lieber Freund!
Ich bitte Dich zu verzeihen, daß ich gestern Deiner liebenswürdigen Einladung nicht Folge gegeben habe. Da ich gestern den ganzen Nachmittag von meiner Wohnung abwesend war und direkt vom Kaffeehaus in die Oper gieng, habe ich Deine Karte erst um ½ 10h nachts zu Gesicht bekommen.
Ich bin sofort ins Löwenbräu gegangen, habe Euch aber leider nicht mehr angetroffen. Auch im Rathauskeller hielt ich Umschau, leider mit ebenso wenig Erfolg. Es würde mich aufrichtig gefreut haben, mit Dir und Herrn Glaser einen Abend verbracht zu haben.
Ich werde dieser Tage - hoffentlich ist Dir der Samstag genehm - mir erlauben Dich zu besuchen. Ich bin sehr gespannt Dein neues Heim zu sehen. Also auf Wiedersehen am Samstag, wenn Du bereit bist und für mich Zeit hast.
Nochmals meine Entschuldigung, mein Bedauern
Ganz Dein ergebener Georg Trakl

136. To the Kurt Wolff Publishing House in Leipzig

Krakow, October 25, 1914

it would bring me great joy if you sent me a copy of my new book sebastian in dream. i am currently lying ill in the local garrison hospital in krakow = georg trakl

137. To Ludwig Von Ficker (In Innsbruck)

Krakau, around October 27, 1914
Dear, esteemed friend!

I am sending you the enclosed transcripts of the two poems I promised you. Since your visit to the hospital, I have been doubly melancholic. I feel almost beyond this world.

In closing, I would like to add that in the event of my passing, it is my wish and will that my dear sister Grete should have everything I possess in terms of money and other belongings. I embrace you, dear friend, most sincerely
Your Georg Trakl

139. To Gustav Streicher in Vienna

Vienna, Winter Semester 1908/09 (?)
Dear friend,

I hope you can forgive me for not accepting your kind invitation yesterday. Since I was away from my apartment the entire afternoon and went directly from the café to the opera, I only saw your card around 9:30 pm.

I immediately went to the Löwenbräu, but unfortunately, I did not find you there anymore. I also checked the Rathauskeller, but with no better luck.

It would have sincerely delighted me to spend an evening with you and Mr. Glaser.

In the coming days - hopefully, Saturday suits you - I will be able to visit you. I am very curious to see your new home. So, I'll see you on Saturday if you are available and have time for me.

Once again, my apologies and regrets.
Your faithful Georg Trakl

144. Irene Amtmann (in Vienna)

Salzburg, Frühherbst 1910 oder 1911

Liebes Fräulein!

Es kommt vor, daß ich tagelang herumvagabundiere, bald in den Wäldern, die schon sehr rot und luftig sind und wo die Jäger jetzt das Wild zu Tode hetzen, oder auf den Straßen in trostlosen und öden Gegenden, oder auch an der Salzach herumlungere und den Möven zuschaue (was noch meine fröhlichste Faulenzerei ist). Aber es ist mehr Unruhe in mir, als ich mir eingestehen mag, und Ihr so freundlicher Brief ist derart ungebührlich lang unerwidert geblieben. Verzeihen Sie es diesem grantigen Sonderling, der lieber in einen Bauer fahren möchte, als im Schweiße seines Angesichtes Verse zu machen. Brauche ich Ihnen zu sagen, daß ich mehr als ungeduldig bin, nach Wien zurückzukehren, wo ich mir wieder selbst gehören darf, was mir hier nicht verstattet ist.

Man könnte mich vielleicht undankbar schelten, unter diesem wunderbaren reinen Himmel der Heimat so zu sprechen - aber man tut gut daran, sich gegen vollendete Schönheit zu wehren, davor einem nichts erübrigt als ein blödes Schauen. Nein, die Losung ist für unsereinen: Vorwärts zu Dir selber! Bisweilen aber gönne man sich Muße, um wenigstens liebenswürdige Briefe liebenswürdig zu beantworten. Wollen Sie Herrn [Ullmann] die besten Grüße entrichten, damit ich verbleibe Ihr sehr ergebener G. Trakl

144. To Irene Amtmann (in Vienna)

Salzburg, Early Autumn 1910 or 1911

Dear Miss!

It happens that I wander around for days, sometimes in the forests, which have already turned quite red and airy, where hunters are now chasing the game to death, or on the roads in desolate and barren regions, or simply loiter along the Salzach, watching the seagulls (which is still my most cheerful idleness). But there is more restlessness within me than I care to admit, and your kind letter has remained shamefully unanswered for so long. Forgive this grumpy eccentric who would rather become a farmer than make verses with the sweat of his brow. Do I need to tell you how impatient I am to return to Vienna, where I can be myself again, which is not allowed to me here.

One might scold me as being ungrateful for speaking this way under the wonderful pure sky of the homeland – but it is wise to resist perfect beauty, which leaves one with nothing but a foolish gaze. No, the motto for someone like us is: Forward into yourself! Yet, from time to time, one should indulge in leisure, at least to answer gracious letters graciously

Please convey my warm regards to Mr. {Ullmann}, as I remain

very faithfully your G. Trakl

People Around Trakl

Boring, Marie (1862–1940) - born in Alsace, she was employed as a governess with the Trakl family starting around 1890. A French "Bonne" was a symbol of high social status, and she conducted most of her conversations with the six children in her own language. As statements from Friedrich Trakl confirm, her dedication, education that stimulated their imagination, and human warmth made her a substitute for their often unapproachable mother, Maria Catherina.

Her influence is difficult to overstate because, as a fervent Catholic, she suffered from a guilty conscience for working in a Protestant household and not being able to lead the entrusted souls to the true faith. She resigned as a result but later returned after two years in her homeland, feeling remorseful. In the interim, a young Parisian woman who had been hired had to leave. After a total of 14 years in the Trakl household, she considered her mission fulfilled as the children were now somewhat grown, and the daughters were placed in boarding schools.

She remained unaware of Georg's posthumous fame until her death in her Alsatian birthplace.

Buschbeck, Erhard (1889–1960) - came from the Salzburg Protestant minority like Trakl, and while in grade school developed a friendship with the poet. He describes the first meeting with Trakl around 1896:

> My memories of Trakl date back to the time of elementary school, and I still see him in front of the Protestant school on the Salzach Quay that I attended, where he was there to obtain a religious education with his sister... a small, well-groomed boy with long, blonde hair accompanied by a French Bonne. For us regular students, those who only came for religious education on some afternoons, it always seemed somewhat 'special,' but with Trakl, there was also a sense of distancing from the others, a shy need for iso-

lation. Somehow, we still got together back then, talked to each other, and knew each other. In high school, he was a grade above me.

A friendship developed during high school, a circle of poets and friends, including Minnich, Kalmár, and Schwab. Buschbeck had already established contacts beyond the region in support of Georg's poetry before he followed him to Vienna in the autumn of 1909 and began studying law.

There he joined "The Academic Federation of Literature and Music," which he led from 1911. Nearly all of Trakl's acquaintances in the avant-garde arts scene, and his publications until 1912 are at least indirectly due to Buschbeck's efforts. This applies to the magazine "Der Brenner," where he promoted Trakl's interests through friend Robert Müller. After numerous publications there and his entry into the inner circle around Ludwig von Ficker, Trakl suddenly broke off their correspondence in 1913. The reason was probably a brief affair with Georg's sister Gretl, whom Buschbeck had been courting for some time. There was apparently no further contact until Georg's death in November 1914.

In 1917, Buschbeck published his memories of Trakl and a short memorial from the New Youth Publishing House entitled "Georg Trakl."

Starting in 1918, Buschbeck was active as a dramatic advisor at the Viennese Burgtheater, published additional books concerning literature and theater, received a Professorship and became at last an honorary member. In 1939, he published Trakl's youthful poems and prose works under the title "From the Golden Chalice."

The closeness of the relationship between Buschbeck and Trakl is documented not only through numerous letters since their youth but also through the dedication of the poem "Three Gazes into an Opal."

Däubler, Theodor (1876–1934) - was the son of a rich merchant family from Augsburg; fluent in the two languages spoken in Austrian Triest, he lived in Italy until 1900. Beginning in 1901, he was often in Paris, where he busied himself with the Arts Academy and the Impressionists. In WWI, he was exempted from military duty and was a war correspondent in Dresden and Berlin. Afterward, he became a wandering poet, between Italy, Greece, Germany and Austria. In 1926, he was chosen President of the German section of the PEN-Club. In 1932, he was diagnosed with severe tuberculosis and succumbed two years later.

Däubler's major- and life's work is the 30,000 verse epic poem *The North Light* (first published in 1910 and continuously expanded), in which he developed his own mythology, whose center is formed around clarifying sunlight as the origin of life. He connected the discipline of classical forms with the eloquence of expressionistic pathos, hymn-like language and extensive symbolism. Other works include *We Do Not Want to Stay* (autobiographical fragments, Munich 1914); *At-*

tica Sonnets (Leipzig, 1924).

A bridge to Trakl was already built through his friendship with Erhard Buschbeck, particularly in Innsbruck, where he participated in the "Brenner" circle around Ludwig von Ficker and held a reading on 11/22/1912. With a further stay in spring of 1914, he engaged Trakl in extensive sit-down discussions and on walks.

He wrote about his spring of 1914 meetings with Trakl in 1921:

> My last excursion with this poet of gentle sadness led us from Innsbruck along a springtime road through villages towards Hall. At that time we became acquainted with each other; he often spoke gentle words with children we encountered,but otherwise he spoke incessantly of death. When we had to part in the evenings, it seemed to me as if I held a filigreed gift from Georg Trakl in my hand: I felt gentle syllables, carefully blooming together, clear as a sense of words unique to him and me. Before the Styx I remembered this sentence precisely: *The manner of death is irrelevant; death is so terrible because it is a fall, rendering everything that precedes or follows it insignificant. We plummet into an incomprehensible blackness. How could dying, the second we pass into eternity, be breif?* I asked him: "Is that why we feel dizzy in profound conversations, on steep slopes, in life as well as at high places?" He nodded: Yes! Only a few months later Georg Trakl had not shied away from the necessary fall. S The saying and the plunge occurred in the spring and autumn of the fateful year 1914. Suddenly I was frightened away from the Styx: Thus the leap into black water! Without being smashed to pieces?

Esterle, Max von (1870–1947) - painter and portrait artist who was on the staff of Ludwig von Ficker's "Der Brenner." He probably met Trakl in Innsbruck starting in 1912 and had frequent contact thereafter. In November 1913, Trakl painted his self-portrait in Esterle's studio.

Esterle represented him in one very appropriate caricature - straightforward in its abstract simplicity - in the Brenner.

Although he was not a close friend of Trakl, the poem "Winter Twilight" was dedicated to him.

Ficker, Ludwig von (Mentor) (1880–1967) - the son of a professor of historical jurisprudence and a teacher from South Tyrol, he moved to Innsbruck in 1896. Studied law based on paternal desire, then art history and German in college. In 1900 his play "Children of Sin" was produced at the Innsbrucker city theater. A "Fervor of the Storm; a Round of Verses" appeared in 1904 in Leipzig.

A large inheritance permitted him a fancy lifestyle and extended stays in Italy while he tried to establish himself as an independent writer. In 1908 he married the Swede Cäcilie Molander. In 1910, Ficker founded the bi-monthly journal "Der Brenner", which soon attracted attention throughout the German-speaking world as a forum for cultural criticism and avant-garde literature. Frequent contribu-

tors included Theodor Däubler, Albert Ehrenstein, Else Lasker-Schüler, Hermann Broch, Rainer Maria Rilke, Theodor Haecker and Ferdinand Ebner, as well as important collaborators Carl Dallago, Karl Röck, Karl Borromäus Heinrich and Max von Esterle.

In 1912, Ficker organized the first reading by Karl Kraus in Innsbruck, who had formally shaped the satires and polemics in the "Brenner." Kraus wrote a statement on the Brenner in his magazine Die Fackel (The Torch).

In 1914 he received a generous donation from Ludwig Wittgenstein of 100,000 crowns to distribute to needy artists, which he passed on to Rilke, Adolf Loos, Trakl and others.

In May 1912, "Der Brenner" helped Trakl break through as an artist by printing his poem "Suburb in Foehn." Ficker described his first meeting with Trakl at the Café Maximilian on May 22, 1912:

> Once again I arrived there soon after noon in order to meet at the so-called Brenner table of friends. I had hardly sat down, however, when at some distance a man stood out, who sat between two windows, which looked out over Maria Theresia Street , on a plush sofa and with open eyes seemed to ponder before himself. His hair was cut short, with a tinge of silver, the face of indeterminable age: oh, thus the stranger sat there, in an attitude, which was instinctively attractive and nevertheless betrayed an aloofness. But I already noticed, he also saw, apparently turned inward, with searching gaze repeatedly over toward us, and, hardly had I appeared , it did not last very long before a waiter handed his card to me: Georg Trakl. I stood up pleased — because shortly before I had published his poem "Surburb in Foehn" –, welcomed him and invited him to join us at our table.

Beginning with "Psalm," dedicated to Karl Kraus, in October of the same year, approximately 60 additional Trakl poems were published, and helped pave the way for book publications with the Kurt Wolff publishing house. More important was the human refuge Trakl found at Ficker's estate, his family and the circle of "Brenner" coworkers. He often stayed in Innsbruck before the outbreak of war. Besides "The Young Maid," Georg also dedicated "Song of a Captured Blackbird" to Ficker, which he developed on a short trip to the Gardasee in the spring 1914. Ficker was the last and only person to visit Trakl before his death in the Krakow garrison hospital, as evidenced by the last letters.

After participating in WWI, Ficker lost financial foundation and integrated "Der Brenner" into the University Publisher Wagner. With his distancing from Kraus, he abandoned literary satire and social criticism in favor of linguistic-philosophical and theological essays and poetry, advocating for a radical Christian inner life. Likewise, he also focused on preserving Trakl's legacy, but this sometimes involved idealizing, eschatological stylizations, and even aspects of a Trakl Church. In 1925, Ficker arranged for the transfer of Trakl's remains from Kraków, burying him in Innsbruck-Mühlau.

In 1940, the Reich Chamber of Literature classified "'Der Brenner'" as "harmful

and undesirable literature." Ficker maintained his contacts in the resistance circles. Ficker maintained contacts with resistance circles, and in 1946, after a twelve-year hiatus, he published the 16th issue of "Der Brenner" with poems by Trakl, Kraus, Gertrud von Le Fort, and Paula Schlier. The final issue in 1954 was dedicated to memories of Ebner, Dallago, Trakl, Wittgenstein, and Rilke. In 1959, he received the Grand Austrian State Prize and witnessed his friend Ignaz Zangerle founding the "Brenner Archive" in 1964 (since 1979, the "Brenner Archive Research Institute"). After his death in 1967, Ficker was buried alongside Trakl.

Geipel, Maria (1882–1973) - Georg's eldest sister, the second child of the marriage between Tobias and Maria Catherina Trakl, following Gustav (born 1880) and preceding Hermine (born 1884) and Georg.

Under the guidance of the governess Marie Boring and during longer stays at boarding schools with her sister Hermine (1897/8 in Neuchâtel and the following year in Hannover), she received the typical education for a daughter of the upper bourgeoisie at that time.

In 1903, she married Wilhelm Geipel from Graz, a private individual who was 16 years older. However, she left him just months later and returned to Salzburg.

There exists a tender letter from Georg to her from the early period after his move to Vienna in 1908.

Until her death, she lived in the former family residence at Waagplatz 3, although it had been sold in 1917.

In 1973, she experienced the opening of the Trakl Memorial in Georg's nearby birthplace at Waagplatz No. 2, where she assisted in furnishing it with original furniture and belongings. These were the remnants of the Trakl family's possessions, which died out with her: none of the seven siblings had any descendants.

Heinrich, Karl Borromaeus (1884–1938) - pursued his studies in a wide range of geographical and academic disciplines, ultimately earning a doctorate with a dissertation on Nietzsche. He emerged as a novelist at a young age, served as an editor for Simplicissimus (1909-1912), and worked as a publishing editor at Langen, Munich. He was one of the main contributors to Ficker's magazine "Der Brenner." Here, he published cultural-philosophical reflections, acted as a friend and editor to Trakl.

Heinrich's narrative, lyrical, and essayistic works were marked by a religious tone, and his life was characterized by pathological melancholy, even suicide attempts. During World War I, he spent most of his time abroad and worked as an attaché at the German embassy in Switzerland. After his marriage in 1921, he and his wife became lay members of the Benedictine Abbey in Einsiedeln in 1925, which provided asylum for him from the Nazis until his death in 1938.

Trakl emphasized a spiritual kinship and intimacy with Heinrich through the

dedication of two poems, where a "brother" is mentioned: "Decline" and "Song of the Departed." In "Der Brenner," Heinrich published notes in 1913 and 1926 under the title "The Apparition of Georg Trakl."

Hauer, Karl (Author) (1875–1919) - a Bohemian and provocateur from an affluent Salzburg family. Trakl became acquainted with him in 1911 in the orbit of the Salzburg "Literature and Art Society Pan," where he was introduced by his former piano teacher, Brunetti-Pisano. It seems he willingly followed Trakl in all kinds of debauchery.

Hauer's publications (in 1910 the collected essays entitled "Of Happy and Unhappy People") attest to a culturally and socially critical tendency marked by a dialectically sharp intelligence. He frequently contributed to the Viennese magazine "Die Fackel" and most likely facilitated the initial contact between its editor, Karl Kraus, and the architect Adolf Loos. Trakl formed a friendship with Kraus and Loos from 1913 onwards, while Hauer remained an episode in his life, although the poem "All Souls' Day" is dedicated to him. This brilliant, yet morbid, polemicist succumbed to tuberculosis in 1919.

Kalmár, Karl von (1887–1958) - a schoolmate of Georg from his Protestant religious education. Along with Erhard Buschbeck and Oskar Vonwiller, they formed an active discussion circle during his high school years that was concerned with questions of literature and world view. By no later than 1905, Kalmár was living in Vienna, where he invited Trakl that year. Trakl declined in a letter that, like another one from the following year in 1906, attests to a trusting relationship that extended beyond aesthetic matters.

During Trakl's time as a student and soldier in Vienna from 1908 to 1911, Kalmár, along with Karl Minnich and Franz Schwab, was the only regular company he kept apart from his friend Buschbeck, who was often unsuccessful in his efforts to make useful acquaintances.

A postcard written in Salzburg to Kalmár is preserved from the 1909 holidays. Afterwards no further contacts between the two are known; Kalmár became a bank clerk and died in 1958 in Vienna.

Kokoschka, Oskar (Painter) (1886–1980) - painter, graphic artist, poet. Kokoschka studied and worked in Vienna, becoming a significant representative of Expressionism through his collaboration with the Berlin magazine "The Storm." Although less well-known than his painting, his plays are considered pioneers of expressionist drama ("The Sphinx and the Stooge" 1907, "Hiob" 1917; "Murderer, Hope of the Women" 1909; "The Burning Thorn Bush" 1911; "Orpheus and Eurydice" 1915).

Kokoschka, along with Karl Kraus and architect Adolf Loos, was one of the artists whom Trakl regularly and amicably associated with during his stays in Vienna from 1913 onwards. He described his relationship with Trakl while painting "The Wind Bride," whose title he derived from the Trakl poem "The Night."

After WWI, Kokoschka worked as a professor at the academy in Dresden until 1923, after which he traveled extensively and created a large cycle of city pictures, then because of the Nazi rise to power emigrates through Prague to London. In 1953, he created the "School of Seeing" in Salzburg as an international summer academy and established himself in Villeneuve. His autobiography "My Life" appeared in 1971.

Kraus, Karl (Publisher and Author) (1874–1936) - a feared journalist, an influencial writer and a public conscience at the beginning of the twentieth century. His Jewish family moved to Vienna, after breaking off studies he was active as a journalist, satirist, and orator. In 1899, he founded the magazine "The Torch," which became a contentious and engaged institution, appearing from 1911 with only his own contributions until the year of his death. Besides brilliant aphorisms, lyric poetry and essays, Kraus also wrote dramas, including his epic masterwork "The Last Days of Mankind," from 1919, standing out as a textual montage and an unsparing indictment of the crimes of WWI.

Karl Kraus first came within reach of Trakl, who had long been an enthusiastic reader of Kraus, in 1911 through his fellow Salzburg writer and drinking companion Karl Hauer, who had frequently contributed articles to "The Torch." In 1912, when Trakl began to publish poems consistently in the magazine "Der Brenner," the connection between the publishers Ficker and Kraus intensified, as Ficker organized several lecture evenings in Innsbruck with Kraus. "Psalm," the second Trakl poem in "Der Brenner" (appearing October 1912) is dedicated to him. Kraus' response appeared in the "Torch:"

To Georg Trakl in gratitude for the poem "Psalm" (published in the magazine "The Torch"):

Seven-month-old babies are the only ones whose gaze holds their parents accountable, so that they sit next to the stolen goods like caught thieves. They have the look that demands back what has been taken from them, and when their thinking stops, it is as if it is looking for the rest and they stare back into the dereliction. There are others who, thinking, adopt such a gaze, but it's the gaze that wants to restore chaos to what they've received too much of. They are the perfected ones who became finished when it was too late. They came into the world with the cry of shame, leaving them with only one, first, last feeling: Back into your womb, oh mother, where things were good!

Trakl answered in a telegram that was printed in Kraus' magazine "The Torch" concerning "Der Brenner" (a biweekly journal published by Ludwig von Ficker beginning in 1910):

That the only honest review in Austria is published in Innsbruck should be well known, if not in Austria itself, then at least in Germany, where

its only honest review also appears in Innsbruck.

In 1913, a friendly relationship developed in Vienna, including the avant-garde architect Adolf Loos, a lifelong friend of Kraus, and Oskar Kokoschka. Without the latter but with Ficker, they embarked on a joint trip to Venice in August of that year. Kraus also actively promoted the subscription of Trakl's poetry collections in "The Torch."

Unique in Trakl's entire body of work is the four-line poem "Karl Kraus" (in the collection "Sebastian im Traum"): Not a single other text is explicitly related to a specific contemporary figure in its title or content. The poem was inspired by a survey conducted by "Der Brenner," where it was first published on June 15, 1913.

Lasker-Schüler, Else (1869–1945) - daughter of a Jewish banker, she started publishing lyric poetry in 1902, which was generally well regarded. Apart from two marriages (1903-12 to Herwarth Walden, the Berlin leader of Expressionism), she lived the life of a vagabond-poet (friendship with Peter Hille), emigrated in 1933 from Switzerland to Palestine, where in 1945 she died impoverished and mentally incapacitated.

Trakl met Lasker-Schüler in Berlin in March 1914, when he visited his sister Grete who was recovering from the effects of a miscarriage. Her impressions of the poet can be found in the poem "Georg Trakl" (1915). Trakl dedicated his poem "The Occident" to Lasker-Schüler. The additional phrase "in admiration" is unparalleled in his dedications.

Loos, Adolf (1870–1933) - Austrian architect and critic, who was one of the pioneers of the international style in Europe. Studied in Dresden, spent 1893-1896 in the USA, then settled in Vienna (the Steiner house, designed in 1910, was one of the first reinforced concrete houses in Europe). In his writings ("Ornamentation and Crime," 1908) he opposed the Art Nouveau movement and the Vienna Secession. From 1924-1928, he lived in the Paris avant-garde scene. His radical approach to functional and rational architecture had a profound influence on many circles of European avant-garde architecture.

Trakl appeared in Loos' horizon around 1910 in Vienna, where he, along with Karl Kraus and Oskar Kokoschka, was associated with the "Academic Association for Literature and Music," where Erhard Buschbeck worked on behalf of Georg and included him. The friendly connection from around 1913, however, was established by Karl Hauer. In addition to frequent meetings in Vienna, he, along with his wife Bessie and Trakl, embarked on a trip to Venice in August 1913.

The poem "Sebastian im Traum," which provided the title for Trakl's second

posthumous collection published in 1915, is dedicated to him.

Loos, Bessie (Wife of Adolf Loos) (Dates unknown) - Englishwoman and former dancer, then wife of the architect Adolf Loos. Trakl's friendly contact with the pair culminated with a trip to Venice in August 1913, documented in letters, and specifically by the dedication of the poem "Kaspar Hauser Song."

Minnich, Karl (Friend of Youth) (1886-1964) - a schoolmate during Georg's high school years starting in 1897, who later also became involved in the circles of adolescent poets called Apollon and Minerva. Literary exchange and various excesses kept their relationship alive after Salzburg, even when Georg moved to Vienna. Minnich was already living there, studying law, when Georg began studying pharmacy in 1908. Along with Franz Schwab and Karl von Kalmár, Minnich was the only regular company he kept.

The efforts of another school friend in Vienna, Erhard Buschbeck, to introduce him to cultural and literary circles, bore little fruit. Starting from 1912, Minnich seems to have lost his standing as a sidekick when Trakl worked in Innsbruck and followed Ludwig von Ficker and began going out with Kraus, Loos and Kokoschka on his visits to Vienna. With the exception of Buschbeck, Minnich is the only acquaintance from youth who Trakl dedicated a poem with "Square by the Forest."

Müller, Robert (Author) (1887 - 1924) The youth and subsequent life stages of this active Expressionist, who worked as a narrator, essayist, publisher, and literary manager, remain in largely unknown. His first publications were in the magazines "Der Brenner" and "Der Ruf." Starting in 1911, he was one of the most fascinating figures on the Viennese literature and cultural scene. In 1914, the pamphlet "Karl Kraus or Dalai Lama. The Dark Priests. A Nerve Deadening." appeared. Until 1914, he served as the literary director of the "Academic Federation of Literature and Music in Vienna," and was friends with Erhard Buschbeck, who was also involved there. At Buschbeck's urging, Müller forwarded Trakl's poems to the "Brenner" editor Ludwig von Ficker and enthusiastically recommended them, leading to the publication of "Suburb in Foehn" in May 1912. It is not confirmed whether Müller ever personally met Trakl.

In 1915, he published the novel: "Tropics. The Myth of the Journey. Documents of a German Engineer. Edited by Robert Müller," which garnered significant attention. As a volunteer, he spent WWI in the news service, subsequently failed at the establishment of a publishing house, and took his own life in 1924.

However, it should be noted that Müller's aesthetic avant-gardism was accom-

panied by cultural imperialist and at times, fascistic tendencies.

Rilke, Rainer Maria (1875–1926) - the world-famous poet from Prague, Rilke, never actually met Trakl, but he took very direct notice of his poetry because he was in correspondence with Trakl's friend and mentor, Ludwig von Ficker. In letters to Ficker in 1915, Rilke condensed some formulations of his impressions as follows:

> Just last night, I found in the envelope (...) Trakl's "Helian," and I thank you very much for sending it. Every rise and advance in this beautiful poem is imbued with an unspeakable sweetness; it moved me deeply through its inner distances. It is, as it were, built upon its pauses, a few enclosures around the boundless wordlessness: that's how the lines stand there. Like fences in a flat land, over which what is enclosed continuously merges into an unattainable vast plain. (...) Trakl's figure belongs to the mythical; instinctively, I grasp it in the five manifestations of "Helian." It could not be more tangible, if it was not from him himself...

> In the meantime, I have received "Sebastian in Dream" and have read much into it: moved, amazed, sensing, and perplexed; for one soon realizes that the conditions of this sounding and resounding were irretrievably unique, like the circumstances from which a dream may arise. I imagine that even those standing close shall still experience these views and insights as if through a window pane: since Trakl's experience moves as if in reflections and fills his whole room, which is unenterable, like the room in a mirror. (Who could he have been?)

Röck, Karl (1883–1954) - A poet and linguist, employed as a civil servant. He was a contributor to the magazine "Brenner" and was the one who engaged most intensely with Georg Trakl alongside the editor Ludwig von Ficker and Karl Borromäus Heinrich. He regularly kept a diary on literary and personal matters after meeting Trakl on June 17, 1912, in Innsbruck.:

Diary entries on Trakl :

6/27/1912
A remark of Trakl's: One is not able to communicate at all. [*also refers to his poems*]

Note of a Trakl sentence from a discussion: ... one does well to resist perfect beauty, because before it there is nothing to do but look on foolishly...

10/26/1913 (*after Georg had borrowed money from him several times*):
He needs 200 K [= Crowns] monthly; 2 K per day for wine drinking and smoking. How many people live entirely on this kind of money.

In contrast to the rather glorified image of Trakl that was maintained within the "Brenner" circles, particularly after his death, Röck also noted his cold and repulsive facets, even suffering two temporary fallings-out with him ("he knew no form of feelings"). Nevertheless, their friendly bond, despite the tensions, is also documented in the dedication of the poem "An Autumn Evening."

At the end of 1913, he worked with Trakl to arrange his mature texts chronologically. He incorporated this into the first complete edition of Trakl's valid works, "The Poems," published in 1919 by Kurt Wolff Publishing House in Leipzig, which he supervised. This edition presents the texts in an arrangement by titled groups that do not follow Trakl's instructions in his self-published volumes "Poems" (1913) and "Sebastian in a Dream" (1915).

Nevertheless, Röck's sequence remained definitive up until the 1969 historical-critical edition by Killy/Szklenar.

Schwab, Franz (1886–1956) - a schoolmate and confidant in Georg's grade school starting from 1897. Literary exchange and various escapades kept their relationship alive even after they both moved to Vienna from Salzburg. In Vienna, Schwab had already begun studying medicine when Georg started studying pharmacy in 1908. Along with Karl Minnich and Karl von Kalmár, Schwab was the only regular companion Georg maintained alongside his friend Erhard Buschbeck, who was often engaged in making useful acquaintances.

Starting in 1912, when Trakl was working in Innsbruck, became associated with Ludwig von Ficker, and spent time in Vienna with Kraus, Loos, and Kokoschka during his visits, it appears that Georg met with his old companion less frequently. However, in 1913, he occasionally stayed at Schwab's apartment. Schwab completed his medical degree and became a doctor. Their last encounter took place in mid-September 1914 during the campaign in Galicia, where Schwab served as a medical officer.

Trakl, Margarethe (1891–1917) - called Grete or Gretl, was the youngest of six children from the marriage of Tobias and Maria Catherina Trakl. The physical and psychological similarities between Gretl and her brother, four and a half years older, were noticeable. The mysteries around the mental and erotic decline that evolved between the two will never be fully understood because their letters to each other have never been found, possibly because the family sought them out to destroy them. In 2011, a German movie entitled *Tabu: The Soul is a Stranger on Earth* was released dramatizing the rumored relationship between Georg and Grete.

Grete is described by those who knew her as unusually vital, passionate, sensual and untamable, paired with a large artistic talent, particularly in music. Like her older sisters she lived more and more frequently outside the house, starting at age eleven, enduring skillfully at boarding schools in St. Pölten and Vienna. In the fall of 1908, she studied piano at the Viennese music academy, paralleling Georg's pharmacy studies at the University of Vienna. They lived separately. Her

tendencies toward excessiveness and immoderation were accentuated by the world of drug abuse she was introduced to by Georg.

In the late summer of 1910, after her father's death, she moved to Berlin and continued her pianistic training with Ernst von Dohnányi. The eldest brother from his father's first marriage, Wilhelm, took over guardianship of the minor, but resigned after long conflicts. After Georg took over, Gretl was able to marry the Berlin bookseller and theater employee Arthur Langen, who was 34 years older than her, on July 17, 1912. From then on she had contacts with the organ of literary expressionism "Der Sturm", whose employees in turn communicated with Ludwig von Ficker and Georg's publisher Kurt Wolff.

In 1913, she is rumored to have had a short affair with Erhard Buschbeck, which may explain why Trakl broke off contact with him. In March 1914, he visited Grete in Berlin while she was recovering from an abortion.

On October 27, 1914, shortly before his death, Trakl bequeathed all his worldly belongings to her in a letter to Ficker, including Wittgenstein's donation of twenty thousand crowns. Even with this support, an inexorable decline began for Grete. She could not resuscitate her career as a pianist. Her husband left her. She plunged ever deeper into the world of drugs.

On September 23, 1917 after a party, she shot herself in Berlin.

Trakl, Maria Catherina (née Halik) (1852–1925) - Georg Trakl's mother; Her father August Halik came from Prague and had been married to Anna Schod in Wiener Neustadt since 1846. The daughter Maria married Tobias Trakl in 1878 and moved with him to Salzburg with her mother, where she gave birth to six children: Gustav (June 25, 1880), Maria (December 21, 1882), Hermine (June 7, 1884), Georg (February 3, 1887), Friedrich (February 27, 1890) and Margarethe (August 8, 1891). It is unclear whether she gave up her Catholic denomination in favor of her Protestant husband.

In Friedrich's insightful reports, Maria Trakl appears as an opaque, isolated personality who felt misunderstood. She supervised the musical education of the well-protected children and gave the family access to cultural and aesthetic spheres. But she did not have the maternal warmth that the children found more in the governess Marie Boring. Maria Trakl often withdrew to her own room for days at a time, where she concentrated on collecting and restoring antiques. However, the tensions resulting from this constellation seem to have had a more subtle effect than ever breaking out openly.

Trakl, Tobias (1837–1910) - Georg Trakl's father was of Hungarian-German descent with Swabian-Protestant roots. He was born as the youngest of 13 children to the merchant Georg Trackel (born 1795), while his mother, Katharina Tremmel, widowed as Laitner, was his second wife. Tobias went to Wiener Neustadt for his business training, where he married Valentine Götz (1841-1870), who gave birth to their son Wilhelm on May 17, 1868. After her death, he married Maria Catherina Halik in 1878 and moved to Salzburg in 1879, where he achieved bourgeois

prosperity as an iron merchant.

Six children were born in various apartments, starting in 1883 in the Schaffnerhaus at Waagplatz No. 2: Gustav (June 25, 1880), Maria (December 21, 1882), Hermine (June 7, 1884), Georg (February 3, 1887), Friedrich (February 27, 1890), and Margarethe (August 8, 1891). In 1893, he opened a large hardware store at Waagplatz No. 3, and the family moved to a more spacious apartment above it. His sudden death in 1910 brought an abrupt end to the business success, and even Wilhelm, as the manager, couldn't prevent the dissolution of the company in 1913.

Tobias Trakl is described in preserved documents as a sociable and uncomplicated jolly person. He enjoyed recognition and respect in Salzburg but remained true to a lower-middle-class lifestyle despite his ascent to the upper-middle class.

Wittgenstein, Ludwig (1889–1951) - philosopher of world renown, youngest son of a wealthy and cultured Austrian industrial family. Wittgenstein studied engineering at first in Berlin and Manchester, before turning to mathematics, logic, and philosophy; close contacts with Gottlob Frege in Jena and Bertrand Russell in Cambridge. Participated in World War I as a volunteer, and was taken as a prisoner of war by the Italians in 1918.

Subsequently, he gave away his fortune, worked as a village schoolteacher and architect, and gained legendary status as a lecturer in Cambridge, where he taught in a highly unconventional manner, focusing solely on his own work. In 1921, he published the "Tractatus Logico-Philosophicus," while his other writings, primarily concerned with philosophy of language, were published posthumously from his estate.

Wittgenstein drew Ludwig von Ficker's attention to Trakl, to whom Wittgenstein donated 100,000 crowns in the summer of 1914 for needy Austrian artists at Ficker's request, with 20,000 of it intended for Trakl. in 1914, Wittgenstein wrote the very quotable:

> I don't understand it; but its tone bewitched me. It is the tone of truly
> ingenious humans.

When Trakl, accompanied by Ficker, wanted to withdraw a first installment from an Innsbruck bank, he broke into a cold sweat and fled due to an anxiety attack. Soon afterward, he was drafted as a reservist to the war in Galicia, and he never received any of the money. In a letter to Ficker from the Krakau garrison hospital on October 27, six days before his death, he bequeathed it to his sister Gretl. At that time, Trakl also sent Wittgenstein a card requesting a visit, as Ficker had informed him that he was stationed in Krakow. When Wittengstein, returning from a reconnaissance mission on the Vistula, received the news, Trakl had died three days earlier and was already buried.

Glossary

Afra – Christian martyr and Catholic saint. According to legend, Afra was given over as a prostitute to the service of the goddess Venus by her mother Hilaria. During the persecution of Roman Emperor Diocletian, Bishop Narcissus of Gerundum in Spain took refuge from his persecutors in Augsburg, Bavaria and found asylum in Afra's house. The bishop converted Afra to Christianity and baptized her. Around 304, Afra was burned at the stake for professing herself to be a Christian and refusing to participate in pagan rites. Her feast is celebrated on the 7th of August.

All Souls' Day – a Catholic day to commemorate the faithfully departed or those baptized souls believed to be in purgatory. It is also sometimes called The Day of the Dead. The theological doctrine is that upon death souls departing from the body who are not cleansed of sin or have not atoned for past transgressions are barred from being one with God, and the faithful on earth can help them through prayer. It is celebrated on November 2nd with requiem masses and visits to cemeteries.

Angelus – a short Catholic devotion in honor of the Incarnation of Jesus Christ repeated three times each day, morning (6 a.m.), noon, and evening (6 p.m.), at the sound of the Angelus bell. It consists in the triple repetition of the Hail Mary, preceded by three introductory versicles and a concluding versicle and prayer. The devotion derives its name from the first word of the first versicle, i.e. *Angelus Domini nuntiavit Maria* (The angel of the Lord declared unto Mary).

Anif – a castle near Salzburg in the proximity of Hellbrunn.

Aphrodite – the goddess of love, beauty and sexual rapture in Greek mythology. Hesiod relates that she was born from sea foam when Uranus, father of the gods, was castrated by his son Cronos who threw the severed genitals into the ocean. Aphrodite arose from the sea as a fully grown woman and was carried by the waves to Cyprus. She was married to Hephaestus, the god of smiths and artisans, but she was the lover of many gods and mortals, perhaps the most famous being Adonis.

Avanti – an Italian word meaning *forward*.

Azrael – the name given the angel of death in the Old Testament. He is depicted as an archangel under the command of God with four faces and four thousand wings. His body is made up of eyes and tongues, matching the number of people residing on earth. He constantly records and erases the names of people at birth and death, and will be the last to die.

Barrabas – the murder that the Roman governor of Judea, Pontius Pilate, freed at the Passover feast in Jerusalem instead of Jesus. Barrabas was sentenced to death by crucifixion, but according to the Passover custom Pilate was allowed to commute one prisoner's death sentence by popular acclaim. The crowd, when offered a choice to release Barrabas or Jesus, picked Barrabas condemning Jesus to crucifixion.

Cain – in the Old Testament, the first son of Adam and Eve who was born after the Fall of Man from the Garden of Eden. He was followed by a brother Abel. Cain became a farmer and Abel a shepherd. Each offered a gift to God, but God only accepted Abel's offering. Cain then murdered his brother Abel out of jealousy. God punished him with a divine curse and the ground would no longer bear fruit for him. He became a wanderer across the earth living in fear of being murdered himself.

Chorale – a church song for a chorus usually performed in the native language of the worshipers.

Condottiere – (kondot-tyara) [Italian=leader], leader of mercenary soldiers in Italy in the 14th and 15th cent.

Confiteor – a Latin word meaning *I confess*. In addition, it is a Catholic prayer of penance where sinfulness is acknowledged and God's mercy and forgiveness is sought. It is recited at the beginning of mass or on various other occasions when as a preparation to receive grace. The prayer begins: I confess to almighty God, etc.

Crucifixus – a Latin word meaning *nailed to the cross*.

Daedalus – architect, inventor and master craftsman in Greek Mythology. He created many objects that are prominent in various myths including the Labyrinth of the Minotaur at Knossos. Daedalus built wings for himself and son Icarus, fashioned with feathers held together with wax. Daedalus warned his son not to fly too close to the sun, because it would melt his wings. Icarus, exhilarated by the thrill of flying, grew careless. Flying too close to the sun god Helios, the wax holding his wings together melted and he fell to his death, drowning in the sea.

De profundis – Latin for *out of the depths (of sorrow, despair, etc.)*; the beginning words of Psalm 130 in the Old Testament, principally used in penitential prayers for the dead, and for souls that are still in purgatory.

Devil – in dualistic religions the embodiment of evil and adversary of God; tempter of mankind; master of Hell. Equated to a large extent in Christianity with Satan and Lucifer.

Dies irae – Latin for *day of wrath*; is a famous Latin hymn written by Tommaso da Celano (about 1190-1260) that describes the Day of Judgment, the last trumpet summoning souls before the throne of God, where the good will be delivered and the evil cast into eternal flames. It is used in the Requiem Mass.

Dionysus – God of wine, intoxication, and fertility in Greek mythology. He invented wine on Mount Nyssa and spread the practice of cultivating grapes around the world. His dual nature is represented in the joy and social benefits of wine as well as the brutality, thoughtlessness and rage that can result from its abuse.

Don Juan – title character of Trakl's fragmentary tragedy Don Juan's Death. Also known as Don Giovanni, this figure has become a synonym for an insatiable sexual seducer. It originates from a drama by Spanish author Tirso de Molina in 1613 and is one of the most

adapted works of world literature.

Dryad – in Greek mythology a type of wood nymph that was thought to inhabit trees and forests. They were especially fond of oak trees. Shy and non-violent they rarely appeared more than a few feet from their individual tree, and can disappear into their tree when frightened.

Eden – Garden of Paradise in the Old Testament from which Adam and Eve are expelled after being lured by Satan in the guise of a snake to eat from the fruit of the Tree of Knowledge. Eden is synonymous with an earthly paradise.

Elai – Aramaic for *my God*; the cry of Jesus before he died on the cross: "My God, my God, why hast thou forsaken me?"

Elis – a myth-like, enigmatic boy character in some of Trakl's poems. The model for the name doesn't originate from the Greek Peloponnesian peninsular, but in the historical fall of Swedish miner Elis Froebom in the 17th century, which E. T. A. Hoffmann (in the novel, "The Miners of Falun," 1818) and Hugo von Hofmannsthal (in the verse drama fragment, "The Miners of Falun," 1906) treated in literature. Elis Froebom met with an accident in the mine on the day of his wedding, and his body was discovered decades later perfectly preserved his youth while his bride had become an old woman.

Endymion – in Greek mythology a handsome shepherd from Asia Minor. He was so beautiful that Selene, the moon goddess, asked Zeus to grant him eternal life so she could be with him always. He consented and Zeus put him into an eternal sleep. Each night, Selene visits Endymion where he is buried and they have over fifty daughters together.

Evoe – typical call of the drunken followers of the Greek god Dionysus.

Exaudi me – Latin for *hear me*; in Old Testament Psalm 69 and 143.

Foehn – a warm dry wind that often blows in the northern valleys of the Alps, due to the indraft of a storm center passing over Central Europe. The wind, heated by compression in its descent from the mountains, reaches the lower levels heated and drained of humidity.

Golgotha – mountain and execution place near Jerusalem where according to the New Testament Jesus was crucified.

Gret – a rough abbreviation for a woman's name; Trakl's favorite sister Margarethe was usually called Grete or Gretl.

Grodek – locality in Galicia, today Eastern Poland; scene of a battle between Austrian and Russian troops at the beginning of the World War I in October 1914, in which Trakl was involved as a medic.

Hauser, Kaspar – (1812–1833) a mysterious, feral boy who appeared on the streets of Nuremberg, Germany. He wore peasant clothes and could barely speak. The boy could only repeat phrases like: "I want to be a rider like my father" or "Horse! Horse!." Eventually it was learned he spent most of his life in a tiny cell that was not large enough for

him to stand, and ate only bread and water. In December 1833, he was lured to a park with the promise of discovering something about his ancestry but was stabbed in the chest by an unknown person. During Hauser's lifetime his fate and parentage had already become an object of speculation and the stuff of literature, which underwent many adaptations in Germany and France. Trakl was particularly affected by Paul Verlain's poem "Kaspar Hauser Sings" (1881) and Jakob Wassermann's novel "Kaspar Hauser or the Lethargy of the Heart" (1908).

Helian – a myth-like, enigmatic character in Trakl's poetry. The name should probably be interpreted as an allusion to Verlaine's "poor Lelian" and the poet Hölderlin.

Helios – the sun god in Greek mythology.

Hellbrunn – a baroque pleasure palace near Salzburg, constructed from 1613–19 by Santino Solari (1576–1646) for Archbishop Markus Sittikus of Salzburg. Its expanded park is well-known for its artfully laid-out ponds and trick fountains.

Hill of Calvary – derived from the Latin word *calvaria* which means skull; a name for Golgotha near Jerusalem, where Jesus was crucified.

Hohenburg – castle near Innsbruck, Trakl's place of residence several times between 1913–4. It belonged at that time to Rudolf von Ficker, brother of his friend and mentor Ludwig von Ficker.

Jerusalem – the holy city of three world religions, Judaism, Christianity, and Islam.

Jesus Christ – the gospels depict him as a Jewish preacher and healer often at odds with Jewish religious authorities. He was crucified outside of Jerusalem during the rule of the Roman governor Pontius Pilate. After his death, numerous followers spread his teachings, and within a few centuries Christianity emerged as a major religion distinct from Judaism. The gospels claim Jesus was the Messiah prophesied in the Old Testament; that he was the son of God; that his mother Mary was a virgin when Jesus was conceived; and that after his crucifixion he rose from the dead to appear to his disciples before ascended into heaven.

Kidron – valley between Jerusalem and the Mount of Olives.

Kristus – rare way of writing of "Christ."

Lans – village near Innsbruck, Austria.

Lucifer – Latin word meaning light-bearer. In the Christian tradition, Lucifer was second in command to God himself, the highest archangel in heaven. But pride and greed motivated him to rebel against God and he was cast out of heaven, along with a third of the host of heaven. He is often referred to as the Devil or Satan, and his fellow angelic rebels are known as demons.

Maenad – in Greek mythology, one of the female worshipers of Dionysus. The name literally means "the raving one." Maenads indulged abundantly in violence, bloodletting, sex, intoxication and mutilation, and were usually depicted as crowned with vine leaves, clothed

in fawn skins and dancing with wild abandonment.

Mary – in the New Testament, the mother of Jesus and at the time of his conception the betrothed wife of Joseph. The Gospels relate that Mary was a virgin when she conceived Jesus through a miracle of God. She was present at the crucifixion along with Mary Magdalene and other women.

Mary Magdalena – in the New Testament, a devoted disciple of Jesus. She is considered a saint by the Catholic Church with a feast day of July 22nd. She is purported to have been a prostitute who had seven demons cast out of her by an exorcism. She became a close companion of Jesus, accompanied him on his last journey to Jerusalem and was a witness to the crucifixion. She remained there until Jesus' body was taken down and laid in the tomb. On the first day of the next week, she and several others brought spices to anoint the body, but the tomb was empty. She was the first person to see the resurrected Jesus.

Mauvaise music – French for *bad music.*

Melusine – beautiful sea fairy from an old French legend; usually depicted as a woman who is a serpent or fish from the waist down. Appeared for the first time in a noted 1387 story by Jean d'Arras where her husband, a count, surprised her in mermaid-form, whereupon she had to return to the sea.

Mirabell – palace with a large ornamental park situated in Salzburg, separated from the old part of town by the river Salzach.

Mönchsberg – part of the long drawn-out, cragged mountain ridge which Salzburg almost completely surrounds.

Mount Calvary – derived from the Latin word *calvaria* which means skull; a name for Golgotha near Jerusalem, where Jesus was crucified.

Narcissus – a beautiful young man from Greek mythology, who fell in love with his reflection in a pond and drowned trying to embrace it. From this myth, the word narcissist evolved for "someone in love with themselves."

Novalis – pen name of the German romantic poet Friedrich von Hardenberg (1772–1801). The death in 1797 of his young fiancé, Sophie von Kühn, led him to write *Hymns to the Night*, a set of six prose and verse lyrics first published in 1800. Seven months after the publication of *Hymns to the Night*, Novalis died of tuberculosis, the same disease that had claimed his fiancé. His "blue flower," introduced in the novel fragment "Heinrich von Ofterdingen," became the emblem of the oneness of dream and reality, the finite and the infinite, and in general of the entire German Romantic movement.

Nymph – female nature divinity in Greek mythology. In "Psalm" from the bequest: the developmental stage of an insect between larva and pupa.

Ophelia – beloved of the title character of Shakespeare's tragedy Hamlet who thinks herself spurned, falls into a frenzy and drowns herself.

Orpheus – famous singer of Greek mythology, who tried in vain to release his beloved, a nymph named Eurydice, from the realm of the dead. Orpheus was taught to play the lyre by Apollo, and his skill on the instrument, combined with the sweetness of his singing voice could charm wild animals and humans equally. He was ultimately killed by the Maenads.

Pan – Greek god of herders and forest, cloven footed and fur-covered, a companion of Dionysus. He is the inventor of the Pan flute and can cause panic-stricken terror.

Pharisees – religious group in Judaism at the time of Jesus which stood in high esteem as scribes. Due to their negative representation in the New Testament became an expression for pedantry and bigotry.

Phoebus – epithet of the Greek god Apollo that emphasizes his aspect as a god of light and sun. In European poetry references are sometimes made to Phoebus and his car or chariot as a metaphor for the sun.

Pilatus – Pontius Pilate, in the New Testament was the governor of the Roman province of Judea from AD 26 until approximately AD 36. According to the accounts in the Gospels, Pilate presided at the trial of Jesus. Passover custom permitted Pilate to commute one prisoner's death sentence by popular acclaim. The crowd chose to release Barabbas the murderer instead of Jesus, allowing Pilate to wash his hands of any responsibility.

Psalm – religious song or poem of praise in the Old Testament collected in the Book of Psalms; from the Greek *psalmós* = string play, chant, song of praise.

Quirinal – one of the Seven Hills of Rome located in the northeast quadrant of the city.

Rachel – Jewish woman's name; in the Old Testament the favorite wife of Jacob.

Rome – capital of Italy and former world empire which during the time of Jesus ruled most of the civilized world. Roman emperors were early opponents of Christianity and lead frequent persecutions against the early church.

Rosary – a certain form of Catholic prayer where Hail Marys are recited in groups of ten with an Our Father in-between. Rosary beads are often used in conjunction as a counting mechanism to ensure the ritual is completed properly.

Sabbath – the Jewish day of rest and religious holiday (Saturday), but in Trakl's youthful poem it is cloaked in the meaning of a witches' celebration.

Saint Peter's Cemetery – a burial place under a steep rock cliff in Salzburg.

Saint Thomas – in the New Testament one of the twelve Apostles of Jesus; known as "Doubting Thomas" who initially does not believe in the resurrection of Jesus and must touch his crucifixion wounds to be convinced.

Saint Ursula – Christian martyr, who according to legend was killed with ten companions during a pilgrimage to Rome near Cologne by the Huns in the 4th Century.

Satan – Hebrew word for *adversary*; leader of the angels in the Old Testament, revolted unsuccessfully against God; in Christianity equated primarily with the devil and Lucifer.

Saturn – in Roman mythology, the king of the golden age; he preceded his son Jupiter who overthrew him as the highest god. In the teachings on the four temperaments going back to the Middle Ages, he stands for melancholy. Also the name given to the 6th planet of our solar system.

Schubert – Austrian composer (1797–1828), considered one of the last masters of the Viennese Classical School and one of the earliest proponents of musical Romanticism. Though he died at the age of 31, he wrote over six hundred romantic songs as well as piano music, many symphonies, sonatas, and operas.

Sea of Galilee – a fresh water lake in Galilee (today a province of Israel), where in the New Testament Jesus often stopped, preached, performed miracles and gathered his disciples.

Sebastian – a Christian martyr and Saint. He was a bodyguard to the Roman emperor Diocletian. His beliefs manifested during the persecution of the Christians and he was probably executed in the 3rd century with arrows. From the 15th century this scene has been frequently depicted in the visual arts. – In Trakl's poetry, he, like Elis and Helian, is a myth-like, enigmatic character.

Sonja – Russian short form of the name Sophia. The associative framework for Trakl's lyric figure is the Sonja Marmeladova from Fyodor Dostoevsky's novel "Crime and Punishment," a harlot by necessity who possesses the character of a holy one, and follows her love, the murderer Raskolnikov, into exile in Siberia.

Sphinx – the Egyptian sphinx is a mythical creature usually made up of a recumbent lion with a human head, usually that of a pharaoh. The Greek sphinx is mythical demon of destruction and bad luck. She was depicted most often as a winged lion seated upright with a woman's head; or as a woman with the claws and body of a lion, a serpent's tail, and wings.

Titan – in Greek mythology, giant divine beings who preceded the Olympian gods. They were defeated by Zeus and the newer gods, and banished into the underworld.

Triton – a water god of Greek mythology and the messenger of the deep. He is usually depicted as a merman, having the upper body of a human and the tail of a fish. He carried a trident like his father, Poseidon. However, Triton's hallmark was a twisted conch shell, which he blew like a trumpet to calm or raise the waves.

About the Translators

Jim Doss is co-editor of the quarterly journal *Loch Raven Review*. He was born and raised in the foothills of the Blue Ridge Mountains, and is a graduate of the University of Virginia. His work has appeared in numerous publications, both on the Internet and in print. Doss has published two books: *Learning to Talk Again* (2011), a book of poems and prose, and *What Remains* (2017). He has also translated Ernst Toller's autobiography, *A Youth in Germany*, and *Letters from Prison*. He earns his living as a software engineer, and lives with his wife and three children in Maryland.

Werner Schmitt was born in Pirmasens in southwest Germany and grew up in a little village near the French border. He began to write poems and prose at the age of 15. In 1984, Schmitt began his study of German and philosophy at the University of Trier, from which he graduated with a Master of Arts degree, highlighted by a dissertation on the ambiguity in the work of the Austrian poet, Georg Trakl. In 1994, Schmitt published *Der Denkgänger*, a book of narratives and short prose. He works predominately with free verse, haiku, stories, and essays which have been published in many anthologies, magazines, newspapers, and read on the radio. Schmitt has performed readings of his work throughout Germany. He maintains the web site www.literaturnische.de which contains the most complete Trakl-Homepage worldwide in both German and English.